Understanding Muslim Mobilities and Gender

Special Issue Editor

Viola Thimm

MDPI • Basel • Beijing • Wuhan • Barcelona • Belgrade

Special Issue Editor
Viola Thimm
University of Hamburg
Germany

Editorial Office
MDPI AG
St. Alban-Anlage 66
Basel, Switzerland

This edition is a reprint of the Special Issue published online in the open access journal *Social Sciences* (ISSN 2076-0760) from 2017–2018 (available at: http://www.mdpi.com/journal/socsci/special_issues/muslim_mobilities_gender).

For citation purposes, cite each article independently as indicated on the article page online and as indicated below:

Lastname, Firstname, and Firstname Lastname. Year. Article title. *Journal Name* Volume number: page range.

First Edition 2018

ISBN 978-3-03842-751-3 (Pbk)
ISBN 978-3-03842-752-0 (PDF)

Table of Contents

Section 1: Moving through Different Gendered Spaces

Section 2: Creating and Negotiating a Transnational Muslim Space

Section 3: From Mobility to Immobility: Intersectional Identifications as Opportunities or Limitations

About the Special Issue Editor

Viola Thimm is Research Fellow at the Department of Languages and Cultures of Southeast Asia, Asia-Africa-Institute, University of Hamburg (Germany). She was awarded her doctoral degree in Cultural Anthropology by the University of Göttingen in 2013 with a dissertation on Gender and Educational Migration in Singapore and Malaysia. Thimm was a guest researcher at Zayed University (United Arab Emirates) (2017–2018), Monash University (Malaysia) (2017), Universiti Kebangsaan Malaysia (UKM) (2009) and at the Institute of Southeast Asian Studies (ISEAS) (Singapore) (2008). Her research interests include cultural practices of mobility; gender relations and intersectionality; kinship and family networks; Islam and its socio-cultural entanglements; consumer culture and consumption, and educational research. Her regional focus lies in Southeast Asia (Malaysia and Singapore) and the Arabian Peninsular (United Arab Emirates). Thimm has been granted several fellowships and awards, such as a Research Fellowship by the German Research Foundation (DFG), a Postdoctoral Fellowship by the "Nachwuchsinitiative der Universität Hamburg" and a Doctoral Fellowship granted by the Hans-Böckler-Foundation.

Editorial

Muslim Mobilities and Gender: An Introduction

Viola Thimm

Asien-Afrika-Institut (Asia-Africa-Institute), Department of Languages and Cultures of Southeast Asia, University of Hamburg, Edmund-Siemers-Allee 1, 20146 Hamburg, Germany; viola.thimm@uni-hamburg.de; Tel.: +49-40-428-387-537

Received: 21 December 2017; Accepted: 25 December 2017; Published: 28 December 2017

1. Mobilities

Mobility represents the common imagination that the current world is in a constant flux, based on, for example, technical development, wide arrays of infrastructure and digital communication (Fábos and Isotalo 2014). The mobile world is constituted through mobile people, objects, narratives, symbols and representations. The common notion is that the world is more mobile than it has ever been before. This understanding approaches mobility with positively attributed meanings, which are based on capitalist and neoliberal discourses: Increasing mobility inheres the ability and freedom to move and the possibility of flexible changes (e.g., Endres et al. 2016a; Uteng and Cresswell 2008). This approach to mobility focuses on transformations of mobile practices, rather than on representations and negotiations linked to mobility and is highly contested (Endres et al. 2016b, p. 2).

The myriad current dynamics of flows of people and their ideas and goods are studied with either a theoretical or empirical mobility approach. Regarding the first strand, using mobility as a concept can be a way of understanding the mobile lives of people (e.g., Endres et al. 2016a; Uteng and Cresswell 2008; Hannam et al. 2006). In this sense, mobility is a lens to research this field with a certain optic and, therewith, ordering it accordingly. The latter strand investigates the diverse kinds of movements by, for example, migrants, refugees, tourists, pilgrims, international students, journalists, NGO personnel and diplomats. This approach has been extended to include research dealing with walking, travelling by train or even electric flows into mobility studies. As part of this approach, John Urry differentiates mobilities as follows:

> 1. Corporeal travel of people for work, leisure, family life, pleasure, migration and escape; 2. Physical movement of *objects* delivered to producers, consumers and retailers; 3. Imaginative travel elsewhere through images of places and people on television; 4. Virtual travel often in real time on the internet, so transcending geographical and social distance; 5. Communicative travel through person-to-person messages via letters, telephone, fax and mobile phone (Urry 2004, p. 28, as quoted in (Uteng and Cresswell 2008, p. 1); emphasis in original).

People have always been mobile, which means that on the descriptive level, mobility is not a new phenomenon. However, the scholarly attention and analytical approach has developed only relatively recently. Many academic centers (e.g., the Scalabrini Institute for Human Mobility in Africa (SIHMA), Cape Town; the European Center for Sustainable Mobility, University of Applied Sciences Aachen; the New Mobilities Research and Policy Center; Drexel University), journals (e.g., *Mobilities*, *Transfers*, *Applied Mobilities*) and conferences (e.g., Nexus of Migration and Tourism: Creating Social Sustainability, ATLAS Asia-Pacific Conference 2018; AAG 2018: Expanding the debate on transport and mobility justice; (Im)mobility: Dialectics of Movement, Power and Resistance, LSE 2018; Inaugural Conference of "Laboratory of City and Mobility": "Arquitectura entre escalas y la ciudad Latinoamericana," Universidad Católica de Chile 2017) focus on mobility which, as a whole, has institutionalized this field of study. Researching social phenomena through the lens of movement—either theoretically or empirically framed—emerged as the *new mobilities paradigm* or *mobility turn* across multiple disciplines, such as anthropology, geography, history, sociology or transportation research (Hannam et al. 2006), as a response to the (assumed) increase of flows of people and objects.

The distinctiveness of mobility studies is not the additive subsumption of various forms of movement under one roof but that it captures the *connections* between human mobility, technology and transportation and, therewith, brings technical development, infrastructure, objects and human movement together. The understanding of entanglements of movements of people, objects and symbols

> [transcends] the dichotomy between transport research and social research, putting social relations into travel and connecting different forms of transport with complex patterns of social experience conducted through communications at a distance (Endres et al. 2016a, p. 1).

Hence, the inclusiveness of the category of mobility opens up the possibility of connecting movement, sedentarism and transportation analytically. Dynamics, for example, in the field of Muslim pilgrimage, such as the higher number of pilgrims, emerging Muslim middle classes in many regions which can afford such journeys and transformations of pilgrimage practices which include more and more consumption activities, can be better understood when taking the development of the corresponding infrastructure, i.e., from ship to airplane, from limited carriers to a wide range of possible routes, into account (Thimm 2017).

Approaching mobility with this lens clearly shows that the common understanding of an increasingly mobile world has its limitations. Not only do the infrastructural and technical possibilities play a crucial role for understanding mobile ways of people but also the embeddedness of these possibilities into power structures, which equally stop people from being mobile or never enable people to move, is another. Focusing power relations regarding mobility leads to the other side of the coin: immobility (e.g., Gutekunst et al. 2016; Glick Schiller and Salazar 2013). Glick Schiller and Salazar (2013) conceptualize mobility in their article "Regimes of Mobility Across the Globe," as a form of physical movement which is contingent on socio-structural constraints, which are an expression of power. They frame mobility as being part of power regimes and, thereby, understand human movement as embedded within sociopolitical, historical and economic relationships. The ability to move based on people's resources and, therewith, on their social position are bound directly to the immobility of other groups of people who cannot refer to such resources and structures. Mobility/mobilization and sedentarism or immobility/immobilization are often not two binary poles but interrelated states for the same people (Götz 2016, p. 10). This understanding marks a turn from a binary, dichotomous understanding of mobility/immobility to a relational one, which emphasizes power constellations and the ways they operate on a discursive level. Using im/mobility as a term of complexity, recognizes power regimes as framings of the connections between human movement and sedentarism. Refugees, for example, cannot cross space and especially borders easily. Their physical movement is slow and limited through their way of transportation, i.e., on foot, hidden in trucks and trains, or in perilous rubber dinghies and depends on segregations by nationality, regional and cultural origin as they are classified by powerful governments in the Western World. The resulting segregation is a decision regarding who gets quickly deported by plane and who can stay, some for a short while only but some other ones forever (e.g., Vigneswaran and Quirk 2015; Ashutosh and Mountz 2012). Governing of movement and institutional control of human movements are fundamental parts of mobility. Including these powerful regulations of mobility into the common understanding challenges the neoliberal notion of the constantly increasing mobility of people, ideas and objects.

Being sensitive of power hierarchies when it comes to movement or to the counterpart—the exclusion from movement—brings us to an understanding that power is an inherent part of mobility. Considering that walking, driving or virtual mobility is equally subsumed under the umbrella term "mobilities" by many scholars (e.g., Papon and Flonneau 2017; Faulconbridge 2015; Kesselring and Clarke 2013), the socio-cultural and political complexity demonstrates that not every form of movement is automatically mobility but needs to fulfill particular criteria. Noel Salazar suggests the following important differentiation between movement and mobility:

> Analytically speaking, movements (as brute acts of motion) become mobilities when they gain meaning as experienced and imagined socio-cultural assemblages. People are moving all the time but not all movements are equally meaningful and life-shaping (both for those who move and those who stay put) (Salazar 2016b, p. 285).

Sara Bonfanti (Bonfanti 2016, p. 185) enhances Salazar's approach by bringing in two additional aspects for a conceptualization of mobilities: "[M]obility [is] constituted not only by movement but also by meaning or ideological representations and by power, be it economic, symbolic or political".

Following Salazar's and Bonfanti's understandings, mobility is movement which acquires meaning through the social actors involved. This meaning-making process is embedded in the power relations in which they interact, however, these power relations are influenced by the mobility of people. In this sense, mobility is not only a form of movement measured empirically but also a form of representation and embodiment.

This approach understands mobility as an analytical category, rather than a descriptive term. It requires an analysis of which movements can be grasped as mobility and why. Working with the concept of mobility, hence, is a way of ordering social phenomena as objects scholars deal with, on the one hand and of ordering research, on the other. Mobility is "as an ever-changing *object of knowledge* co-shaped and co-constituted by social sciences" (Endres et al. 2016b, p. 3, emphasis in original). This means that the way scholars systematize and order social phenomena is the reason why the mobility paradigm emerged, not the analyzation of descriptive facts.

Mobility studies deal with the manifold ways in which people get involved in transregional, transnational or global networks, or how they are excluded from them and how people and objects cross time and space (Salazar 2016a, p. 3; Sheller and Urry 2016, p. 12). Hence, this field of investigation, furthermore, entails the category of space. Spaces are constituted through social relations and social action (Schroer 2006; Löw 2001; Werlen 1987). The meaning of places and the spatiality of conditions are constituted *in relation to* and as *a result of activities* simultaneously (Werlen 2010, p. 63). Social spaces are, in turn, bound to materiality and lived in geographical places (Werlen 2005). The socio-spatial relationships reflect territorially based mechanisms of appropriation and allocations of different discourses. Hence, space is a place of social order, which brings us back to the aspect of power as part of mobility.

Through using space as an analytical tool, discourses, practices and aspirations become issues of globality. Human movements are better analyzed and understood with and not in contrast to other types of movements, considering not only human movements but also the massive flows of capital and goods which are, simultaneously, an expression, trigger and result of globalization. The global space reminds us that social debates and practices are not locally split but transcend regional and national borders and boundaries. This space between different regions or nation states arises from mobile subjects passing through it, which can be related to each other socially. The linkages between the categories of space and globalization, furthermore, have changed conceptualizations of space: Processes of globalization, which become evident in new information technology and infrastructure, induce "time-space-compression" (Harvey 1989), hence, spatial and temporal overlaps and entanglements. New perceptions of geographical distances and social relationships, which people have over such distances, are constantly developing. Social relationships can by now be maintained over hundreds to thousands of kilometers. Through telecommunications and the World Wide Web, hurdles of time difference and geographical distance are reduced with one click in the Internet.

2. Muslim Mobilities and Gender

Mobility as a lens bridges human mobility and transportation and analyzes these entanglements in their embeddedness in meaning-making and power hierarchies. Structural factors, such as sociopolitical and economic circumstances and backgrounds, play huge roles when it comes to questions such as who can be mobile at which particular historical time and why. With its specification of "Muslim" mobilities (see Fábos and Isotalo 2014), this special issue deals with the im/mobile lives of Muslims, especially regarding the religious or spiritual backgrounds to, influences of and reasons or motivations for their im/mobility. Dealing with this field, we should differentiate between religion and spirituality. The religious side relates to practices based on religious guiding principles or obligations such as going on pilgrimage. People do not only go on hajj (pilgrimage) or umrah ("small pilgrimage") for religious purposes but also for spiritual motivations, which is getting closer to Allah or losing one's ego, for example. Both sides, the religious and the spiritual, form the motivation of Muslims to be mobile. Performing hajj or umrah due to religious obligations and spiritual enhancement leads to further spatial ordering of the Muslim world, which encourages many Muslims to migrate or visit other Islamic places or regions with a high Muslim and Islamic influence. The idea of a "Muslim center" and of a "Muslim periphery" is crucial for the orientation of Muslims in an imagined Muslim world. Exemplarily, Mecca in today's Saudi Arabia is regarded as the center of the Muslim world (Abaza 2011) by most Muslims, as the Kaaba—the black cube in Mecca which symbolizes the house of God (*baitullah*)—is believed to be located at the center of the world. Muslims from all over the world visit these sites for their pilgrimage; 300–330 million pilgrims currently perform their religious obligations at the key sites on the Arab Peninsular every year (Vukonić 2010, p. 33). Based on this concept of sacred regions, Muslims in Asia, Africa or Latin America are positioned and position themselves on the margins of these regions. The ordering based on spiritual reasons becomes evident when considering the numerical side: Indonesia has the world's largest Muslim population but is regarded as part of the "Muslim periphery" (see (Lücking and Eliyanah 2017) in this issue).

Religion is not only a theological or institutional expression of certain imaginations and ideologies but a specific interpretation of social reality and, therewith, a socio-cultural approach to the world (Sandıkcı and Jafari 2013; Schielke 2010). This specific interpretation of reality gets its expressions in institutions (organizations), traditions (oral and material traditions such as symbols, songs, scriptures) and social practices (prayers, moral behavior). Religion offers a comprehensive worldview and, therewith, produces and projects meaning, forms identities, offers orientation for daily activities and legitimizes or delegitimizes power. This special issue deals with these different approaches to Islam and Muslim ways of life: On the one hand, it deals with the sense of "religion," which has its roots, in a Western way of thinking, as an understanding of a human relation to (a) divine being(s). On the level of social processes, this understanding is especially related to institutions and institutional power. On the other hand, it deals with Muslim notions of religion which can be better grasped by the concept of *din*. From a Muslim perspective, *din* includes the obligations Allah imposes on humans, i.e., rational beings. *Din* is the mutual obligation between Allah and Allah's followers, who submit to Allah's authority (Sandıkcı and Jafari 2013, p. 412). This concept includes the way of living, the mental, spiritual and intellectual attitude and the behavior and practices an individual or society follow. It comprises the whole human life in its fullness.

Understanding Islam as a complex net of meaning-making (not only for the im/mobile lives of people), it is, furthermore, a cultural practice entangled with other categories of difference. According to this understanding, Islam as a religion and a way of seeing the world is interwoven with, among other things, gender. Regarding religion and gender as axes of differentiation means focusing them as social constructs that have inflected the varied and unequal lives of people throughout the world for generations. Religion and gender express identifications which are mutually constitutive and inform how people interact with one another. "Identifications" are personal and collective senses of belonging which are culturally constituted, embedded in sociopolitical and historical conditions and, therewith, not anything naturally given (Brubaker and Cooper 2000). The term "identification" extends the static notion of "identity" by adding a perception of dynamic social relations. In this regard, this special issue deals with the intersections of Muslim mobilities and gender (see Uteng and Cresswell 2008), in the sense of negotiating belonging, identity and relations between women, men and other genders based on the respective identifications as a woman, a man or a transgender, for example.

In their entangled effectiveness, religion and gender influence the degree to which people can be mobile (see, e.g., Werbner 2015; Falah and Nagel 2005). The analytical approach to understanding mobility in this respect is popularly termed the "intersectionality" framework (e.g., Thimm et al. 2017; Phoenix and Pattynama 2006; Hooks 2000; Crenshaw 1989). This framework, stemming from the black feminist movements in the US, has become a useful tool for analyzing linkages between social locations, identities and social power structures. Religion could be the only lens applied to analyses of people's im/mobile lives. It is useful to engage with other axes of differentiation, such as gender—but it can be race, ethnicity, class, or sexual orientation, to understand the complexity and richness of social processes. In other words, to analyze how religion interacts with gender and one another and how, in turn, this influences mobility or sedentarism.

It is this understanding that provided the inspiration for this special issue. The aim has been to analyze social relations, identifications and power in im/mobility when it is rooted in religious and/or gendered backgrounds and social structures by bringing together scholars from different disciplines and regional contexts who are interested in engaging in a dialogue between Islamic concepts, Muslim practices and gender and mobility theories. The articles illustrate complex, multiple and even contradictory perspectives on the connections between Islam, gender and mobility. For this special issue, I was particularly interested in works that incorporate historical and sociopolitical understandings into the analysis of the realities of Muslim "movers." Research that employs interdisciplinary investigations of contemporary gender orders, norms and practices in this regard, as part of a net of social relations organizing power and inequality, were particularly welcome. Consequently, I invited contributions that explore the multiple and complex ways that religion, gender and mobility inform and are informed by one another in the call for this special issue. I hope that the articles will accomplish this aim and inspire further research on religion-gender-mobility intersections especially and encourage a critical, situated and dynamic engagement with identities and power hierarchies in order to advance mobility theory in general.

3. Contributions in This Issue

The composition of the articles of this special issue show the variety of how Muslim mobility and gender can be studied as dynamic social fields, on the one hand (Byng 2017; Giuliani et al. 2017; in this issue). On the other hand, it provides insight into the possibilities of using it as theoretical lens to investigate the respective other fields: Mobility can be used as a theoretical lens (and, therewith, as an inclusive category, see (Kramer 2017) in this issue) to investigate gender (Daoud 2017; Golkowska 2017; in this issue). A theoretical gender optic (Lücking and Eliyanah 2017; Shanneik 2017; Wagner 2017; in this issue) or a more complex theoretical approach, i.e., intersectionality, can be used as a lens to approach im/mobility (McLean and Higgins-Opitz 2017; Bianchi 2017; Amin 2017; in this issue).

The first section of this special issue, *Moving through Different Gendered Spaces*, shows what being mobile in everyday life can mean to mobile people themselves and how they navigate through different spaces. In this section, "movement" is key for understanding relations between different social spaces and, therewith, serves as an analytical tool for understanding the connections between gendered spaces. Suheir Abu Oksa Daoud (Daoud 2017) analyzes connections between space, place and identity in general and how transportation (driving cars) relates to space and gender especially in her article *Negotiating Space: The Construction of a New Spatial Identity for Palestinian Muslim Women in Israel* (Daoud 2017). Using in-depth interviews, Daoud examines the impact of space on Muslim Palestinian women living in ethnically divided cities and how ethnicity and patriarchy make a difference in shaping their spatial experiences. Muslim women in Israel have not usually been very present in spaces outside their homes or villages but they have engaged in new spaces in economic, social and educational fields. One strategy for challenging limitations in the public realm is driving private cars, as this "opens new spaces for women and increases women's freedom, confidence, independence, mobilization and involvement in the public space," Daoud argues. The author, therewith, introduces this special mode of transportation to the investigation of women's mobility. In the second article of this section, *Qatari Women Navigating Gendered Space* (Golkowska 2017), Krystyna Golkowska challenges conventional understandings of gendered spaces by examining Qatari women's agency within existing frameworks of the gender–space nexus. Referring to data gathered from the literature as well as ethnographic observation and shared narratives, the author reveals a significant increase in women's presence in the public sphere based on moving into traditionally male dominated spaces, such as education, employment and sports and, thereby, gaining visibility and agency within these spaces.

Whereas the articles in the first section deal with gendered spaces within one nation state, the next section of this issue, *Creating and Negotiating a Transnational Muslim Space*, analyzes the reverse: Firstly, this section deals with a global or transnational space, i.e., the analysis goes beyond one nation state and secondly, the authors do not focus on how this space is gendered but rather "religionized," as I want to put it, based on shared Islamic beliefs and practices. The articles in this section investigate formations of transnational religious space with a theoretical gender approach. Mirjam Lücking and Evi Eliyanah deal with different forms of mobility (pilgrimage, labor migration) in their article *Images of Authentic Muslim Selves: Gendered Moralities and Constructions of Arab Others in Contemporary Indonesia* (Lücking and Eliyanah 2017) and with transnational engagements and negotiations with global discourses in the Muslim World and how these intersect with notions of morality. Based on ethnographic research in Indonesia and a cultural analysis of cinematic representations of Indonesian students in Cairo, the authors examine how Indonesian Muslims, who have traveled to or lived in Western Asia or Northern Africa, define and negotiate their identifications in relation to Arab others. This process takes place against the backdrop of imaginations of a "Muslim Center" (the Arab World) and "Periphery" (the other Muslim majority regions of the world). Within this global sphere of Muslim localizations, gendered moralities—as conceptions of what constitutes good Muslim men and women—are central to images of authentic Muslim selves, Lücking and Eliyanah argue. In the next article of this section, *Shia Marriage Practices: Karbala as* lieux de mémoire *in London*, Yafa Shanneik deals with diaspora and migration, conceptualized in a transnational or global field, as she researches engagements with ideas and practices in the Shia Muslim world (Shanneik 2017). Shanneik shows how Iraqi Shia women in the UK contest and negotiate identity and belonging by referencing to places and spaces that relate to their identity and self. Hence, these identity negotiations in a transnational field become possible based on the past mobile lives of the social actors. The author conceptualizes the transnational aspects of cultural memory expressed in Shia marriage practices as examples of transnational Shia *lieux de mémoire* (which refer to spaces, objects or events that have a significant meaning to a particular group's collective memory as theorized by Pierre Nora). She investigates how marriage rituals, images and objects are used by Iraqi Shia women as a means to preserve religious and cultural memory simultaneously and challenge existing marriage practices. Shanneik enhances Nora's concept by bringing in the transnational as the field of identity-making. The third article of this section, *Mattering Moralities: Learning Corporeal Modesty through Muslim Diasporic Clothing Practices* by Lauren B. Wagner, examines how gendered Muslim corporeality (through clothing practices) is negotiated in a transnational field by constantly physically mobile European-Moroccans (Wagner 2017). The author researches how moral bodies materialize with and through clothing by observing and following the constant mobilities of social actors who are moving back and forth across spaces dominated by "Muslim" and "Western" "regimes of modesty and morality," as Wagner puts it. She investigates particularly how modesty is constructed and constituted through Muslim Moroccan women's bodies across transnational spaces and argues that bodies, clothes and gazes are entangled agents which produce modesty in the transnational field.

The third section of this special issue, *From Mobility to Immobility: Intersectional Identifications as Opportunities or Limitations*, deals with mobility's counterpart: immobility, based on power hierarchies. The interplay of mobility and immobility functions here as a field of investigation. The authors in this section examine the im/mobility nexus with a theoretical gender or intersectionality optic. This is similar to the approach in the previous section *Creating and Negotiating a Transnational Muslim Space* but the fields of mobility and gender are extended in this section by immobility and intersectionality. Michelle McLean and Susan B. Higgins-Opitz (2017) examine gender as a limitation for physical and social mobility (the latter in the form of professional careers) in their article *Male and Female Emirati*

Medical Clerks' Perceptions of the Impact of Gender and Mobility on Their Professional Careers (McLean and Higgins-Opitz 2017). The authors analyze the "feminization," i.e., the increase in the number of women, of medicine by investigating how gender influences the career of medical students in the United Arab Emirates based on semi-structured interviews. McLean and Higgins-Opitz argue that gender intersects with mobility at the point of the student's opportunities, as these are limited for female students based on travel restrictions in the context of a patriarchal, gender-segregated but rapidly changing society in the Gulf. Despite having aspirations and opportunities of specializing abroad, most of the female final year medical students did not take the chance because of the fact or assumption that this would not be possible, as they either need a chaperone or the permission to travel granted by their fathers, brothers or husbands. As more women take up studies in medicine and practice their profession successfully, the young women in McLean's and Higgins-Opitz's study are actors in the field of a changing profession and challenge gender-related values of their broader society, the authors argue. In the next article of this section, *Reimagining the Hajj* (Bianchi 2017), Robert R. Bianchi deals with Muslims who are on the move for religious reasons (hajj and umrah pilgrimage) and how they encounter limits and boundaries in this mobile phase. The author analyzes death rolls made public by whistle blowers in the Saudi Ministry of Health in 2016: The data accessed reveals details about pilgrim deaths in Mecca from 2002 to 2015 (90,276 victims from more than 100 countries), such as the names, nationalities, genders, ages and dates of death. Bianchi reveals that the most vulnerable pilgrim populations are poor people, women and children from across Africa and Asia, as well as foreign workers, refugees and illegal migrants living in Saudi Arabia. In the sense of an intersectionality informed lens, he shows how gender intersects with class, for example. Whereas Muslim pilgrims from affluent societies, such as the Gulf countries, benefit from ongoing medical attention, indigent pilgrims from Mali, Mauritania, Myanmar and Yemen have difficulty helping themselves. Bianchi proposes to reform and reinvent the hajj by lengthening the hajj season from five days to several months to improve the situation drastically. In the third article of this section, *Gender, Madness, Religion and Iranian-American Identity: Observations on a 2006 Murder Trial in Williamsport, Pennsylvania* (Amin 2017), Camron Michael Amin takes "regimes of mobility" and the mobility–immobility nexus as a lens to study intersectional interwoven dynamics. In his microhistorical case study, he deals with the intersection of ethnicity, religion and gender in constructing the social identity of Iranian-Americans. Amin uses particularly Iranian-American/diaspora Studies and im/mobility (regimes of mobility) as an approach to study the case of Brian Hosayn Yasipour, who was sentenced for murdering his daughter. The author argues that the judgment "transformed [Brian Hosayn Yasipour] (...) from an Iranian immigrant, who was free to move between Iranian/Muslim and (White) American/Christian contexts, into an American murderer who was confined to prison" (Amin 2017, p. 2). Therewith, he shows clearly how intersectionally embedded perspectives and circumstances influence social positioning, expressed in possibilities and limitations of individuals.

The next section of this issue, *Intersecting Forms of Im/mobility*, investigates gender through a mobility lens. Hence, the approach in this section is contrary to the investigation of mobility with a gender lens in both sections *Moving through Different Gendered Spaces* and *From Mobility to Immobility: Intersectional Identifications as Opportunities or Limitations*. Max Kramer deals with the interplay of mobility and immobility and with different forms of mobility in *Mobilizing Conflict Testimony: A Lens of Mobility for the Study of Documentary Practices in the Kashmir Conflict* (Kramer 2017) and savors the inclusiveness of the category of mobility. He applies a lens of mobility to the study of documentary film practices and gender in zones of conflict (Kashmir, Northern India) by carrying out ethnographic research. Kramer argues that different mobilities intersect in the filmic practices of filmmaker Iffat Fatima, who discusses representation of Kashmiri Muslim women's agency in conflict zones: When the filmmaker travels with her film and screens it at various places, the audiences get emotionally and intellectually mobilized through the experience of watching it and debating about its subject (Kramer 2017). Against the backdrop of representations of Muslim women in conflict zones as (religiously) immobilized victims, the filmmaker Fatima challenges this narrative by showing female subjects in their everyday (im-)mobility and their participation in demands for political autonomy.

The last section of this issue, entitled *Moving and Settling: Identity Negotiations in Muslim Migration Contexts*, deals with forms of mobility, in this case, with the special form of migration which serves as the field of investigation here. Michelle Byng works on transnational migration from various Muslim majorities countries to the West and how this form of movement is informed by intersectionality in *Transnationalism among Second-Generation Muslim Americans: Being and Belonging in Their Transnational Social Field* (Byng 2017). Using qualitative interview data, the author investigates what experiences second generation Muslim Americans face when visiting their parents' country of origin and how this influences their perceptions of their US American identity. On the macro level, the national and global conflicts around Islam raise important questions about the citizenship of Muslims in the West. On the micro-level, being an American is central to the identity of second-generation Muslims in the United States, which is shaped predominantly by debates and practices regarding religion, ethnicity and nationality within their transnational social field, Byng argues. The second article in this section, *Being a "Good" Son and a "Good" Daughter: Voices of Muslim Immigrant Adolescents* by Cristina Giuliani, Maria Giulia Olivari and Sara Alfieri (Giuliani et al. 2017), similarly studies migration from Muslim majority countries (Morocco, Egypt and Pakistan) to the West (Italy). In contrast to Byng's study on second generation Muslims, this article considers the case of immigrant adolescent children who moved to Italy through family reunification. The authors examine how notions of morality (being a "good" son and a "good" daughter) intersect with gender. They argue that being obedient and respectful of parents' desires is differently articulated by Muslim immigrant girls and boys. Girls must and do focus themselves on staying at home and preserving heritage culture, whereas boys emphasize the importance of educational success to develop the possibility of becoming the breadwinner in their own prospective families. The authors clearly point out that their respondent's post-migration experience is highly influenced by identity negotiations based on the cultural and social expectations of their migrant parents and host country.

Apparently, these four sections are meant to be a starting point for the comparative analysis of the phenomenon in question but they do not cover the entangled processes of Muslim mobilities and gender in its entirety. The present special issue of Social Sciences intends to give a first in-depth analysis which, it is hoped, will be complemented and expanded by future research.

Acknowledgments: I am grateful to the editorial team of Social Sciences for taking care of the publication of this special issue. Managing Editor Siyang Liu supported the whole process with valuable assistance. I would also like to thank the anonymous peer reviewers who took their time to review the manuscripts. They made a generous and valuable contribution and helped to improve the quality of the special issue as a whole.

Conflicts of Interest: The author declares no conflict of interest.

References

Abaza, Mona. 2011. Asia Imagined by the Arabs. In *Islamic Studies and Islamic Education in Contemporary Southeast Asia*. Edited by Kamaruzzaman Bustamam-Ahmad and Patrick Jory. Kuala Lumpur: Yayasan Ilmuwan, pp. 1–28.

Amin, Camron Michael. 2017. Gender, Madness, Religion, and Iranian-American Identity: Observations on a 2006 Murder Trial in Williamsport, Pennsylvania. *Social Sciences* 6: 85. [CrossRef]

Ashutosh, Ishan, and Alison Mountz. 2012. The Geopolitics of Migrant Mobility: Tracing State Relations through Refugee Claims, Boats and Discourses. *Geopolitics* 17: 335–54. [CrossRef]

Bianchi, Robert R. 2017. Reimagining the Hajj. *Social Sciences* 6: 36. [CrossRef]

Bonfanti, Sara. 2016. Dislocating Punjabiyat: Gendered Mobilities among Indian Diasporas in Italy. In *Bounded Mobilities: Ethnographic Perspectives on Social Hierarchies and Global Inequalities*. Edited by Miriam Gutekunst, Andreas Hackl, Sabina Leoncini, Julia Sophia Schwarz and Irene Götz. Bielefeld: Transcript, pp. 183–205.

Brubaker, Rogers, and Frederick Cooper. 2000. Beyond 'Identity'. *Theory and Society* 29: 1–47. [CrossRef]

Byng, Michelle. 2017. Transnationalism among Second-Generation Muslim Americans: Being and Belonging in Their Transnational Social Field. *Social Sciences* 6: 131. [CrossRef]

Crenshaw, Kimberlé. 1989. Demarginalizing the Intersection of Race and Sex: A Black Feminist Critique of Antidiscrimination Doctrine, Feminist Theory and Antiracist Politics. *University of Chicago Legal Forum* 140: 139–67.

Daoud, Suheir Abu Oksa. 2017. Negotiating Space: The Construction of a New Spatial Identity for Palestinian Muslim Women in Israel. *Social Sciences* 6: 72. [CrossRef]

Marcel Endres, Katharina Manderscheid, and Christophe Mincke, eds. 2016a. *The Mobilities Paradigm: Discourses and Ideologies*. London and New York: Routledge.

Marcel Endres, Katharina Manderscheid, and Christophe Mincke, eds. 2016b. Discourses and Ideologies of mobility: An Introduction. In *The Mobilities Paradigm: Discourses and Ideologies*. London: Routledge, pp. 1–7.

Fábos, Anita H., and Riina Isotalo. 2014. Introduction: Managing Muslim Mobilities: A conceptual Framework. In *Managing Muslim Mobilities: Between Spiritual Geographies and the Global Security Regime*. Edited by Anita H. Fábos and Riina Isotalo. New York: Palgrave Macmillan, pp. 1–18.

Falah, Ghazi-Walid, and Caroline Nagel. 2005. *Geographies of Muslim Women: Gender, Religion, Space*. New York: Guilford Publications.

Faulconbridge, James. 2015. Changing practices: A key role for temporality and spatiatlity—James Faulconbridge. *Mobile Lives Forum*. October 28. Available online: http://en.forumviesmobiles.org/video/2015/10/28/changing-practices-key-role-temporality-and-spatiatlity-james-faulconbridge-2958 (accessed on 17 December 2017).

Giuliani, Cristina, Maria Giulia Olivari, and Sara Alfieri. 2017. Being a "Good" Son and a "Good" Daughter: Voices of Muslim Immigrant Adolescents. *Social Sciences* 6: 142. [CrossRef]

Glick Schiller, Nina, and Noel B. Salazar. 2013. Regimes of Mobility across the Globe. *Journal of Ethnic and Migration Studies* 39: 183–200. [CrossRef]

Götz, Irene. 2016. Mobility and Immobility: Background of the Project. In *Bounded Mobilities: Ethnographic Perspectives on Social Hierarchies and Global Inequalities*. Edited by Miriam Gutekunst, Andreas Hackl, Sabina Leoncini, Julia Sophia Schwarz and Irene Götz. Bielefeld: Transcript, pp. 9–11.

Golkowska, Krystyna. 2017. Qatari Women Navigating Gendered Space. *Social Sciences* 6: 123. [CrossRef]

Miriam Gutekunst, Andreas Hackl, Sabina Leoncini, Julia Sophia Schwarz, and Irene Götz, eds. 2016. *Bounded Mobilities: Ethnographic Perspectives on Social Hierarchies and Global Inequalities*. Bielefeld: Transcript.

Hannam, Kevin, Mimi Sheller, and John Urry. 2006. Editorial: Mobilities, Immobilities and Moorings. *Mobilities* 1: 1–22. [CrossRef]

Harvey, David. 1989. *The Condition of Postmodernity. An Enquiry into the Origins of Cultural Change*. Oxford: Blackwell.

Hooks, Bell. 2000. *Feminist Theory: From Margin to Center*. London: Pluto Press.

Kesselring, Sven, and Elly Clarke. 2013. On the Move: In the Virtual and the Physical Worlds. *Mobile Lives Forum*, March 1. Available online: http://en.forumviesmobiles.org/crossed-perspectives/2013/03/01/move-virtual-and-physical-worlds-611 (accessed on 17 December 2017).

Kramer, Max. 2017. Mobilizing Conflict Testimony: A Lens of Mobility for the Study of Documentary Practices in the Kashmir Conflict. *Social Sciences* 6: 88. [CrossRef]

Löw, Martina. 2001. *Raumsoziologie*. Frankfurt am Main: Suhrkamp.

Lücking, Mirjam, and Evi Eliyanah. 2017. Images of Authentic Muslim Selves: Gendered Moralities and Constructions of Arab Others in Contemporary Indonesia. *Social Sciences* 6: 103. [CrossRef]

McLean, Michelle, and Susan B. Higgins-Opitz. 2017. Male and Female Emirati Medical Clerks' Perceptions of the Impact of Gender and Mobility on Their Professional Careers. *Social Sciences* 6: 109. [CrossRef]

Papon, Francis, and Mathieu Flonneau. 2017. The future of cars: Triumph or decline? *Mobile Lives Forum*. January 13. Available online: http://en.forumviesmobiles.org/arguing/2017/01/13/future-cars-triumph-or-decline-3411 (accessed on 17 December 2017).

Phoenix, Ann, and Pamela Pattynama. 2006. Intersectionality. *European Journal of Women's Studies* 13: 187–92. [CrossRef]

Salazar, Noel. 2016a. Keywords of Mobility: What's in a Name? In *Keywords of Mobility: Critical Engagements*. Edited by Noel B. Salazar and Kiran Jayaram. New York: Berghahn, pp. 1–12.

Salazar, Noel. 2016b. Conceptual Notes on the Freedom of Movement and Bounded Mobilities. In *Bounded Mobilities: Ethnographic Perspectives on Social Hierarchies and Global Inequalities*. Edited by Miriam Gutekunst, Andreas Hackl, Sabina Leoncini, Julia Sophia Schwarz and Irene Götz. Bielefeld: Transcript, pp. 284–89.

Sandıkcı, Özlem, and Aliakbar Jafari. 2013. Islamic encounters in consumption and marketing. *Marketing Theory* 13: 411–20. [CrossRef]

Schielke, Samuli. 2010. *Second Thoughts about the Anthropology of Islam, or How to Make Sense of Grand Schemes in Everyday Life*. ZMO Working Papers 2010; Berlin: ZMO.

Schroer, Markus. 2006. *Räume, Orte, Grenzen: Auf Dem Weg zu Einer Soziologie des Raums*. Frankfurt am Main: Suhrkamp.

Shanneik, Yafa. 2017. Shia Marriage Practices: Karbala as *lieux de mémoire* in London. *Social Sciences* 6: 100. [CrossRef]

Sheller, Mimi, and John Urry. 2016. Mobilizing the New Mobilities Paradigm. *Applied Mobilities* 1: 10–25. [CrossRef]

Thimm, Viola, Mayurakshi Chaudhuri, and Sarah J. Mahler. 2017. Enhancing intersectional analyses with polyvocality: Making and illustrating the model. *Social Sciences* 6: 37. [CrossRef]

Thimm, Viola. 2017. Commercialising Islam in Malaysia: *Ziarah* at the intersection of Muslim pilgrimage and the market-driven tourism industry. In *Siri Kertas Kajian Etnik UKM (UKM Ethnic Studies Paper Series Bil. 56*. Bangi: Institut Kajian Etnik, Universiti Kebangsaan Malaysia.

Uteng, Tanu Priya, and Tim Cresswell. 2008. Gendered Mobilities: Towards an Holistic Understanding. In *Gendered Mobilities*. Edited by Tanu Priya Uteng and Tim Cresswell. Aldershot: Ashgate, pp. 1–12.

Darshan Vigneswaran, and Joel Quirk, eds. 2015. *Mobility Makes States: Migration and Power in Africa*. Philadelphia: University of Pennsylvania Press.

Vukonić, Boris. 2010. Do We always Understand Each Other? In *Tourism in the Muslim World*. Edited by Noel Scott and Jafar Jafari. Bingley: Emerald, pp. 31–45.

Wagner, Lauren B. 2017. Mattering Moralities: Learning Corporeal Modesty through Muslim Diasporic Clothing Practices. *Social Sciences* 6: 97. [CrossRef]

Werbner, Pnina. 2015. Sacrifice, Purification and Gender in the Hajj. In *Hajj: Global Interactions through Pilgrimage*. Edited by Luitgard Mols and Marjo Buitelaar. Leiden: Sidestone, pp. 27–39.

Werlen, Benno. 1987. *Gesellschaft, Handlung und Raum: Grundlagen Handlungstheoretischer Sozialgeographie*. Stuttgart: Steiner.

Werlen, Benno. 2005. Raus aus dem Container: Ein sozialgeografischer Blick auf die aktuelle (Sozial-)Raumdiskussion. In *Grenzen des Sozialraums: Kritik Eines Konzepts—Perspektiven für Soziale Arbeit*. Edited by Netzwerke im Stadtteil Projekt. Wiesbaden: VS-Verl. für Sozialwissenschaften, pp. 15–35.

Werlen, Benno. 2010. *Gesellschaftliche Räumlichkeit 2: Konstruktion Geografischer Wirklichkeiten*. Stuttgart: Steiner.

Section 1:
Moving through Different Gendered Spaces

Article

Negotiating Space: The Construction of a New Spatial Identity for Palestinian Muslim Women in Israel

Suheir Abu Oksa Daoud

Department of Politics, Coastal Carolina University, Conway, SC 29528-6054, USA; sdaoud@coastal.edu; Tel.: +1-843-349-6513

Received: 22 April 2017; Accepted: 5 July 2017; Published: 8 July 2017

Abstract: This article examines the impact of space on Muslim Palestinian women living in ethnically divided and deindustrialized cities and the roles ethnic marginalization and patriarchy play in shaping their spatial experiences. It examines how women negotiate their roles within space and establish themselves as actors therein. This study also explores the connection between mobility and space in the case of Palestinian Muslim women in Israel. It considers whether and how space and mobility are connected for this minority group. Muslim women in Israel, who were once rarely involved in spaces outside their homes, fields, and villages, have broken existing boundaries to enter new economic, social, and educational environments. However, the gendering of space for these women has been profoundly changed and challenged by a variety of factors, namely state interference, modernization, and Islamism.

Keywords: women; space; place; Palestinian Muslim; identity; mobility; Israel

---

1. Introduction

Little or no existing research addresses this area of discussion, reflecting the dearth of scholarship on Israeli Palestinian women in general (Daoud 2009). This paper thus aims to fill an existing void while hopefully inspiring further research on the topic. The article is based on an analysis of in-depth interviews with six Muslim women living in religiously and ethnically mixed Muslim-majority cities in Israel.[1] It analyzes women's stories related to their perception of place/space and identity. Examining women's voices enhances current research models and methodologies (Belenky et al. 1986) and highlights women's narratives, activities, concerns, and ideas, thereby enabling us to gain an understanding of what shapes their spatial identities.

The research sample includes the following women: Esheh, Amal, Zuhriyyeh, Raghda, Maha and Susan. All these women are highly educated.[2]

These women come from different localities and regions in Israel and represent different religious ideologies: three are secular, one is a member of the outlawed Islamic Movement,[3] and two view themselves as ideologically similar to the Islamic Movement but are not members. Geographically, one comes from Umm el-Fahm,[4] a predominantly Muslim city and the stronghold of the outlawed

---

1 Interviews with women in this paper were conducted by the author between January and April 2017.

2 Esheh is a Ph.D. student and a mother of one child, in her 30s; Amal is a Kindergarten teacher and mother of five, in her late 40s; Zuhriyyeh is a project manager in her town, single, in her 50s; Raghda, is a student, single, in her 20s; Maha is an instructor, a mother of two, in her 50s; and Susan, is a lawyer and mother of two, in her 40s.

3 In 1996, the Islamic movement in Israel split. The more pragmatic Southern Faction (IMSF) recognized the Oslo Accords and members ran for national elections as part of a coalition of other Arab parties. The Northern Faction (IMNF) on the other hand, opposed the Oslo Accords and active participation in national elections. The latest faction was outlawed by the state in 17 November 2015. On this topic see (Daoud 2016a).

4 It is the second majority Palestinian city after Nazareth with over 52, 000 resident citizens of Israel.

Islamic MovementNorthern Faction. A second woman is from Kuf-Qare', another predominantly Muslim city in the Triangle area. One is from Nazareth, the largest Arab Palestinian city in Israel, which is a Christian-Muslim mixed city in the North,[5] and one is from Haifa,[6] a mixed city of Jewish and Arab residents (Christian, Muslim and Druze). One woman is from Tamra, an entirely Muslim city in the North, and one is from Raineh, a mixed village of Muslims and Christians in the North.

The interviews were based on open-ended questions such as: Tell me about your city; do you feel it is accommodating for women and their needs? What does your city mean to you, and would you consider moving? What does "home" mean to you? What obstacles do you face in private and public spaces? How does politics affect both spaces? Do you believe place affects attire and freedom for women? What are the physical conditions in your locality? Do you think your case represents other cases? As a minority, how does your nationality affect your space and identity?

My experience of conducting research with Palestinian women in Israel on a variety of topics over a period of more than two decades allowed me to carefully select appropriate female participants for this project. I chose women with whom I had previously worked who can speak on the topic and are familiar with terms such as "identity," "public spaces," and "private spaces." Two interviewees, Amal and Raghda, were recommended by prominent activists. The interviewees were excited about this research; however, the topic of space/place was a little new to them and complicated even to educated participants. In total, I contacted ten women, but only six were willing to participate. I would suspect that uneducated or inactive women would have some difficulty speaking on this topic. Interviews were conducted in Arabic via phone, and I translated them to English. In most cases, I had to follow up with participants for clarification and to ensure my translation was accurate. The follow-up communication occurred via email and WhatsApp (WhatsApp Inc. Mountain View, CA, USA). Having known these women for many years. I believe I was able to accurately convey the exact meaning of their sentiments.

One consideration presents itself in this analysis: can the study of a few Muslim women capture the significance of place in women's lives and the identity of the entire female Muslim population in Israel? Five out of the six women interviewed said their cases represent the cases of most women they know. As an initial study on the topic, this project offers insight into women's shifting spaces and identities. It explores how individuals' ethnic and gender identities as Palestinians and as women (religious or secular and city or village dwellers) are formed and affected by their life experiences and relationships.

Understanding Palestinian Muslim women living in a Jewish state and their relationship to space requires contextualizing their experiences within the general Israeli Palestinian population and their relationship to public space in Israel, as will be demonstrated in the following section.

2. Public Space and Palestinian Identity: The Historical-Political Context

Following the 1948 War, Palestinians[7] remaining in the newly established state of Israel became a minority dominated by the Jewish majority and alienated from public space, which was seized by the state's aggressive policies designed to control them. The Jewish state automatically excluded non-Jewish citizens with respect to nation-building, identity definition, political power, and national priorities and goals (Rabinowitz 2001, p. 66). Urban cities and centers shank or disappeared as a result of rapid expansion of Jewish settlements aimed to absorb the new immigrants. The old Palestinian metropolis was erased. Public spaces and poor infrastructure in Palestinian localities became a clear indicator of the group's marginal status, exclusion, and alienation (Rabinowitz 2001, pp. 66–67).

---

[5] A city of about 80,000 Christians and Muslim Palestinians.

[6] Haifa is the third-largest city in Israel located on the Mediterranean, with a population of over 270,000 in 2015. About 82% of its population is Jewish, almost 14% are Palestinian Christians, and some 4% are Muslims.

[7] Palestinians constitute about 21% of the 8.615 million citizens of Israel in 2016; among them, 84.4% are Muslim. See (CBS 2016).

Over the years, institutionalized discrimination became one of the major factors blocking the development of Arab localities in Israel. Since the establishment of the state, not even a single new Arab community has been established.[8] According to *Adalah*—The Legal Center for Arab Minority Rights in Israel, the severe housing crisis facing Arab citizens of Israel is a direct result of long and systematic discrimination in state zoning regulations and land distribution policy (Adala 2017). A letter sent by *Adalah* to various state authorities, including Prime Minister Benjamin Netanyahu, illustrates this problem:

This discrimination has been expressed via massive state land expropriations from Arab citizens, the shrinking of jurisdictional boundaries of Arab municipalities, lack of distribution of state land for the purposes of development, budgeting earmarked for Judaization of the landscape, as well as discrimination in the state budgeting of Arab municipal authorities (Adala 2017).

With no expansion of the existing communities' jurisdictional areas, the population density in Arab localities has increased 11 times over and has significantly contributed to the housing shortage. While local authorities play an important role in the planning and development of their towns, only five Arab local authorities (out of 110) are granted the right to control local planning. Regional committees, mostly Jewish, do most of the planning for Arab towns. This system prevents Arab communities from having development plans designed to address the unique needs of their residents (Adala 2015).

Danny Rabinowitz argues that the spatial discontinuity of Palestinian citizens in Israel damaged their ability to develop a coherent identity (Rabinowitz 2001). However, Abu-Rabia-Queder and Weiner-Levy go one step further, arguing that the discussion of Muslim women in Israel should be put into a context of a minority that resides in separate Arab geographic and cultural spaces, a fact that allows women of this minority to maintain their unique culture (Abu-Rabia-Queder and Weiner-Levy 2008). Complexity of identity of Palestinians in Israel has been largely discussed in the literature about this minority. Some suggest their identity stems from four elements: citizenship (Israeli), ethnic (Arab), national (Palestinian) and religion (Muslim, Christian or Druze)[9]. Other scholars view this minority's ongoing identity dilemma as deteriorating into a crisis.

3. Beyond Location: Space as Identity

In his landmark 1979 essay "Space and Place: Humanistic Perspective," the eminent geographer Yi-Fu Tuan proposed a more humanistic perspective of geography than that to which we are accustomed. Notions of both place and space are core factors in the discipline of geography. While geographic literature historically gave different definitions to any given place, scholars mostly associated it with location. However, argued Tuan, place should be explained within the broader frame of space, and it should not strictly signify location, for it conveys a very real sense of "history and meaning." In his words, then, the study of space is the examination of "a people's spatial feelings and ideas in the stream of experience" (Tuan 1979, p. 388). This experience is how we come to know the world through "feeling, perception and conception." (Tuan 1979) Others have argued that the importance of space should be examined based on human interaction and according to group experiential and social position. Further, the space we construct varies from one individual to another and cultural group to another. Moreover, spaces are "gendered" (Low 1996; Spain 1993; Nakhal 2015, p. 17). Jana Nakhal, who examined gendered space in the case of Beirut, argues that "the capitalist patriarchal system[10] we live under dictates our roles and relations to the place." Nakhal further argues that women are subjugated within "economic and social structures at home, in the street, and in

---

8 This is aside from forced communities of Bedouins in the Negev area, south of Israel. More on this topic, see (Ismael 2005).
9 For further discussion on this topic, see for example (Ghanem 2001; Rouhana 1998).
10 This phrase largely refers to the assumption that the capitalist system feeds on a pre-existing system of oppression, patriarchy, and enforces women's oppression in economy and beyond. See (Comanne 2010).

cafes" and suggests that both women and men living in developing countries need places that fulfill their needs.[11]

Other areas of study, such as environmental psychology, propose that identities form in relation to environments. Place and identity are inextricably bound to one another as people identify with where they live, shape it, and are shaped by it. Examining the relationships among people and places contributes to the understanding of identity formation and the role of place in social and psychological development (Giesek et al. 2014a). Place identity is a sub-structure of a person's self-identity and consists of knowledge and feelings developed through everyday experiences of physical spaces. A sense of place identity derives from the multiple ways in which place functions to provide a sense of belonging, construct meaning, foster attachments, and mediate change.

The public or private character of space is contested politically, economically, socially, psychologically, and spatially. Since the emergence of the notion of "public" in ancient Greece, access and use of public space has always been limited and disputed. Space is always layered in the way it is perceived and regulated, as well as in the way it is physically constructed (Giesek et al. 2014b). According to architectural historian Dolores Hayden, place makes memories cohere in complex ways. People's experiences, she says, focusing on urban landscape, intertwine the sense of place and the politics of space (Hayden 2014). According to her, some identities are hidden from certain narratives of place. Geographer Don Mitchell makes a compelling argument that access to public space is a right, and this right can be examined according to people's right to inhabit that space. He suggests that our ability to occupy public space is a fundamental human right, rather than a right to property (Hayden 2014).

As for the discussion of home, theoretical approaches reveal that the meaning of "home" is rather complicated. A complex distinction has been made between the physical nature of the household and the concept of home, which encompasses interaction between place and social relationships. However, even home is not one-dimensional and is far from being ideal. Idealizing home does not reflect the diverse experiences of people and provides a false description of the meaning of home (Mallet 2004).

The following sections analyze the interviews and discuss the factors that shape Muslim women's relation to space, both public and private.

4. Shifting Space-Shifting Experiences

College education, especially in mixed cities, has increased Palestinian women's experiences, their national identities, and in some cases their feminist awareness. In some cases, these experiences pose challenges when these women go back to their closed spaces and localities; they have to abide by social norms and lose some of the freedoms they enjoyed in the big cities during their college years. Examining the case of Esheh, a young Palestinian woman living in the city of Umm el-Fahm, which is the stronghold of the outlawed radical wing of the Islamic Movement in Israel,[12] we see traces of that assertion.

In particular, the importance of space is reflected in Esheh's undergoing of the traditional move to the home of her new husband's family after marriage, whereupon her social outlook is profoundly changed although she never actually leaves Umm el-Fahm. Esheh said:

> Just recently, I started to feel the importance of place in my life. This especially happened after I got married and moved away from the center of the city, Umm el-Fahm, to live in another neighborhood far from the center. My parents' house is located in the center, and all services are available including a school, a bus, and a store. My new home has no internet connection, no paved street, and no adequate electricity. I realized that I cannot adapt to these changes. Prior to that, I had lived in Haifa for five years as a student. The people I used to deal with were students and academic professionals. The people I have to deal with

[11] See (Nakhal 2015, pp. 24–28).
[12] More on the Topic see, (Daoud 2017; Rubin 2015).

> now are my mother-in-law and my husband's family and their friends. I even have to go to the hair stylist that they go to. This started to bother and affect me much. Before, I used to wonder why women in our society disappear after marriage and used to criticize this phenomenon. I am starting to understand the reason now.

Esheh's example also reinforces the idea that patriarchal values can be held just as easily by women as they are by men, giving shape to their common perception of gender roles See (Daoud 2009, p. 112). Amal, from Tamra, a predominantly Muslim city in the north of Israel, expressed a very similar experience to that of Esheh:

Women live close to the husband's family and relatives; there is no freedom, and the woman is obligated to fulfill all social duties with them. There are a lot of problems because of that. The woman does not have much freedom and choice. Many women are deprived of education and still subject to family violence. There are social centers for women, but women do not go there because of social norms and pressures.[13]

However, the meaning of place for Zuhriyyeh, a Palestinian woman from Kufr Qare', a predominantly Muslim city only a few kilometers from Umm el-Fahm, involves much more than location; it carries spirit, personality, and even a "holiness."[14] In fact, it is often the case that physical, historical, national, and personal experiences come together in an emotionally charged combination in such a space. Zuhriyyeh's experiences were determined, among other factors, by her lifelong physical disability. She recalled the following:

> Unlike other kids of my age, I was not born in a hospital but at home. This is probably why I am still connected to this place and the umbilical cord hasn't fallen until this moment. When I became seven months old, I was given the wrong immunization, like all kids my age in my city. They either died or had some kind of disability. My case was the worst. The state just recently (I am now in my late 40s) acknowledged its responsibility and compensated us. However, my connection to this place is also connected to history, to my late father's story of our dislocation as Palestinians following the 1948 war. Then, all women left, and my father and other men stayed to protect the village (it was not a city yet that time). Every "Independence Day," my father used to tell us this story. It accompanied me all my life. They (the Israelis) got their independence, but at the same time, they took our homeland.

The connection to the land was another type of connection to Zuhriyyeh had with her place. She continues:

> My father was a peasant, and he loved his land and cultivated it and cherished it and his olive trees. He taught us that the land has a higher value. I lived and studied in Haifa for six years, but while I was there, I used to see my town in everything.

5. Physical Buildings and the Politics of Space

Nahkal has argued that architectural standards also matter. They "recreate gender, racial and class hierarchies, just as local cultural productions reinforce specific notions of women-as-space" (Nakhal 2015, p. 18). As a result, Nakhal says, "we are left with an unchallenged reproduction of gender binaries and a reinforcement of what women are 'supposed' to be and do."[15] However, while the physical design features were the focus of many studies, there are few studies focusing on gendered space within the home (Towsend 2000, p. 40). Modern architectures, for example, position

---

13 Interview by Author, 30 March 2017.
14 See for example discussion of Tu Fu on the emotional meaning of space, pp. 409–11.
15 (Nakhal 2015, p. 22).

the kitchen, which is defined as a woman's space, at the rear of the house, which reflects the division of front/back of the house or public/private. However, in more expensive houses, larger kitchens are located in the front of the house.[16] The design of the home thus does not give space to women, although her home is supposed to be her private space. This is illustrated in the case of Esheh, who criticized the culture of buildings and housing in her city that do not take into consideration women's needs, arguing that her case represents so many other cases in her city:

> The culture of buildings and architects are very different in the Arab communities than in Jewish or mixed towns. We build huge houses: villas. My house is 250 meters, and it is not considered above standard. In Haifa, I am ready to live in a 60-meter house. It takes half of my daily energy, about six hours, cleaning. The moment I enter my home, I see the kitchen, and I hate that. It is a reminder that this is the primary space for woman. The absurdity is that the kitchen is open to the living room, so it has to always be clean and tidy, something that is almost impossible. The social environment does not accept those who are different, and the community does not give support. Women have no control over the place. When a woman gets married, her house is already built and prepared by her husband and his family. It is not acceptable by the society that a woman says what she wants from her house or controls the way it is built. No woman I know had a say on her house.

However, Maha from Haifa, a mixed city in the North of Israel, had a different experience and has told a different story. Unlike Esheh, she had a say in choosing her married home and where to live. She also says that other women she knows moved from the village to Haifa, and they also had a say in that decision:

> I don't think you can always assume that the houses in the village are bigger, because that is not always the case. It is true that usually there are more family members there. In my case, our apartment is adequate for two people, and we have a spare room for guests and an office.

Maha admitted, though, that Arab families in Haifa with school-age children have to negotiate their location and space and make compromises. Segregation based on ethnicity is another issue she mentioned:

> Families with children do make sacrifices. Indeed the apartments are smaller, and parking is an issue. This is especially the case when the woman is a professional and the household owns two cars. We live in a mixed neighborhood, but it is one of the few mixed neighborhoods in Haifa. It used to be more mixed, but more Jews have moved out over the years and it has become mostly an Arab neighborhood. There are a lot of segregated Jewish areas in Haifa because Arabs cannot afford to buy or rent homes there and because they are far away from the Arab schools where Arabs prefer to live close to.

The discussion of space and gender brings into examination the spatial dichotomy of private/public spheres, a central consideration in gender theories. Public spaces are considered to be areas occupied by large numbers of people where business and other interactions take place. Private spaces, on the other hand, are areas that involve privacy, intimacy, comfort, a sense of freedom, and liberation. Public spaces, such as the workplace, are viewed as masculine spaces, while private spaces, such as home, are viewed as the female's domain/the domestic sphere. However, strong critiques challenged the "idealized" view of home as a refuge (Mallet 2004, p. 71). This dichotomy was also challenged by feminist theory, which argues that the personal is political. However, some feminists (Davis-Yuval 2003) have fallen into that categorization of personal vs political, associating the

---

16 (Towsend 2000, p. 44).

personal/private with the home and family, where most women are located, and the public as political.[17] In addition to the personal space that does not meet women's needs, public spaces also do not take into account women's and gender needs (Nakhal 2015, p. 17). This shortage is apparent in the case of Zuhriyyeh:

> Our "Arab" localities still lag in their basic infrastructures. For example, here there are no sidewalks. A disabled woman, like me, or a mother who wants to go for a walk with her baby in a stroller, isn't able to do so. Moreover, buildings are very close to each other, and neighborhoods are crowded. There is unbelievable daily traffic, especially in the only entrance to the city, due to state policies and lack of land allocations to public spaces. Our infrastructure suffers in all areas. No one wants to give up any meter of his private land, not out of selfishness but because we are politically trapped. Something has to change about state policies.

Moreover, this research shows that private/personal is not always a free space for women because husbands and different members of the family and extended family have varied positions, interests, and powers. Many of the challenges women face in their public spaces are a result of state policies rather than bad internal local planning.

It is the family and relations between kin rather than the tangible structure of the house that matters most.[18] In examining several cases of Palestinian Muslim women and their relationship to space, it becomes clear that the physical building can create meaning in shaping women's spaces. As Tuan has suggested, piles of bricks and stones become places because they possess life and create meaning. Others have referred to the relation between home and identity and suggested that home is an expression of the self, reflected in interior design, decorations, etc. (Mallet 2004, p. 82) This was the case for Zuhriyya, who was so bound to her house:

> My home is my space; it means so much to me. I built it the way I wanted from my own money. I am strongly attached to my family, to my aging mother, to my brothers and their kids. We are becoming more and more of an individual and consuming society; the fertility rate is decreasing, everyone gets an education and gets a job, and people live on welfare and have overstated amenities. I built a wall around me and do not let anyone interfere with my life. Recently, my brother tried to interfere and dictate something on me. I was shocked at this masculine patriarchal attempt but stood firmly against it.

Raghda, from the city of Nazareth, the largest Arab Palestinian city in Israel, expressed suffocation resulting from the crowded neighborhoods and crowded streets that affect relationships, increase tensions between family members and neighbors, and cause private/public boundaries to disappear:

> Streets are very crowded, and car jams and traffic became so suffocating. I now prefer to walk than to use a car. This traffic is not normal. It causes people stress and nervousness and sometimes leads to trouble. I live in the biggest neighborhood in Nazareth. Houses are very close to each other. It is like they are piling on top of one another. People cannot breathe. The atmosphere is uncomfortable, which causes problems with relatives who live right next door. It is suffocating, noisy, and has negative implications on all areas of our lives, especially the psychological ones.[19]

Spaces have an immense impact on women and their daily lives. Amal from Tamra, a predominantly Muslim city in the North, recalled,

[17] (Towsend 2000, p. 40).
[18] See also (Towsend 2000, pp. 2, 40).
[19] Follow-up interview with Raghda, 25 March 2017.

> My neighbor's house is so close to my balcony that I can literally enter their house. Housing and building land areas are very scarce, and there is very little freedom on where to build. Thus, men live usually above their parent's houses. My house is built above my in-laws' house, and this limits my freedom to a big extent. I have to share everything with them, even their emotions, regardless of my own mood or emotions. Moreover, because there are few houses to rent or for sale, a divorced woman may be forced to live with her kids in her divorced husband's parents' house. My friend lives above her husband and his new wife. She and her kids have no other option. Rental prices are very expensive, and at the same time, it is not accepted socially that divorced women live far from their parents or their ex-husbands' parents.

Even a large central city such as Umm el-Fahm suffers as a result of state policies. While Umm el-Fahm is considered the social, cultural and economic center for residents of the Wadi Ara and Triangle regions, an area in Israel with a concentration of Arab Palestinian towns and villages with a predominantly Muslim population, it is just a periphery town. Indeed, Arab localities and their living structure in Israel have changed dramatically in recent years from small traditional villages to a unique hybrid rural-urban type called "urbanized villages." As Esheh described it in Umm el-Fahm,[20]

> Umm el-Fahm is a periphery; it is not what people expect to see. The neighborhoods have very poor infrastructures, and the local council suffers from a poor budget. The current mayor was a former member of the Islamic Movement who ran as an independent after the Islamic Movement decided it wouldn't run again. The state is responsible, but the local council is also responsible because it works without any planning or efficiency. Additionally, the council establishes projects in a sloppy manner. Residents are also responsible because they build driveways for their houses and use the street while doing so, causing trouble for anyone driving or even walking through the area.

One of the key questions that emerges here is: how do women challenge their spatial relationships? How do they deal with their frustration? Blunt Alison and Jillian Rose, who have also discussed public versus private space, suggested that different individuals interact and experience different spaces depending on their gender and other identities (Blunt and Rose 1994).

Gender, no doubt, plays a role here, but education, character, relationship with the male and male characters, and many other factors should be taken into account when analyzing how women behave when living in suffocating space experiences. The trap that many studies fall into when introducing gender as an aspect of research is that they treat "gender" as only concerning women. McDowell has argued that often women are "slotted-in" in order to satisfy a claim for a gendered approach. What is really required is a consideration of the relationships between and among men and women, boys and girls, in order to gain an understanding of how the home may be experienced differently according to gender (Towsend 2000, p. 40).

Esheh, for example, would not hesitate to move with her hijab and deep Islamist roots to another city like Tel-Aviv, a predominantly Jewish city. This is just to illustrate the amount of frustration and alienation Esheh experiences in her own space, location and society. Still, highly educated women like Esheh wait for the right moment to pursue their dreams. She tries to balance her husband's and society's expectations with her own plans and aspirations:

> When I was single, I had a lot of freedom in my parents' house, as they valued individualism and supported me. I got married to a family with old values. Before marriage, my soon-to-be husband supported the idea of my studying for my PhD in Jerusalem, but after we got married, his mother opposed that, and I did not pursue my PhD. She was very sick, and I

[20] For more on the urbanization of Arab communities in Israel, see (Shmueli and R 2015).

> had to take care of her and take shifts with other family members every day. The husband's family in my society expects things from the woman, but they do not give her anything in return. The woman is considered their daughter in duties but not in rights. Shortly before my mother-in-law passed away, I applied for my PhD. But it is very hard, especially because I have a little kid; it takes me five hours to get to the Hebrew university in Jerusalem and come back home. It is very hard to pursue education after marriage without support. Although this is my city and these are my people, I started to feel alienated. When I sit with my female friends, we all talk about this and all have similar problems and feelings.

Similar to Esheh, Raghda also expressed her desire to move outside of Nazareth and even to a place outside the state:

> Nazareth is beautiful, but it also has a lot of ugly things. Its streets are not comfortable, violence and crime has increased, there is less security, and people do not care for each other like before. There is unseen racism, and sometimes it gets out in a very ugly way (between Muslims and Christians and between different classes). It is also very hard to find a job, and if we do, salaries are very little. Under a Jewish manager in the mall, for example, a girl younger than me could get paid better. There is more appreciation. Here, girls work long hours and accept a salary below the minimum wage. If I get an opportunity to live outside, I am not going to hesitate.

Davis-Yuval identified two important points. First, in welfare states, no society can be free from state intervention, direct or indirect; second, cities or urban spaces offer more freedom and fluidity than villages or towns (Davis-Yuval 2003). Maha, no doubt, has found more freedom in Haifa:

> I live in Haifa, and I consider myself a city person. I've never lived in a village. The city to me is the place that I can be relatively more anonymous and where I feel freer to be who I am. Haifa provides me with a fair amount of diversity and a fair amount of access to culture (theater, film, lectures, etc.) It is a place I feel at home because of the climate and the presence of a certain percentage of Palestinian/Arab citizens.

Despite finding more freedom and opportunities living in mixed cities, Palestinians in Israel face several challenges. Indeed, the images of the ethnic divided and deindustrialized city have been very influential in studies of conflict and critiques (Low 1996). As an ethnic minority in Israel, people in Arab cities suffer from neglect and different types of discrimination.[21] Even in mixed cities, Arabs suffer from unemployment, crowded neighborhoods, failed health systems and unequal allocation of resources in the education system (Shmueli, Deborah F. and Khamaisi R, ibid) Maha said:

> I can say that my personal experience and the experiences of other women friends in Haifa point to a severe shortage in jobs for Arab women, and living in the city does not really open up doors that are closed to Arab women in Israel in general.

Maha asserted that Haifa is "still not a place that I feel that I own." She was talking about a different type of alienation:

> Over time, Haifa has become physically more crowded and has attracted intolerance. In July 2014, during Israel's war against Gaza and in the midst of joint Arab-Jewish peaceful protests against the war, the protesters were violently attacked by right-wing, pro-war outsiders of the city who came loaded in buses. These attacks took place just a few minutes away from my neighborhood. However, no violators were caught or prosecuted. This event was very telling about the illusion of Haifa as a place where tolerance and diversity thrive, and that affected my sense of security.

---

[21] There are Arab 17 cities in Israel, among them 6 mixed of Arabs and Jews.

Maha expressed her impatience as the place keeps impacting her life in many ways:

> I have changed as well, as I find myself being more and more impatient as the city gets to be more crowded and the general political environment in the country becomes more aggressive toward Arabs. Only recently, in November 2016, and during the fires in Haifa,[22] the prime minister announced that this was Arab terrorism, when in fact the police continue to announce that they still do not have any evidence of that. The general atmosphere is poisoned.

Maha accused the Israeli government of causing this alienation: "The government is ultimately responsible for the intolerance and the fact that Arab citizens feel that belonging is lacking."

A space had changed over time, and nostalgia is something people talk about not only in literature, but in their daily lives:

> Everyone speaks about nostalgia, about a city that many leaders and graduates came from. My mother says the only thing in common between our city today and forty years ago is ignorance. People still value a strong person and do not dare to challenge him. She is a remarkable woman.

Mobility and the Search for New Opportunities

Mobility has been defined as "freedom for movement across physical space" (Rosen 2011). It is the process of striking out for new prospects; it indicates liberation, self-reliance, exploration, and reinvention (Rosen 2011). Mobility enhances capabilities, increases opportunities and is an important component of women's freedom (See (Hanson 2010)). Lack of reliable public transportation, limited ownership of private vehicles by women, and poor road conditions limit or deprive women of access to certain public spaces, mainly work places and other opportunities. In some cases, these conditions also increase harassment against women and make women's journeys unsafe (Mahadevia et al. 2016).

One question to be asked in this study is whether Muslim women in Israel drive their own cars and how safe it is for them to move around.

Cultural and social restraints have been given to explain the lack of Palestinian women's access to work places in Israel and the limited mobility of these women using private cars. However, cultural explanations alone ignore the impact of state policies on the economic status of large segments of Palestinians in Israel who suffer from economic difficulties and cannot afford to buy cars or who lack proper public transportation in their Arab localities. A study conducted by Kayan, a feminist organization based in Haifa, has shown that while an increasing number of Palestinian women have driver's licenses, between 37 and 44 percent cannot afford to buy a car, and 23 percent do not have their own cars because of social reasons (In (Daoud 2012)).

All the women in this research have driver's licenses and private cars except for Raghda. She commented:

> I've had my driver's license for nine years, but I do not have a car yet. I use my father's car or walk. Someone has to bear in mind the many expenses of having a car before they buy a car, yet lately, I have started thinking of buying one.

This connection is confirmed by all the women in this study. Amal commented that having a private car increases women's independence and the opportunity to participate in the workplace, and Maha, who has been driving a car for 38 years, said that "no doubt it increases women's freedom and creates opportunities." According to Esheh,

---

[22] A wave of fires in Israel during November 2016 that affected various regions, mainly Haifa.

> Having a car is one of the most useful things I've ever experienced. Before I got a car, I had to use public transportation or walk to my workplace, which consumed a large portion of my time. This also made it harder to stay out in the evenings because it is not safe. No doubt having private cars increases women's freedom and mobility, especially for women who cannot do their basic errands such as going to the store or to the doctor without asking the help of others. That is especially true in our city as well as most Arab localities, where public transportation is not adequate.

While Zuhriyyeh echoes Esheh's assessment, she stresses the connection among mobility, personal freedom and time: "These three components are connected to each other." She also adds that in recent years, there has been improvement in public transportation inside her city and between her city and the Jewish main centers, which facilitates mobility for all.

Raghda said that transportation in Nazareth is not an issue, yet she elaborated on the transportation difficulty in other Arab localities, especially those that are not recognized by the state of Israel, such as Ein Houdh,[23] where buses provide service every few hours. There are no schools either, so students have to walk a long way to other localities to seek education.

Interestingly none of the women experienced sexual harassment while using public transportation. Some, however, experienced a different kind of harassment when they became drivers. "Women do not know how to drive" is a general assumption by males in her society, says Esheh:

> I was not harassed in the past when I took public transportation. Now, as a driver, I face harassment from male drivers who shout at me to move although they are the ones who are not following the rules. Lately, I have started to shout back at them and use the same phrase they use against my driving: 'Who gave you a driver's license?'

Zuhriyyeh speaks about a different type of harassment:

> Racist treatment against us [Palestinians in Israel] is becoming a phenomenon in the Israeli society today, especially after the right wing government took over. It has become more frequent that Palestinians with religious appearances are the subject of racist harassment.

Safety is another issue that was raised in the women's discussion about mobility. Women from several cities including Nazareth, Umm el-Fahm and Kufr-Qare' said their mobility is very limited at night because of the growing violence, frequent shootings and murder cases in their cities. "Our localities are not safe anymore. In the evening, it is not safe even for my kid to stand in our front yard," says Esheh.

The situation in other localities seems better. For example, Amal says that in Tamra, a predominantly Muslim city in the north part of the country, public transportation is acceptable and safety prevails in the city:

> Tamra is a small city, and recently the local authority introduced a new transportation system that eased mobility. Some roads are still not safe and lack proper lighting or sidewalks. But generally speaking, I am not afraid to walk at night. It is a safe place, and the people of my city are peaceful.

Maha commented that Haifa, too, is a city with multiple means of transportation and that there are no problems with mobility in this area. She also said that Haifa feels particularly safe although she does not usually walk late at night in the downtown area.

In sum, Palestinian women's mobility opens new spaces for women and increases women's freedom, confidence, independence, mobilization and involvement in the public space; it also provides

---

[23] In 2012, Israeli authorities shut the only school in this un-recognized Arab Muslim small village in Israel. Israel does not recognize more than 40 Arab localities that existed prior to the foundation of Israel and does not provide them with any basic services including electricity, water, paved roads and education. More on this topic, see (Ismael 2005).

some safety by allowing them to avoid walking at night. However, this mobility is also affected by women's status as part of a marginalized ethnic group in Israel.

6. Publicizing the Personal: Space and Islamism

To what extent is the space of Palestinian women shaped by the rise and the existence of the Islamic Movement (IM) and its dominance or lack of dominance in their cities? To what extent does the IM or nationalism affect women's dress and their private-public spheres?

Surprisingly to many, the IM in Israel, which organized legally in early 1980, heavily mobilized Muslim women, unlike the long-argued fundamentalist approaches that suggest women's limitation and confinement to their homes and roles as mothers and wives. Before the IM, there were few attempts to establish associations to absorb religious Muslim women and to incorporate them in the public life. With this involvement, the public-private dichotomy was cracked open; women in the IM became immersed in charitable, educational, religious, social, and national activities. The movement strongly advocated women's education (although it supported separation in some places) and involvement in politics (although not in high- ranking positions). Online activism in social media, mainly Facebook, and blogs opened a new space for these women to publish their ideas and feelings and to promote their agendas, opinions, and activism (Daoud 2016b, p. 21).

Nabila, an activist from the Democratic Front for Peace and Equality (DFPE),[24] a fierce opponent party to the Islamic Movement, commented on the new phenomenon of Muslim women becoming active in the public sphere in Nazareth:

> Suddenly these women began to have a life outside their homes. You see them participating in all kinds of activities and meetings in the town. The hijab is not very widespread–maybe because the Islamic Movement itself is not strong here or maybe because of our closeness to the Jewish centers. Although some might think that the last factor might push people more toward religion or conservatism as a reaction to the Jewish influence, this did not happen.

Women's roles were further emphasized by the Islamic Movement's factions, in both the North and the South, especially around election times, when competition for the Arab vote is very intense. Even women in the radical faction of the movement that split in 1996 were largely mobilized.

Mobilization of women in the IM came amid accusations that the IM aims to take women backward and that it imposes the hijab on them. For women interviewed for this research, place definitely affects attire and experiences; however, traditions can play a stronger role than Islamism, as Esheh suggested:

> In Umm el-Fahm, a city where tradition is stronger than religion, the city does not encourage face covering but the hijab with light makeup. The place definitely affects attire. Most women my age wear the hijab with jeans. They prefer the Turkish style.

Zuhriyyeh made an important comparison of her town and Umm el-Fahm, both in the same geographic area and both predominantly Muslim. Her comments confirm that Muslim communities and locations are diverse and that the politics of place differ from one community to another. She said:

> Umm el-Fahm is geographically close to us, but it is oppressive toward women. Unlike women there, women in my city are a model for change and leadership. Many political and active women brought change and are deeply involved. Here, the Islamic Movement has negative and positive impacts on women and people. One example is IM's support for the poor. Women of the Islamic Movement here also participate in remarkable activism. Unlike other women's groups from other parties, they work quietly and effectively.

---

[24] DFPE is an umbrella organization including several Palestinian groups with a dominant Israeli Communist party leadership.

> Still, there is a social pressure of the place that expects women, especially the married with older kids and the elderly, to veil. But I believe that the hijab and religion are not related. I do not wear a hijab but view myself as religious.

While an increased number of Muslim women wear the hijab in Israel, earlier research has suggested that this increase is not always connected to the rise of the Islamic Movement in Israel. It was a choice mainly connected to two factors: religion and nationalism (Daoud 2016b). None of the women interviewed by the author has worn the hijab by force. The case of Amal from Tamra, who admitted that she was forced to wear the hijab, portrays women's personal space as shaped and constructed by the political. Amal recalled,

> I did not want to wear the hijab. My husband forced me. He joined the Islamic Movement and it was not acceptable that a wife of an IM member goes unveiled. All my sisters are unveiled. Now, with the IM outlawed by the government, I suspect the younger female generation won't be under such pressure. My friend was pressured in a different way. She was beaten by her husband because she refused to vote for his political nominee.

However, it seems again that in mixed cities, including Jewish/Arab such as Haifa or a Christian/Muslim city such as Nazareth, women enjoy more personal space and freedom of dress. Raghda asserts that in Nazareth, a lot of freedom is given to women in the area of dress and movement:

> We go to cinemas and cafes at night, and more and more women in the past years have enjoyed entertainments in the city. We also have a lot of freedom in our dress. We do not face any issues in these matters.

Maha also spoke about the politicizing of women's personal space, not necessarily by the Islamic Movement, which is weaker in Haifa, but by the internal Palestinian political forces in the city. She points out that some Arab parties contribute to the increasing alienation and separation of women in an ethnically divided city:

> I do not see the influence of the Islamic Movement in Haifa. The Democratic Front for Peace and Equality (DFPE)/Communist party is definitely weaker and has lost its influence on the city. The National Democratic Alliance (NDA) has a presence here, and due to NDA's influence, there is a general tone of competition regarding who is more loyal to the Palestinian heritage and who is more patriotic. NDA also feeds a sense of us (Palestinians) vs. them (Israeli Jews) and contributes to a sense of separation between Arabs and Jews in Haifa. The election of Ayman Odeh (DFPE and a resident of Haifa) to the Knesset and his lucid and inclusive rhetoric have helped ease tensions and raised a feeling of pride among the Arabs in Haifa.

While the spread of the hijab is clear, there is no evidence it affected women negatively in their communities; it did not hinder Islamist women from public activism. In fact, the opposite happened.[25] Moreover, supported by the IM male-dominated leadership, many Muslim women view fundamentalist movements as vehicles for socioeconomic advances. A member of the outlawed radical faction stated: "Similiar to other societies, our society undermines women. I am criticized for my education and work that requires me to travel. It is true there is a general support for women's work, but there are still restrictions. To me, the only framework that encourges my activities, including the political ones, is the Islamic Movement". (Daoud 2016b)

[25] (Daoud 2016b, pp.39–41)). A similar conclusion was reached by Arar and Shapira, who noted that the hijab can enable Muslim women to break into the public sphere and to become part of society's influential circles. See, (Arar and Shapira 2016).

Not surprisingly, Muslim women are alienated from the public space outside of their communities because they wear head covers and speak Hebrew with an accent. They also suffer discrimination when seeking employment in Jewish centers.[26]

7. Conclusions

Examining several cases of Palestinian Muslim women and their relationship to their place and space, it is clear that space, gender and ethnic identity are entangled. The private/public dichotomy proves to be artificial. Personal space is shaped and constructed by multiple factors: the physical, the family/friend relationships, the political/religious/local, and the state. Political interference in the private/personal realm has jeopardized its security and privacy. Public and private are intertwined, and boundaries between them are difficult to distinguish. Further, interviews have shown that physical space and familial relationships are important factors in shaping gender spaces.

Even in what is supposed to be their private space (the home), Arab Muslim women face significant intervention from different family members. Their personal space often does not offer them refuge and comfort. The space is not in favor of these women's aspirations for more freedom to pursue their dreams of higher education, a better job, or a peaceful life. In the public arena, they are not part of the space planning, the architecture of the city, or the streets that do not meet their needs as women and mothers and disabled community members. The community offers little space for women to speak out their frustrations, their suffocation, and their preferences for the space. In larger mixed cities, encompassing different communities, cultures and ethnicities, Muslim women have a greater margin, and their space is shaped by similar and yet different problems: divided cities, marginalization as an ethnic group, and sometimes a feeling of lack of belonging (Rendell 2003).

This research has also shown that Palestinian women's mobility is connected to several issues. Owning private cars opens new spaces for women and increases women's freedom, confidence, independence, mobilization and involvement in the public space; it also provides some safety by allowing them to avoid walking at night. However, this mobility is also affected by women's status as part of a marginalized ethnic group in Israel. In Muslim majority cities, state authorities do not work to address safety problems or interfere by imposing the law against the growing violence and acquisition of arms by the citizens. This environment significantly affects women's mobility, as it causes them to be fearful of going out after the sun sets.

Daphne Spain has argued that spatial perspective points out the reciprocity between status and space (Spain 1993). This is true to some degree, but not completely. Women in this research were mostly educated; however, their impact over space was limited due to a variety of factors. Changes in economic and educational factors have not always empowered Muslim Palestinian women in Israel or led them to challenge their spatial boundaries. Living in majority Muslim cities and in mixed cities, Palestinian Muslim women face a variety of factors that limit their freedom and alienate them because of their gender, their ethnicity, or both. "Humanist findings," argued Tuan, promote self-knowledge that is essential to examine our lives. Examining the meaning of place in the case of Palestinian Muslim women and the challenges they face in their personal and public spaces are the first steps to overcome their spatial alienation and to find meaning in their lives.

Conflicts of Interest: The author declares no conflict of interest.

References

Abu-Rabia-Queder, Sarab, and Naomi Weiner-Levy. 2008. Identity and gender in cultural transitions: Returning Home from Higher Education as 'Internal Immigrants' Among Bedouin and Druze Women in Israel. *Social Identities* 14: 665–82. [CrossRef]

[26] For obstacles facing Palestinian women in Israel face in workplaces, see (Daoud 2012).

Adala. 2015. Deliberate Obstacles, Not Failures: Adalah's Response to The State Comptroller's Report on the Housing Crisis in Israel. *Adala*. April 28. Available online: https://www.adalah.org/en/content/view/8536 (accessed on 29 April 2017).

Adala. 2017. Israeli State Policy Prevents Legal Construction in Arab Towns, Creates Dire Housing Crisis. *Adala-The Legal Center for Arab Minority Rights in Israel*. January 19. Available online: https://www.adalah.org/en/content/view/9003 (accessed on 29 April 2017).

Arar, Khalid, and Tamar Shapira. 2016. Veiling and Management: Muslim Women Managers in Israel. *International Journal of Cross Cultural Management* 16: 367–84. [CrossRef]

CBS. 2016. Central Bureau of Statistics. Available online: http://www.cbs.gov.il/reader/cw_usr_view_Folder?ID=141 (accessed on 29 April 2017).

Belenky, M., B. Clinchy, N. Goldberger, and J. Tarule. 1986. *Women's Ways of Knowing: The Development of the Self*. New York: Basic Books.

Blunt, Alison, and Jillian Rose. 1994. Introduction: Women's Colonial and Postcolonial geographies. In *Writing Women and Space*. New York: the Gilford Press.

Comanne, Denise. 2010. How Patriarchy and Capitalism Combine to Aggravate the Oppression of Women. *CADTM*. Available online: http://www.cadtm.org/How-Patriarchy-and-Capitalism (accessed on 13 February 2017).

Daoud, Abu Oksa Suheir. 2009. *Palestinian Women and Politics*. Gainesville: University Press of Florida, p. 2.

Daoud, Suheir Abu Oksa. 2012. Palestinian Working Women in Israel: National Oppression and Social Restraints. *Journal of Middle East Women's Studies* 8: 78–101.

Daoud, Suheir Abu Oksa. 2016a. Islamism, Nationalism and Modernization: The Case of the Islamist Movement in Israel. *Politics, Religion & Ideology* 17: 18–32.

Daoud, Suheir Abu Oksa. 2016b. Women in the Islamic Movement in Israel. *Gender and Islamism-Special Issue, Frontiers: A Journal for Women Studies* 37: 21–46.

Daoud, Suheir. 2017. Islamism in Israel, between Integration and Clash. *Middle East Online*. March 27. Available online: www.middle-east-online.com/?id=245072 (accessed on 13 April 2017).

Davis-Yuval, Nira. 2003. Citizenship, Territoriality and the Gendered Construction of Difference. In *State/Space: A Reader*. Edited by Neil Brenner, Bob Jessop and Martin Jones. Malden: Blackwell Publishing, p. 320.

Ghanem, As'ad. 2001. *Palestinian Arab Minority in Israel, 1948-2000*. Albany: State University of New York Press.

Jen Jack Giesek, William Mangold, Cindi Katz, Setha Low, and Susan Saegert, eds. 2014a. Place and Identity. In *The People, Place and Space Reader*. Abingdon: Routledge, Available online: http://peopleplacespace.org/toc/section-3/ (accessed on 2 May 2017).

Jen Jack Giesek, William Mangold, Cindi Katz, Setha Low, and Susan Saegert, eds. 2014b. "Public" and "Private" Realms. In *The People, Place and Space Reader*. Abingdon: Routledge.

Hanson, Susan. 2010. Gender and mobility: new approaches for informing sustainability. *Gender, Place and Culture* 17: 5–23. [CrossRef]

Hayden, Dolores. 2014. Urban Landscape History: The Sense of Place & Politics of Space. In *The People, Place and Space Reader*. Abingdon: Routledge.

Ismael, Abu Sa'ad. 2005. Forced Sedentarisation, Land Rights and Indigenous Resistance: The Palestinian Bedouin in the Negev. In *Catastrophe Remembered, Palestine, Israel and the Internal Refugees*. Edited by Nur Masalha. London: Zed Books.

Low, Setha M. 1996. The Anthropology of Cities: Imagining and Theorizing the City. *Annual Review of Anthropology* 25: 383–409. [CrossRef]

Mahadevia, Darshini, Aseem Mishra, Anurita Hazarika, Yogi Joseph, and Tinam Borah. 2016. *Safe Mobility for Women, Case of Guwahati*. CUE Working Paper; Ahmedabad: Centre for Urban Equity, p. 33.

Mallet, Shelly. 2004. Understanding Home. *The Sociological Review* 52: 62–84. [CrossRef]

Nakhal, Jana. 2015. Women as Space, Women in Space: Relocating our Bodies and Rewriting Gender in Space. *Kuhl, Journal for Body and Gender* 1: 15–22.

Rabinowitz, Danny. 2001. The Palestinian Citizens of Israel: The Concept of Trapped Minority and the Discourse on Transnationalism in Anthropology. *Ethnic and Racial Studies* 24: 64–85. [CrossRef]

Rendell, Jane. 2003. Introduction: 'Gender, Space'. In *Gender Space Architecture: An Interdisciplinary Introduction*. Edited by Jane Rendell, Barbara Penner and Iain Borden. New York: Routledge.

Rosen, Christine. 2011. The New Meaning of Mobility. *The New Atlantis* 31: 40–46.

Rouhana, Nadim. 1998. *Palestinian Citizens in an Ethnic Jewish State: Identities in Conflict*. New Haven and London: Yale University Press.
Rubin, Lawrence. 2015. Why Israel Outlawed the Northern Branch of the Islamic Movement? *Brookings*, December 7.
Shmueli, Deborah F., and Khamaisi R. 2015. *Israel's Invisible Negev Bedouin: Issues of Land and Spatial Planning*. Switzerland: Springer International Publishing, pp. 13–20.
Spain, Daphne. 1993. Gendered Spaces and Women's Status. *Sociological Theory* 11: 137–151. [CrossRef]
Towsend, Poula. 2000. Gendered Space? An Exploration of the Gendered Meaning and Experience of "Home" in Contemporary British Society. *Gender and Home* 3: 40–46. Available online: http://research.ncl.ac.uk/forum/v3i1/gendered%20space.pdf (accessed on 13 February 2017).
Tuan, Yi-Fu. 1979. Space and Place: Humanistic Perspective. In *Philosophy in Geography*. Edited by S. Gale and G. Olsson. Berlin: Springer, p. 388.

Essay

Qatari Women Navigating Gendered Space

Krystyna Golkowska

Faculty of Premedical Education, Weill Cornell Medicine-Qatar, Education City, P.O. Box 24144 Doha, Qatar; krg2005@qatar-med.cornell.edu; Tel.: +974-4492-8223

Received: 27 July 2017; Accepted: 12 October 2017; Published: 16 October 2017

Abstract: ADespite growing interest in the lived experience of Muslim women in Arab countries, there is still a dearth of studies on the Gulf region. This article focuses on Qatar, a Gulf Corporation Council (GCC) country, to explore its changing sociocultural landscape and reflect on Qatari women's agency within the framework of the traditional gendered space model. Applying Grounded Theory methodology to data collected from a variety of scholarly and non-scholarly sources, the author offers a themed overview of factors that facilitate and constrain Qatari women's mobility. The findings testify to a significant increase in female presence and visibility in the public sphere—specifically in the spaces of education, employment, and sports. They also show that young Qatari women exercise agency through navigating the existing systems rather than question traditional socio-cultural norms. The paper identifies this search for a middle ground between tradition and modernity and its ideological underpinnings as the area of future research that should be led by Qatari women themselves.

Keywords: Qatar; gender; space; tradition; modernization; globalization; women; agency; mobility; transformation

---

1. Introduction

Recent years have seen growing interest in exploring the lived reality of Muslim women in Arab countries (Gonzalez 2013; Falah and Nagel 2005; Sonbol 2003; Sedghi 2007). In this context, the scarcity of studies on the Gulf Corporation Council (GCC) countries is striking, especially since modernization and globalization have been dramatically changing the region and bringing with them a host of social issues that remain understudied (Gonzalez 2013, p. 210). Qatar, a small but important Gulf state due to its strategic location, resources, and political positioning, has so far received even less attention than its neighbors. The country's ambition to play a leadership role in the region usually gets a fair deal of attention locally and internationally, but its changing sociocultural landscape has not been fully examined yet. Among the few studies of the lived experience of women in GCC countries (Sonbol 2012; Pandya 2013; Benn et al. 2011; Gonzalez 2013; Le Renard 2014; Bristol-Rhys 2016), none concentrates on Qatar. There is a clear need for quantitative and qualitative research on the country's socio-cultural transformations, especially from a gender perspective. The present paper aims to identify a gap in the literature on Qatari women's mobility and agency and map the territory for future inquiry.

The lens used in the present discussion is shaped by feminist geography. Although in the literature on Muslim women the spatiality of gender relations has not been fully explored (Falah and Nagel 2005, p. 3), feminist geography seems to provide the best perspective for analyzing the complex relationships between bodies, identities, places, and power. Since the 1980s, feminist geographers have been emphasizing the importance of examining the lived experience of particular women at a particular time and in a particular place. Adopting this approach helps to move beyond the perspective of the white, middle-class Western woman—the bias in early feminist research identified by, for example, bell hooks (1984) and Chandra Talpade Mohanty (1984); it also helps to avoid the risk of downplaying differences and defining the subject as "the Arab/Muslim woman" (for challenges to Orientalist representation of Muslim women see Mahmood 2005; Falah and Nagel 2005; Abu-Lughood 2016). Moreover, from the beginning, feminist geographers have been interested in the interplay between gender and space (both physical and symbolic), particularly in the division between the public and private spheres and spatial constraints facing women (Ardener 1981; Domosh and Seager 2001; Moss 2002; Torstrick and Faier 2009). Such theorizations are very relevant in exploring Arab cultures, and are especially useful in examining issues at the intersection of gender, space, and religion in the Gulf.

Since Qatar is a Sunni monarchy with Sharia law as its main source of legislation, Qatari women's present day mobility needs to be viewed in the context of the established patterns in Islamic gender relations. While historically the level of human mobility was high for Muslims, tribal order and strict interpretation of the Qur'an resulted in a rigid spatial organization (Hidemitsu 2003). For a follower of Islam, space and movement in it are imbued with both social and religious significance. A faithful Muslim makes every effort to live in Dar al-Islam, Muslim space, a binary opposite of Dar al-Harb, a non-Muslim space. This kind of life means literal and metaphorical orientation towards Mecca. Indeed, one of the five religious duties of Muslim is a religious pilgrimage to the holy city and the bodily performance of daily prayers involves facing that direction. Moreover, in Muslim societies religion intersects all types of space. With regard to social relations, a strict interpretation of the Qur'an enforces gender segregation. Hence the division into male and female domains and allotment of roles corresponding to them. Traditionally, public space is perceived as exclusively male; women are confined to the household, where they act out their roles of wives and mothers. Moreover, spatial separation exists within domestic space as well, with parts of the house designated for exclusive use of women and men. Even weddings and funerals are celebrated separately. In brief, as Belk and Sobh (2009) notice, in addition to a more prominent boundary between public and private space marked by walls and windows facing inward, "within Arab Muslim homes, there is a sharper distinction between men's and women's spaces as well as transitional spaces in moving from one to another" (p. 34).

In Islam, the principle of gender separation is further signaled through spatial practices related to clothing. The rule of modesty requires that a woman covers her body and wears a hijab (a headscarf). Likewise, the prohibition against attracting the male gaze regulates female body language and behavior in a mixed gender environment. Perhaps no other concept has been more hotly contested in the literature on Muslim women than the veil (Mernissi 1992; Secor 2010; Ahmed 2012). Nowadays, especially in the diaspora, the practice of wearing a hijab can be interpreted as signaling a variety of attitudes; it can function as a sign of religiosity, respect for tradition, political beliefs or a combination of any them (Secor 2010). Originally, however, the practice of veiling used to denote the status of Muslim females and shelter them when they ventured outside their domestic sphere. Thus, by symbolically upholding the division between the male and female space it allowed women some mobility while enforcing the rule of avoiding the male gaze.

Since women are perceived as bearers of the family honor, their movement outside the household is controlled and restricted (Sharabi 1988; Barakat 1993). Many females in the Gulf still travel only with a family member. Under Sharia law, a woman is not allowed to travel the distance of "three days and three nights/48 miles" without her husband or a Mahram, a male guardian for whom it would be unlawful to marry the woman due to blood relation or marriage (Central Mosque 2003). Nowadays, a single Qatari woman under the age of 25 needs to obtain her father's or husband's permission to travel abroad; this can be seen as a sign of progress as previously this age limit used to be 50 years of age. On the other hand, male Qataris need a guardian's permission only until they reach the age of 18 (Ministry of Interior Qatar 2013). Married women are entitled to travel without permission irrespective of their age, but in case the husband does not want his wife to travel, he can approach the competent court to prevent her journey. Overall, although in general Qataris travel a great deal, women's freedom of movement remains regulated.

Now that advances in transportation and communication have increased global connectivity and interdependence, traditional spatial boundaries need to be constantly renegotiated. In the case of Qatar, industrialization and modernization resulted in an influx of expatriates from all over the world, all arriving with different beliefs regarding gender and spatial practices. More importantly, the government's decision to pursue modernization and build a knowledge-based economy meant importing Western models of education and modern patterns of social life. Hence, the newly created physical and symbolic space offers opportunities for growth as well as potential tension between Western liberalism and local conservative interpretation of Islam. This situation gives rise to many questions, chief among them being how Qatari women navigate between modern and traditional codes of conduct and spatial practices.

The present paper begins with a brief overview of factors that facilitate Qatari women's advancement and hamper their progress. The section on the government policy and public discourse on gender is followed by a brief discussion of female presence and gender identity performance in public space. Available data gathered from the literature as well as ethnographic observation and shared narratives suggests that Qatari women operate within the traditional gendered space model and show little desire to question it. Instead, they try to find agency in modifying established codes of conduct or spatial practices. It is this search for the middle ground and the potential emergence of a culturally defined notion of agency that the paper identifies as the area for future research. The author suggests that this type of inquiry should be led by Qatari women themselves.

2. Parameters of Qatari Women's Mobility

This section gives an overview of the government-sponsored narrative of change and discusses the challenges and opportunities it affords Qatari women.

2.1. *Qatari Government's Agenda and Public Discourse on Gender*

In Qatar, like everywhere in the Gulf, the oil and gas boom of the 1950s created a new physical and sociocultural landscape. The most immediate change was urbanization and an influx of foreigners. At present, 92% of the country's residents live in the country's capital, Doha (Ministry of Development Planning and Statistics 2016). Moreover, in a short period of time, the Qataris became a tiny minority in their own country. For example, in 2016 there were 313,000 Qatari nationals in Qatar, which means that expatriate Western "experts" and a cheap labor force from East Asia and Africa accounted for approximately 88% of all residents (Ministry of Development Planning and Statistics 2016). As the skyline keeps rising, the expanding space of the city is becoming progressively more complex and multilayered, filled with diverse and sometimes conflicting discourses.

Qatar's present-day geopolitical agenda favors the advancement of women. To build a knowledge-based economy, become a regional leader in research and innovation, and play an important role on the international scene, the country needs to mobilize the potential of all of its citizens. A roadmap to Qatar's human, social, economic, and environmental development was drawn by its leadership in *Qatar National Vision 2030* (*QNV 2030*), a document made public in October 2008. As it is officially stated in *QNV 2030*, the national narrative is shaped by the desire to balance a push for modernization with respect for tradition. This principle underlies all government-sponsored reforms or initiatives and shapes the design of the newly created public places. It also clearly defines the parameters within which gender roles are being rewritten.

The ambitious goals spelled out in *QNV 2030* meant opening new vistas for Qatari women. Gender equality was guaranteed in 1999, when Sheikh Hamad Al-Thani approved a new constitution enabling women to vote, hold elected offices, and exercise other rights given to all citizens. Under the leadership of HH Sheikha Mozah Almissned, the emir's wife, education and employment opportunities for women became a national priority. An impressive investment was made to reform primary and secondary schools, and build Education City (later renamed Hamad Bin Khalifa University), a mega campus that hosts six top ranking American universities. Due to this bold initiative, women who could not travel abroad were able to pursue world-class education in their own country. In addition to establishing gender equality in the job market, legislative measures were adopted to support women's entrepreneurial initiatives. Furthermore, Qatari women's entry into public space was deemed complete when in 2012 for the first time in its history Qatar sent female athletes to the Olympic Games in London. Again, the reasons for this move were complex and intertwined. In Qatar's vision for the future, building a sports culture and increasing women's physical activity are important for the nation's physical well being as well as for economic and political reasons. Like in other regions of the Gulf, obesity and lack of regular physical activity are prevalent in Qatar and result in a very high incidence of diabetes, hypertension, and cancer. In view of this health crisis the government must take action to foster a healthier lifestyle. At the same time, sponsoring major sports events such as the Asian Games in 2006 or FIFA 2022 is important for financial and leadership reasons, whereas promoting gender equality in sports empowers women and helps to brand Qatar as a modern country. Overall, it is such a combination of political, economical and ideological motives that now creates a favorable climate for Qatari females' advancement.

In the space of public discourse, the government-sponsored narrative of modernization is promoted by the local media that highlight the progressive agenda and individual success stories. At the same time, the message of change is counterbalanced by a strong emphasis on the traditional role of women in the domestic sphere. *QNV 2030* clearly highlights the importance of female contribution to nation-building through keeping the family strong, both physically and mentally. It also appoints women as the guardians of moral values and the country's cultural heritage. The existence of the tradition–modernity dichotomy and tension related to it is openly acknowledged in the document, as reflected in the following statement:

> Qatar's very rapid economic and population growth have created intense strains between the old and new in almost every aspect of life. Modern work patterns and pressures of competitiveness sometimes clash with traditional relationships based on trust and personal ties, and create strains for family life. Moreover, the greater freedoms and wider choices that accompany economic and social progress pose a challenge to deep-rooted social values highly cherished by society (General Secretariat for Development Planning 2008, p. 4).

In brief, the model promoted in *QNV 2030* affirms gender equality in legal terms but also leaves women with the task of bridging the divide between modern practices and local custom regarding gender relations.

2.2. *Shifting Socio-Cultural Landscape: Qatari Women in Public Space*

To what extent have Qatari women availed themselves of the opportunities unknown to the generations of their mothers and grandmothers? The available statistics paint a picture of increased small- and large-scale mobility. Progress has been especially evident in the areas of education and employment.

As observed by Willoughby (2008), "it is within the GCC countries that the sharpest rise of educational achievement has been witnessed for women in the whole Arab world" (p. 85), and in Qatar the gains have been spectacular. Not only in Qatar University, the single national tertiary level school in the country, but also in the institutions following North-American curricula, Qatari females outnumber and outperform males academically (Ridge 2014; Walker 2014). RAND, the renowned research institution commissioned by Qatar to oversee its educational reform, highlighted this fact in its 2007 report stating, "the educational attainment is trending in opposite directions for men and women, with women becoming better educated over time while men's level of education declines" (Stasz et al. 2007, pp. 14–15).

Recently, the gains in education have begun to translate into participation in the job market. Women's employment rates have increased to 36% (Al-Tamimi 2016; Ministry of Development Planning and Statistics 2016). This rate is the highest in the Gulf region, but still disappointing considering that 88% of Qatari females pursue higher education (Al-Tamimi 2016). Remarkably, 44% of women cite cultural reasons as an obstacle in pursuing professional goals (Walker 2016). Moreover, Qatari women still occupy only certain segments in the job market. Not unlike their counterparts in other GCC countries (Willoughby 2008), they continue to seek a narrow range of employment opportunities, either jobs traditionally considered female (for example, teaching) or highly-valued prestigious careers such as medicine (Stasz et al. 2007). Some professions are still deemed inappropriate or less desirable for women. Thus, for example, there are very few Qatari females working as lawyers, flight attendants, hospitality workers, or nurses (Bahry and Marr 2005). Although a number of women study chemical engineering, many choose not to pursue their careers once they realize that employment in construction companies or petroleum and petrochemical industries requires frequent visits to the site and work in a dominantly male environment. Similarly, although women outnumber men among students of political science at Qatar University and Georgetown University School of Foreign Service, they occupy very few important political positions. For example, there are no women on Majlis Al Shura, the legislative body of the Monarchy of Qatar, and there are only two women on the Municipal Council and one female ambassador out of 100 (Al-Tamimi 2016). Furthermore, restrictions on showing photographs of females or even posting pictures on social media limit women's participation in the media. In the workplace, gender stereotypes often continue to prevent women from reaching their full potential. During the 2010 conference organized by Qatar University, the panelists acknowledged the existence of bias against women. Nouf Al Sulaiti, Director of Legal Affairs Department at Vodafone stated, "For women in the Arab society, there is a cap on the level of achievement they can reach, there isn't a level of surety of how high women can reach in the workplace in Qatar" (Toumi 2010). In this situation, enterprising women who establish their own small business companies, usually related to marketing women's products or services, seem best placed to combine traditional familial obligations with individual aspirations.

In the space of public discourse, a new way of thinking about gender is signaled by attempts to reevaluate Arab women's agency. Thus, for example, a recently published study on the spatial organization of Qatari households emphasizes the dynamic and modern nature of female space in contrast to a more static male space (Belk and Sobh 2009, p. 34). Likewise, the desire to deconstruct stereotypical notions of Arab women as passive and oppressed guides a number of analyses of cultural products (Al-Ghadeer 2009; Al-Malki et al. 2012) and reverberates in conversation with women of all ages. Qatar has seen an effort to validate women's experience by publishing anthologies of women's narratives (Henderson and Rajakumar 2008, 2010). Last but not least, one needs to acknowledge the effort lead by Sheikha Al Mayassa, the daughter of Sheikha Mozah, to document and preserve the work of women artists in the region.

In the cityscape, signs of change include the normalization of Qatari women's presence in advertisements related to business, commerce, banking, and other services. It is not too far-fetched to link everyday physical movement in public space with social mobility, so one can also point here to the results of the government's push to increase Qatari women's participation in physical activity. There is not enough data yet to ascertain that gains at the elite level of sports have been accompanied by an increase in sports activities in the community, but the government's campaign to raise awareness of the benefits of regular exercise has had some success. This can be seen in the growing popularity of walking, the easiest and least controversial form of exercise for women. Campaigns such as *Walk for Health, Every Step Counts* have legitimized the idea of women engaging in some form of physical activity in a mixed-gender multicultural public space. Modification of clothing practices can serve as yet another example of embodied cultural change that has become noticeable in the last decade. In public, Qatari females used to wear a long black overcoat called abaya and a black headscarf called sheila. Even though outside the country some women would substitute modest attire for their abayas and keep just their sheilas, in Qatar they continue to wear abayas as a sign of ethnic and national identity. While for more conservative women the dress code remains unchanged and even includes a full-face veil, Doha has recently seen the emergence of "the new abaya." No longer plain and uniform in style, this garment can be elaborately ornamented as well as vary in cut and lately even in color.

In other words, it resembles more an evening gown than a plain, identical garb and thus reflects individual taste, creativity, and awareness of latest fashion.

Despite some real change, a great deal of public space in Doha maintains the traditional divisions. Hair salons, hospitals, and clinics remain gender segregated, and many establishments have separate waiting rooms for men and women. Some restaurants have family rooms, and all gyms and swimming pools observe "ladies only" hours or activities. Although the branch universities in Education City and private secondary level schools are co-educational, public schools and Qatar University—the only national tertiary level educational institution—are gender segregated. There have been intermittent attempts to enforce the rule barring single men from entering malls on Friday (a religious holiday and day free from work) to ensure more privacy for women, and in 2012 conservative backlash resulted in a public campaign against immodest clothing practices. Negative gender stereotypes are still prevalent in Qatar, and many women have internalized them. For example, a recent study confirmed that three out of four Qataris believe that men are better qualified than women to play an active role in politics, and 40% of Qatari of men and women (with no significant difference between the sexes) believe that it is not acceptable for a woman to run for a political office (Al-Tamimi 2016). Finally, in the space of public discourse, some topics remain taboo. For example, there is little public acknowledgement or discussion of issues related to marriage and family life that run counter to modern practices such as arranged marriages, polygamy, consanguinity (marriage between first cousins), or misyar marriages (short-term contracts allowing for legal cohabitation without the stigma of prostitution).

To sum up, although the leadership's agenda has given Qatari women access to public space, it is not clear how the increased women's participation in the job market and sports and their spectacular gains in education have impacted gender relations in the private space or transformed commonly held beliefs about gender roles.

3. Qatari Women's Perceptions of Their Mobility and Agency: The Case of Female Students

The least researched area in studies on Qatari women—and Gulf women in general—is the area of their perceptions. It would be important to establish how young Qatari women view their mobility and agency; specifically, what obstacles they think they have to overcome in the process of entering and appropriating the traditionally male space, how much agency they believe they have, and what changes in gender roles they see or would like to see in the future. Such an inquiry could begin with female undergraduate and graduate students, since they are at the forefront of socio-cultural changes in their country, and the affective domain of their experience is worth exploring. Especially females studying North American curricula in Education city—a transnational mega campus—find themselves in a space filled with disparate and often conflicting discourses; thus, they are most likely to experience the tension between modernity and tradition identified in *QNV 2030*. The preliminary exploration presented here results from applying Grounded Theory methodology to data collected from the literature, ethnographic observation, and shared narratives of Qatari women.

The dominant theme that emerges from the data is appreciation of access to education and professional careers. The authors of essays published in *Qatari Voices* (Henderson and Rajakumar 2010), *Qatari Narratives* (Henderson and Rajakumar 2010), or WCM-Q and TAMU-Q anthologies highlight the contrast between the students' lives and the lives of their mothers and grandmothers, and pride in pursuing a college degree. This is hardly surprising, considering that 50 years ago there was no public education system in Qatar and most women were illiterate (Al-Misnad 1985). In informal and public statements, young women students also point to their role models, HH Sheikha Mozah and other members of the royal family, as evidence of change. In general, they seem to have internalized and acted upon the message of female empowerment spelled out in *QNV 2030*.

In terms of obstacles hampering progress, balancing culturally defined familial obligations with professional duties remains the biggest concern for young women and their families. In fact, young women worry more about satisfying expectations associated with gender roles in private space than about being recognized or rewarded for fulfilling professional obligations. Although maids and nannies are easily available and commonly used in Qatari households, professional women still face a double burden. Qatari tradition requires attending numerous family celebrations, making social calls, and taking care of younger siblings and sick or elderly family members. Generally, prioritization of the familial and tribal obligations over individualistic goals is expected of all members of the society, yet the burden of emotional work that it requires falls disproportionally on women. Understandably, younger women may find it hard to deal with the pressure from conservative family members. Understandably, inability to live up to the internalized norms and expectations can result in a feeling of guilt and inadequacy, the invisible cost of visible gains.

Although Qatari female students state that their aspirations are hampered by societal expectations, they do not acknowledge (or choose not to talk about) the existence of any significant restrictions on their agency (Qutteina et al. 2016). Neither do they question the traditional division between males and females in private or public space. On the contrary, even in the school's coeducational setting, division between genders is respected and observed through self-segregation, modifying verbal and non-verbal behavior (for example, no hand shaking with members of opposite sex) to comply with the Islamic principle of modesty.

On the other hand, there are signs of change and indications that young Qatari females seek agency through modification of traditional gender rules. This strategy is reflected in new marriage contracts that contain clauses allowing for travel and study (Rajakumar and Kane 2016). Evidently, such modifications of existing social norms give women more direct control over their lives. One can argue that if a girl views a college degree as a way of increasing her marriageability rather than a step towards a career, she can hardly be called liberated—at least in the Western meaning of the word. On the other hand, any assertion of a woman's right to education cannot but be seen as positive, regardless of its motivation. Another example of altering traditional practices is the young females' preference for the new abaya. Trivial as it may seem, this modification of the traditional garment shows how some Qatari women try to satisfy the need for self-expression without rejecting customary norms.

One would be remiss not to point to another positive development. From its inception, Education City was envisaged as a research hub, an incubator of ideas and training grounds for future leaders. Through grants and event sponsorship, the Qatar Foundation encourages students and faculty to engage in research. Even a cursory look at the *Annual Research Conference Proceedings* will reveal a positive trend with regard to women's issues. In the period of 2010 to 2015, only a small percentage of papers in the *Social Science, Art and the Humanities Pillar* section focused on women. To be specific, in 2010 there were three such papers, in 2011 two, in 2013 one, and in 2014 again two (no *Proceedings* available for 2015). However, in 2016 there were already seven papers discussing a broad range of women's experience, three of them resulting from projects involving female undergraduate students.

A recent study argues that young Qatari females "are caught between their own beliefs about gender equality and larger Qatari societal norms" (Qutteina et al. 2016). That certainly sounds true; however, it is still not clear what these beliefs really are and what shapes them. Overall, young Qataris lack the terminology and preparation to discuss gender issues from a feminist perspective. Moreover, as shown by Qutteina et al. (2016), their understanding of concepts such as freedom or agency differs from the way these concepts are understood in the West. As elsewhere in the Gulf, in Qatar secular feminism is viewed by many as alien or suspect. At the same time, it is not at all clear how Qatari women position themselves vis-à-vis Islamic feminism. In general, any type of feminism still has negative connotations in Qatar, as illustrated by the reaction of the audience to a recent lecture in Education City (Lindsey 2017) or last year's campaign to fire a Qatar University professor espousing Islamic Feminism (Badawi 2016; Al Fassi 2017). Discussing Gulf women's attitudes, Gonzales argues that Islamist feminists "are finding ways to negotiate for progressive women's rights within the conservative constraints of their culture" and are most successful when they present their arguments for women's rights as legitimately sanctioned by "the sociological sources of legitimate authority within Islamic contexts, namely religious texts, the community, and authority figures" (Gonzalez 2013, p. 2). Right now, at least on the surface young Qatari women' behavior seems pragmatic rather than ideologically inspired. But that may be changing. As Al-Malki et al. (2012) observe, every day Arab women have to make choices between the value systems of globalization and Islam, and the challenge for them is not to reject either but to "take reflective ownership over the complex hybrid identities they have tacitly accepted" (p. 233) in search of a new way of being. If there are signs that Qatari women are ready for a change from within and finding a middle ground between tradition and modernity, they need to be documented and explored.

4. Concluding Remarks

One can conclude that at present change in Qatar is elite-led, and female mobility—as understood in the Western sense of the word—is exercised unevenly. For the most part, Qatari women have availed themselves of the unprecedented opportunities created by the government-sponsored narrative of change. The biggest gains have been made by the younger generation of college educated females who have been moving into traditionally male dominated spheres and increasing their visibility in public space. Some of these women appear to seek autonomy through navigating the existing social systems and spaces rather than trying to question or deconstruct them. Thus, they seem to have embarked on the way towards creating a culturally shaped definition of agency and mobility. If Qatari women begin to create a third space between Western feminist ideology and traditional female Arab identity, exploration of this process and its affective domain should come from the women themselves. Research incorporating oral history methodology and principles would be particularly relevant in this context. Collecting oral narratives would give voice to women of different age groups and communicative competence, and thus provide a more balanced and complete picture of the ongoing transformations. Additionally, Qatari females' perceptions of their effort to establish themselves in the traditionally male space could also lead to new policies and initiatives providing them with much needed support.

Conflicts of Interest: The author declares no conflict of interest.

References

Abu-Lughood, Lila. 2016. The Cross-publics of ethnography: The Case of "the Muslimwoman". *American Ethnologist* 43: 595–608. [CrossRef]

Ahmed, Leila. 2012. *A Quiet Revolution: The Veil's Resurgence, from the Middle East to America.* New Haven: Yale University Press.

Al Fassi, Hatoon. 2017. Why We Need to Embrace Women's Rights and Open Debate. *Doha News*, March 9. Available online: https://medium.com/dohanews/why-i-believe-qatr-should-embrace-women\T1\textquoterights-rights-and-open-debate (accessed on 4 September 2017).

Al-Ghadeer, Moneera. 2009. *Desert Voices: Bedouin Women's Poetry in Saudi Arabia.* London: Tauris Academic Studies.

Al-Malki, Amal, David Kaufer, Suguru Ishizaki, and Kira Dreher. 2012. *Arab Women in Arab News. Old Stereotypes and New Media.* Doha: Bloomsbury Qatar Foundation Publishing.

Al-Misnad, Sheikha. 1985. *The Development of Modern Education in the Gulf.* London: Ithaca Press.

Al-Tamimi, Noor Khalifa. 2016. Qatari Women's Engagement in Politics. *Qatar Foundation Annual Research Conference Proceedings* 2016: SSHASP2414. [CrossRef]

Ardener, Shirley. 1981. *Women and Space: Ground Rules and Social Maps.* Kent: Croom Helm.

Badawi, Nada. 2016. Saudi Scholar Comes Under Fire in Qatar for Feminist Views. *Doha News.* Available online: https://dohanews.co/saudi-scholar-comes-under-fire-in-qatar-for-feminist-views/ (accessed on 4 June 2017).

Bahry, Louay, and Phebe Marr. 2005. Qatari Women: A new generation of leaders? *Middle East Policy* 12: 104–19. [CrossRef]

Barakat, Halima. 1993. *The Arab World: Society, Culture and State.* Berkeley: University of California Press.

Belk, Russell, and Rana Sobh. 2009. Behind Closed Doors: Gendered Home Spaces in a Gulf Arab State. In *AP-Asia-Pacific Advances in Consumer Research*. Duluth: Association for Consumer Research, Vol. 8, p. 34. Available online: http://www.acrwebsite.org/volumes/14874/volumes/ap08/AP-08 (accessed on 8 June 2016).

Benn, Tansin, Getrude Phister, and Haifaa Jawad, eds. 2011. *Muslim Women and Sport*. New York: Routledge.

Bristol-Rhys, Jane. 2016. *Emirati Women: Generations of Change*. Oxford: Oxford University Press.

Central Mosque. 2003. Ruling on Women Traveling without a Mahram. Available online: https://www.central-mosque.com/fiqh/wtravel1.htm (accessed on 13 March 2016).

Domosh, Mona, and Joni Seager. 2001. *Putting Women in Place. Feminist Geographies Make Sense of the World*. New York: The Guilford Press.

Falah, Ghazi-Walid, and Caroline Nagel, eds. 2005. *Geographies of Muslim Women*. New York and London: The Guilford Press.

General Secretariat for Development Planning. Qatar National Vision 2030. Available online: https://www.mdps.gov.qa/en/qnv/Pages/QNVDocument,aspx (accessed on 12 April 2016).

Gonzalez, Alessandra. 2013. *Islamic Feminism in Kuwait: The Politics and Paradoxes*. New York: Palgrave Macmillan.

Henderson, Carl, and Mohanalakshmi Rajakumar. 2008. *Qatar Narratives*. Doha: Bloomsbury Qatar Foundation Publishing.

Henderson, Carl, and Mohanalakshmi Rajakumar. 2010. *Qatari Voices*. Doha: Bloomsbury Qatar Foundation Publishing.

Kuroki Hidemitsu, ed. 2003. *The Influence of Human Mobility in Muslim Societies*. New York: Routledge.

Le Renard, Amelie. 2014. *A Society of Young Women: Opportunities of Place, Power, and Reform in Saudi Arabia*. Redwood City: Stanford University Press.

Lindsey, Ursula. 2017. Women and Islam: A Topic that Troubles. Al_Fanar Media, March 10. Available online: https://www.al-fanarmedia.org/2017/03/women-islam-topic-trouble (accessed on 10 June 2017).

Mahmood, Saba. 2005. *Politics of Piety: The Islamic Revival and the Feminist Subject*. Princeton: Princeton University Press.

Mernissi, Fatima. 1992. *The Veil and the Male Elite: A Feminist Interpretation of Women's Rights in Islam*. New York: Basic Books.

Ministry of Development Planning and Statistics. 2016. Available online: http://www.mdps.gov.qa/en/statistics (accessed on 7 February 2017).

Ministry of Interior Qatar. 2013. Exit Permits. Available online: https://www.moi.gov.qa/site/english/departments/APD/news/2013/06/02/29458.html (accessed on 7 February 2017).

Moss, Pamela, ed. 2002. *Feminist Geography in Practice: Research and Methods*. Oxford and Malden: Blackwell Publishers Ltd.

Pandya, Sophia. 2013. *Muslim Women and Islamic Resurgence: Religion, Education and Identity Politics in Bahrain*. London and New York: I.B. Tauris.

Qutteina, Yara, Laurie James-Hawkins, Buthaina A. Al-Khelaifi, and Kathryn M. Yount. 2016. Meanings of Women's Agency: Improving Measurement in Context. *Qatar Foundation Annual Research Conference Proceedings* 2016: SSHAQP2331. [CrossRef]

Rajakumar, Mohanalakshmi, and Tanya Kane. 2016. Measuring Qatari Women's Social Progress through Marriage Contracts. *Qatar Annual Research Conference Proceedings* 2016: SSHAOP 1335. [CrossRef]

Ridge, Natasha. 2014. *Education and the Reverse Gender Divide in the Gulf States: Embracing the Global, Ignoring the Local*. New York: Teachers College Press.

Secor, Anna J. 2010. The Veil and Urban Space in Istanbul: Women's Dress, Mobility and Islamic Knowledge.Gender Place & Culture. *A Journal of Feminist Geography* 9: 5–22. [CrossRef]

Sedghi, Hamideh. 2007. *Women and Politics in Iran: Veiling, Unveiling and Reveiling*. Cambridge: Cambridge University Press.

Sharabi, Hisham. 1988. *Neopatriarchy—A Theory of Distorted Change in Arab Society*. New York: Oxford University Press.

Sonbol, Amira El-Azhary. 2003. *Women of the Jordan: Islam, Labor and the Law*. Syracuse: Syracuse University Press.

Sonbol, Amira El-Azhary, ed. 2012. *Gulf Women*. Doha: Bloomsbury Qatar Foundation Publishing.

Stasz, Cathleen, Eric R. Eide, and Paco Martorell. 2007. *Post-Secondary Education in Qatar: Employer Demand, Student Choice, and Options for Policy*. Arlington: Rand Corporation. Available online: http://www.rand.org/pubs/monographs/MG644 (accessed on 12 October 2010).

Torstrick, Rebecca L., and Elizabeth Faier. 2009. *Culture and Customs of the Arab Gulf States*. Westport: Greenwood Press.

Toumi, Habib. 2010. Qatar Women Work to Change Tradition. *Gulf News*. December 23. Available online: http://gulfnews.com/news/gulf/qatar/qatar-women-work-to-change-tradition-1.734457 (accessed on 2 September 2017).

Walker, Leslie. 2014. Female University Students in Qatar Outnumber Men 2:1. *Doha News*. June 12. Available online: http://dx.doi.org/105339/qfarc.2016 (accessed on 7 June 2016).

Walker, Leslie. 2016. Qatar Home to Highest Proportion of Employed Women in the Gulf. *Doha News*. March 15. Available online: https://dohanews.co/qatar-home-to-highest-proportion-of-employed-women-in-the-gulf (accessed on 20 May 2017).

Willoughby, John. 2008. Segmented Feminization and the Decline of Neopatriarchy in GCC Countries of the Persian Gulf. *Comparative Studies of South Asia, Africa and the Middle East* 28: 184–99. [CrossRef]

Section 2:
Creating and Negotiating a Transnational Muslim Space

Article

Images of Authentic Muslim Selves: Gendered Moralities and Constructions of Arab Others in Contemporary Indonesia

Mirjam Lücking [1,*] and Evi Eliyanah [2,*]

1 Department of Social and Cultural Anthropology, University of Freiburg, Breisgau, Fahnenbergplatz 79085, Germany

2 School of Culture History and Language, The Australian National University, Canberra, ACT 0200, Australia

* Correspondence: mirjam.luecking@ethno.uni-freiburg.de (M.L.); evi.eliyanah@anu.edu.au (E.E.)

Received: 30 June 2017; Accepted: 29 August 2017; Published: 3 September 2017

Abstract: In contemporary Indonesia, Muslims increasingly define themselves by othering fellow Muslims, including Arab Muslims. This article examines how Indonesian Muslims, who have traveled to and/or resided in the Middle East, construct their social identities in relation to Arab others. Ethnographic research with labor migrants and pilgrims, and a cultural analysis of cinematic representations of Indonesian students in Cairo, show that conceptions of gendered moralities feature strongly in the ways in which these particular Indonesian Muslims define their authentic Muslim selves, as distinct from Arab others. They attribute ideal male and female characteristic features to Asian Islamic identities, while they portray objectionable ones as Arab culture. This implies that self-representations play a crucial role in the ways in which Indonesian Muslims relate to a region, culture and people long viewed as the "center" of Islamic culture. The representations of Arab others and Indonesian selves eventually lead to contestations of religious authenticity and social class.

Keywords: gender; moralities; mobilities; othering; Indonesian Muslims; Arab Others; social identity; Islamization; authenticity

1. Introduction

Indonesia—like other Muslim regions in Asia and Africa—is considered to be at the "Islamic periphery" because of its remoteness to the region where Islam was revealed. For Muslims in these "peripheral" regions, the question to what extent Arab culture and customs are part and parcel of authentic Islamic lifestyles appears to be more topical than ever in the post 9/11 era. While some Indonesians promote "Arab" Islamic traditions as purer versions of Islam, others denounce them as cultural derivations from the "true" teachings of Islam. Between these two standpoints are shades of grey, and religious authenticity is the subject of controversial debate in Indonesia.

Gender is a prominent category in these debates. By analyzing how Indonesian Muslims engage with ideas of religious authenticity in relation to Arab others, this article contributes to an understanding of the complex contestation over authentic Islamic lifestyles in contemporary Indonesia, in particular in contexts of spatial mobility to the Middle East. We argue that in these mobile contexts, gendered moralities—as conceptions of what constitutes good Muslim men and women—are central to images of authentic Muslim selves. As the conception of gendered moralities originates from Indonesians' own culture and is represented as superior to Arab gender features, the established concepts of center and periphery in defining authentic Islamic lifestyle crumble. This implies that socially belonging to the domestic context plays a crucial role in the ways in which Indonesian Muslims relate to a region and people beyond Indonesia, including the Middle East as the so-called center of Islamic cultures.

Pilgrimages to the holy sites in Mecca and Medina, working opportunities and education are the three most widespread reasons for Indonesians' journeys to the Middle East. In this context, spatial mobility is intertwined with the construction of social identities. Renegotiations of social identity happen through the representations of self and other in the course of these travels and become relevant even for those who stay put. Indonesian society engages in discourses about Indonesian selves and Arab others through persons who do travel to the Middle East and through popular culture.

Therefore, this article brings cinematic representations and everyday representations of Indonesian selves and Arab others together. This exemplary selection provides a crosscut of the interplay of popular culture representations and everyday representations of social identities. In a combination of cultural analysis and anthropological field research, we aim at providing a complementary description of popular images of self and other that serve as reference points in the making of contemporary Indonesian Muslim identities. Moreover, the juxtaposition of on- and off-screen representations and of three groups of Indonesians who draw on first-hand experiences in the Middle East highlights the relevance of social class in contemporary Islamic lifestyles in Indonesia. Thus, the analysis relates to the interdependencies between spatial and social mobilities, gender, religion and images of self and other.

We unpack the argument by first discussing how ideas of Arabness in Indonesia relate to claims of religious authenticity. Secondly, we provide an overview of the fields and the films examined. Next, we analyze the gendered representations of Arab others and Indonesian selves and the contexts in which these representations occur. Finally, we present conclusions regarding what the complex negotiations of gendered representations indicate about social frictions and gender dynamics inherent in contemporary Muslim identity making in Indonesia.

The analysis draws on data from our research projects on cinematic representations of contemporary Indonesian masculinity (Eliyanah) and on images of the "Arab World" among labor migrants and Mecca pilgrims (Lücking) as well as our joint investigations.[1]

2. Claims of Authenticity

The negotiation of social identities among Indonesian Muslims must be considered against the backdrop of historical and contemporary debates on Islamic authenticity. Heterogeneity between and within Islamic communities continues to pose challenges to the establishment of a united Islamic community, the *ummah*[2]. At times, this heterogeneity sparks acts of identification and differentiation among Muslims, through which claims to authenticity are hotly contested. In such contests, believers and academics question a common premise of authenticity: geographical proximity to the birthplace of the religion (Kahn 2015). In Indonesia, intensified Islamization deepens the contestation of authenticity, one of the most crucial dynamics of social change since the early 1990s. As an example, Woodward et al. (2012), observe that some religious leaders publicly make claims to religious authenticity by ridiculing other Muslims' practices. Among those other Muslims are Arab Muslims.

In this process of othering, various Arabic cultures are subsumed under the label "Arab", which refers to the region in the Middle East and also means "being Arabic" (Abaza 2007; Lücking 2016; Slama 2008, 2015). Clearly, "Arab" culture is not only homogenized and generalized in Western orientalist representations (Said 1978), but also in non-Arab Muslim regions. However, as some parts of "Arabness", such as the language of the Qur'an, are part and parcel of Islamic religious practice, the othering is only partial. "Arab" is a rather vague category that carries multiple connotations referring to language, ethnicity, culture, outward appearance, region and also ideological streams such as the radical or Wahhabi interpretations of Islam. In rendering attention to these emic generalizations of

1 We combined insights from our individual PhD projects in the framework of the Go8-DAAD Joint Research Cooperation Scheme.

2 Ummah refers to all people united by the Islamic faith. It encapsulates the global Islamic community.

"Arab", this article examines the ways in which particular groups of Indonesian Muslims who have traveled to and/or lived in the Middle East define their authentic Muslim identities through processes of othering people and ideas that they label as "Arab".

The terrorist attack of 9/11 and other acts of violence committed in the name of Islam intensified the tension among various groups of Muslims in Indonesia and globally. Muslims who abhor the violence claim that the perpetrators have failed to grasp the true teaching of Islam. This is exemplified in the view of the late Abdurrahman Wahid, the fourth president of Indonesia, who was also a notable Muslim leader in the country and globally. Wahid (Wahid 2005) not only claimed that acts of violence do not represent authentic Islam, but also pinpointed the ideology behind them:

> "An extreme and perverse ideology in the minds of fanatics is what directly threatens us (specifically, Wahhabi/Salafi ideology—a minority fundamentalist religious cult fueled by petrodollars)" (p. 5) (brackets in original).

Underlying Wahid's statement is an implicit claim of his own superior understanding of Islam and what is considered "authentic" Islamic practice. Blaming Wahhabi/Salafi ideology as inspiring violence indirectly suggests a hierarchy between Indonesian Muslims and other Muslims, in this case the followers of Wahhabi/Salafi ideology, who are perceived as being predominantly Arab. In Indonesian public discourse, Wahhabism is usually associated with violence, religious bigotry and misogyny (Rohmaniyah and Woodward 2012, p. 2). In the global context, the involvement of Wahhabi Muslims from Saudi Arabia in the 9/11 terrorist attacks has resulted in a tendency to equate Arab Islamic traditions with violence. This tendency is termed the Arabization of Terrorism by Ronald Hall (Hall 2003). Different from Islamophobia in the Western world, many Indonesian Muslims perceive not religion (Islam) but ethnicity (Arabness) as the cause of violence. Therefore, localized manifestations of Islamophobia among Muslims in Indonesia can be described as "Arab-phobia" (Lücking 2017, p. 198).

In Indonesia, the phenomenon of the Arabization of terrorism materializes in renewed anxiety concerning Arab Muslims in the wake of Islamization and the power vacuum in post-New Order Indonesia. The ethnicization of terrorism is related to the argument that Saudi Arabia supports Wahhabism in Indonesia, and that leading figures in Indonesian Jihadist groups such as Ja'far Umar Thalib, Habib Rizieq Shihab and Abu Bakar Ba'ashir are of Arab descentAbaza (2007) and Slama (2008) highlight the growing racism against Hadhrami people (Indonesians of Arab descent) in relation to the accusation of radical tendencies. The high proportion of Arab descendants among the leadership positions in Islamic radial groups such as the Islamic Defenders Front (FPI) (Woodward et al. 2012), the growing religious intolerance seen as resulting from the spread of Wahhabi teachings (Wieringa 2006, p. 3; Rodemeier 2009, p. 54), the rising support for Sharia law in the wake of decentralization (Wieringa 2006; Bush 2008), and the increasing media reports of violence experienced by Indonesian migrant workers in the Arab World (Silvey 2012, p. 427; Chan 2014) have arguably fueled the contemporary anxiety about Arab Muslims in Indonesia.

Interestingly, this renewed anxiety about Arab Muslims occurs simultaneously with renewed interest in the Arab World and Arab Muslims. More and more Indonesian Muslims participate in various religious gatherings led by Hadhrami descendants (Slama 2008, 2015; Woodward et al. 2012) and there is growing interest in the exploration of Middle Eastern Muslim fashion in Indonesian fashion culture, such as *abaya* and the face veil (Nef Saluz 2007), for similar trends in Malaysia (Thimm 2015). Moreover, travel to the region for the *hajj* pilgrimage has increased, as seen in the long waiting list for first-time pilgrims (Directorate of Hajj and Umrah of Ministry of Religious Affairs of Republic of Indonesia 2015) and the exponential increase of *umrah*, the minor pilgrimage, that can be done at almost any time of the year, in contrast to the *hajj*, which falls on specific dates in the Islamic calendar (Harian Umum Pelita 2014). Since the 1980s, the Middle East has also been a major destination for Indonesian Muslim labor migrants (IRIN 2009; Silvey 2004, p. 250). Furthermore, Indonesian Muslims sustain interest in studying in Middle Eastern educational institutions, especially in Cairo and Mecca (Abaza 2007; Schlehe and Nisa 2016). This ambivalent relationship with the "Arab World" provokes the question: What role do the actual experiences of mobility towards the Middle East play in contestations over authenticity?

Our analysis of how Indonesian Muslims engage with ideas of authenticity in relation to Arab others departs from the understanding that authenticity is a matter of perspective. However, there are conflicts over different perspectives because the social actors do not understand them as individual opinion but as objective fact. Lambek (1993) demonstrates how people claim objectivity of knowledge by putting their ideas into practice, which creates social realities. He argues that "embodiment provides the ultimate ground for legitimating objective knowledge, rendering it experientially real and conforming its presence in and for the bearer or recipient" (Lambek 1993, p. 307). We consider mobility as an opportunity for such embodied experiences and shall analyze the interdependence of discursive and experiential dimensions in claims of authenticity. Here, we carefully consider the power relations in defining authenticity (cf. (Winarnita 2016)). Unraveling various components in defining authentic Muslim selves, such as religious, gender and class identities, serves to provide understanding of contemporary Muslim lifestyles in Indonesia.

The issue of Indonesian Islamic authenticity has captivated Indonesian Muslim intellectuals as well as Western social scientists since the 1960s. Well-known scientists such as Geertz (Geertz 1976), Jay (Jay 1969), and Anderson (Anderson 1972) allude to Indonesian Islam's nominal and/or syncretic characteristics, and deny its authenticity due to its distance from the center of Islamic civilizational force in the Middle East (Hefner and Horvatich 1999, p. 8). Although this argument has many times been refuted (i.e., by (Abaza 2007; Bowen 1993; Hefner and Horvatich 1999; Newland 2000)), the authenticity of Islam, as adhered to by Indonesians, continues to be a recurring theme regarding Indonesian Islam. Van Bruinessen (2013) shows that the religious move against Middle Eastern as well as Western-influenced Muslim scholars continues to center around claims of authenticity. We would like to contribute to this conversation by showing that claims of authenticity among Indonesian Muslims who have experienced direct contact with Arab Muslims is gendered, class segmented and substantially shaped by the socio-cultural values in the domestic context.

Instead of investigating the opinions of Indonesian Muslim scholars, we are interested in understanding the perspectives of the general public. Most of the pilgrims, labor migrants (mainly domestic workers), and students are ordinary people who seek to make sense of their encounters with Arab culture in their everyday life and personal biography rather than consciously nourishing a public discourse or engaging in a theological debate. Nevertheless, public debates do have an impact on their personal interpretations. With this interest in everyday practices and popular culture, we look at on- and off-screen representations.

3. The Fields and the Films

We combine the perspectives of cultural studies and anthropology by focusing on Indonesians who have had direct contact with Arab culture and customs through different experiences of mobility. This joint project sprung from our respective PhD projects and was enabled through a cooperation between the Australian National University and the University of Freiburg, funded by the Go8-DAAD Joint Cooperation Scheme. Eliyanah undertook the cultural analysis of the texts and production of two contemporary Indonesian films: *Ayat-Ayat Cinta* (Bramantyo 2008) (The Verses of Love, hereafter abbreviated as AAC) and *Ketika Cinta Bertasbih* (Umam 2009a, 2009b) (When Love Glorifies God, hereafter abbreviated as KCB)[3]. To do so, Eliyanah carried out a close reading of the films to understand how Indonesian Muslims, men and women, are depicted cinematically in relation to their Arab counterparts. In order to complement the close reading, Eliyanah also conducted a series of in-depth

[3] This film is a duology: *Ketika Cinta Bertasbih 1* and *Ketika Cinta Bertasbih 2*. Both were made by the same principal crew of filmmakers and were produced by the same film company. They were released in March and September 2009 respectively. Since they constitute a single plot, this article refers to them as a single entity with the name *Ketika Cinta Bertasbih* (KCB).

interviews with nine principal filmmakers, comprising a director, scriptwriters, and producers involved in the films. Eliyanah also conducted interviews with two actors involved in the production of the films. As suggested by Hall (Hall 1997, p. 17), representations work as much as through "what is seen", in the context of this article the cinematic representations, and "the unseen". The interviews were the means to understand the latter aspect of representation, particularly in the context of how such cinematic representations of Indonesian Muslim selves and Arab others were possible to produce and were considered relevant by the creative minds behind the production at this particular moment in history.

We believe that commercial representations are not produced in a social vacuum. They are in part inspired by their contemporary social realities. The people involved in the production of the films are members of contemporary Indonesian society. Their filmmaking practice is a form of cultural practice intended to give meaning to events taking place around them at that moment in history. Intentionally or otherwise, they constitute a collective statement of what is considered "normal", and conversely, "not normal": the odd, the attractive, the scary, or the humorous within a certain regulated social setting (Heryanto 2014, p. 51). Indeed, the meanings offered by the filmmakers behind both films may not represent the heterogeneous Indonesian Muslims. The fact that both films were well received, as indicated by their stellar sales (Film Indonesia 2013), and also positive public testimonies from important figures, including then President Yudhoyono himself (Hasits 2008) and deputy leader of the Indonesian Muslim Cleric Council (MUI) (Wijoseno 2008), show that the films represent significant viewpoints shared by a great number of Indonesians at that time.

We selected the films firstly because both are based on novels written by an Al-Azhar graduate, were made by mostly Muslim filmmakers, and prominently feature experiences of Indonesians living and studying in the Middle East. We consider that the experience of Muslims behind the production of these films substantially informed how certain forms of "becoming Muslim" were represented cinematically. Secondly, they were produced and distributed in the period in which Islamization intensified in post-authoritarian and post-9/11 Indonesia (see previous section). Thirdly, AAC and KCB are milestones of Islamic-themed films in Indonesia. Films in this category tend to emphasize religiosity in their titles and content (Imanda 2012, pp. 92–93). The narratives are likely influenced by the novelists' experience of being in the Middle East, as reflected in the films' male protagonists (Sakai 2012, pp. 13–15). In fact, AAC and the first half of KCB are set in Cairo and the protagonists are mostly educated at Al-Azhar.

AAC revolves around Fahri, a postgraduate student at Al-Azhar University. The plot is driven primarily by his quest for an ideal wife. Fahri represents the "ideal" Muslim man: educated, pious, affectionate, and respectful of women. Fahri also represents a perfect match between Islam and modernity. As an "ideal" Muslim man, he is the love interest of many women, Muslim and non-Muslim. Fahri is a counter-representation of violent Muslim men, who in this film are mostly depicted as Arabs. However, despite being very resourceful in religious knowledge, he still needs to learn from more senior male Muslim scholars, mostly Arabs. He eventually marries a German-Turkish pious Muslim lady through a *ta'aruf*[4], arranged by his religious mentor.

KCB revolves around Azzam, a male Indonesian undergraduate student at Al-Azhar. Coming from a poor family, Azzam struggles to balance entrepreneurial work and study, which seems also to have been the experience of the writer (Sakai 2012, p. 14). Azzam is an "ideal" Muslim man, idolized by several Muslim women. Like Fahri in AAC, through *ta'aruf* Azzam marries Anna, the representation of an ideal Muslim woman: educated, independent, pious, affectionate, and pretty.

Lücking conducted fourteen months of anthropological fieldwork in Central Java and Madura in 2013 and 2014. A substantial part of the fieldwork was residence with labor migrants and pilgrims in

4 Islamic match-making process, in which a man (with his family) meets a woman through a religious teacher or family member and in the presence of the woman's family.

two villages and two urban areas. Participation in everyday life enabled conversations that developed from natural daily interactions. More formalized interviews—a form of conversation alien to many research participants—were conducted to a lesser extent. With the research participants' consent, the data was documented in research logs and where possible recorded and transcribed. This written material has been coded in the methodological tradition of Grounded Theory (Corbin and Strauss 1990). In the article at hand, we present the findings through "ethnographic snapshots" of the experiences of five research participants:[5] Dewi, a University student in urban Yogyakarta who participated in the hajj in 2012 as one of the youngest pilgrims; Ibu Anwar[6], an elderly lady in rural Madura who accomplished the umrah in a group of fellow widowed women, Pak Mariadi[7], a hajj returnee in rural Yogyakarta, Siti, a thirty-year old labor migrant who has been working in Kuwait and Abu Dhabi, and Ibu Anisa, who lives in the same village as Siti and worked in Saudi Arabia. Despite their different ages, genders and residence in urban and rural areas, all five persons can be considered members of the middle class when it comes to their living standards and their self-perceptions. However, many fellow Indonesians, especially urban middle class members who work in high skill sectors, do not consider migrant returnees such as Siti and Ibu Anisa as belonging to the same social class. This is evident in the terminology used to refer to one's own as well as others' social status. Siti and Ibu Anisa argued that others labeled them *buruh migran* (migrant workers). Indeed, their village had been introduced to me as *kantong TKW*,[8] which literally means "female labor migrant pocket". The academics, civil servants and labor rights activists who told me about the village had used the term "*kantong*" metaphorically for "village". As something small, insignificant and compact, the term evokes the image of a secluded place with a high concentration of migrant workers. Siti and Ibu Anisa, who emphasized their material wealth and their savoir-vivre, complained about the stigma of being labeled as migrant workers. This highlights that the definition of who belongs to the middle class is subjective and contested. Interlocutors from urban environments who work in service delivery or white collar jobs argued that migrant women would have a consumptive lifestyle and would not invest their earnings sustainably.

Dewi, Ibu Anwar and Pak Mariadi are respected members of their communities. Dewi became the leader of a students' organization at her university. Ibu Anwar took over the role as head of the family after her husband died and is active in neighborhood meetings. Pak Mariadi held the position of neighborhood chief during the time of inquiry. This indicates that social status is not only related to materiality but also to prestige, education and social networks. Terms such as "middle class" and "migrant worker" are emic categories that mark social hierarchies. The pilgrimage significantly boosted the status of Dewi, Ibu Anwar and Pak Mariadi, while Siti and Ibu Anisa are labeled lower class migrant women, even though they accomplished the pilgrimage more than once during their stays abroad.

Thus, despite having the same destination, the experiences, especially the return experiences, of migrants and pilgrims differ remarkably. In the attempt to make the journey meaningful upon return, different images of the Arab World and of Arabness serve as guiding references in the identity constructions of labor migrants and pilgrims (Lücking 2014, 2016, 2017). These guiding references are rather heterogeneous, for instance the image of the Arab World as the Holy Land in advertisements for pilgrimage travel agencies or the Arab World as a harsh environment in reports about the ill treatment of labor migrants.

The common thread running through the ethnographic fieldwork and the films is travel to the Middle East, which has often been associated with increased piety and also with intensified

5 Pseudonyms are used to name the interlocutors, except the filmmakers. The interviews were conducted in Bahasa Indonesia. For the purpose of this article, the excerpts from the interview are presented in English translation. Lücking translated the fieldwork interviews with labor migrants and pilgrims, and Eliyanah translated those with the filmmakers.

6 "Ibu" literally means "mother" and is the common address for married women in Indonesia, comparable to Mrs.

7 "Pak," an abbreviation of "Bapak," literally means "father" and is the common Indonesian address for men, comparable to Mr. or Sir.

8 TKW is an abbreviation for *Tenaga Kerja Wanita* (female labor migrant).

identification with Arab Islamic practices, which are sometimes considered more authentic than Indonesian Islamic practices (Berg 2011, p. 231). We do not intend to make a systematic comparison between everyday life and cinematic representations by putting the cultural analysis and ethnography side by side in this article. We rather deal with the complementary and interdependent notion of on- and off-screen representations. Returnees from the Middle East often display their enlightenment by adopting Arabic language, clothing style and customs. However, on a discursive level, students, migrants and pilgrims question the authenticity of Arabness. In order to highlight the ambivalent and sometimes contradictory meanings of the term "Arab", we use inverted commas whenever we refer to the concept of Arabness in emic or ambivalent categories. In contrast to the emic use of the term "Arab", our etic category of "Arab others" refers to the results of our analysis of stereotypical representations of Arabness.

4. Gendered Moralities and Religious Authenticity

Our analysis reveals that gendered moral visions—ideas of what constitutes good Muslim men and women—feature prominently in the ways Indonesian Muslims in our investigation construct authentic Muslim selves in relation to their Arab others. There is no outright admiration of, or aversion to Arab others, but there certainly is constant questioning of their religious authenticity. The simultaneous admiration and aversion to Arabs' gendered moral visions signify the complex social relationship developed by Indonesian Muslims to their Arab counterparts. Arab Muslims on the one hand are models of authentic Islamic practice. Yet, on the other hand, they are also cast as un-Islamic. As Indonesian Muslims other Arab Muslims primarily by depicting the latter's gendered moral visions as contradictory to (Indonesian) Islamic values, they undermine the authenticity of the version of Islam performed by their Arab counterparts, and promote their own superior version of Islam as more authentic. Whereas Indonesians perceive that there are positive and negative stereotypes of Arab men and women, many Indonesians believe that the "true" (or pious) versions of men and women are prevalent in their own society. In other words, the concept of authenticity among Indonesian Muslims at this point in history is anchored at "home" despite their experience of contact with the region and people long believed to be central to Islamic culture. The established distinction between central and peripheral Islam can no longer be sustained, as the so-called periphery also claims to be as authentic, if not more authentic, as the center.

4.1. *Representations of Arab Muslim Men*

Our research participants and the protagonists of the films hold a complex view of Arab men. On the one hand, Arab men are cast as the ideals, whose morality is to be emulated by Indonesian Muslims. On the other hand, Arab men are viewed as immoral because they are perceived as expressing their manliness in harsh verbal expressions and violence, including violence against women and minority groups. This negative view of Arab men represents the perception of the other, as distinct from Indonesian Muslim men.

When pilgrims and labor migrants discuss spirituality and authentic Islam in Saudi Arabia, they mainly refer to public practices of Islamic norms and rituals by Arab men. In pilgrimage preparation courses, Dewi and Ibu Anwar had learned that Arab people are particularly pious:

> "At the time of prayer, all shops will close and everyone heads immediately to the mosque for prayer. In Saudi Arabia people do pray on time, and will stop all other activities."[9]

This image of the Arab world as a particularly pious society is represented on the cinema screen too. In both of the films we analyzed, the protagonists are students at Al-Azhar, the oldest Islamic education institution in the world and one of the primary destinations for Indonesian scholars in

9 Pilgrimage preparation course at Hasuna Tour Yogyakarta, 2 March 2013, translation by Lücking.

their pursuit of Islamic knowledge since the 19th century (Laffan 2004, p. 2). Orienting the pursuit of knowledge of Islam towards the Arab world is a strong representation of the position of Indonesian Muslims as inferior to the Arab Muslims. Moreover, male Arab Muslim scholars, in particular, are depicted as role models and thinkers whose views and practices are to be emulated by Indonesian Muslims seeking to express their authentic Muslim selves. The male protagonists look up to their male lecturers and mentors, who are mostly Arabs. Fahri in AAC greatly respects Syech Usman, who serves as a model Muslim man for him. Fahri learns from him about the importance of marriage and man-woman relations in Islam. Moreover, in both films, the works of Middle Eastern male scholars, such as Ibnu Qudamah in KCB, are often cited to justify certain gendered religious practices as authentically Islamic.

However, this does not mean that Indonesian men are represented as less knowledgeable, and thus less authentic, than Arab men. AAC, for example, depicts Indonesians as pious and educated Muslim men, as a resource of authentic Islamic knowledge. This is shown through a scene in which Fahri provides information to a female non-Muslim American journalist on the status and rights of women in Islam. An Indonesian Muslim man becoming a producer of knowledge about Islam in the land in which the oldest Islamic studies center is located is a strong statement of authenticity. Fahri's ability to convey knowledge of a more authentic version of Islam makes him an ideal Muslim man in the eyes of both non-Muslim and Muslim women. The film thus makes a strong statement that Indonesian Muslim men can be as authentic as their Arab mentors.

The positioning of an Indonesian Muslim as a representation of authentic Islam in this context deserves further critical exploration. An interview with the director of photography of AAC, Faozan Rizal, revealed that he and his Muslim filmmaking team considered that it was timely to produce a representation of Indonesian Islam as authentic as, or even more authentic than, the Arab version. According to Rizal:

> "We are concerned because after *reformasi*, we tend to be Arabized. We are the country with the largest Muslim population in the world, why do we have to emulate the Arabs? It is they who have to emulate us."[10]

The term "Arab" in the interview quote refers to a bifurcated meaning. Firstly, it refers to people of Hadhrami descent in Indonesia who hold increasingly significant public roles in the public expression of religious piety in the post-authoritarian period, or in Rizal's term *reformasi*. In the previous section, we explained about the increasing anxiety about Hadhrami-led radical Islamists, in contrast with the more culturally based Hadhrami Islamists in Indonesia. The concern about violent Arabs within Indonesia inspired the production of Indonesian exemplars of Muslim men, such as Fahri in AAC, whose Muslim masculinity is in fact more desirable.

Secondly, taking into account the fact that the novel and film were produced in the aftermath of 9/11, the "Arab" in the above quote also represents the Arabization of terrorism. Through Fahri's exemplary Muslim character, the film distances Indonesian Muslims from the violence committed in the name of religion by "Arab" Muslims.

Representations of Arab men being violent contrast with the image of their piety. This ambivalence is also prevalent in migrants' and pilgrims' narratives. While on the one hand travel guides explain that Arabs are particularly pious, as in the statement above, on the other hand, they warn pilgrims of their harshness. Dewi recounted:

> "They like to shout. They enjoy being harsh. In Indonesia we don't do that. We keep our anger inside. They pointed at me, when accidentally my skirt was lifted a bit, shouting "*haram, haram*," but it was not on purpose. They are so rude."[11]

---

[10] Personal communication with Faozan Rizal, 22 May 2014.
[11] Personal communication with Dewi, 25 January 2013.

Ibu Anwar explained that she had heard about harassment of women and the pilgrimage guide had advised her to remain in a group at all times. Moreover, she argued that Arabs and also Africans had no sense of hygiene or politeness. "They don't know how to behave and they are wild,"[12] she claimed. The racial stereotypes of tall, big and coarse Arab and African men are also visually depicted in pilgrimage comic guidebooks (Luqman 2000, p. 100).

Furthermore, Indonesian pilgrimage returnees portrayed Arab Muslim men as self-centered. Dewi illustrated this by describing how Arab men would selfishly make their way through the crowds during pilgrimage rituals and mock pilgrimage groups from other countries. Dewi recounted how an Arab man had asked her if she would like to become his second wife. "They consider Asian women as maids and prostitutes," she said in outrage, and continued: "polygamy is not acceptable and fortunately not very common in Indonesia, he was crazy."[13] Moreover, she depicted Arab men as verbally *kasar* (harsh), speaking loudly, acting in a *sombong* (arrogant) way, looking down on Asians and Africans. Pak Mariadi described Arabs' prejudice against Indonesians in the following way.

> "(...) The person who does the call to prayer in our local mosque here is a graduate from Universitas Gadjah Mada (UGM) with the best grades. He got cum laude in almost everything. Then he went to Saudi Arabia for two years and became a driver. Even though he is a technical engineer, he became a driver there. I asked him why he did not get a work permit as an architect. Why? Because the Arabs said: 'Sorry brother, the work permits for architects and technical engineers are only given to Arabs, French people or Russians,' that's what they said, no work permits for Indonesians."[14]

A feeling of solidarity with fellow Indonesians who work in the Gulf nourishes criticism of alleged Arab superiority. This is especially relevant with regard to the treatment of women. Many pilgrims claimed that Arab men were potentially violent and treat women badly. Therefore, male pilgrims positioned themselves as protectors of female pilgrims. Ibu Anwar, who accomplished the umrah in a group of widowed women, also considered the Indonesian nation state and the travel agencies, who guide pilgrims' journeys, as protectors in this matter.

The most widespread image of female victims of Arab harshness are, however, female migrant workers (Brenner 1999, Chan 2014, 2015). From their own observations within the intimacy of family life, female labor migrants recounted that Arab men treated their wives badly, were likely to be polygamous and sexually attracted to Indonesian domestic assistants. Siti, who had worked in Kuwait and Abu Dhabi, concluded that the Arabs were really "harsh" and it required bravery to go there. She described herself as "*pemberani*", which means the brave one, and further explained that she considers it important not to allow the Arabs to "step on Indonesians" (in Indonesian "*menginjak*"), which is a phrase frequently used to refer to behavior that is discriminatory against Indonesians. Obviously, our research participants doubted the alleged piety of Arab men and also emphasized their own dignity. Pak Mariadi, for instance, concluded:

> "But really, the Arab people are just crazy, aren't they? The Arabs are harsh. It's not me saying that the Arabs are crazy; it's the holy book. The holy book says that al-Arabīyūn, the Arabs, are people that really like to argue and are hypocrites. It's the holy book that states that. That's why all the prophets were sent there, because they need that there. Here we do not need a prophet, you know. Because we are just good."[15]

In expressing his doubts about the authenticity of Arab piety, Pak Mariadi refers to a higher authority, namely "the holy book". This legitimization of views often occurs through a distinction

---

12 Personal communication with Ibu Anwar, 3 July 2014.
13 Personal communication with Dewi, 25 January 2013.
14 Personal communication with Pak Mariadi, 1 March 2013.
15 Personal communication with Pak Mariadi, 1 March 2013.

between culture and religion. Migrants and pilgrims acknowledge male Arab Muslims' religiosity but they criticize their cultural habits, judging them to be un-Islamic. They conclude that Arabs would probably fulfill the five pillars of Islam but they would not represent ideal moral Muslim men, in contrast to caring, polite and responsible Indonesian men.

This idea of a need for protection against Arabs corresponds with the narrative of both films, which challenge the contemporary popular media images of Islam and propaganda campaigns related to the war against terrorism in the aftermath of 9/11. In international mass media, Islam is often depicted as a religion which discriminates against women and which gives license to Muslim men to commit violence against and subjugate women (Haddad 2007). AAC and KCB contradict this discourse through their Indonesian male protagonists. The male protagonists are counter-representations of the violent and harsh Muslim men, cinematically represented mostly as Arabs. Male Indonesian Muslim scholars on screen reinterpret and reinforce their own sense of Muslim identity, as they engage with male and female Arab others.

In both films, Arab men constitute all the primary antagonists to be morally corrected by the Indonesian Muslim male protagonists. These Arab men are portrayed as physically, verbally, and sexually abusive to women, intolerant to difference, manipulative, criminal, and often violent. These negative stereotypes co-exist with the positive ones discussed above.

AAC is remarkable in representing Indonesian Muslim men as the image of "authentic" Muslimhood and Arab Islam as less authentic. A scene of a scuffle on a train involving a pious Arab man and Fahri clearly suggests the superior social status of pious Indonesian Muslim men in relation to violent Arab others. In the scene, Fahri corrects what is portrayed as the "un-Islamic" behavior of Arab men in the treatment of (female) foreigners and a Muslim woman by bringing up a *hadith*-based justification. This scene represents Fahri's doubt about the authenticity of the Arab man's Islamic view. Just as in the statement by Pak Mariadi, "the holy book", the Qur'an, is used to legitimize the criticism of Arab behavior. It is again clear that gender is central in defining the authenticity of Indonesian Muslims and the othering of Arab Muslims. Whereas Indonesian men stand up for women's rights, Arab men are the opposite, and are in fact seen as the cause of the problem of women's rights violations. To be a morally authentic Muslim man, as suggested by the films and the pilgrims' narratives, one has to be able to protect and speak up for Muslim women.

This is where the complexity lies, where the state of contradiction is encountered by Indonesian Muslims, on- and off-screen, when they travel to the Middle East and negotiate their Muslim social identity in relation to the Arab others. They learn from and greatly respect pious male Muslim models, but they criticize what they perceive and represent as narrow-minded and potentially abusive Arab men, whom they seek to correct through their own morally superior behavior.

4.2. Representations of Arab Muslim Women

Like the ambiguous representations of Arab Muslim men, Arab Muslim women are also portrayed in a contradictory manner. In fact, encounters with Arab Muslim women appear to be even more nuanced. Each sub-group has quite different experiences of encounters with female Arab Muslim others.

Generally, pilgrims and labor migrants mentioned gender segregation as one of the biggest differences between Indonesia and Saudi Arabia and other countries in the Gulf. As an example, the pilgrimage returnees Dewi and Ibu Anwar, like many others, recounted that encounters with Arab people during pilgrimage are in fact restricted to men, as women are "hidden" behind veils and in the private sphere (cf. (Sidani 2005, p. 500)). Labor migrants who happened to work in the private sphere had much to say about Arab women as their employers. Instead of empathizing with these women, migrant women's evaluation of their female Arab employers is highly critical. In fact, perceptions of Arab women as passive victims of patriarchal and violent structures are extended into an overall critical view of female Arabs. Against the backdrop of employer-employee power relationships, migrant domestic workers described their female Arab employers as immoral, lazy, pampered, full of suspicion and jealousy, and as ungenerous. Siti argued that beneath the full body veil, Arab women would wear expensive jewelry and sexy clothes. In women-only environments, they would talk and behave "dirty". The expensive clothing and immoral mindset totally contradicted the Islamic ideal of modesty and chastity. Siti, like other migrant women, denounced Arab female dress codes as hypocritical, and not related to sincere piety (cf. (Sidani 2005, Le Renard 2008)). In line with questioning the authenticity of dressing habits, Siti and Ibu Anisa pointed out that Arab women would rarely perform the daily prayers and if they did, they would only be allowed to do so at home, in contrast to Indonesian Muslim women who are used to performing prayers at mosques just as Indonesian Muslim men do. In general, Siti and Ibu Anisa praised Asian culture as more woman-friendly and thus superior. Other popular criticisms mentioned by the migrant workers were hygiene, lifestyle, and a general lack of modesty and shame. Ibu Anisa illustrated this by saying:

> "There, they [the Arab women] do not take care of themselves; the women there, they just sleep and eat, so their physical appearance isn't good. They never work, so they become loose and slack. They never do sports. They are just at home. Men do the shopping and everything, the daily needs. There is nothing that the women do. Just sleep and bear children."[16]

The othering of Arab Muslim women in post-migration narratives goes hand in hand with an idealization of images of Javanese moral femininity, involving softness, refinement, restraint, humility, and politeness (Mulder 1997; Winarnita 2016, p. 24). Moreover, migrant women emphasized greater freedom in exercising their female agency in their hometowns in Java without fear of reprimand from their husbands or a strict patriarchal system. These qualities and opportunities in Java were seen as more fitting representations of Islam than those attitudes displayed by Arab Muslim women and Arab culture, supposedly representing "authentic" Islam.

In the films, Indonesian students interact with Arab Muslim women both in their homes and in the public sphere, such as in educational institutions. To this group of Indonesian Muslims, some Arab Muslim women, such as the female lecturers and wives of the male lecturers, are models of feminine piety and morality. There is no questioning their authentic Muslimhood, and Indonesian women are encouraged to emulate these women's examples of feminine Muslimhood. In the films, female Indonesian students at Al-Azhar see their female lecturers and the wives of their mentors as feminine role models. They admire these Arab Muslim women. Anna, the female protagonist of KCB, for instance, greatly respects her female lecturers at Al-Azhar's campus for female students. Anna admires the depth of her lecturer's knowledge and femininity. In AAC, Aisyah, the female protagonist, is half Middle Eastern and she becomes the most ideal candidate to be Fahri's wife. Aisyah represents an ideal Muslim woman in the film. She is pretty, intelligent, independent, pious, supportive of her husband, and dresses modestly.

However, few other women are cinematically depicted as victims of the patriarchy and/or perpetrators of crime and violence. Most female antagonists in the films are Arab women who are to be corrected by the ideal Indonesian Muslim men. In KCB, an Arab woman represents the commonly perceived Arab moral decadence: she makes sexual advancements on an Indonesian Muslim male student, and then blackmails him by falsely accusing him of adultery. In AAC, Arab Muslim women are also portrayed as victims of the patriarchal Muslim Arab men. One female Arab Muslim is a victim of domestic violence and her frustration leads her to be a manipulative character. Against these Arab Muslims, Indonesian Muslim men and women are counter-representations who can provide corrections and lead them to a perceived "better" version of Islam.

The representation of Arab women as victims of gender-based violence and discrimination apparently resonates with the stereotypical view of the Arab world. Over the years, the Indonesian

[16] Personal communication with Ibu Anisa, 21 March 2014.

media have covered myriad stories on the restrictions imposed on women in the gulf countries. A hashtag search on Indonesian media with Islamic backgrounds such as *Republika Online*, for instance, produces more articles on the restrictions imposed on women in Saudi Arabia than on their rights. The media have also been inundated by stories of abuses experienced by Indonesian female domestic workers working in the region (Hugo 2003). Therefore, according to the novelist, who was also involved in the film production of KCB, the film version of KCB was intended to provide visualization of the respected status and position of women in Islam:

> "In the film *Ketika Cinta Bertasbih*, women are represented as holding high status in Islam and are liberated. They have the liberty to choose whom to marry and set conditions to be fulfilled by their future husbands in order for the marriage to take place, as long as the conditions guarantee the wellbeing of the women, her families and their future husbands." (Habiburrahman El Shirazy in an interview with (Nuh 2008)).

Taking into account the stereotypical treatment of women in the Arab world, the statement given by the novelist strengthens the assertion that the version of Islam represented through Indonesian Muslim characters in KCB, as well as in AAC, is premised more strongly on the authentic version of Islam which respects women, affords them agency and is non-discriminatory.

However, despite reservations regarding the lifestyles of Arab women, Indonesian Muslim women mark their identity as pious followers by adopting and creatively modifying Arabic fashion styles. We will discuss this in more detail in the following section.

4.3. Arab Style

The experience of mobility manifests in the embodiment of style, which is gendered and divided by class. In this case, we will show a slightly different experience of the embodiment of mobility among the three groups of travelling Indonesians. While veiling is prevalent as a marker of feminine piety among pilgrims and students, it is denounced as a less significant Islamic teaching and a symbol of hypocrisy by female labor migrants. As for male students represented in the films, unlike the male pilgrim returnees they do not adopt distinct clothing styles to mark their increased piety.

Despite discursive critique of Arab culture and customs, many Indonesian pilgrims, both male and female, mark their status as pilgrimage returnees through distinct clothing, which is often labeled as an Arab style. For outside observers, it causes some confusion that the exact same term, namely "Arab", is used in different emic categorizations: in reference to ideology, culture and fashion. The last of these has much more positive connotations than the first two categories.

Among male pilgrimage returnees, white, ankle-long garments called *jubbah* are popular at special occasions, and among women the long *abaya* robes are in vogue. Especially in orthodox regions such as Madura, Arab accessories, such as the checked *kufiyah* cloth, are popular for marking one's status as a *hajj* returnee. Likewise, other fashion styles, which originate in Indonesia's lively Muslim fashion industry, are labeled as Arab-inspired, and have become synonymous with piety among consumers. Dewi, Ibu Anwar and Pak Mariadi brought home Arab souvenirs from their journeys, including Arab clothing, which they would wear as a sign of their completion of the pilgrimage.

However, a slightly different experience of embodiment of Arab style is depicted by the male protagonists in AAC and KCB. The screen representations of ideal Muslim men are more heterogeneous. No Indonesian male Muslim graduate of Al-Azhar in the films is depicted as wearing typical traditional Middle Eastern long dress, such as the *jubbah*, and nor do they wear the Indonesian *sarong*. They mostly wear pants and shirts, including when performing religious rituals such as praying. Unlike the women, their clothing is not portrayed as symbolic of who is most Islamic.

To further explore notions of piety and fashion, Indonesian Muslim women arguably face greater pressure to express their religious authenticity through fashion than Indonesian Muslim men (cf. (Jones 2010)). In reference to Thimm (2015) who shows for Malaysian Muslims that the Arabic *abaya* can be a symbol of modernity as well as piety and in fact carries different meanings for different actors, we confirm that the alleged authenticity of dress is particularly controversial. Exploring "Arabic" fashion culture, such as wearing *abaya* and large veils, can become an embodied experience to express religious authenticity as well as modernity and—given the pressure to consume—social class. Off-screen, female pilgrims face more pressure to change their style upon return from pilgrimage, while male pilgrims do not face equal pressure. On-screen, the representations of ideal Muslim women, Arab and Indonesian, are homogenously veiled. The unveiled women are either non-Muslims or less ideal Muslim women. Fahri's second wife, upon her conversion, adopts veiling to affirm her authentic feminine Muslimhood (Paramaditha 2010). According to Eliyanah (2016), the increasing significance of veiling in symbolizing feminine piety in Indonesian cinema is a recent phenomenon, which started in the 1990s and has become an almost mandatory visual code in the twenty-first century. Although the veiling fashion adopted by female Muslim characters in Indonesian cinema varies, it is hard not to notice the increasing prevalence of *abaya* and large veils as symbols of superior feminine piety (Eliyanah 2016).

However, the expression of feminine morality and piety through the adoption of modest and decent dress, which is often reduced to straight cut *abayas* and large veils, albeit of various colors, is strongly questioned by most of the labor migrants taking part in this research. As these migrant workers assessed their female employers' modes of fashion in relation to morality and piety, they tended to denigrate the *abayas*, large veils, especially the face veils worn by their female employers as expressions of being *munafik* (hypocritical) and as mandatory clothing that is imposed upon women. While not denying that such fashion is Islamic, they tended to see the expression of piety in fashion as superficial.

The labor migrants carefully separated culture from religion, attributing negative stereotypes to Middle Eastern culture and not to Islam. Consequently, Siti, Ibu Anisa and other migrant women were not generally in favor of fashionable veiling practices. They would wear veils rather sporadically when traveling or attending official meetings, unlike the female pilgrims, such as Dewi and Ibu Anwar, and the female students on screen who wore them whenever they were in public and invested time and money in headscarf fashion. What labor migrants, pilgrims and students have in common is a distinction between culture (Arabness) and religion (Islam). Culture, rather than religious practice, is seen as problematic. However, the estimation of where to draw the boundaries between culture and religion obviously differs and therefore contradictory types of "Arabness" emerge: "Arabness" is a synonym for fundamentalism and harsh Middle Eastern culture as well as a symbol for superior Muslim morality and modernity. In emic conceptions and everyday language, these types are often not differentiated terminologically. What "Arab" means depends on the context.

4.4. Images of Femininity and Claims of Authenticity

In the representations of gendered moralities, the role of women is particularly central. Moral or immoral behavior and religious authenticity are mostly exemplified in representations of femininity and men's ability to preserve the "honor of women". Competing discourses battle over claims of authenticity, marking frictions in the broader socio-political context at the national and global levels. Strikingly, these claims of authenticity are male-dominated discourses both on- and off-screen, while moral femininity becomes the object of the discourses. Yet women are not merely passive participants; they actively negotiate the discourses at the level of practice.

Compared to other nations, Indonesia has a high percentage of female participation (approx. 50%) in the hajj (Bianchi 2004, p. 69). Robert Bianchi relates Indonesian women's presence in commerce, land owning and their position in customary law in rural areas to the high level of female participation in the pilgrimage (Bianchi 2015, p. 74). However, in the ethnographic fieldwork from which we drew our data, it is evident that the decision makers in the context of the pilgrimage, such as civil servants in the Ministry of Religious Affairs and pilgrimage guides, are mainly male. As they are not only in charge of technical questions but also spiritual and cultural ones, these men obviously have remarkable influence in shaping leading discourses concerning Arab others and Indonesian selves.

Indonesian labor migration to the Gulf is a female domain and many women are involved in the preparation and administration of labor migration, though the key decision makers appear to be men. Public discourse about the role of migrant women is linked to judgmental views of modesty in behavior and clothing style. These discourses revolve around migrant women's potential (im)morality as an indication of their economic success (Chan 2014, 2015; Silvey 2006; Winarnita 2016, p. 77).

Film production in Indonesia is also male-dominated, with the majority of films being directed by male filmmakers. Between 1998 and 2010, women filmmakers comprised only 13% of the total 184 directors working in mainstream cinema (Kurnia 2014, p. 8). The films examined in this article were both adapted from novels written by a male graduate of Al-Azhar, and were directed and written by male Muslim filmmakers. Women occupied only minimal roles in the production, either as co-scriptwriters or co-producers. These roles provide the women with limited power to shape the story and characters. In fact, the female co-producer of KCB was not involved in story development at all, as suggested by the KCB scriptwriter Tantowi in an interview with Eliyanah[17]. In other words, the production is very much male-dominated.

Furthermore, in both films the prime protagonists are male. They are representations of ideal male Muslim masculinity and religious authenticity. They are both knowledgeable in terms of religion. Other people, Muslims and non-Muslims, men and women, often consult them about Islam. Fahri in AAC, for example, becomes the representation of Muslims, if not Islam, in terms of treatment of women in Islam. Not only does he set an example, but he can also explain the status of women in Islam. In short, knowledge about Arab others is mostly constructed by men although it often revolves around women and men-women relationships. This implies the underlying perception of hierarchy not only between Arab and Indonesian Muslim men but also between Muslim men and Muslim women more generally.

The migrants' and pilgrims' recollections of their experiences of mobility and the cinematic depictions of students' experiences in Egypt mirror how personal identity making is related to the general global and national controversies about religious authenticity, in which the role of women is equally central. At the national level, the distinction between Arab others and Indonesian Muslim selves is often expressed through statements about the status and treatment of women, as for instance in a statement by the Indonesian minister of religious affairs:

> "For example, in many Middle Eastern countries, women have less freedom. They can't drive; they can't go anywhere on their own, they are not even admitted in religious sites. In Indonesia, they have more freedom." (Majalah Tempo 2015)

The minister of religious affairs is a prominent figure in the relationship between Indonesia and Saudi Arabia. The quote comes from an interview with a major print magazine on the state's support of a certain form of Islam that claimed to be more compassionate and accommodating of differences. This version of Islam is called *Islam Nusantara*, which means the Islam of the Indonesian archipelago. Thus, in this statement it is implied that Indonesian Muslim selves are socially constructed as superior to Arab others because the latter tend to treat women a discriminatory manner, i.e., women cannot drive or enter certain religious sites, unlike in Indonesia where women have more liberty.

In the domestic politics of Indonesia, especially in the post-authoritarian era, gendered conceptions of morality have become an important arena for the articulation of social identities in the intensified Islamization of contemporary Indonesia. As argued by Brenner (1999), control over public (gendered) moralities can lead to the acquisition of political power. Intertwined with claims of religious authenticity, these gendered moralities function as symbolic capital in the religious and political spheres (Winarnita 2016, pp. 33, 90). As an example, political power gambling has occurred through the implementation of partial Sharia law in several regions in Indonesia since the decentralization law

[17] Personal communication with Imam Tantowi, 14 April 2014.

was passed in 2001. Many sharia regulations contain recommendations for women's dress. In this undertaking, religious symbolism and the promotion of a certain image of femininity becomes a capital that various political actors—religious as well as secular parties—try to exploit.

However, even though it seems to be mainly men who compete in the discourses about Arab others and the morally superior Indonesian self, women are active at a practical level in their consumption and dress practices. In the transnational context of migration, pilgrimage and education abroad, mobile actors may relate to more than one dominant discourse. This is especially relevant in the context of migration. Winarnita (2016) argues that migrant women subvert dominant discourses in a playful manner. In her case study on migrant women dancers in Australia this took place through the exaggeration of stereotypes, which "was done for the pleasure and hilarity of being able to shock, as well as for the sense of power and popularity that accompanied it" (Winarnita 2016, p. 90). In the area of Islamic lifestyle consumption, women are joining in to define, reproduce, affirm, or contradict the discourses produced by men. This means that women are not the passive objects of male-dominated discourses but agents in the quest for authenticity and identity construction. As representations and practices are interrelated, we have to consider that women are not merely acting upon the male-dominated discourses but also challenge them. This is most obvious, for example, in the case of female labor migrants who do not adopt Arab-Islamic fashion culture to appear pious. This indicates that the "new" Indonesian Muslim identity is not only related to gender ideals but also to class. Who belongs to a certain class is a matter of negotiation. Female labor migrants cannot so easily access the social capital that Arabness entails, they do not promote Arabness and the ideas related to it in a similar way to female pilgrims, but challenge the discourse of a modern, economically successful, and fashionable Muslim along with its gender ideals.

5. Conclusions

Coming back to the question of how Indonesian Muslims engage with ideas of authenticity in relation to their Arab others, our analysis shows that gendered moralities are a significant demarcation of social identities and religious authenticity. They are markers of distinction between us and them. As the Indonesian Muslims we came across in our research strongly anchor the conceptions of gendered moralities to the idea of domestic culture, they transform the conceptions of gendered moralities into markers of superior authenticity in Islamic practice. Through their conceptions of superior Indonesian Islamic lifestyles, the subjects of our analysis socially depict Indonesia as central to contemporary Islamic cultures and knowledge. In this context, the boundary between center and periphery, which has been pivotal in the discussion of Islamic authenticity, crumbles.

The experiences of mobility substantially inform the justification for boundary making. Mobility provides an opportunity to engage with contemporary national and global issues, including Islamic authenticity. This engagement is discursive as well as practical. Through experiences of mobility, new opportunities for enactment and discussion open up. "Arabness" is embodied as much as it is narrated. Strikingly, adaptations of and demarcations from what is labeled as "Arab" in emic categories go beyond Arabness in the Middle East and are also directed at competitors within Indonesia. Identity making in the context of migrants', pilgrims' and students' experiences is consequently not only inspired by actual encounters with Arab others but also by international and national discourses. Representations of "Arabness" are embedded in these discourses and reveal social undercurrents in the construction of Muslim identities in contemporary Indonesia. There is a tendency to adopt an ambivalent view in constructing Arab others, and in reinforcing one's own notions of identity. In the context of our research, Indonesians represent Arab others both as models of authenticity and as people whose culture undermines important aspects of Islam, such as respect for women and humility. This means that the practice of othering in this context is partial and selective. There is an effort to become the "better Muslims", especially with regards to gender ideals. This partial othering comes along with a narrative of "taking the good" from outside influence and "leaving the bad elements" aside. In combination with Javanese culture this results in morally good Muslim individuals.

Through the representations of Arab others, Indonesians position themselves as morally superior and as practicing more authentic Islam, thereby challenging the concept of geographical proximity to Mecca as the defining point in determining "authentic" Islam. At the core of Indonesians' ability to both accept and reject aspects of Arabness is the distinction between Arab cultural and religious practices. This distinction runs through narratives surrounding Arabness, and allows Indonesians to critically determine what they consider "authentic" Islam, rather than adopting all aspects in a wholesale manner. Thus, while the embodied mobile experiences appear to contribute to a differentiation between culture and religion, the question of what is perceived as culture and what is perceived as religion—in emic categories—remains controversial. It is this aspect that indicates social tensions in the negotiation of authentic Islamic lifestyles.

This is especially evident concerning women and womanhood as central to the respective discourses. Indonesian Muslims tend to use gendered moral visions to ground their claims to authenticity. The agents involved in the production of these moral visions are, for the most part, dominated by males. Gendered moral visions are shaped by staging an image of "modern Indonesian Muslim men and women" who claim to be the role models for "other" Muslims in Indonesia and the Middle East, if not globally. This version is promoted in films and among the urban middle class. Yet the case of the female labor migrants challenges these images of authentic and superior Islamic lifestyles. Their denunciation of hypocritical Islamic style hints at the conflictive notions of contemporary Muslim identity making. Obviously, spatial and social mobility do not go hand in hand. The physical embodied mobile experience becomes a source of legitimization in the endeavor to exploit various forms of capital from normative representations. However, in order to experience upward social mobility, the representations of Arab others have to fit in the home context.

The analysis of on- and off-screen representations of Arab others and Indonesian selves indicates that Indonesians critically engage with the globalized discourse of the Arabization of terrorism. By associating Arab culture with radical interpretations of Islam, Indonesian Muslims locate the problem of violence committed in the name of religion outside Indonesian society, although such acts of violence are also committed within Indonesia.

The distancing from religious radicalization and violence leads to the stylization of an image of harmonious, modern Indonesian Islam. Here, the films' narratives provide imagined solutions. The middle class pilgrims obviously engage with these imagined solutions. However, the stylization of a modern Indonesian Islam goes along with a claim of superiority that does not only concern the religious sphere.

We revealed that the "Arab style" of urban middle-class Muslims is not only a statement about piety but also about being rich and being removed from the working class (cf. (Jones 2010)). This is obvious in people's self-ascriptions as middle class and the stigmatization of working migrants. Clearly, there is another other in this context, namely the lower class, the poor and rural population from which the urban, formally educated middle-class Muslims distance themselves. Thus, the story about Indonesians' engagement with Arab others is also a story about othering and dealignment within their own society. Here, the adoption of Arab-Islamic style is a criterion of distinction for the middle class. The case of the labor migrants challenges the imagined solutions and dreams of a modern Islam and reveals how contested Muslim identities in Indonesia are at the nexus of the frictions and conflicts concerning the right interpretation of Islam, class affiliation, and gender roles.

We conclude that othering Arabness goes beyond encounters with Middle Eastern Arabs. The representations of the journey or residence abroad and of something potentially "foreign" are also a way to discuss issues related to inner-Indonesian tensions without directly pointing at them.

The analyses of on- and off-screen representations of travel experiences have shown that they are not dichotomous but rather are interrelated. Just like stories on the screen and stories in real life, mobile experiences are not detached from the home context. The juxtaposition of on- and off-screen representations and different mobile groups reveals fissures between different versions of "authentic" Muslim religiosity. Considering the competing claims of authenticity and the seemingly decentered position of the Arab World within the Muslim World, as shown in the example of Indonesians' relationships with Arab culture at the alleged center of the Muslim World, the idea of a global Muslim *ummah* continues to be contested. We agree with Hassan (Hassan 2006), that the future of the Muslim *ummah* will most likely be a wide range of differentiated regionalized *ummahs*, embodying the specific regions' unique characteristics of Islam, which have been socially and culturally molded and are nationally and internationally contested.

Acknowledgments: This joint publication is the result of the collaborative research exchange "Social Identities in Contemporary Indonesia: A New Framework of Studying Asia", led by Prof. Ariel Heryanto (The Australian National University) and Prof. Judith Schlehe (University of Freiburg) and funded by Go8-DAAD Joint Research Cooperation Scheme. We appreciate the feedback provided by Prof. Heryanto, Prof. Schlehe, and other project members: Meg Downes, Paritosha Kobbe, Maria Myutel, and Evamaria Sandkühler. Furthermore, we thank Alec Crutchley and Jennifer Plaistowe for their competent proofreading.

Author Contributions: Both authors equally contributed to the article at hand, from data collection, research design and analysis to preparing the manuscript for publication. The data stems from our individual PhD projects. Eliyanah collected data through close readings of the films and interviews with principal filmmakers and actors. She also carried out the cultural analysis on the films and their production politics. Lücking undertook anthropological research among labor migrants and Mecca pilgrims in rural and urban areas in Central Java and Madura. Throughout 2014 and 2015, we identified overlapping research interests and developed joint questions and arguments during meetings in Indonesia, Germany and Australia. Previous versions of the article were presented at conferences and workshops at the Australian National University and the University of Freiburg.

Conflicts of Interest: The authors declare no conflict of interest.

References

Abaza, Mona. 2007. More on the Shifting Worlds of Islam. The Middle East and Southeast Asia: A Troubled Relationship? *The Muslim World* 97: 419–36. [CrossRef]

Anderson, Benedict. 1972. The Idea of Power in Javanese Culture. In *Culture and Politics in Indonesia*. Edited by Claire Holt. Ithaca: Cornell University Press, pp. 1–69.

Berg, Birgit. 2011. "Authentic" Islamic Sound? Orkes Gambus Music, the Arab Idiom, and Sonic Symbols in Indonesian Islamic Musical Arts. In *Divine Inspirations: Music and Islam in Indonesia*. Edited by David D. Harnish and Anne K. Rasmussen. New York: Oxford University Press, pp. 207–40.

Bianchi, Robert. 2004. *Guests of God: Pilgrimage and Politics in the Islamic World*. New York: Oxford University Press.

Bianchi, Robert. 2015. The Hajj and Politics in Contemporary Turkey and Indonesia. In *Hajj: Global Interactions through Pilgrimage*. Edited by Luitgard E. M. Mols and Marjo Buitelaar. Leiden: Sidestone Press, pp. 65–84.

Bowen, John R. 1993. *Muslims through Discourse: Religion and Ritual in Gayo Society*. Princeton: Princeton University Press.

Brenner, Suzanne. 1999. On the Public Intimacy of the New Order: Images of Women in the Popular Indonesian Print Media. *Indonesia* 67: 13–38. [CrossRef]

Bush, Robin. 2008. Regional 'Sharia' Regulations in Indonesia: Anomaly or Symptom? In *Expressing Islam: Religious Life and Politics in Indonesia*. Edited by Greg Fealy and Sally White. Indonesia Update Series; Singapore: Institute of Southeast Asian Studies, pp. 174–91.

Chan, Carol. 2014. Gendered Morality and Development Narratives: The Case of Female Labor Migration from Indonesia. *Sustainability* 6: 6949–72. [CrossRef]

Chan, Carol. 2015. In Sickness and in Wealth. Inside Indonesia. Available online: http://www.insideindonesia.org/in-sickness-and-in-wealth (accessed on 2 August 2015).

Corbin, Juliet M., and Anselm L. Strauss. 1990. *Basics of Qualitative Research: Techniques and Procedures for Developing Grounded Theory*. Los Angeles: Sage.

Directorate of Hajj and Umrah of Ministry of Religious Affairs of Republic of Indonesia. 2015. Hajj Waiting List. Available online: http://haji.kemenag.go.id/v2/basisdata/waiting-list (accessed on 15 September 2015).

Eliyanah, Evi. 2016. Cinema: Representations on Commercial Films. In *Encyclopedia of Women and Islamic Cultures: Supplement XIV*. Edited by Suad Joseph. Available online: http://referenceworks.brillonline.com/entries/encyclopedia-of-women-and-islamic-cultures/cinema-representations-in-commercial-films-COM_002068 (accessed on 29 July 2017).

Film Indonesia. 2013. Data Penonton: 10 Film Indonesia Peringkat Teratas dalam Perolehan Jumlah Penonton pada Tahun 2007–2013 Berdasarkan Tahun Edar Film. Available online: http://filmindonesia.or.id/movie/viewer/2007-2013#.Ui6JPG37Qik (accessed on 18 May 2013).

Geertz, Clifford. 1976. *The Religion of Java*. Chicago: University of Chicago Press.

Haddad, Yvonne. Y. 2007. The Post-9/11 Hijab as Icon. *Sociology of Religion* 63: 253–67. [CrossRef]

Hall, Stuart. 1997. The work of representation. In *Representation: Cultural Representations and Signifying Practice*. Edited by Stuart Hall. London, Thousand Oaks and New Delhi: SAGE Publications, pp. 13–64.

Hall, Ronald E. 2003. A note on September eleventh: The Arabization of terrorism. *The Social Science Journal* 40: 459–64. [CrossRef]

Harian Umum Pelita. 2014. Peserta Umrah Meningkat Satu Juta Jamaah. *Harian Umum Pelita*, May.

Hasits, Muhammad. 2008. Nonton Ayat-Ayat Cinta, SBY Nangis. *Okezone*. March 28. Available online: http://news.okezone.com/read/2008/03/28/1/95655/nonton-ayat-ayat-cinta-sby-nangis (accessed on 20 February 2015).

Hassan, Riaz. 2006. Globalisation's Challenge to the Islamic Ummah. *Asian Journal of Social Science* 34: 311–23. [CrossRef]

Robert W. Hefner, and Patricia Horvatich, eds. 1999. *Islam in an Era of Nation-States: Politics and Religious Renewal in Muslim Southeast Asia*. Honolulu: University of Hawaii Press.

Heryanto, Ariel. 2014. *Identity and Pleasure: The Politics of Indonesian Screen Culture*. Singapore: NUS Press.

Hugo, Graeme. 2003. Information, Exploitation and Empowerment: The Case of Indonesian Overseas Workers. *Asian and Pacific Migration Journal* 12: 439–67. [CrossRef]

Imanda, Tito. 2012. Independent versus Mainstream Islamic Cinema in Indonesia: Religion Using the Market or Vice Versa? In *Southeast Asian Independent Cinema: Essays, Documents, Interviews*. Edited by Tilman Baumgärtel. TransAsia: Screen Cultures: Hong Kong: Hong Kong University Press.

IRIN. 2009. *Indonesia: Tough Times for Returning Labor Migrants*. Jakarta: Integrated Regional Information Networks (IRIN).

Jay, Robert R. 1969. *Javanese Villagers: Social Relations in Rural Modjokuto*. Cambridge: MIT Press.

Jones, Carla. 2010. Images of Desire. *Journal of Middle East Women's Studies* 6: 91–117. [CrossRef]

Kahn, Joel S. 2015. Foundational Islams: Implications for Dialogue. *Arena Magazine* 134: 22–26.

Kurnia, Novi. 2014. Women Directors in Post-New Order Indonesia: Making a Film, Making a Difference. Ph.D. Thesis, Flinders University, Bedford Park, Australia.

Laffan, Michael. 2004. An Indonesian community in Cairo: Continuity and Change in a Cosmopolitan Islamic Milieu. *Indonesia* 77: 1–26.

Lambek, Michael J. 1993. *Knowledge and Practice in Mayotte: Local Discourses of Islam, Sorcery and Spirit Possession*. Anthropological Horizons; Toronto: University of Toronto Press.

Le Renard, Amelie. 2008. "Only for Women:" Women, the State, and reform in Saudi Arabia. *The Middle East Journal* 62: 610–29. [CrossRef]

Lücking, Mirjam. 2014. Making 'Arab' One's Own. Muslim Pilgrimage Experiences in Central Java, Indonesia. *International Quarterly for Asian Studies* 45: 129–52.

Lücking, Mirjam. 2016. Beyond Islam Nusantara and "Arabization": Capitalizing "Arabness" in Madura, East Java. *The German Journal on Contemporary Asia* 137: 5–24.

Lücking, Mirjam. 2017. Indonesians' and Their Arab World—Guided Mobility among Labour Migrants and Mecca Pilgrims. Ph.D. Thesis, University of Freiburg, Freiburg im Breisgau, Germany. unpublished.

Luqman, A. 2000. *Komik Haji: Cara Mabrur naik Haji & Umroh*. Jakarta: Nirmana.

Majalah Tempo. 2015. Ini Bukan Dearabisasi. *Majalah Tempo*. July 13. Available online: http://majalah.tempo.co/konten/2015/07/13/LU/148623/Ini-Bukan-Dearabisasi/21/44 (accessed on 16 July 2015).

Mulder, Niels. 1997. Images of Javanese Gender. In *Images of Malay-Indonesian Identity*. Edited by Michael Hitchcock and Victor T. King. Kuala Lumpur, Oxford and New York: Oxford University Press, pp. 138–47.

Nef Saluz, Claudia. 2007. *Islamic Pop Culture in Indonesia: An Anthropological Field Study on Veiling Practices among Students of Gadjah Mada University of Yogyakarta*. Arbeitsblatt/Institut für Sozialanthropologie, Universität Bern Nr. 41; Bern: Institut für Sozialanthropologie.

Newland, Lynda. 2000. Under the Banner of Islam: Moblising Religious Identities in West Java. *The Australian Journal of Anthropology* 11: 199–222. [CrossRef]

Nuh, Muhammad. 2008. Dakwah di Balik Ketika Cinta Bertasbih. Available online: http://www.eramuslim.com/berita/silaturrahim/dakwah-di-balik-ketika-cinta-bertasbih.htm#.VQzzKuHoTcc (accessed on 21 March 2015).

Paramaditha, Intan. 2010. Passing and Conversion Narratives: Ayat-Ayat Cinta and Muslim Performativity in Contemporary Indonesia. *Asian Cinema* 21: 69–91. [CrossRef]

Rodemeier, Susanne. 2009. Zartes Signal einer Wende. Aktueller arabischer Einfluss auf Java. *Südostasien. Zeitschrift für Politik, Kultur, Dialog* 4: 52–55.

Rohmaniyah, Inayah, and Mark Woodward. 2012. Wahhabi Perspective on Pluralism and Gender: A Saudi-Indonesian Contrast. In *Center for Strategic Communication*. Tempe: Arizona State University.

Said, Edward W. 1978. *Orientalism*, 1st ed. New York: Pantheon Books.

Sakai, Minako. 2012. Preaching to Muslim Youth in Indonesia: The Dakwah Activities of Habiburrahman El Shirazy. *Review of Indonesian and Malaysian Affairs* 46: 9–31.

Schlehe, Judith, and Eva F. Nisa. 2016. The Meanings of Moderate Islam in Indonesia: Alignments and Dealignments of Azharites. In *Southeast Asian Studies at the University of Freiburg*. Occasional Paper Series, No. 31; Available online: http://www.southeastasianstudies.uni-freiburg.de/publications/op-series (accessed on 24 August 2016).

Sidani, Yusuf. 2005. Women, Work, and Islam in Arab Societies. *Women in Management Review* 20: 498–512. [CrossRef]

Silvey, Rachel M. 2004. Transnational domestication: State power and Indonesian migrant women in Saudi Arabia. *Political Geography* 23: 245–64. [CrossRef]

Silvey, Rachel M. 2006. Consuming the Transnational Family: Indonesian Migrant Domestic Workers to Saudi Arabia. *Global Network* 6: 1–18. [CrossRef]

Silvey, Rachel M. 2012. Gender, Difference, and Contestation: Economic Geography through the Lens of Transnational Migration. In *The Wiley-Blackwell Companion to Economic Geography*. Edited by Trevor J. Barnes, Jamie Peck and Eric S. Sheppard. Paperback Edition. Wiley Blackwell Companions to Geography; Chichester: Wiley Blackwell.

Slama, Martin. 2008. Islam Pribumi. Der Islam der Einheimischen, seiner "Arabisierung" und arabische Diasporagemeinschaften in Indonesien. *ASEAS—Österreichische Zeitschrift für Südostasienwissenschaften* 1: 4–17.

Slama, Martin. 2015. In Between and in the Middle: Multiple Positions of the Hadhramis in Indonesia. Paper Presented at FRIAS Conference, University of Freiburg, Freiburg im Breisgau, Germany, unpublished.

Thimm, Viola. 2015. Die arabische Abaya in Malaysia. Verhandlungen von muslimischen Kleidungspraktiken weiblicher Körperlichkeit, und Modernität. *Paideuma* 61: 95–116.

Van Bruinessen, Martin. 2013. "Ghazwul fikri" or Arabization? Indonesian Muslim Responses to Globalization. In *Dynamics of Southeast Asian Muslims in the Era of Globalization*. Edited by Ken Miichi and Omar Farouk. Tokyo: Japan International Cooperation Agency Research Institute, pp. 47–70.

Wahid, Abdurahman. 2005. Right Islam vs. Wrong Islam. Available online: https://www.wsj.com/articles/SB113590649048834335 (accessed on 24 June 2016).

Wieringa, Saskia. 2006. Islamization in Indonesia: Women Activists' Discourses. *Signs: Journal of Women in Culture and Society* 32: 1–8. [CrossRef]

Wijoseno, Gagah. 2008. Din Syamsuddin: Lawan Fitna dengan Ayat-Ayat Cinta. Available online: http://news.detik.com/read/2008/04/07/164434/919701/10/din-syamsuddin-lawan-fitna-dengan-ayat-ayat-cinta (accessed on 30 January 2015).

Winarnita, Monika S. 2016. *Dancing the Feminine: Gender and Identity Performances by Indonesian Migrant Women*. Brighton: Sussex Academic Press.

Woodward, Mark, Inayah Rohmaniyah, Ali Amin, Samsul Ma'arif, Diana Murtaugh Coleman, and Muhammad Sani Umar. 2012. Ordering What is Right, Forbidding What is Wrong: Two Faces of Hadrami Dakwah in Contemporary Indonesia. *Review of Indonesian and Malaysian Affairs* 46: 105–46.

Bramantyo, Hanung. 2008. *Ayat-Ayat Cinta*. Directed by Hanung Bramantyo. South Jakarta: MD Pictures.

Umam, Chaerul. 2009a. *Ketika Cinta Bertasbih 1*. Directed by Chaerul Umam. Jakarta: SinemArt.
Umam, Chaerul. 2009b. *Ketika Cinta Bertasbih 2*. Directed by Chaerul Umam. Jakarta: SinemArt Pictures.

Article

Shia Marriage Practices: Karbala as *lieux de memoire* in London

Yafa Shanneik

Department of Theology and Religion, University of Birmingham, Birmingham B15 2TT, UK; y.shanneik@bham.ac.uk

Received: 14 June 2017; Accepted: 14 August 2017; Published: 1 September 2017

Abstract: Muslim marriages have gained much attention in public debates and academic research. This article examines marriage practices among displaced Iraqi Shia migrants in the UK. Only a few studies have examined this group and fewer by investigating their marriage practices as a way to preserve their religious and cultural memory (Halbwachs 1992). The article is based on Pierre Nora's concept of *lieux de mémoire*, which refers to spaces, objects or events that have a significant meaning to a particular groups' collective memory (Nora 1989, 1996). I argue in this paper that the transnational aspects of cultural memory expressed in Shia marriage practices such as rituals, images, and objects among the Iraqi Twelver Shia women in the UK can be regarded as examples of transnational Shia *lieux de mémoire*. These marriage practices, although appropriated for various personal, social, and religious memories outside of any national framework, are still highly politicized. The article focuses on the practice of *sofrat al-'aqd* (for short *sofra*) that provides women with the ability to articulate their religious and social identity through material objects placed on the *sofra* that act as women's transnational Shia *lieux de mémoire*.

Keywords: Muslim marriages; Shia Islam; *sofra*; *lieux de mémoire*; collective memory

1. Introduction

Twelver Shia (Momen 1985) remember annually the death of Imam Husayn, who is believed to have been killed together with his supporters at the battle of Karbala by the Umayyad's Caliph troops in southern Iraq in 680CE, through the performance of various commemorative ritual practices, theatrical performances, and the production of numerous literary and artistic productions (al-Haidari 1999; Chelkowski 2010; Shanneik 2015). The article examines the transnational aspects of cultural memory expressed in marriage practices[1] such as rituals, images, and objects and analyses how they are used by women as a tool to preserve the religious and cultural memory (Halbwachs 1992; Misztal 2003) of Iraqi Shia women in the diaspora. This article uses Pierre Nora's concept of *lieux de mémoire*, which refers to spaces, objects, or events that have a significant meaning to a particular groups' collective memory (Nora 1989) and argues that, through these commemorative practices, Shia are able to present the Karbala narrative as *lieux de mémoire* allowing the construction of a coherent Shia identity around the persecution, displacement, and maltreatment of Shia throughout the centuries. Marriage ritual practices are appropriated for personal, social, and religious memories outside of any national framework but are nevertheless highly politicized. Various spaces of marriage practices are used to articulate different kinds of memories among and across various generations. Performing

[1] Research on marriages in public debates, see (Abaza 2001; Arabi 2001). There are a number of academic work on various forms of Muslim marriages such as on unregistered (*urfi*) (Shahrani 2010; Walby 2010), visiting (*misyar*) (Arabi 2001), temporary (*mut'a*) marriages (Haeri 1989, 1992; Mervin 2008); tourist marriage (Abou el Magd 2009). On the legal aspect of Muslim marriages in Europe, see (Nielsen and Christoffersen 2010; Bowen 2011).

Shia marriages feeds into the individual and communal efforts of Shia in the UK to keep the memory of Karbala alive and the understandings of Shia communal identity in the diaspora functioning throughout generations. The performance of Shia marriage ceremonies functions thereby as an identity marker. For the first generation of Shia living in a diasporic context, it acts as a 'signifier of stability' (Bhabha 1994, p. 102) and, for the second generation, as a way to connect with their parents' and Shia communities' religious and cultural practices. Marriage practices are usually performed in female-only spaces in which women assume authority and leadership in all aspects of organising the marriage. What to include in a marriage ceremony and what meaning and function the various elements and aspects have are negotiated between the generations and influenced by various religious and political beliefs, socio-economic and educational backgrounds, and individual migratory experiences.

The French historian Pierre Nora uses the term *lieux de mémoire*, translatable as sites, places, or realms of memory, to denote certain places in which we could anchor our memories. Being primarily concerned with collective and national memory, he argues that we need to construct and share sites that are material and symbolic 'to stop time, to block the work of forgetting, to establish a state of things, to immortalize death, to materialize the immaterial' (Nora 1989, p.19). Nora's definition of *lieux de mémoire* involves material spaces and places as well as abstract ideas of enabling connections to the past for the purpose of avoiding oblivion. There are various types and ways of remembering that are continuously reconstructed and represented on an individual and collective level. What is remembered and how it is remembered is crucial in making sense of our past, present, and future identity (Erll 2011). Nora's term represents the change in historical consciousness and public efforts in identifying with the nation and the nation-state. The identification with a particular nation-state and the construction of a national identity, likening it to a specific past, is the focus of Nora's concept. He developed it specifically to anchor French national memory and to prevent it from oblivion. The purpose of the French *lieux de mémoire* is to identify particular sites that have a specific historical meaning and to construct a narrative around these sites to develop a French national memory (Nora 1996). Monuments, texts, and other anchors of memory in contemporary society are turned into national icons and gain status in order to form a clearly defined French national memory (Nora 1989). The concept of *lieux de mémoire* assumes the nation to be a clearly definable entity and to be based on specific images and notions of gender, class, and ethnicity.

The model of *lieux de mémoire* can, however, be transferred and modified to suit other memory cultures (Grever 1997). In this article, I will take the conceptualization of individual and collective memory beyond Nora's framework of a fixed imagined community of a nation-state (Anderson 1983) and adapt a more complex transnational religio-cultural and political dimension to it. It focuses on the practice of *sofrat al-'aqd* (for short *sofra*), which is an all-female activity performed during an *'aqd* in which a table cloth is spread either on the floor or on a table on which various objects are presented such as a mirror, candles, a copy of the Qur'an, and also food items such as nuts, eggs, corn, and honey (see Figure 1, below). These food items are either symbols of fertility or seen as aphrodisiacs. The practice of *al-mashy* or *al-mashaya* (al-Sharqi 1978) literally means 'the walk' or 'the walking' and refers to a selection of mainly menfolk, chosen in most cases by women, who walk to the bride's family home to ask for her hand. Whereas particularly the younger generation of Iraqi Shia women insist on including the *sofra* as part of their wedding performance, the older generation holds onto the performance of the *mashaya* as they are both used to articulating women's Shia identities in the UK. They are both an expression of the women's *lieux de mémoire* since the women associate the objects placed on the *sofra* with various aspects related to the memory of the battle of Karbala and the *mashaya* with the collective unity of the Shia community and the preservation of Shia history, articulated through marriage practices performed in the diaspora. This construction of memory has the function of creating identities on diverse levels. Marriage practices become a useful tool to articulate identities that sometimes refer to an Iraqi/Iranian hybrid heritage, an Arab Shia (as opposed to Iranian Shia) identity, or a more nationalist Iraqi Shia identity. Such identity construction can also foreground its religious dimension by being collectively and individually identifiable and recognized as part of a wider translational Shia community. The performance of the *sofra* in the UK (Spellman 2004) resonates in its form and also its meaning with practices performed in the Gulf. Through social media and transnational networks and ties, young women are connected transnationally, thereby confirming and challenging existing marriage practices and also building new practices and marking their own Shia *lieux de mémoire.* One of the first generation of Iraqis in London explains: 'We did not have all these practices in Iraq, these young girls here started improvising with new forms of rituals they gather and put together from here and there.'

Figure 1. A *sofrat al 'aqd* provided by Um Zahra in London.

2. Shia Communities in London

The article is based on four years of ethnographic fieldwork among various Shia women communities in the UK. There are no precise numbers on the Iraqi population living in the UK, which includes the second and third generation. According to the 2011 census, there are an estimated 73,000 Iraqis living in the UK, with the vast majority residing in London (Office for National Statistics 2013). Unofficial sources, however, estimate a much larger number of Iraqis living in the UK. The International Organisation for Migration (IOM) estimates the number to be around 240,000 (International Organisation for Migration 2007, p. 8). The Iraqi Embassy, as well as a number of Shia community centres, estimate between 350,000 and 400,000. The religious and political factions and the ethnic, national, economic, and educational backgrounds of Shia communities in London are very diverse. Most came to the UK during the 1980s and early 1990s (Communities and Local Government 2009, p. 7). Some of the first generation of Iraqi women I interviewed were born and raised in Iraq and moved directly to the UK, but others had to go to so-called transit countries such as Iran, other Gulf countries, the Netherlands, or other European destinations first and then settled in the UK. This article examines marriage practices among 84 first generation Iraqi Shia, who both came from Iraq directly or through transit countries, as well as among 54 second generation Iraqi Shia, who were born and raised in London. The interviews with the first generation of Iraqi women were mainly conducted in Arabic.[2] The second generation, however, used a mix of Arabic and English. In this article, the interview responses are not categoraized or placed into a certain pattern but rather dealt with on an individual basis in order to demonstrate the complex diversity of the Shia community. One could, though, observe some general similarities in the responses from each generation. The article, however, does not intend to reduce responses to particular groups since the cultural and religious memory of each woman differs according to where her socialization occurred and to the degree to which the religio-cultural surroundings of her host societies impacted on her own religious practices. Not only the women's religio-cultural memory before migrating to the UK but also the women's interaction with Shia now living in London coming from other national and cultural contexts contribute to the Iraqi Shia women's understanding of identity expressed through marriage practices. Due to the diverse nature of Shia communities in London sharing the same religious spaces, different religious and cultural practices encounter and interact with one another and in some cases result in new forms of practices that are specific to Shia in Europe (Shanneik Forthcoming).

The politics of remembering is central in the upbringing of their children, as one of the women I interviewed explains: 'We had to leave Iraq when I was still a little child. So I did not remember what life is like in Iraq. However, my mother always kept telling us stories about Iraq, our families, friends and our neighbourhood. These stories gave me the Iraqi identity I felt very attached to when growing up in Iran. I do the same with my own children here in London. I tell them about life not only in Iraq but also in Iran. I want my children to be attached to their Iraqi/Iranian Shia heritage.' The various details involved in and around the concept and practices of marriage are deeply positioned within a clearly defined understanding of a religio-cultural narrative that is articulated through particular material spaces and objects, as well as interpersonal relations and social networks. Similar to Nora's concept of *lieux de mémoire*, the first generation of Iraqis living in London identify certain practices they remember from their own life and marriage experience before migrating to the UK and construct a particular religio-cultural narrative of memory around them. The collective recognition and acceptance of marriage practices plays a prominent role among Iraqi Shia in diasporic spaces, as one of the Iraqis I interviewed confirms: 'We all do it this way. This is what we are and this is how it should continue. It is part of being an Iraqi and it belongs to marriage'.

3. 'It belongs to marriage'

The different social and communal steps prior to proposing to marriage are important within a marriage context and also become markers of identity. How the suited marriage partner should be found, how to propose, whom to bring along when proposing, the bridal gift, or the marriage ceremony all are constructed in a form to suit the socio-religious context back 'home' as it is remembered, as one of the women explains: 'Everything needs to be done as they used to be done back home. Everything according to its roots (*kolo ala 'usulo*). Particularly in marriage issues there is no playing around. No compromises are allowed. This is our family reputation. Everything needs to be done according to how they used to be done. Living in the UK now does not change the way we perform marriages.' The reputation but also the religious, socio-economic, and the political background of the family is important when it comes to finding a suitable match (Haeri 1989). Certain women known as *khattaba*[3], who usually have wide access to the various community members and who enjoy social and religious capital (Bourdieu 1986), act as matchmakers. Very often this role is occupied by the female religious leader, *mullaya*, of the community, who, because of her religious role, is invited to various family and

2 I have provided my own translation for interviews conducted in Arabic but kept the structure as close to the original as possible to avoid divergent meaning through translation.

3 Some call them *mashayya, dallaya*. For a historical account of matchmakers in Iraq and in Najaf in particular see (al-Sharqi 1978, pp. 89–90).

religious occasions such as events marking the rites of passage of family members[4]. At these events, the *mullaya* is allowed access to very personal and private spaces, enabling her to build an opinion of a family and its various members (Sharif 2005). This opinion is valued a lot within the community to the extent that it influences the decision whether or not the proposed groom is suitable for marriage, as one of the women explains: '*Mullaya* [her name] is a pious person. We've known her for over 20 years now and we value her opinion. When she says go away from this boy and don't give him to your daughter. We accept it'.

The concept of marriage is still seen among many Iraqis in London as, not only a marriage between two individuals alone, but also a marriage between wider families. Transnational links to the country of origin but also to the countries where this family might have migrated before ultimately coming to the UK play an enormous role in investigating the religious, socio-economic, and political circles with which this family might have been involved at their various diasporic locations. Various phone calls, skype meetings, and conversations through numerous social-media channels such as WhatsApp, Snapchat, Facebook, Telegram, etc. are used as tools to investigate the history of not only the proposed groom's but also the bride's family.

The process of proposing to a woman is a communal and social act that is expressed through mainly men's capital. The performance of the *mashaya* practice (al-Sharqi 1978), which is the walking to the bride's family home to ask for her hand, is an essential part of the marriage process. Who to asks to be part of the *mashaya* is crucial, and the higher an individual's rank within the community, the better, as one of the women explains: 'You show your respect towards the family and the degree you value them as well as how much proposing to their daughter means to you when you bring people with you who are respected within the community.' She continues by saying how challenging this step is now in the UK as back in Iraq you can chose the highest ranked men from your own family members in addition to other key figures in the community. Since, however, extended family members are not always available in diasporic places, the proposing grooms usually rely on present community members like high-ranking religious scholars. In some cases, other family members living in other European countries are asked to fly to the UK and be part of the *mashaya*. Such a step is highly appreciated and 'increases the chances of their proposal of marriage being accepted', as one of the women explains. Transnational links and networks are therefore used to support one's religious and social capital within diasporic spaces in marriage contexts. At one occasion, as I was told, the eldest of the extended family back in Iraq, also called *kbeer el 'ele*, was skyped in during a *mashaya* visit. This was seen as an enormous step in proving not only the seriousness of the proposal and the respect towards the family they were visiting and to whom they were proposing marriage but also their degree of 'respecting tradition', as the woman explains. The socio-religious positioning of the extended family in the Middle East both has an impact on and also, in some cases, shapes the position of the family and its intra-communal relations with other families in Europe.

The wider transnational positioning of the two families becomes sometimes more important than the local situation of the two individuals themselves, which is something that the prospected couple would be more interested in as it is more relevant to their lives together in the UK, as one of the women explains: 'The problem that we Iraqis face here in the UK when it comes to marrying our children off is that we are more concerned about the wider family (from where they come from, which political and religious party they belong to, which *marje'* [source of emulation] they follow, how many religious scholars in the family they have, etc.) and neglect the fact that we need to ask about the two who are actually going to marry each other. We need to concentrate more on the couples (what are their degrees of religiosity, how is their behaviour, who are their friends, what did they study, where do they

---

4 Birth or *taklif* parties for girls (marking the transition of young girls into puberty). For more on this topic, see (Eftikhar 2015, pp. 67–77; Torab 2007, pp. 169–70).

work, where do they spend their free time and with whom, etc.) than looking to what their ancestors were like back in Iraq or Iran or anywhere else.'

Another woman adds and points to the phenomenon of the dramatic increase of divorce cases among Iraqis of the second generation living in the UK: 'I feel sorry for our children. They are trapped in-between. We [the older generation] have a concrete view on how they should lead their lives without taking into account that they were brought up in a different time and different place. Here the upbringing is usually the responsibility of the mother. The influence of other family members such as grandmothers and aunts, by whom we were influenced when we were children, is not present. How to respect the elders and even the way to talk to them is different among the kids who were brought up here. The main problems newly-wed couples face are usually in relation to in-laws who have concrete expectations how the relationship between them and the couple should be.'

The problem however, as I heard repeatedly, lies mainly in the first generation's expectations, which were formed in a different time and place. The respect that is expected to be expressed towards the older generation should be, from their point of view, unconditional and is unnegotiable. The younger generation however, arguing from a freedom of speech and freedom of choice point of view, do not see a problem in, for example, disagreeing with the older generation and articulating this to them very clearly. The younger generation does not regard these generational disagreements as an act of disrespect but more a case of different viewpoints, which is something that the older generation regard as a fundamental issue of personal and socio-cultural attitude. The following example of an old Iraqi marriage practice, which some parents insist in following, illustrates this generational conflict more clearly. It, however, also presents how Iraqi Shia women in diasporic spaces adhere to particular marriage practices as anchors of memory, thereby constructing what Nora calls *lieux de mémoire* in order to articulate a, for them, clearly defined religious and national identity.

4. Marriage Ceremonial Practices

The fear of losing one's identity in the diaspora urges some Iraqi Shia in London to search for anchors of memory in the hope of providing them with the feeling of stability and security. One such anchor is the *'aqd*, signing the marriage contract. Some of the mothers and mothers-in-law insist on the *'aqd* being done 'as in the old days' as I was told in Arabic. After the *'aqd* has been signed by the groom, the witnesses, and the bride's representative (*wakil*), the groom enters the room where the bride and other female family members and guests are celebrating, as one of the women describes: 'Traditionally in the old days, the bride wears a white [nightgown]. Neither the bride nor anyone in the room is allowed to have anything knotted. No hair-ribbons are allowed and the bride will have her hair down.' This is an old Iraqi practice that some of the mothers performed when they were brides back in the Gulf. It is a practice they remember from back 'home', which they associate with their 'roots', and it acts therefore as an anchor of memory, avoiding the oblivion of these 'roots'[5]. Particularly as part of marriage practices, as the peak of the rite of passage of a woman, certain cultural signs (Assmann 2002; Assmann and Czaplicka 1995) such as the white nightgown, provide stability for individuals and articulate their belonging to a particular community. Communal confirmation of the meaning of such cultural signs adds another layer to the individual's construction of not only the individual's identity but also a wider communal identity. These particular cultural sings are used as a tool to communicate a certain cultural memory that belongs to a certain group of people, which provides them with the 'roots' and the feeling of 'home', which my interviewees repeatedly referred to in our conversations.

These cultural signs, which some women of the first generation of Iraqis insist in using as part of their children's marriage practices, refer to a memory that goes back to their own childhood and was performed in a different geographical and societal space. These spacio-temporal social

[5] The words 'home' and 'roots' were often used among first generation Iraqi women in London when talking about the performance of the *'aqd*.

differences are not taken into consideration when it comes to contemporary diasporic marriage practices. These cultural signs are often of high importance to the women and become part of what Nora calls *lieux de mémoire* and inform their transnational Shia Iraqi identity in the UK. Through these cultural signs performed during a marriage ceremony, women are able to make a connection and link to their past in order not to forget what it means to be an Iraqi Shia. As Nora argues, the purpose of *lieux de mémoire* is to anchor our memories of a different space and time to the present and avoid the oblivion of one's roots. The importance of roots and of lineage has been repeatedly mentioned by my interviewees and is linked to the concept of Shia Islam that goes back to the narrative of Karbala.

The *lieux de mémoire* expressed through the performance of marriage ceremonies are, however, part of women's imagined authenticity of marriage practices, as one of the second generation Iraqi women explains: 'Wearing a nightwear [nightgown] during a marriage ceremony! How odd is this and who does that these days? This might have been performed in the 60s or 70s in Iraq but certainly not in the Twenty-first Century. This is embarrassing. I cannot see myself doing that in front of everyone. In front of my mother-in-law? No way.' Another young woman adds: 'And above all this is not done these days in Iraq anyway. I haven't been to a wedding party in Iraq but my friends and relatives there sent me their pictures on WhatsApp or I have seen them on Facebook and no one was wearing a nightwear [nightgown]. I don't understand why we should here?' Social media is used by the younger generation of Iraqi Shia in London to question, to a certain extent, their mothers' views and ideas on marriage practices and to negotiate new marriage practices that they want to integrate into existing ones in the UK such as *sofrat al-'aqd*.

5. *Sofrat al 'aqd* among Iraqi Shia in London

The function and symbolism of the *sofra* varies according to one's degree of religiosity and belief in the ritual itself. In terms of symbolism and structure, it parallels general sacrificial rites as there is an offering of food, an expression of intension (*niyya*), a dedication to the Shia Imams and other members of the Prophet's family (*ahl al-bayt*. See (Haider 2014), and communal consumption of the food. Food and eating in a ritualized context involve meaning generated through the collective and individual translation of signs and symbols and reflect the 'beliefs, values, cosmology, history, hierarchical structures, and other aspects of the religious culture' (Soileau 2012). During the *sofra* ritual, a religious female reciter, *mullaya*, recites passages from the Qur'an, various prayers, and pieces of poetry, and recalls particular historical Shia narrations. Through these prayers, poems[6], and sacred stories, which are recited over the meal, the food is transformed into a powerful repository of blessing (*baraka*). The belief in the power of food that has been consecrated is wide spread in the various religious gatherings (*majalis*) I attended in Europe and the Middle East. The collective consumption of food is regarded as *barakat*, which is transformative and can be transferred to any person who partakes in the food. Through these readings, women transform the dishes on the *sofra*, opening channels to others to connect to the transcendental. Through the food, not only the bride, but also all the women who consume the food will be given the opportunity to establish a link to the sacred. Foods on the *sofra* are therefore votive dishes that have been prepared and cooked for the event of transition and connection to the transcendental (Torab 2005, 2008).

Sally Promey and Shira Brisman refer to the term 'sensory cultures' (Promey and Brisman 2010), which describes the interaction between objects and individuals through their association with different smells, sounds, touches, and sights: 'Sensory culture, like material culture, concerns not simply perception and its histories and theories but also things perceived and things produced for sensory apprehension' (Promey and Brisman 2010, p. 198). Rituals involve the utilization of a combination of

---

[6] A well-known wedding song I repeatedly heard says: This is who he wanted and who he wished for .... The daughter of the shaykh is brought to the son of the shaykh: hay el radha we hay elly temanaha bint el shekh libnel shekh jibnaha. هاي الرادها وهاي التمناها ... بنت الشيخ لابن الشيخ جبناها. See also (al-Hajjiyye 1967, p. 28).

senses '[b]ut it is only when some substance is ingested that all of the senses can operate together' (Soileau 2012). Rosewater and saffron, which are key ingredients of sweet votive dishes, are sometimes used to wash the bride's feet on the day of the *'aqd*. Some add to the *sofra* the old tradition of what is called the 'tray of luck; (*seniyyet bakht*), which contains various herbs and incense[7] displayed decoratively on a tray (see Figure 2) and is sometimes burned in a censer over charcoal, causing an intensive and pleasant smell in the room.

Figure 2. Also referred to as *seniyyet bakht* (tray of luck) taken by Shanneik 2017 in London.

It is believed that this incense offers protection from the evil eye to prevent jealousy and envy. Women refer to Shia sources highlighting the religious importance of these herbs and thereby refer to the symbolic but also religious importance of using these ingredients before entering wedlock and starting a new life. There are various ways of displaying these herbs on the tray. Some have only the function of symbolic decorations, while some others are used because of the belief in their effect. Some younger Shia only use them because their parents or new in-laws want them to be used, as one of the younger Shia women explains: 'I don't necessarily believe in them. But they look good and our families think they will provide us with a good and happy life. Anything to make them happy really. If it's only about burning some herbs or putting some underneath my pillow then go for it.' Her mother, however, thinks that these practices are important not only for protection and for a happy marriage but also to express their 'roots', as she explains: 'I did it. My mother did it and therefore I want my daughter to do it too. This has been always part of the marriage ceremony and this is how it should continue'.

The fragrant aroma spread in the room through the rosewater, the saffron, the herbs, and the incense becomes a somatized experience for the other women present, as one of the women explains: 'Can you smell Karbala? The minute you enter the room you can smell Karbala.' Another woman adds: 'I don't know if I should laugh or cry. I always have mixed feelings in such *majalis*.' This somatized experience during a *sofra* in combination with the Qur'anic and poetry recitations is linked back to the Karbala narrative. The *mullaya*, through her readings, activates particular memories and thereby directs the congregation to a certain line of memory. The *mullaya* translates each object on the *sofra* in terms of its local, transnational, and diasporic significance in order to make it relevant to everyone in the room. By doing so, the *mullaya* generates a collective memory and thereby strengthens the group's general identity of being Shia outside of any nation-state. Some of the women I interviewed, for example, chose sacred Shia days for the wedding ceremony such as on the day that it is believed Sayyida Fatima, the daughter of the Prophet Muhammad and the mother of Imam Husayn, married Imam

7 Also referred to as *bakhur* or *harmal*.

Ali[8]. This would be a key topic the *mullaya*, for example, would focus on in the *majlis*, contributing to the generation and direction of memories towards women in Shia Islam, emphasizing the role that Sayyida Fatima played in securing a happy marriage with Imam Ali. Female religious authoritative figures such as Sayyida Fatima are taken as role models and a reference point, particularly for younger Shia living in minority contexts (Shanneik 2015; Pierce 2012; Aghaie 2005).

6. Sofra as Contested *lieu de mémoire*

Sofra becomes a space in which various memories are activated and to which different layers of meanings, symbolism, and religious functions for each individual are associated. The *sofra* as a whole, but also each object on the *sofra*, brings various concrete and abstract memories alive for the women. Each individual interprets the *sofra* and its objects in her own terms and is affected in various ways by the *sofra's* somatized experience, as one of the women describes: 'Saffron is magical and should always be part of the *sofra*. Its discrete taste reminds you of Iran and its deep orange colour transfers you to the beauty and warmth of our homeland Iraq.' On the one hand, the individual's interpretation of and association with the *sofra* is influenced by the *mullaya*, while, on the other hand, each individual makes her own links depending on their biographic experiences. Some of the women, for example, had the feeling of being back in Najaf or in Karbala, others in Qum or Mashhad and also in Kuwait or Bahrain, as these were there places in which they were brought up or are regarded as being sacred in Shia Islam. The *sofra* was able to transfer the women emotionally to the places they left but also to bring these memories to the *majlis* in London. In regard to the younger Shia women, the *sofra* brought them back to a Shia pilgrimage trip to Karbala that they performed a year or a couple of months ago. These religious memories are sometimes linked with personal memories of having met their current husbands or having visited certain relatives while being in Iraq or Iran or have a political dimension to them as others remember the Shrine of Sayyida Zaynab in Damascus, associating it with the killing of Shia under the so-called *Islamic State* (*IS*). As such, these triggered memories support the general narrative of the historical persecution of Shia and thereby create a link to the mythico-historical events of Karbala. These different layers of memory are generated in varying degrees through different objects on the *sofra*, embedded within its religious votive context. The *sofra* can therefore be regarded as a place as it represents a way of intersecting various places (Iraq, Iran, Kuwait, Bahrain) and ideas (the historical persecution of Shia starting with the narrative of Karbala up to Shia's present-day persecution under IS-rule) as well as time (historical memories with contemporary migratory experiences) (see also (Foucault 1984)). Memories are eternalized through objects. The *sofra* is a place of eternity as it functions as a tool to keep the memory of Karbala alive and assures the continuation of various layers of individual memories. It represents the accumulation of various memories that have been gathered over time and through various places. The *sofra* is a tool to eternalize the memory of Karbala, which is transmitted through the temporal representation of the *sofra*. The *sofra* is mobile and has a beginning and an end, thus making its physical presence temporal. Through the various memories generated during a *sofra*, however, the *lieux de mémoire* are made eternal through the distribution of votive presents and the consumption of the food from the consecrated *sofra*. It becomes a form of transmission to present various memory narratives, allowing the construction of a coherent identity category within a religious and festive space. The *sofra* is a form of *lieux de mémoire* as it generates numerous layers of memories accumulated over time and from different places.

During a marriage ceremony, which is regarded as an event of transitional phase, the *sofra* provides security and stability through the various objects that generate particular *lieux de mémoire*, thereby constructing a collective Shia identity in the diaspora. The particular gendered Shia identity is highlighted through linking Shia marriage practices with historical female Shia figures. References are

[8] There are certain days that are regarded as being sacred but others that are referred to as 'bad' days such as 3, 5, 13, 16, 21, 24, 25. For more see (al-Sharqi 1978).

made to particular Shia historical figures such as Sayyida Fatima, who is the genealogical connection of the Shia Imams to the Prophet Muhammad, and her daughter Sayyida Zaynab, who is remembered as the one who kept the memory of Karbala alive through the performance of religious ritual gatherings remembering the death of her brother and his supporters. The *mullaya* in a marriage *sofra* refers to such female authoritative figures, who are remembered as strong and active members of society fighting for justice urging other women in the gathering to follow their example and be 'ambassadors of Shia Islam in the UK and in Europe' as heard in one *majlis*. Particularly when the marriage falls on one of the days on which these Shia female figures are remembered, the narrative of the *mullaya* would be directed to such heroic female figures. The display of nuts, eggs, and corn (see Figure 3) are symbols of fecundity, renewal, and continuity. Female fecundity is represented as the female ability, and therefore religious obligation to human reproduction in order to 'increase the number of good Shia' as the *mullaya* continues. It is through giving birth and raising up good Shia children that the message of Karbala can continue, as the mullaya highlights: 'It is in your hands .... In our hands as women to carry on the message of Imam Husayn. We can let the world know for what Imam Husayn was standing for through raising up children who would serve the Shia community in Europe'. Here, the woman's body is used to express collective agency and a particular female ability to nurture and create life, which is relevant particularly within a marriage context.

Figure 3. Bread in the shape of flowers, corn, and eggs. Picture delivered by Um Zahra in London 2017.

7. Karbala as *lieu de mémoire* in London?

Shia women in London preparing a marriage ceremony consciously and actively decide what to use in terms of the objects and narratives to be included as part of the marriage practice. One of the women, who is a wedding planner in London, explains: 'Women do not randomly decide which date the *'aqd* is to be performed or what to put on a *sofra* or which *mullaya* to invite to lead the *majlis*. It all depends on the family and their background, whether from Iraq (and then the question is from Najaf or Karbala or elsewhere) or Iraqis who migrated to Iran or Kuwait before coming to Europe. Whether you have a *sayyid* (descendent of the Prophet Muhammad) in your family. It all depends. At the end of the day ... It is all politics. To get married is not the business of the bride and the groom but the business of the whole Shia community here and back home. Even if the couple does not see it or they do not care, their parents care. The couple, they need to understand this, and they very often do not understand it, but they do not live alone, they live within a community, and they need to respect this. Every step needs to be thought through. It takes months to organise a wedding. People from back home are very often incorporated in the wedding planning here. They even sometimes send over some objects to display on the *sofra* or send stones or tiles from the holy shrines. Marrying is not an easy business.'

The power dynamics among Shia community members in London relate back to intra-national relations belonging to the particular religious and social spheres in their countries of origin. Historical rivalries between the two shrine cities of Najaf and Karbala in Iraq play an enormous role within Shia communities in London. Historical transnational conflicts between countries such as Iran and Iraq also play a role in the wider positions of families within Shia communities in London. The changing political and religious climate in the Middle East has an additional impact on family networks in the diaspora. Some young British Shia are outside of these power dynamics, but others are and insist on being part of it by either confirming the continuation of the status quo or changing some of these intra-communal relations. Marrying from the community requires, in the latter case, a lot of political intra-communal considerations. This is also relevant when thinking about what practices to include in a marriage ceremony.

Regarding *sofrat al 'aqd*, there are various opinions around the existence of the *sofra* within Iraqi folkloric traditions (al-Sharqi 1978; al-Hajjiyye 1967). Whereas a number of women referred to the *sofra* as being part of 'what Shia do', others deny its importance and urge women to refrain from including it in their marriage ceremonies. Those who regard it as a continuation of a long Iraqi Shia tradition argue, though, that how the *sofra* is laid out nowadays, what objects are placed on it, and what meaning each object has for the wedding organizers differs from what the women remember from the time they were married in the 60s and 70s in the Gulf, as one of the women explains: 'Now these young girls they pay a lot of attention to details. Everything needs to be set up for a reason. It looks like a piece of art.' Another woman adds: 'In our days it was only a *seniyya* (see Figure 2, above) but now it is a whole *sofra*'. There are some Shia who reject the concept of the *sofra* in itself, as one of the women explains: 'Some people do a *sofra* saying to God that if you make this couple happy, I will dedicate a *sofra* to you next time. This is as if you are making a condition to God. This I reject. If you want to do a *sofra* and donate what is on it to your guests then it is fine but you cannot make a *sofra* and connect it to a condition made to God. If God wants to make the couple happy, He will, with or without a *sofra*.' Another woman supports this opinion by saying: 'People do not get the idea of the *sofra* and use it for their own good. Not only during a wedding but also during other occasions. The whole idea of the *sofra* nowadays is being used to show off. The young girls they compete in who makes the better *sofra* on their wedding. They hire people to do it professionally. They pay them money. Imam Husayn would not have accepted this. Take the example of Sayyida Fatima, her wedding was simple and our daughters' weddings should be simple too.' The *sofra* also has a political dimension to it. Whether the family is close to, for example, the Islamic Republic of Iran or whether they want to disassociate themselves from the Iranian regime determines whether to place certain objects on the *sofra* that are regarded as 'typical Iranian' or whether to do a *sofra* at all, as some regard it as an Iranian practice, which, out of political reasons, some decide to refrain from performing. Certain objects or practices such as honey (see Figure 3), which the bride and the groom feed each other with their little fingers, is regarded by some as Iranian. Placing the honey on a *sofra* would generate for some memories of Iran. Those families who oppose the Iranian regime would therefore reject using honey as an object on the *sofra* to express their political stance regarding the Iranian government and its particular ideological orientation.

Young Shia women's usage of the *sofra* in their wedding ceremony can be seen as their conscious orientation and declaration of belonging to a Shia heritage. The *sofra* is a material and symbolic tool to express their identity of being Shia and to link their present with their historical Shia past in general and with Imam Husayn and the Karbala narrative in particular. The *sofra* becomes a form of *lieux de mémoire* for the young generation of Shia in the UK as it connects and links them to a Shia history and provides them with a religious identity they regard as important during a rite of passage. They constantly renegotiate and reproduce their identities as Shia and what it means for them to be Shia in Europe increasingly through material expression, be it through the *sofra* in a marriage ceremony or through the various other religious practices they perform during the year in which they either commemorate or celebrate their Imams and other Shia religious figures. Young Shia constantly build various *lieux de mémoires* integrated within their local British context of living in a highly diverse Shia community in London. Different to the older generation of Shia, who might orient themselves to belonging to a particular nation-state, following a certain *marja'*, or being part of a specific tribe or family, the younger generation moves usually back and forth across these borders. They connect to Karbala as their *lieux de mémoire* but fuse it within their local context. One woman of the older generation sums it up in regard to marriage practices by saying: 'Nowadays Shia marriages are a mix of everything: the *sofra* is Iranian, the poetry Iraqi, the dress Indian, and the cake English'. Another woman refers to a marriage that took place this year, where 'the bride had an Iraqi wedding à la British style. The bride was wearing a hatinator and looked like Kate, the Duchess of Cambridge, and this before entering a *sofrat al 'aqd* ... this is their world, it is their reality and we need to accept it as well.'

8. Conclusions

This article illustrated the complex transnational religio-cultural and political dimensions of Pierre Nora's *lieux de mémoire* through adapting it, for the first time, to the study of Shia Islam. It demonstrated how particular Shia ritual practices performed by and for women such as *sofrat al 'aqd* can be regarded as a form of Nora's *lieux de mémoire*. The *sofra* serves as the site of memory, allowing the individual and the community in general to build a sense of a Shia historical continuity generated out of the Karbala narrative (see also (Nora 1989, p. 7)). The *sofra* itself but also all the arrangements around it such as the various objects on the *sofra*, the poetry recited, the food consumed, and the herbs burned all are tools for the various activations of numerous memories. As Aleida Assmann explains, '[t]he site is all that, what one seeks in it, what one knows of it, and what one relates to it' (Assmann 2002). Iraqi Shia women in diasporic spaces construct an imagined authenticity of marriage practices to ensure the continuation of individual and collective memories. Whether taking the different spacio-temporal contexts into consideration or not, Iraqi Shia women very often adhere to practices they remember from their own childhood and youth, presenting them as authentic, even if they have changed or been abandoned in Iraq, in order to keep the memory of an imagined past alive. The Shia ritual practice of *sofra* is a place that combines different (non-)virtual and (re)contextualized spaces that find their origin in a particular Shia narrative interwoven with personal, individual, and biographical memory. Material objects displayed on the *sofra* relate to Shia historical sites and narratives of Shia history, which function in making the past tangible and which act as a meaning-making apparatus for the present (Assmann 2002, pp. 201–2). Each individual, however, relates to these historical narratives differently, resulting in a plethora of Shia memories, all connected in one way or another to the narrative of Karbala. These memories are individually and collectively constructed, allowing various layers of memories to be associated with the same place. The activated memories are not randomly chosen by the organizers of a marriage ceremony but rather are consciously decided upon and reflect the socio-political and religious orientations of the hosts of the marriage. Transnational networks and family ties have an influence on the local intra-communal structures and relationships in the UK. Marriage practices in Europe are one of many other communal activities that are influenced by the geo-political and religious developments in the Middle East.

The first and second generation of Iraqi women in the UK search consciously for anchors of memory to construct a particular narrative of their Shia past that determines and defines their present and future. These anchors of memory are individually but also collectively (re)constructed and (re)defined and are influenced by the past as well as current political, socio-economic, and religious changes in the Middle East and in Europe. As Aleida Assmann argues, the politics of memory provides a group with its genealogy (Assmann 2006, p. 138), legitimized through symbols 'across space and time' (Assmann 2006, p. 132). Memory pluralizes and blurs the boundaries of identity but provides Shia women in Europe with a reference point that they articulate through material objects that act as *lieux de mémoire* of a Shia transnational identity. It is the female space of the *sofra* that provides women with the ability to articulate their religious and social identity as women connected and even rooted within a Shia past, which is expressed through ritual practices that are transnationally transmitted and influenced but locally performed.

Acknowledgments: The research for this article was partly funded by the ERC Project 2013-AdG-324180 'Problematizing 'Muslim Marriages': Ambiguities and Contestations', lead by the principle investigator Prof Annelies Moors and held at the University of Amsterdam, as well as by the University of South Wales Research Institute for the project 'Shia Marriage Practices and Changes in the UK'.

Conflicts of Interest: The author declares no conflict of interest.

References

Abaza, Mona. 2001. Perceptions of Urfi Marriage in the Egyptian Press. *ISIM Newsletter* 7: 20–21.

Abou el Magd, Nadia. 2009. Outcry in Egypt over 'marriage tourism'. *The National*, August 17. Available online: https://www.thenational.ae/world/africa/outcry-in-egypt-over-marriage-tourism-1.546799 (accessed on 29 August 2017).

Aghaie, Kamran S., ed. 2005. *The Women of Karbala: Ritual Performance and Symbolic Discourses in Modern Shi'i Islam.* Austin: University of Texas Press.

al-Haidari, Ibrahim. 1999. *Trajidiyat Karbala: Susiyulujiyat al-khitab al-Shi'i* [The Tragedy of Karbala. The Sociology of the Shii Speech]. London: Dar Al Saqi.

al-Hajjiyye, Aziz Jasim. 1967. *Baghdadiyyat. Taswir lil hayat al-ijtima'iyye wal 'adat al-baghdadiyye khilal ma'at 'am.* Baghdad: Mudiriyet al-funun wal thaqafa al-sha'biyya. Wizarat al-thaqafa wal Irshad.

al-Sharqi, Talib Ali. 1978. *Al-Najaf al Sharif. 'Adatuha wa taqaliduha.* Al-Najaf: Matba'at al-Adab.

Anderson, Benedict R. 1983. *Imagined Communities: Reflections on the Origin and Spread of Nationalism.* London: Verso.

Arabi, Oussama. 2001. *Studies in Modern Islamic Law and Jurisprudence.* Leiden: Brill.

Assmann, Aeida. 2006. *Erinnerungsräume: Formen und Wandlungen des kulturellen Gedächtnisses*, 3rd ed. München: Beck.

Assmann, Aleida. 2002. Das Gedächtnis der Orte—Authentizität und Gedenken. In *Firma Topf & Söhne—Hersteller der Öfen für Auschwitz: Ein Fabrikgelände als Erinnerungsort?* Edited by Aleida Assmann, Rank Hiddemann and Eckhard Schwarzenberger. Frankfurt: Campus, pp. 197–212.

Assmann, Jan, and John Czaplicka. 1995. Collective Memory and Cultural Identity. *New German Critique* 65: 125–33. [CrossRef]

Assmann, Jan. 2002. Das kulturelle Gedächtnis. *Erwägen, Wissen, Ethik* 13: 239–47.

Bhabha, Homi K. 1994. *The Location of Culture.* London: Routledge.

Bourdieu, Pierre. 1986. The Forms of Capital. In *Handbook of Theory and Research for the Sociology of Education.* Edited by John G. Richardson. New York: Greenwood, pp. 241–58.

Bowen, John R. 2011. Islamic Adaptations to Western Europe and North America. *American Behavioral Scientist* 55: 1601–15. [CrossRef]

Chelkowski, Peter J., ed. 2010. *Eternal Performance: Ta'ziyeh and other Shiite Rituals.* London: Seagull books.

Communities and Local Government. 2009. *The Iraqi Muslim Community: Understanding Muslim Ethnic Communities.* London: Communities and Local Government.

Eftikhar, Tina. 2015. *The Birth of a Celestial Light: A Feminist Evaluation of an Iranian Spiritual Movement Inter-Universal Mysticism.* Newcastle: Cambridge Scholars Publishing.

Erll, Astrid. 2011. *Memory in Culture.* Translated by Sara B. Young. Hampshire: Palgrave Macmillan.

Foucault, Michel. 1984. Of Other Spaces: Utopias and Heterotopias. Translated from the French by Jay Miskowiec. *Architecture /Mouvement/ Continuité*, October. [CrossRef]

Grever, Maria. 1997. The Pantheon of Feminist Culture: Women's Movements and the Organization of Memory. *Gender & History* 9: 364–74.

Haeri, Shahla. 1989. *Law of Desire. Temporary Marriages in Shi'i Iran.* Syracuse: Syracuse University Press.

Haeri, Shahla. 1992. Temporary Marriage and the State in Iran: An Islamic Discourse on Female Sexuality. *Social Research* 59: 201–23.

Haider, Najam. 2014. *Shi'i Islam: An Introduction.* Cambridge: Cambridge University Press.

Halbwachs, Maurice. 1992. *On Collective Memory.* Translated by Lewis A. Coser. Chicago and London: The University of Chicago Press.

International Organisation for Migration. 2007. Iraq Mapping Exercise. Available online: http://unitedkingdom.iom.int/sites/default/files/doc/mapping/IOM_IRAQ.pdf (accessed on 27 July 2017).

Mervin, Sabrina. 2008. Normes religieuses et loi du silence: Le marriag temporaire chez les chiites du Liban. In *Les Metamorphoses du Marriage au Moyen-Orient*. Edited by Barbara Drieskens. Beyrouth: IFPO, pp. 97–118.

Misztal, Barbara. 2003. *Theories of Social Remembering*. Maidenhead: Open University Press.

Momen, Moojan. 1985. *An Introduction to Shi'i Islam: The History and Doctrines of Twelver Shi'ism*. New Haven: Yale University Press.

Nielsen, Jörgen, and Lisbet Christoffersen, eds. 2010. *Shari'a as Discourse: Legal Traditions and the Encounter with Europe*. New York: Ashgate Publishers.

Nora, Pierre. 1989. Between Memory and History: Les Lieux de Mémoire. *Representations*. Special issue: Memory and Counter-memory 26: 7–24. [CrossRef]

Nora, Pierre. 1996. General Introduction: Between Memory and History. In *Realms of Memory: Rethinking the French Past*. Edited by Pierre Nora and Lawrence Kritzman. New York: Columbia University Press, pp. 21–26.

Office for National Statistics. 2013. Detailed country of birth and nationality analysis from the 2011 Census of England and Wales. Available online: http://www.ons.gov.uk/ons/dcp171776_310441.pdf (accessed on 27 July 2017).

Pierce, Matthew. 2012. Remembering Fatimah: New Means of Legitimizing Female Authority in Contemporary Shi'i Discourse. In *Women, Leadership, and Mosque. Changes in Contemporary Islamic Authority*. Edited by Masooda Bano and Hilary Kalmbach. Leiden and Boston: Brill, pp. 345–62.

Promey, Sally, and Shira Brisman. 2010. Sensory Cultures: Material and Visual Religion Reconsidered. In *The Blackwell Companion to Religion in America*. Edited by Philip Goff. West Sussex: Blackwell Publisher.

Shahrani, Shahreena. 2010. The Social (Re) Construction of 'Urfi Marriage. Ph.D. dissertation, University of Ohio State, Columbus, OH, USA.

Shanneik, Yafa. 2015. Remembering Karbala in the Diaspora: Religious Rituals among Iraqi Shii Women in Ireland. *Religion* 45: 89–102. [CrossRef]

Shanneik, Yafa. Forthcoming. *Gendering Shia Religious Rituals from Europe to the Middle East*. Leiden: Brill.

Sharif, Tahya Hassan Al Khalifa. 2005. Sacred Narratives Linking Iraqi Shiite Women across Time & Space. In *Muslim Networks from Hajj to Hip Hop*. Edited by Miriam Cooke and Bruce B. Lawrence. Chapel Hill and London: The University of North Carolina Press, pp. 132–54.

Soileau, Mark. 2012. Spreading the Sofra: Sharing and Partaking in the Bektashi Ritual Meal. *History of Religions* 52: 1–30. [CrossRef]

Spellman, Kathryn. 2004. *Religion and Nation: Iranian Local and Transnational Networks in Britain*. New York and Oxford: Berghahn Books.

Torab, Azam. 2005. Vows, Mediumship and Gender. Women's Votive Meals in Iran. In *Gender, Religion and Change in the Middle East. Two Hundred Years of History*. Edited by Inger Marie Okkenhaug and Ingvild Flaskerud. Oxford: Berg, pp. 207–23.

Torab, Azam. 2007. *Performing Islam. Gender and Ritual in Iran*. Leiden and Boston: Brill.

Torab, Azam. 2008. Conditional Agreements with Saints: Gift and Commodity in Shi'a Muslim Votive Practices. In *Women and the Gift*. Edited by Morny Joy. Bloomington: Indiana University Press, pp. 139–58.

Walby, Joanne. 2010. Extended Holiday in Hurghada: Russian Migrant Women and 'Urfi Marriage. *Surfacing* 3: 39–70.

Article

Mattering Moralities: Learning Corporeal Modesty through Muslim Diasporic Clothing Practices

Lauren B Wagner

Technology and Society Studies, Maastricht University, Grote Gracht 90-92, 6211SZ Maastricht, The Netherlands; l.wagner@maastrichtuniversity.nl

Received: 15 June 2017; Accepted: 31 July 2017; Published: 24 August 2017

Abstract: Questions of 'coveredness' in Islamic codes of dress, particularly as they apply to women, are often framed through the symbolic statements that they enable or disable, or through discourses on public versus private spaces. Rather than focus on these disciplining dimensions, this article explores observations about embodied practices for clothing oneself 'modestly', and some of the paradoxes thereof, which emerged in the context of research about diasporic mobilities of European-Moroccans in Morocco. Drawing heavily on Karen Barad and a materialist phenomenological approach to corporeality, this approach produces an understanding of how moral bodies materialize with and through clothing. By observing and following the mobilities of participants across spaces dominated by 'Muslim' and 'Western' regimes of modesty, certain dissonances of their practices in these differentiated spaces indicate ways bodies, clothing and moralities are intra-actively entangled. Proposing ethnography as a diffractive apparatus, the analysis incorporates participant reports, as well as embodied learning through ethnographic time. By approaching this 'disciplining' diffractively, all agents–knowledgeable bodies, malleable clothes and spatially moral gazes–are considered as intra-actively influencing each other, mattering into 'modesty' where 'subjected' bodies, as well as clothing and regimes of modesty are adapting.

Keywords: Barad; corporeality; shame; phenomenology; intra-action; diffraction; Islam; Morocco; ethnography; embodiment

---

1. Introduction: Feeling Covered

The extract of talk represented in Box 1 comes from an interview between myself, Anissa and Shirin, which took place in a cafe in Den Haag, Netherlands. Anissa and Shirin are longtime friends and Dutch-Moroccans; they were recruited for participation for this ethnographic research about European Moroccans visiting Morocco when I asked them for directions while they were on a pleasure trip in Marrakech. We met again several months later, when we were all 'back home' in Europe, from Morocco.

In the context of research about diasporic negotiations of belonging in Morocco, I asked them about wearing djellabas, a loose-fitting, dress-like silhouette that is worn, with many variations in color, style and decoration, by both men and women in Morocco. This question addressed style practices around an object (djellaba) that is widely understood as indexing 'Moroccanness'. Some Moroccans who have lived most or all of their lives in Europe wear a djellaba as everyday clothing, in Europe or in Morocco. Anissa and Shirin, evidently, do not. Yet, Shirin's unusually complex answer as to why she does not usually wear them was an exceptional elicitation of how European Moroccans visiting Morocco might experience their bodies and clothing.

Box 1. Interview extract: Walking in a djellaba[1].

Anissa and Shirin, Den Haag 10 April 2008, 1m

1 LW do you ever wear djellabas and things like that there? or do-
2 S there? ya eh:::::: no I can't walk with the h-djellaba-h-h,=
3 LW no?
4 S =but I la- I love to wear- wear it sometimes/ if I go to the **hammam** or something eh near,(.4) I eh wear a djellaba
5 LW you can't walk? or you can-
6 S no eh, w- ya, it's- it's- it's- **diff**icult, I don't know, it's eh em (.) if you have the long djellaba, it's (.) *ja en je loopt toch een beetje:, je bent niet gewend, ik weet niet*
you walk like a little: you are not used to it, I don't know
7 A *bijna nooit (aandoen)*
I hardly (wear them)
8 S it's not that I cannot walk with it, but *ja het zit niet echt eh je moet 'r effe aan wennen, want hier doe je 't nooit aan dus ja*
yeah, it doesn't sit right, you have to get used to it because you don't wear them here so yeah
9 LW it's different feeling, you have to walk slower hehahhah
10 S ya! it's **diff**erent ya. but it's **comfortable** because everything, (.3) you have the feeling everything is emm: (1.0)
11 A [[covered
12 S [[*bedekt/* covered
13 S yeah, but *je moet 'r aan wennen*
you have to get used to it

Shirin explains over several conversational turns about her preference for, but difficulty in walking in a djellaba. Though Anissa interjects that she "hardly [wears them]" (Line 7), Shirin continues her efforts to explain her meaning: she is able to walk, but it requires "getting used to" (Line 8) because she is not in the habit of wearing them here (in Europe). After I laughingly comment that "you have to walk slower" (Line 9), Shirin agrees, then contradicts the discomfort expressed in her previous statements by emphasizing that it (the djellaba) is "comfortable". Identifying how that 'comfort' manifests, both women simultaneously utter "covered", in English and Dutch (Lines 11 and 12).

'Feeling covered' here becomes an important intersection between place, material body, and social dimensions of modesty enacting particular gazes and creating felt reactions, recognizable to all three interlocutors, in these emergent corporealities. The fact that Shirin is both uncomfortable in a djellaba because she is not 'used to' it, and comfortable in it because she feels 'covered' (a feeling that Anissa seems aware of as well, in how she simultaneously voiced its English translation) demonstrates a spatial dimension to 'wearing a djellaba' as a clothing practice. It is something both women are unaccustomed to doing in one diasporic node (Europe), but Shirin has attempted in another diasporic node (Morocco), in alignment with her activities there. While her body may not be used to it, in terms of the movements permitted by its shape, her corporeal materiality also appreciates 'feeling covered'.

1 The interview is transcribed using adapted conversation analysis conventions (see Atkinson and Heritage 1984). In contrast to many common methods for analyzing interviews, this approach will include analysis based on the sequential and interactive nature of talk (Sacks 1992; Schegloff 2007), beyond the lexical content. Participants were told they can speak in English or their native Dutch, whichever might be easier. The interviewer question in line 1 that begins this section of talk, was following other questions about objects and clothing they like to buy in Morocco, including the elaborate dresses (*takshetas*) that many women have tailor-made in Morocco.

Transcription conventions:

Bold = emphasis; italic = Dutch; - = hesitation/stop; : = elongation; h = breath; [[= simultaneous turn-taking; = = continuous speech over turns; ? = strong rising tone; , = weak rising tone; . = strong falling tone; / = weak falling tone; () = uncertain transcription; (.#) = length of pause

Questions of 'coveredness' in Islamic codes of dress, particularly as they apply to women (like Anissa and Shirin, as Muslims), are often framed through the political statements that they enable or disable, or through discourses on public versus private spaces (Secor 2002). They become readable as a set of (masculine) gazes, composed by and enforcing rules of moral order defining a feminine 'private', to which women resist and innovate to assert subjective expression. In this paper, I would like to expand on discussions about how Islamic modes of clothing can be fashionable, cosmopolitan and mobile (Tarlo 2007; Gökarıksel 2012; Gökarıksel and Secor 2010a, 2010b; Mahmood 2005; Falah and Nagel 2005), by engaging the corporeal materialities of bodies that absorb and enmesh with gazes, rules, spaces, environments, and fabrics that cover their flesh. This framing is built on an understanding of bodies as generative and productive as much as reactive, in intra-action (Barad 2007) within and without.

This orientation, I contend, can be productive for understanding how corporeal discomforts negotiate and intra-act a shame::modesty spectrum as they move with their clothing across spaces shaped by different gazes and discourses. Within the scope of this paper, I will be purposefully vague about what those discourses may include, as an effort to avoid producing or attributing 'context' to these processes beyond the social ordering experienced in the practice of 'feeling covered' (Katz 1999; Turowetz et al. 2016). Instead of characterizing this as a process of disciplining onto and through bodies via 'discourse', I want to take all of these agents–knowledgeable bodies, malleable clothes, and spatially moral gazes–as intra-actively influencing each other, so that the bodies are reshaping and reforming along with 'discourse'. In short, I want to explore how 'modesty' matters, including and beyond the 'subjected' bodies (Barad 2007).

My suggestion for this orientation to bodies becoming 'modest' is based in ethnographic exploration that was not analytically focused on this topic as the core investigation. Rather, these observations about embodied practices for clothing oneself 'modestly', and some of the paradoxes thereof, emerged in the context of research about diasporic mobilities of European-Moroccans in Morocco. Both the performance of this research as ethnographic and the fact that it focused on mobile agents, regularly traveling in and out of Morocco as members of a European-born and raised diaspora, play a role in how the examples below can be analyzed. My mobility as a non-Muslim, non-Moroccan woman and their mobility as Moroccan-origin Muslims come into play as we all cross back and forth between European and Moroccan regimes of morality, and how they can infuse into our bodies as a way of knowing the world.

To analyze these intra-actions incorporating my own ethnographic apparatus to understand how 'comfort' can be achieved for different Muslim Moroccan women across diasporic space, I draw upon Karen Barad's framework for agential realism as diffraction: inserting myself as observer/apparatus in this dynamic and exploring onto-epistemologically how I am able to know such practices by absorbing them (Jackson and Mazzei 2011). After a short discussion on agential realism, I present an object of study in how modesty can be produced through clothing practices engaged in by Muslim women, with a discussion of how these might be subjected to different regimes of morality across spaces. I address only religion as a morality regime here–not education, political climate, or other social variables–because across the quoted and many other diasporic women who might experience 'feeling uncovered', these spaces are characterized between enforcement of 'religiousness' or 'secularness'. Next, I discuss how my ethnographic apparatus, through a process of learning how to dress in Morocco in my own female body, substantiates a framework through which I can diffractively observe the practices and moralities of others around me. My observations, along with those expressed by women who participated in the research and are quoted here, diffract into an analysis of how certain clothing, corporeal lived bodies, and fluid regimes of morality entangle in a Moroccan summertime landscape filled with diasporic visitors. This diffraction resolves, finally, into an intra-active modesty: not conclusive, directional, or necessarily readable through ways that certain women choose to (or feel forced to) cover or uncover their skin, but emergent and entangling as intra-actions of all these elements.

2. Object: Modesty of Dress for Muslim Women

Whether about putting clothes on or taking them off, how Muslim women's bodies are clothed draws social attention. This attention is composed and constructed not only through moral gazes, but in how those gazes materialize, rendering acceptable or unacceptable certain entanglements of bodies and clothing, taking place in certain spaces. While the de-clothing of that woman on the beach (Box 2 below) is enmeshed in ongoing evolutions of a political, moral, and securitized landscape that draws links between the coveredness of a Muslim body and physical and ideological risks to France, Noura's sense of being required to wear a djellaba when going out in Fez (Box 3 below) is likewise entangled with ongoing debates in the political, cultural and religious landscape across Morocco. These two examples illustrate how modesty of dress for a Muslim woman becomes an object that changes shape and matters along with dispersed spaces, clothing practices and diverse corporealities. This section builds a formulation of 'modesty' in relation to the spaces, practices, and corporealities that become relevant for the Muslim Moroccan-European women under discussion here.

Box 2. Wearing a burkini

On 23 August 2016, global news websites were plastered with images of a woman being pressured by police to remove layers of her clothing. Sitting on a beach in Nice, France, she was ticketed 'for not wearing "an outfit respecting good morals and secularism"' (Quinn 2016); a witness attested that some onlookers applauded the police while the woman's young daughter cried.

Box 3. Interview extract: going out in a dress.

Noura, Arena Palace Cafe, Fes, 29 July 2008 40 s

```
         ... nous je vais dire euh:  moi je vous dire eh:  la journée je peut pas
1 N      sortir en robe comme ça.  la journée je-suis obligée de mettre un djellab-
         une djell[aba
         us, I'm saying, I'm telling you eh:  during the day I can't go out in a
         dress like this, during the day I'm obligated to put on a djellab-
         a djell[aba
2 LW                                  [ouais °ouais°
                                    [yeah °yeah°
3 N      parce que:  sinon c'est toute la journée eh (.4) les::  va dire eh/les gens
         d'ici nous abordent, mais eh
         because:  otherwise it's all day eh (1.4) the::  let's say eh/the people
         from here talk to us but eh
4 LW     ouais
         yeah
5 N      avec eh (.)  sans respect quoi.
         with eh (.)  without respect
```

Before addressing the interpretative moralities of Islam or the clothing practices, I need to clarify how bodies here are understood as malleable and knowledgeable, themselves mattering intra-actively with other elements, through agential realism.

2.1. Mattering Barad and Agential Realism

Matter, Barad asserts, "is the sedimenting historicity of practices/agencies and an agentive force in the world's differential becoming" (Barad 2007, p. 180). For the present case, 'feeling covered', observed through the ways individual women intra-act with their clothing, 'matters' here as a triangulation of how these different agents meet in harmonious cooperation, and how different forms of 'discomfort' manifest and indicate their dissonance. Attending to these entanglements of matter, and the matter they iteratively produce, enables ineffable corporeal sensations and experiences, especially those, like a sense of feeling 'covered', that are difficult for an observer to record, to take part in an analysis of how modesty is produced through these (Muslim, female) bodies. The 'agents' thus include intangible, ineffable and indescribable sensations of corporeal comfort as well as the human and non-human actors that convene in observed moments and reported perceptions as mattering: literally making materiality in the intra-activity of all participating tangible and intangible entities.

Construing 'modesty' ethnomethodologically as an intra-active process enables an analysis of how corporeal materialities integrate gazes, how gazes produce clothing styles, and how clothing styles respond with and to corporeal manifestations. Such intra-actions might include how others experiencing the same trouble as Shirin (above) have adapted djellabas (shortened lengths, added longer slits, incorporated matching trousers) so they are more easily walkable. Such adjustments of clothing, as well as the intra-action between body and clothing experienced by Shirin and Noura, and recognized by myself and Anissa, become observable as entities enmeshed in the social ordering of 'modesty'. Combining this kind of data on practical activity with Barad's formulation of agential realism, enables an empirical examination of how bodies formulate possible gazes and how clothing, as well as discourses, institutions and other potential agents involved, formulate possible bodies. Ontologically and methodologically, I attempt to approach this emergent mattering from the event outwards (Katz 1999), taking seriously Shirin's sense of 'coveredness' as matter rather than discourse, and attempting to trace what agents and intra-actions contribute to it.

To apply this framework specifically to bodies and clothing, I find myself aligning with Hanson (2007), who is frustrated with the theoretical means at hand to discuss how clothing and bodies interact in both material/physical and discursive ways, all of which become part of corporeal physicality beyond simply a layer of clothing to cover one's skin. Discussing drag-kinging women, she approaches their clothing practices as sensory sites of the 'felt' effects of transformation, where the work of producing masculinized female bodies materializes other social forces of dominance and liberation (Hanson 2007, p. 78). The 'becoming' of this is, for her, a palimpsest of visual and carnal layers interacting with each other, from the physical body through the layers of clothing and costuming (Cavallaro and Warwick 1998). Transformations enacted through these bodies become molecular in their layering, as interactions between the tingling of exposed skin, gazes of proximate others and the fabric of clothing wherein all aspects to this assemblage are malleable, and any one has the potential to become agentive in this complex interaction. That is, rejecting the some of the prevailing ways of examining the (re)production of masculinity through similar sites of embodied transformation, she demonstrates the dynamic untenability of conventionally imagined boundaries to a corporeal body by embracing the "ambiguous and irreducible relationship that exists between dress and the body" (Hanson 2007, p. 103).

Drawing heavily on Barad (Barad 2003, 2007) and a post-humanist phenomenological approach to embodiment, this theoretical approach produces an understanding of how bodies, through their desires, affects, mutabilities and creativities, materialize social relations. It has a different starting place than parallel research on embodied subjectivity and the symbolic identity of clothing, such as the 'material culture' field reflected in work like that of Dick Hebdige and Daniel Miller, by presuming agency on the part of human and non-human actors in assemblage as opposed to reading bodies primarily as a canvas for mapping social expressions and relations. Instead of tracing the genealogical history of a style through its uses and referents, here the focus is on the materiality and corporeality within a new materialist ontology that approaches bodies and their clothing (or clothing and their bodies) as emergent, lived matter (Coole 2010).

2.2. Shame: Modesty

Modesty is itself thus a meeting point of material corporealities and moral regimes. It can be conceived in response to an emotion of 'shame', itself describing both an immediate and an internalized sense of inadequacy or inappropriateness, intertwined with social norms and values defining adequacy and appropriateness. Modesty is one reaction to shame, or to an anticipation of shame. These are, as Dolezal argues in *The Body and Shame*, a set of emotions that depend on self-reflexivity, but are also inherently social, arising 'in the interaction between bodies; [involving] an intensification of the body's surface and its visibility' (Dolezal 2015, p. 5) and a corporeal affective experience of physical changes (heat, blushing, goosebumps, etc.) (Dolezal 2015, p. 6). In other words, shame::modesty, as a spectrum of emotion, require intra-action with a social world, with moralities and expectations, and with a corporeal material self to emerge.

Dolezal further claims that women's bodies are more frequently a site for shame than men's (Dolezal 2015, p. 7). That observation extends into anthropological literature on Islamic communities, where an 'honor/shame' dichotomy was an entrenched framework for analysis (cf. Bauer 1985; Abu-Lughod 1986), often focusing on the regulation and production of honor. This anthropological attention has, historically, often rested on what has been codified as a defining characteristic of Muslim societies: the production of gender separation whether spatial (Bourdieu 1979), emotional (Abu-Lughod 1986) or through female clothing practices (El Guindi 1999), all of which seek to 'protect' women's visibility by regulating when, where, and how (e.g., what physical parts of their bodies) might be visible. While, as Dolezal indicates, women's bodies anywhere have been subject to production as 'shameful' in a multitude of ways (Dolezal 2015, p. 106), the particular configurations of visibility of women's bodies in an Islamic moral framework create specific conditions for visibility–of their bodies as whole or as bodies in components, like hair, skin or limbs–that enter into an intra-action of modesty.

Of these various visibility practices, veiling is often discussed as a key example of how Islam interacts with shame and modesty in regulating female behavior. The many variations on wearing a veil reflect many possible interpretations on what the Qur'an (Surah 24: 30–31) requires as a modestly covered body. Both sexes are enjoined to cover the 'awrah, or parts of body that should not be public, which includes the area from the navel to the knee for both men (though male negotiations of this requirement seem to be less frequently researched) and women (Badr 2004). Manifesting as an interpretation of a religious text, like any parallel practice, veiling is not related to only one dimension of social life: veiling or not-veiling can be a stylistic, pragmatic, or unreflective choice, based as much in a social, political, or economic environment as it might reflect spiritual beliefs, or sacralization (El Guindi 1999) or politicization (Badr 2004) of a woman's body. As Secor (2002) argues, veiling acts as part of a symbolic order that configures spatialities in complex ways, both as fashion-conscious stylistic expression and as a corporeal form for negotiating external political realities. Furthermore, wearing a veil cannot be simply equated to creating a 'modest' body to the extent that being 'modest' by covering one's head can be done in a showy and immodest way (Secor 2002, p. 10; White 1999). As it travels along with a body, veiling reflects one of the many ways women negotiate moral regimes on the visibility of their bodies and their access to both public and private spaces.

In this sense, veiling, along with modes of regulating visibility of women, can be interpreted ultimately as spatial regimes. Visibilities that might produce 'shame'—such as showing the area from the navel to the knee—are of course possible among certain gazing others within enclosed or private spaces, where the form of enclosure or privacy is also itself a negotiation of perceptions. Fernea (1998) recounts shooting sequences of an ethnographic film on women in Marrakech in a hammam, while the women participating were taking part in their normal acts of bathing; knowing full well that the images of their uncovered bodies, normally restricted to the vision of other women alone, would be visible to a broad and unknowable public. While spatialities of visibility can be regulated by doors and walls defining public from private, they can also be reformulated through technologies and other interpretive materialities in ways that become acceptable as 'modest' to those who interact with a given moral regime.

In short, shame and modesty need to be taken as not merely an event of a consciousness, more or less directly related to an assumed problematic visibility, but a complex interaction of events, corporealities, and reactions that are material and cognitive as much as emotional and affective (Dolezal 2015, p. 119). As Barad would contend, these are intra-actions: "not a thing but a doing, a congealing of agency" (Barad 2007, p. 151) that matters. The mattering of this intra-action—which I am focused on here as producing 'modesty'—leaves marks on the entities and bodies involved.

These explorations point to how modesty and immodesty are imprecise moralities, even in Muslim-dominant spaces where they appear more delineated and fixed. Though many of these discourses relate to women's bodies, as does much of the data I discuss here, notions of modesty and appropriate dress may also apply to Muslim men. In this sense, what becomes 'modesty' here is a negotiation between Islamic spaces, bodies and practices of being covered rooted in Morocco and, for these visitors, practices that travel with them from Christian-dominant public spheres in Europe. That is, 'modesty' is not a definable object outside the intra-actions it produces through (gendered) bodies, clothing, and (spatial) gazes, none of which can be entirely separated from the other in this entangled object. The next section presents Barad's methodology for approaching such an object through entanglement might be constructed through an 'apparatus'.

3. Apparatus: Ethnographic Learning across Diasporic Space

Seeing the succession of images widely published showing an anonymized woman removing a shirt to reveal her bare arms underneath, I felt a visceral shiver of modesty in my own skin. Though I cannot claim affinity with her position or circumstances in almost any other way, I can recognize the sense of feeling de-clothed: of having an instinctive, practiced sense of how one's own body should be covered, of how that covering becomes connected with one's body as a single organism, and of the sense of violence when that layer is forcibly removed. Via Barad, my intimate knowledge and experience of 'uncoveredness' becomes part of my apparatus for knowing in this assemblage (Jackson and Mazzei 2011).

When Noura explained to me her embodied preference to be covered by a djellaba when out in the city during the day (as opposed to within the enclosed café where we were sitting; see Fernea (1998), I expressed sympathetic and empathetic affect in my response. Not only was her answer recognizable from other reports by other diasporic Moroccan women about their clothing choices in Morocco, it was recognizable through my personal clothing choices, learned over accumulated visits, interactions, gazes, admonishments, and goosebumps as a non-Moroccan visitor in Morocco.

An attempt to analyze an embodied experience of modesty is itself an epistemological project. While we can interview individuals about such experiences, discursive descriptions are inevitably removed from some of the ineffable and ephemeral dimensions of how that experience manifests in through bodies. They provide evidence that the phenomenon exists, but relatively limited data on how it might be felt. Alternately, an attempt to track how such embodied reactions are produced in naturally-occurring encounters—such as recording heart rates or perspiration (Dolezal 2015, p. 12)—would be technologically challenging, and still may not produce meaningful data on the phenomenon. Because a manifestation of modesty (e.g., through an experience of shame) involves many simultaneous interactions (e.g., increasing heart rate along with some discursive narrative of a cause), we need to examine it through a more complex apparatus that considers both how self-reflexive subjects understand their own shame and how un-reflexive bodies experience it.

Along these lines, ethnographic attention works as an apparatus, in the way Barad defines it, for producing a diffractive analysis. Diffraction poses a distinctive analysis from the social constructionist effort at reflexivity:

> Whereas reflexivity, based on the visual metaphor of reflection, calls on the researcher to recognize and disclose her positionality by reflecting on her raced, classed, gendered, and geographic characteristics (among others), diffraction attends to the ways in which actors intra-act with, interfere with, and reinforce one another to produce difference in those bodies (and their positionalities) and in research. It is a relational method where process and change are constitutional. (Neely and Nguse 2015, pp. 141–42).

By proposing ethnography as a diffractive apparatus, this analysis incorporates ways that participants like Shirin and Noura report their experiences as well as ways that an embodied and learning ethnographer (Hasse 2014) develops understandings of such experiences over time. Following Barad, this apparatus is an open-ended practice (Barad 2007, p. 170): an instrument that is part of observation, not separate from it, producing '*dynamic (re)configurings of the world through which bodies are intra-actively materialized*' (Barad 2007, pp. 169–70, italics original).

For the purposes of this project, the apparatus has two key dimensions: *ethnographic time*, documented below through the ongoing and long-term learning process involved in executing this research, and the agential cut of *diasporic space*, incorporating emergent configurations of places and borders that participants encounter as Muslim Moroccan women from Europe. This agential cut is integral to how the ethnographic apparatus is designed, in the sense that it is "a constructed cut between the object and the agencies of observation" (Barad 2007, p. 196), "mark[ing] off a particular instance of wholeness" (Barad 2007, p. 197) from other kinds of wholeness in the environment. In other words, the multifaceted, material and discursive production of these spaces is both the object of study and interfered with (and interfering in) how the study is executed. Engaging these spaces through this apparatus presumes that they can be studied as an object, while simultaneously presuming their malleability and interrogating when, how, and why they might exist. Both these aspects of apparatus combine for a diffractive analysis that specifies the time spaces through which I have come to observe and learn about embodied senses of modesty and the fixity and malleability of how clothing practices and discourses of modesty are enacted across physical locations.

3.1. Ethnographic Time

The ethnographic timeline for this project could begin in the summer of 1999, when I first visited Morocco as a tourist, first encountered many Moroccans from Europe travelling to Morocco for summer holidays, and first purchased a gondorra (see below) as a 'local' item of clothing to wear myself. In a more scientifically rigorous sense, it could begin at the summer of 2003, when I began interviewing Moroccans from Europe about their experiences of visiting during my stay in Fez as a language student. Since then, I have been in perennial communication with Morocco and Moroccans (from Europe and from Morocco) in face-to-face conversations and friendships, via mediated distances (telephone, chat, social media, news media), and through academic research (Minca and Wagner 2016; Wagner 2017). Through all these modes of contact, I have been a learning ethnographer (Hasse 2014) in innumerable aspects of being and becoming 'Moroccan' (Wagner 2017), which cannot be enumerated here.

Limiting this timeline to the topic of this analysis–clothing, bodies and discourses of modesty about women–I can recount some moments when I have learned how to wear clothing 'correctly' within environments where I was participating. Some moments were through expressed attention to my clothing, like the time I was wearing a sleeveless shirt, waiting outside for a visitor to arrive to a friend's house, and my friend came out to tease me about sitting on the street "practically naked". Other moments were in attention to other people's clothing: the way I have seen women get dressed and undressed at homes and at hammams through a series of layers, from a decorative outside through cotton pyjamas and underwear; the way mothers, daughters and sisters tugged down at each other's shirts to make sure all of their stomach skin stays carefully covered; the way a group of male tour guides jokingly called an unsuspecting European tourist a prostitute (in Moroccan Arabic) while indicating to me how her breasts were visible through her shirt; and, of course, the way I have been catcalled on the street in Morocco, no matter what kind of clothing I wear. Beyond Morocco and beyond a research context, my ethnographic understandings of these intra-actions have been influenced as well by conversations with friends about their own choices for clothing practices: about when, where and how to wear a veil, for example, or about what regimes of morality in proximity (like parents) or globally (like Wahhabism) are affecting their behavior.

My own perspective as an ethnographer has, of course, evolved over time through this process. When I first purchased items of Moroccan clothing (a djellaba in 2003, a gondorra in 1999), I wore them like Western-style dresses, with no layer of clothing underneath. From watching others, I learned that I had been walking around "practically naked" because of the ways these items are designed to be worn with other layers: the open pocket-holes in a *djellaba* offer a portal to interior hidden pockets, presuming there is more clothing underneath; gondorras, often made from very lightweight cotton, are generally effectively translucent, and cannot be 'modestly' worn without additional layers.

As an ethnographer engaging with participants across different spaces, and myself living in European cities since 2004, I have also learned, and had opportunities to observe, how these practices persist across diasporic borders. For myself, I can recognize at least one instinctive embodiment of 'Moroccan' modesty that I practice whether in Morocco or elsewhere: the sense that my stomach should be covered. Though I often prefer to wear sleeveless shirts, I find myself tugging down at my clothes to make sure my abdominal skin is completely covered, even considering that as a factor when shopping for new shirts. While this development may not be entirely attributable to learning how to become 'Moroccan', it is certainly imbued with my participation in this environment, and contributes to how I become a diffractive apparatus to analyze what sort of clothing practices contour diasporic spaces.

3.2. Diasporic Space

The broader project through which these data were collected was an investigation of linguistic and leisure practices by Moroccan-origin Europeans who visit Morocco during their summer holidays, called diasporic visitors (DVs). Within a framework of migration studies, and persistent questions about post-migrant generations sense of 'belonging' in a sending or receiving country, the objective was to investigate how 'belonging' is pursued, enacted, negotiated, and abandoned in face-to-face encounters between individuals coming from a diaspora of descendants of Moroccan emigrants to Europe and Moroccans living in Morocco. By investigating these interwoven practices of what kinds of activities they do in Morocco, during what is effectively their vacation leisure time, and how they are able to interact with others–in what languages, to what purposes–this project analyzed how diasporic mobilities between spaces contribute to regenerating practices of visiting a homeland and producing discourses about others through those visits.

Implicitly, these visits involve crossing political borders between places that have historically produced themselves as different along a parameter of religion. Whether these imaginations involve secularism in contrast to theocracy or differentiate between Christianity(ies) and Islam(s), religion (present or absent) is a parameter through which moral behavior is differently contoured across these spaces. While embodiment of religion was not a topic directly investigated in the research, it was a dimension of practice that participants indicated as relevant to their sense of space in Morocco versus in Europe. That differentiation was often made relevant by participants through practical means–such as, as one participant identified, being able to eat at any McDonald's in Morocco because all the meat would be halal, as opposed to Europe (Wagner 2017)—rather than as a discursive or imaginative condition that might 'attract' them to Morocco. Effectively, while they might have access to spaces and places in Europe that acknowledged Islamic moralities and customs, in Morocco that space was not as practically confined, and assumed to be everywhere.

The 'everywhereness' of Islamic moralities in Morocco as opposed to Europe is also embodied through practices that participants would choose *not* to do, or feel they needed to 'hide' while in Morocco. One example is found in the different practical contours of 'safety' in public space for diasporic women in Morocco, where gazes, masculinities, and norms of leisure practices might contrast to how they participate in public space in Europe (Wagner and Peters 2014). Importantly, the way that 'safety' might be perceived and embodied across the differentiated morality of Islamic or Western spaces is by no means universally agreed upon: to the extent that moral transgression is negotiated through many interwoven, intra-acting dimensions, embodied performances of moral responsibility (or transgression) are malleable, complex, and necessarily incorporate borders that might otherwise be invisible to an observer. The agential cut performed by examining diasporic practices across political borders, therefore, is not an examination of how those political borders delineate practices related to religious moralities, but how practices may produce, define, or diminish the importance of those borders; and possibly produce entirely different borders themselves (Wagner 2017).

In relation to clothing as embodied practice that recognizes both religious morality and the habituated individual body, using diasporic space as an agential cut is a means to observe how embodied practices circulate within this space, incorporating influences and antagonists from different nodes within it. Building the examples used above, this cut recognizes how both Noura and the woman on the beach are dressing 'normally' for some nodal position where they might otherwise find themselves; whether in wearing dresses that expose more skin when going out in France, or in wearing burkini-style covering to the beach in Morocco. Likewise, they are both negotiating negative responses when repeating that practice in a different node; both, effectively, being told how to dress by the reactions of men in proximity. By considering both examples within a spectrum of diasporic space, we can interrogate how their clothing, embodied practices, and environments produce manifestations of Islamic morality about female modesty.

4. Diffractions: Clothing, Publics, Corporealities

Examining clothing practices, public moralities, and diasporic corporealities as a learning ethnographer in this context, I continue to build on Barad's framework by approaching this analysis as diffractive. As Mazzei (2013, p. 779) describes it,

> in a diffractive process of data analysis, a reading of data with theoretical concepts (and/or multiple theoretical concepts) produces an emergent and unpredictable series of readings as data and theory make themselves intelligible to one another. Such knowing on the part of the researcher and her world requires a rethinking of agency as distributed between and among the human and non-human.

While previous sections have discussed various forms of clothing styles (djellaba, burkini), the analysis below focuses on a particular silhouette, what I will collect here to under the name gondorra, which has become particularly noticeable as a non-human agent moving through different diasporic spaces across the ethnographic timeline over which I have observed them. In terms of moralities, this particular style also sits between a djellaba and a burkini, as a way that Muslim diasporic Moroccan visitors have developed to negotiate 'coveredness'. It is reflective of their leisure activities as holiday visitors–such as, quite often, going to the beach, where a burkini might be a 'normal' mode of attire–and sense of modesty as understood and enacted in Morocco, in the same spaces where Shirin and Noura felt themselves needing to be more 'covered' by a djellaba. The agency here thus is distributed between these clothing styles and silhouettes, the moralities of public gazes, and affective sensations of corporeality lived through knowledgeable bodies.

Having formulated above an object of study–the production of corporeal and sartorial modesty in Islamic contexts—I use three formulations below that each combine two of the three non-human agents—clothing, publics and corporealities—to explore how this entanglement produces between human and non-human actors. First, I examine how wearing gondorras emerges as a material corporeality, engaging body with clothing, within diasporic spatial networks of Moroccans from Europe when they visit Morocco (and as they return with them to Europe). Taking this emergent practice through the lens of ethnographic experience, I demonstrate how it becomes recognizably, affectively dissonant with the kinds of moralities of clothing and gazes I have learned to respond to in Morocco. Finally, by pulling one participant as a self-reflexive agent into this diffractive analysis process, I can revisit and revise Shirin's (and Noura's) sense of needing more covering with one woman for whom a *gondorra* means she needs less.

4.1. Wearing Gondorras

Gondorras are a common piece of clothing found in markets anywhere in Morocco that comes in forms for both genders, differentiated mostly by vibrant colors for women and greys, browns and blacks for men. The basic shape is a long and rectangular loose-fitting sheath, made from light cotton or polyester, with arm openings that cover shoulders without a separate sewn sleeve, and sometimes pockets or side holes positioned to access interior pockets. The armholes and collar may be embroidered, giving some stylistic variation beyond the fabric to what is otherwise a very simple garment. It has different names in different parts of the country, and I have heard it be called a 'marrakshia', 'b'daya', 'gondorra' or pyjama, depending on the region and gender. They are generally interior, household clothing for women, and more often worn outside by men (Box 4).

Box 4. Field notes: Oasiria aquatic park, Marrakech, 9 August 2008.

we get up to leave, and Nawel is in her 3rd ensemble—from a shorter pattern dress to an ample marrakshia with the sides tucked in...I'm wondering, where she got that idea from? is this everywhere?

Though gondorras were a common and available clothing style long before I started this research (I myself purchased one on my first visit to Morocco in 1999), they have emerged at some point as an article of clothing that all DVs have one or more of in their closet. Within my ethnographic times cape, during summer fieldwork in 2007 and 2008 I noticed this style seemingly springing up as leisure clothing worn outside primarily by young DVs, as I remarked in the field note above. From north to south, in many cities, beaches, and leisure sites around Morocco where European-Moroccans visit their family homes, it became easier to observe that item of clothing and reliably suspect that the wearer was a diasporic visitor. In this field note, my comment not only addresses her ownership of this item, now seemingly 'everywhere', but also her manner of wearing it 'tucked in at the sides' (see Figure 1 below), that seems to also be 'everywhere'.

Figure 1. This participant still wears her gondorra, while her friend has his folded on the chair next to him. The woman in bright pink in the distant background is also wearing a gondorra over layers (used with permission).

Both men and women invested in them: one male participant referred to his preference for 'traditional' clothing in an interview, and I later discovered he meant a gondorra, while another woman, buying presents for her female cousins who were checking on her house while she was on holiday, chose several colors of *gondorra,* since, as she explained, a new color would always be welcome in their collection. During that same visit, her sister was searching for a new one to buy for her growing son. While many of them seemed to be bought for use primarily during the summer holidays in Morocco, I also noticed, in April 2011, a woman in a *gondorra* at a shopping mall in Liège, Belgium, searching for a car in the parking lot.

Though the inception point would be impossible to trace, owning, shopping for, buying, and wearing gondorras has embedded itself as a practice within the Moroccan summer holiday time space for diasporic visitors much in the same way a 'suit' becomes a recognizable corporeal grammar of clothing for Mazzei (Mazzei 2013). Costing between seven and fifteen Euros, made of lightweight fabrics in colors that resonate with the beach and poolside leisure activities that take place during most visits, gondorras have become emblematic of certain affects and part of how the practice of 'being in Morocco' is achieved. In some ways they may reflect a sense of authenticity and tradition, as an item of clothing that comes from Morocco in several profound ways: using fabrics that are supposedly produced there, and often featuring embroidery that repeats across different Moroccan textiles and clothing styles. Yet, the emergence over ethnographic time of this garment as *de rigeur* for any DV to have, in multiple colors, indicates how its practice exceeds its symbolic meaning. While they may index traditionality, they function for the summer heat, for their colorful decoration, and for me, as well as for DVs themselves, as a sign for recognizing other diasporic visitors in the streets. It becomes a corporeal, fashion practice through which the summer time space of diasporic Morocco is mattered.

4.2. Malleable Moralities

This field note (Box 5 below) indicates both a recognition of how gondorras were taking place as a clothing practice in this environment, and how I was learning to understand them ethnographically. This was the first moment I recorded thoughts about this practice, which I had noticed a year earlier, of DVs wearing gondorras to the beach. At the time, I registered my impression of this practice as 'bizarre': an ethnographic judgement that comes after my previously discussed experiences in Morocco about what is appropriate clothing to wear on the street. While this commentary concerned male beachgoers wearing gondorras, and the rest of my argument focuses on feminine modesty, they were nevertheless wearing them in what seemed a risqué fashion: with only swim shorts underneath.

Box 5. Field notes: Sabadia Beach, near Al Hoceima, 22 July 2008.

I'm noticing more and more men wearing gondorras to go to the beach: to my mind, there's a feeling of strutting in this kind of native outfit, something the same men probably would never wear in EU. Also, they all look fresh and new, the gondorras, and they are often not wearing full clothing underneath, instead wearing it as a sort of beach cover-up. Bizarre

Calling that practice 'risqué' is a diffractive judgement made through ethnographic experience. While for DVs gondorras may seem an ideal beach cover-up—long, loose, comfortable, yet unique and fashionable—for others in Morocco they are more commonly worn in the same way most 'traditional' Moroccan clothes are worn, as the topmost in a series of layers. They may be similarly associated with leisure and comfort for resident Moroccan men, to the extent that in families where I have been present I observed men wearing them on their day off from work. In parallel, I have seen resident Moroccan women wearing them as they work around the house, or visit nearby neighbors, but not to go further than the immediate neighborhood; not out into the city, or to the beach, as DVs do. In addition, they have material features that, to maintain 'modesty', require them to be worn over something else: male versions, for example, come with side holes instead of pockets so that one can access an interior trouser pocket, and female versions, though more bright and colorful, are still too thin of a material to wear solo.

These factors of design and materiality of the clothing itself are part of the reason why Figure 1 above and the observations noted at Sabadia Beach registered to me, through ethnographic experience, as 'immodest'. Unlike the clothing practices I have been trained to embody in Morocco, these seem to use a gondorra as if it itself is sufficiently 'covering'; these bodies do not seem to feel the sensation of shame of skin that might be visible through a thin fabric. The sense of being 'covered', as identified by Shirin and Anissa above, is fulfilled for them as it is not for me, producing a diffractive moment where the corporeal capacities of their bodies and of mine create dissonance. Much like how Mazzei (2013) hones in on one participant's description of buying and wearing a 'suit' as an expression of power, these diffractive observations engage both my knowledge about 'gondorra-wearing', discourses about it, and how I understand it to be an expression of self, as well as how I have experienced subjectivities through that practice:

> I could feel the affect, what it produced in us as women trying to assert ourselves and to be taken seriously and our compliance to norms and resistance in ways that brought the material back into my reading and knowledge making–both intellectually and physically. The suit intra-acted with my discursive constructions to produce a different subjectivity, both then and now. I therefore, at some level, can continue to read this intra-action as a result of a discursive construction that prescribes a specific list of do's and don'ts in order for women (and men) to be taken seriously in the work place. (Mazzei 2013, p. 783)

Yet, instead of showing how DVs are conforming to the prescriptions of their 'suit', these observations indicate how, in this intra-action, they are forging a specific, possibly 'diasporic', mode of clothing practice that ignores (or is ignorant of) moralities that might impinge upon it.

Of course, not all DV wearers of gondorras would be using them in the same way, as much as they might serve as a cover over a bikini, they might also serve as a cover over a burkini, part of the way to move between home and beach that embodies diasporic modesties and belongings simultaneously. The combined need for some kind of covering (which may be, relating to local gazes and moralities, inadequate) with a sense of the body underneath it, slightly visible through the fabric, or through the way that 'tucking in' establishes the waistline, hipline, and possibly contours of the legs, become entanglements of clothing and corporeality that challenge a gaze I had learned to practice. This is by no means to suggest that there is any intention for 'immodesty' on the part of *gondorra*-wearers; in fact, the tucking practice may be also related to enabling a longer and faster stride to walk in a gondorra, often made too long and too narrow to move quickly. Tucking in to reduce its length is a strategy among women working at home as well, using ropes or apron strings to pull it up around the waist.

These diffraction patterns incorporate elements of cross-border corporealities as practiced in Morocco, through how their modes and manifestations incorporate elements from across diasporic space. DVs are not purposefully rejecting a spatially-formulated corporeal modesty, but collectively they are challenging and shifting what becomes 'acceptable', both as visible for women beyond their own neighborhoods, and on their own bodies.

4.3. Diasporic Corporealities

As the diffractive analysis of this paper has developed over years of ethnographic attention and observation, it has also developed along with participants' feedback. In that sense, the diffraction pattern incorporates some aspect of mirroring reflexivity, reverberating ideas and practices between my learning experience as an ethnographer and their learning experience as participants.

The woman pictured in Figure 2 has played such a role, responding to not only questions about where and when she has seen gondorra in use, but also her reaction to the argument of this paper. She was one who, along with myself and a few others, noted that gondorra seemed to appear suddenly everywhere in this landscape; not a fashion from her youth, but one that has emerged in the last several years and become ubiquitous.

As a woman who veils, choosing to continue that practice out of habit and moral attention of her parents as much as out of her interpretation of its religious morality, she is normally dressed in more covering attire than as she is pictured above. In the Netherlands, I always see her in layers of long sleeves and long dresses, comfortably embodying the kind of 'coveredness' reflected by the woman on the beach in Nice. Yet, while discussing how gondorra enable a different kind of corporeality on the street, she observed that, for herself, it has become an acceptable way to be dressed beyond the house: on city streets, on the way to the beach. As much as the 'coveredness' she senses through her normal style of dress involves covered arms, covered legs, covering her neck and shoulders, the visible exposure of skin by a gondorra is not felt as such, as that item has entangled into her practice of DV corporeality in Morocco.

Figure 2. Women walking in central Tangier, summer 2015 (photograph by the author).

5. Conclusions: Intra-Actions

> My "own" body is material, and yet this vital materiality is not fully or exclusively human. My flesh is populated and constituted by different swarms of foreigners. The crook of my elbow, for example, is "a special ecosystem, a bountiful home to no fewer than six tribes of bacteria ... " The *its* outnumber the *mes*. In a world of vibrant matter, it is thus not enough

> to say that we are "embodied." We are, rather, an *array of bodies*, many different kinds of them in a nested set of microbiomes (Bennett 2010, pp. 112–13).

> The langue of Sera, the suit, discursive constructions, textual practices, and becoming selves are mutually implicated in a production of possibilities both thought and unthought, actualised and unactualised. What matters is not the origin, but an opening of a different type of 'knowing produced in a co-constitutive relation between matter and discourse where it is impossible to pull apart the knower from the known' (Mazzei 2013, p. 784; citing Lenz Taguchi 2013, p. 715).

While Bennett frames the 'vibrant matter' of embodiment through the visceral molecular sensation of 'its' populating an array of 'mes', these 'its' are not only swarms of foreign bacteria. They include, I contend along with Mazzei, the integration of matter and discourse to become an intra-active 'mattering' of corporeality. In order to explore that process, I have drawn together what arrived as quite disparate moments of 'feeling uncovered', where Moroccan Muslim bodies were encountering some kind of clothing, de-clothing, or re-clothing, through my own ethnographic apparatus of experience over time. What this shows is how these diasporic bodies are producing their own gazes, publics, and moralities through corporeal clothing practices, as much as they are responding and resisting when they move between different regimes of morality across borders. Effectively this is a 'mattering' of modesty, in the ways these bodies pass through different spaces and contour a sense of coveredness that resonates inwards and outwards.

Yet this analysis is not directed at equating either of these regimes with 'secularism' or 'Islam', to solidify what either of these do to define the spaces they control. Instead, this approach focuses on the practices engendered through how these regimes are malleable along with the mobilities of bodies crossing between them, and how these embodiments and their clothing become malleable as well. In that sense, this analysis has closer links to discussions of drag queens and their production of bodies through layers of clothing (Hanson 2007) than with the way veiling becomes a social, stylistic, or political statement. What is at issue here is not the symbolism of a gondorra as a traditional item of Moroccan material culture, nor of 'feeling covered' an indicator of Muslim regimes over women's bodies, but how it intervenes into other modes of practice (incidental to its 'authenticity') to reconfigure regimes of morality across diasporic space.

By using diasporic mobilities across space as an agential cut through which to observe 'modesty' as it can be produced in and through Muslim women's bodies, this approach embraces the molecular and agentive fluidity of mattering. Questions about how moral gazes, women's bodies, and clothing becoming analyzable from the site of discomfort or 'trouble' outwards, engaging many possible dynamic directionalities, materialities, discourses, institutions and actors. Using Barad's proposal that these entanglements of entities are 'mattering' as much as they are (materially) mattered, enfolding in an ongoing generativity in and of the world embraces how these bodies matter. It rejects the implicit analytical or perceptual layering of tangible against intangible, separating bodies from clothing from gazes, and imagines these as single, intra-active organisms (arrays) with sometimes perceptible thresholds acting in assemblage. Each intra-active element manifests in the complex triangulations of clothing, gazes, visibilities, and corporeal materiality.

Using this as my initial framing, the analytical questions about entities enfolded in this dynamic equally address how the bodies involved are differentially iterating, *and* how the other mattering entities–gazes, perceptions and clothing itself–iterate to produce modesty that is 'enough' in some circumstances, for some bodies, and 'not enough' for others. It embraces how many different Muslim (Moroccan) women matter their clothing practices differently, "redefine[ing] objects as more in networks than in single sites, to trouble identity and experience, and what it means to know and to tell." (Lather 2016, p. 126). By approaching this topic ethnomethodologically, as an exploration of the achievement of social order, as well as through Barad's agential realism, I trace the production of shame: modesty from trouble outwards. This perspective provides a theoretical reframing with potential for much further productivity in approaching and analyzing the trajectories and experiences of shame: modesty as political, corporeal, and vibrant matter to those who experience its effects.

Acknowledgments: I owe a debt of unpayable gratitude to several individuals who invested energy into previous versions and submissions of this paper, including Meghann Ormond, Dan Gilman, David Bissell, J. D. Dewsbury and Alan Latham. The Body Reading Group organized at Maastricht University has enabled the current version to take shape. I thank Viola Thimm and the three anonymous reviewers for accepting it to this special issue, as well as the other journal editors and many anonymous reviewers for the time, energy and insight contributed to previous versions. Aspects of this analysis are discussed along different theoretical lines in *Becoming Diasporically Moroccan* (Clevedon: Multilingual Matters).

Conflicts of Interest: The author declares no conflict of interest. Funding for this research was provided by the University of London Central Research Fund.

References

Abu-Lughod, Lila. 1986. *Veiled Sentiments: Honor and Poetry in a Bedouin Society.* Berkeley: University of California Press.

Atkinson, J. Maxwell, and John Heritage, eds. 1984. *Structures of Social Action: Studies in Conversation Analysis.* Paris: Cambridge: Maison de Sciences de l'Homme, Cambridge University Press.

Badr, Hoda. 2004. Islamic identity re-covered: Muslim women after September 11th. *Culture and Religion* 5: 321–38. [CrossRef]

Barad, Karen. 2003. Posthumanist performativity: Toward an understanding of how matter comes to matter. *Signs: Journal of Women in Culture and Society* 28: 801–31. [CrossRef]

Barad, Karen. 2007. *Meeting the Universe Halfway: Quantum Physics and the Entanglement of Matter and Meaning.* Durham: Duke University Press.

Bauer, Janet L. 1985. Sexuality and the Moral "Construction" of Women in an Islamic Society. *Anthropological Quarterly* 58: 120–29. [CrossRef]

Bennett, Jane. 2010. *Vibrant Matter: A Political Ecology of Things.* Durham: Duke University Press.

Bourdieu, Pierre. 1979. *Algeria 1960: The Disenchantment of the World: The Sense of Honour: The Kabyle House or the World Reversed: Essays.* Cambridge and New York: Cambridge University Press.

Cavallaro, Dani, and Alexandra Warwick. 1998. *Fasioning the Frame: Boundaries, Dress and Body.* Oxford: Berg.

Coole, Diana. 2010. The inertia of matter and the generativity of flesh. In *New Materialisms: Ontology, Agency, and Politics.* Edited by Diana Coole and Samantha Frost. New York: Duke University Press, pp. 92–115.

Dolezal, Luna. 2015. *The Body and Shame: Phenomenology, Feminism, and the Socially Shaped Body.* New York: Lexington Books.

El Guindi, Fadwa. 1999. *Veil: Modesty, Privacy and Resistance.* Oxford: Berg.

Ghazi-Walid Falah, and Caroline Rose Nagel, eds. 2005. *Geographies of Muslim Women: Gender, Religion, and Space.* New York: Guilford Press.

Fernea, Elizabeth Warnock. 1998. *In search of Islamic Feminism: One Woman's Global Journey.* New York: Doubleday.

Gökarıksel, Banu. 2012. The intimate politics of secularism and the headscarf: The mall, the neighborhood, and the public square in Istanbul. *Gender, Place & Culture* 19: 1–20. [CrossRef]

Gökarıksel, Banu, and Anna Secor. 2010a. Islamic-ness in the life of a commodity: Veiling-fashion in Turkey. *Transactions of the Institute of British Geographers* 35: 313–33. [CrossRef]

Gökarıksel, B Banu, and Anna Secor. 2010b. Between Fashion and Tesettür: Marketing and Consuming Women's Islamic Dress. *Journal of Middle East Women's Studies* 6: 118–48. [CrossRef]

Hanson, Julie. 2007. Drag Kinging: Embodied Acts and Acts of Embodiment. *Body Society* 13: 61–106. [CrossRef]

Hasse, Cathrine. 2014. *An Anthropology of Learning: On Nested Frictions in Cultural Ecologies.* Dordrecht: Springer.

Jackson, Alecia Youngblood, and Lisa A. Mazzei. 2011. *Thinking with Theory in Qualitative Research: Viewing Data across Multiple Perspectives.* London: Routledge.

Katz, Jack. 1999. *How Emotions Work.* Chicago and London: University of Chicago Press.

Lather, Patti. 2016. Top Ten+ List: (Re)Thinking Ontology in (Post)Qualitative Research. *Cultural Studies? Critical Methodologies* 16: 125–31. [CrossRef]

Lenz Taguchi, Hillevi. 2013. Images of thinking in feminist materialisms: Ontological divergences and the production of researcher subjectivities. *International Journal of Qualitative Studies in Education* 26: 706–16. [CrossRef]

Mahmood, Saba. 2005. *Politics of Piety: The Islamic Revival and the Feminist Subject*. Princeton: Princeton University Press.

Mazzei, Lisa A. 2013. Materialist mappings of knowing in being: Researchers constituted in the production of knowledge. *Gender and Education* 25: 776–85. [CrossRef]

Minca, Claudio, and Lauren Wagner. 2016. *Moroccan Dreams: Orientalist Myth, Colonial Legacy*. London: I.B. Tauris.

Neely, A., and T. Nguse. 2015. Relationship and Research Methods: Entanglements, Intra-Action, and Diffraction. In *The Routledge Handbook of Political Ecology*. Edited by Tom Perreault, Gavin Bridge and James McCarthy. London: Routledge, pp. 140–49.

Quinn, Ben. 2016. French police make woman remove clothing on Nice beach following burkini ban. *The Guardian*. Available online: https://www.theguardian.com/world/2016/aug/24/french-police-make-woman-remove-burkini-on-nice-beach (accessed on 14 August 2017).

Sacks, Harvey. 1992. *Lectures on Conversation: Volumes I & II*. Edited by Gail Jefferson. Oxford and Cambridge: Blackwell.

Schegloff, Emanuel A. 2007. *Sequence Organization in Interaction: A Primer in Conversation Analysis I*. New York: Cambridge University Press.

Secor, Anna J. 2002. The Veil and Urban Space in Istanbul: Women's dress, mobility and Islamic knowledge. *A Journal of Feminist Geography* 9: 5–22. [CrossRef]

Tarlo, Emma. 2007. Hijab in London Metamorphosis, Resonance and Effects. *Journal of Material Culture* 12: 131–56. [CrossRef]

Turowetz, Jason, Matthew M. Hollander, and Douglas W. Maynard. 2016. Ethnomethodology and Social Phenomenology. In *Handbook of Contemporary Sociological Theory*. Handbooks of Sociology and Social Research; Edited by Seth Abrutyn. Cham: Springer International Publishing, pp. 387–410.

Wagner, Lauren B. 2017. Viscous automobilities: Diasporic practices and vehicular assemblages of visiting "home". *Mobilities* 1–20. [CrossRef]

Wagner, Lauren. 2017. *Becoming Diasporically Moroccan: Linguistic and Embodied Practices for Negotiating Belonging*. Clevedon: Multilingual Matters.

Wagner, Lauren, and Karin Peters. 2014. Feeling at home in public: Diasporic Moroccan women negotiating leisure in Morocco and the Netherlands. *Gender, Place & Culture* 21: 415–30. [CrossRef]

White, Jenny. 1999. Islamic chic. In *Istanbul: Between the Global and the Local*. Edited by Çağlar Keyder. Oxford: Rowman & Littlefield, pp. 77–94.

Section 3:
From Mobility to Immobility: Intersectional Identifications as Opportunities or Limitations

Article

Male and Female Emirati Medical Clerks' Perceptions of the Impact of Gender and Mobility on Their Professional Careers

Michelle McLean [1,*] and Susan B. Higgins-Opitz [2]

1 Faculty of Health Sciences & Medicine, Bond University, Gold Coast, QLD 4226, Australia
2 College of Health Sciences, University of KwaZulu-Natal, Durban 4041, South Africa; acsb@xsinet.co.za
* Correspondence: mimclean@bond.edu.au; Tel.: +61-7-5595-5536

Received: 4 July 2017; Accepted: 5 September 2017; Published: 9 September 2017

Abstract: Background: Medicine has undergone profound changes in terms of the number of women entering the profession with postulated implications of this 'feminization' for the profession. The present phenomenological study sought to gain insight into the experiences of final year male and female Emirati medical students (clerks) in terms of the impact of gender on their careers. Methods: Semi-structured interviews were conducted with 24 of the 27 clerks. Interviews were transcribed and analyzed thematically. Findings: There was consensus that the gender profile of medicine in the United Arab Emirates was changing as opportunities emerged for Emirati women to branch into different medical specialties. These opportunities were, however, local or regional due largely to travel restrictions on women. Females would thus receive a less highly regarded board certification than males who were encouraged to specialize abroad. On their return, males would be appointed as consultants or as high-ranking administrators. Participants also acknowledged that like their roles in their society, some medical specialties were 'gendered', e.g., surgery (male) and pediatrics and obstetrics and gynecology (female). Conclusion: Although religious and cultural traditions around gender and mobility will influence the professional careers of male and female Emirati medical graduates, the situation is, however, changing.

Keywords: career intentions; Emirati; gender; medical students; mobility; Muslim

---

> "Any situation in which some men prevent others from engaging in the process of inquiry is one of violence; ... to alienate humans from their own decision making is to change them into objects." —Freire (2005, p. 85)

1. Introduction

In most parts of the world, female medical students now generally outnumber their male counterparts, contributing to an increasing female medical workforce. This so-called 'feminization' of the medical profession has been well documented in the UK, Europe and North America, where females account for more than 50% of medical school intakes and practicing physicians (Paik 2000; Searle 2001; Sibbald 2002; Van der Reis 2004; Levinson and Lurie 2004; Reichenbach and Brown 2004; Allen 2005; Heru 2005; Kilminster et al. 2007; Dacre 2008; McKinstry 2008; Riska 2008; Drinkwater et al. 2008; Maiorova et al. 2008; Phillips and Austin 2009; Babaria et al. 2009; Weizblit et al. 2009; Roskovensky et al. 2012; Bleakley 2013; Mudaly and van Wyk 2015; Van Wyk et al. 2016). Although much less has been reported in developing countries, this trend appears similar (Al-Jarallah and Moussa 2003; National Association of Universities and Higher Education Institutions (ANUIES); Breier and Wildschut 2006, 2008; Mudaly and van Wyk 2015; Van Wyk et al. 2016). In Kuwait, for example, female medical post-graduates have outnumbered males since 1993

(Al-Jarallah and Moussa 2003) and in Mexico since 1999 (National Association of Universities and Higher Education Institutions ANUIES). In South Africa between 2002–2005, the number of registered female medical practitioners increased by 24%, while female medical students increased from 51 to 56% (Breier and Wildschut 2008).

In its simplest, context-free sense, 'feminization' describes the shift in the numerical composition of medical practitioners in a profession that has long been the domain of males. The implication of this increased female medical workforce has been widely discussed (Searle 2001; Levinson and Lurie 2004; Allen 2005; Heru 2005; Kilminster et al. 2007; Riska 2008; Riska and Novelskaite 2008; Dacre 2008; McKinstry 2008; Maiorova et al. 2008; Weizblit et al. 2009; Mudaly and van Wyk 2015; Van Wyk et al. 2016). Riska (2008) contends that using the term 'feminization' to describe an increasingly female medical workforce embodies *"predictions about qualitative changes in the practice of medicine"* (p. 3). She discusses several potential outcomes for the medical profession, including gender differences in terms of how medicine is practiced, deprofessionalization of the profession and the 'ghettoization' of women into certain specialties. Although Kilminster et al. (2007) concluded that little evidence exists to suggest that women practice medicine differently from men, Heru (2005) has argued that since female practitioners are reputedly superior in domains such as communication skills and empathy, a more 'feminized' medical workforce will restore a culture of humane and caring doctors.

The 'deprofessionalization' view of an increasingly feminized medical workforce portends that because of the socialized gender stereotype associating men with power and authority and women with nurturing and powerlessness, the profession's status will decline as a result of women entering the profession or a specialty in increasing numbers (Haug 1975; Levinson and Lurie 2004). Examples cited are those of the status of medicine in several Eastern European countries, where women have been in the majority for more than 70 years (Barr and Boyle 2001; Riska 2008; Riska and Novelskaite 2008).

Probably the most noticeable outcome of the increased number of women entering the profession is that of gender-dominated specialty niches which Riska (2008) referred to as 'ghettoization'. These niches are reflective of extensions of biological and stereotyped roles. In Riska and Novelskaite (2008) post-Soviet Lithuania study, gender stereotyping and differential salaries and perceived rewards in specialties has culminated in the horizontal and vertical segregation of male and female physicians into specialties seen to embody prototypical characteristics of each sex. To this end, pediatrics is an extension of motherhood, while surgery requires physical strength and hard work and is therefore better suited to males. Even across other contexts, for one or more reasons (e.g., patient refusal, negative experiences as students (Salter 2007; McLean et al. 2010, 2012), same gender mentoring), a similar segregation has led to a situation today in which obstetricians and gynecologists are generally women and surgeons are predominantly men (Heru 2005; Riska 2008; Wildschut 2010).

Today's medical students have thus chosen a career in a 'gendered' profession (Riska 2008; Mudaly and van Wyk 2015), but a profession in which the gender profile is changing or has already changed in some contexts. One might argue that this trend has been towards a situation that once was, a profession in which women were revered as goddesses of medicine, healers and saints before being deemed inferior and vilified as witches. This then left the profession to become one of prestige dominated by men (Wynn 2000). Irrespective of where students study medicine, it is likely that during their clerkships, which, for many might be their first immersion in the medical 'culture', they will surely find themselves in an environment in which 'gender' is part of almost every facet of their clinical work, from their relationship with nurses and doctors to their interactions with patients. It is well documented, for example, that females may not choose a surgery specialization, due, in part, to their experiences as students in a discipline that is under male control (Salter 2007; Drinkwater et al. 2008; Babaria et al. 2009, 2011; Wildschut 2010). Similarly, in obstetrics and gynecology (O&G), the increasing number of women refusing to be examined by male students and physicians is often cited as a reason for this specialty becoming almost exclusively serviced by female physicians (Magrane et al. 1994, 1996; Ching et al. 2000; Grasby and Quinlivan 2001; O'Flynn and Rymer 2002; Higham and Steer 2004; Hamilton 2006; Salter 2007; Wildschut 2010).

While these reports of 'gendered' student experiences appear to be universal, they reflect largely Western contexts. For the purposes of this study, gender has been defined as *"the socially constructed characteristics of women and men—such as norms, roles and relationships of and between groups of men and women … While most people are born either male or female, they are taught appropriate norms and behaviours—including how they should interact with one others of the same or opposite sex within households, communities and work places"* (World Health Organization 2017). Thus, in cultural contexts in which men and women have clearly delineated roles, it is not difficult to imagine that 'gender' will be a social construct that will influence how they will ultimately practice medicine. The present study set out to explore how the social construct of 'gender' impacts on the experiences and career trajectories (including opportunities to study abroad) of male and female medical students raised in a traditional, gender-segregated Muslim society.

1.1. Study Context

The United Arab Emirates (UAE) is a relatively young country. In less than half a decade, it has rapidly evolved from a nation of pearl divers and Bedouins to one in which a traditional culture rubs shoulders with modern cities of skyscrapers and engineering masterpieces. UAE society, as is the case for many Muslim countries, is, however, conservative and is described as traditional and patriarchal (Goby and Erogul 2011). Islam teaches that men and women have different biological roles and social responsibilities, with males being the providers, protectors and defenders of females, who are the mothers, nurturers and educators (Alromaithy et al. 2007). Islam also requires that a woman's purity and image be maintained, a responsibility which begins with her father, brothers, uncles and family and is then transferred to her husband (Barakat 1993). As part of this protectionist value is the religious *hadith* (a narrative originating from the words or deeds of Prophet Muhammad) restricting unaccompanied women from travelling, as this would expose her to numerous risks. If she needs to travel, she must be accompanied by a male companion who is either her husband or a close *mahram* (non-marriageable) relative. Men, on the other hand, are free to travel at liberty (Alromaithy et al. 2007).

Although in Islam men and women are equal in human dignity, this spiritual equality is not always reflected in *Shari'ah* law, where women may have restricted rights when it comes to choosing marriage partners, getting divorced and having custody of their children (Dhami and Sheikh 2000). According to Islam, men and women have equal rights in terms of employment, education and ownership of land and business, but for a woman, her family comes first (Gallant and Pounder 2008). Although the UAE rulers have recognized the value of modernization and promoted education for all its citizens, they have, however, tried to retain the regional cultural integrity and Islamic values by maintaining sex segregation (Schvaneveldt et al. 2005).

In just one generation, many Emirati women have been catapulted from (future) wives, mothers and home-makers with little or no formal education to now accounting for about 70% of tertiary education enrolments, sometimes in fields (e.g., information technology, engineering, medicine) that have traditionally been the domain of men (Ridge 2009; World Economic Forum 2012). With female employment outside the home a relatively new and modern concept in the UAE (Itani et al. 2011), these tertiary education enrolment figures for women have, however, not translated into the employment market. Despite a 548% increase in the number of women entering the labor market in the UAE between 1960 and 2000 (Metcalfe 2006), the country's roots in religious fundamentalism and the need to conform have hindered women from taking certain jobs. A 2003 United Nations Development Programme (UNDP) report concluded that the UAE culture supports *"the development of human capabilities of women but not for their utilization"* (p. 19). This is not surprising considering that gender roles in the Middle East have been shaped by four elements: the centrality of the family (vs. the individual) as the main unit in society, the man as the sole breadwinner, a code of modesty that rests on family dignity and the reputation of women, and the unequal balance of power in the private sphere that is anchored in family laws (United Nations Development Program UNDP; World Bank 2003a, 2003b; Metcalfe 2006). In response to this social and religious order, women have navigated the patriarchy and structural and attitudinal organizational barriers by engaging in business development amongst themselves, such as the Arab Women' Society, a Gulf Co-operative Council organization dedicated to Arab women's business (Metcalfe 2006) and have also become entrepreneurs (Goby and Erogul 2011; Itani et al. 2011; Marmenout and Lirio 2014; Tlaiss 2015). Notwithstanding these activities and despite the UAE setting up a Gender Balance Council with plans to improve maternity leave, the latest 2016 Global Gender Gap report ranks the UAE 124th (out of 144 countries) in terms of gender inequality (World Economic Forum 2016; Arabian Business.com 2016). The highest ranked Middle Eastern country is Qatar (119th).

1.2. The Study in Context

The study was conducted in the Abu Dhabi Emirate. Participants in the study were final year medical students in a medical college established in 1984 to train Emirati doctors. The medium of tuition was English. Although male and female students were segregated (like Emirati society in general), the syllabus was the same. As a result of the socio-cultural context, male students, however, had limited access to female patients during their obstetrics and gynecology rotations (McLean et al. 2010). At the time of the study, students completed two years of medical sciences, two years of an organ system course (mainly problem-based learning; clinical skills training) followed by the two-year Clinical Sciences Course. During this clerkship phase, students spent most of their time in local public hospitals and primary healthcare clinics where they encountered both male and female patients in a gender-segregated healthcare system. Following a year-long internship, many continued with post-graduate studies (residency) locally or abroad. It is more likely that males would specialize abroad while females, because of the requirement for a male chaperone to travel, would generally specialize locally or within the region. The highly regarded (by local authorities and patients) North America Board certifications made Canada and America desirable destinations for specialization and sub-specialization. Prior to 2007, when the college began offering post-graduate programs (e.g., urology, surgery, medicine, dermatology and pediatrics), family medicine had been the only available local residency for most female graduates who were not permitted to travel to study. At the time of the study, the certifying body was the Arab Board (Jordan).

1.3. UAE Patient and Physician Profile

With expatriates accounting for approximately 85% of the UAE population, patient and physician profiles are diverse. The extensive male, semi-skilled labor force originates mainly from Asia and South-East Asia, while the skilled sector comprises professionals from the Middle East as well as from North America, Europe and Asia. To meet the healthcare needs of a growing local and expatriate population, male and, to a lesser extent, female physicians too have had to be recruited (Schiess et al. 2015) from Western countries, the Middle East (e.g., Syria, Jordan, Egypt) and also South-East Asia (e.g., India, Pakistan).

1.4. Research Framework and Questions

In the context of a conservative, patriarchal, gender-segregated but rapidly developing Middle Eastern society, this study set out to gain insight into final year male and female Emirati medical students' experiences and perceptions of how gender has or could influence their career aspirations and ultimately how they might practice medicine. The study has been informed by the discourse relating to the 'feminization' of the medical profession (Heru 2005; Riska 2008), a traditionally 'gendered' profession in which women now generally outnumber men. Cognizance was also taken of Ridgeway (2009) conception of gender as *"A multilevel structure, system, or institution of social practices that involves mutually reinforcing processes at the macro-structural, institutional level, the interactional level, and the individual level"* (p. 146). Within the context of the present study, 'gender' as a social construct was therefore likely to affect every facet of the lives of Emirati men and women in this study and would certainly impact on how and where they eventually practiced medicine.

The study was also informed by the literature on social groupings in human societies. While such groupings are most commonly structured along sex, class, ethnic, racial or religious lines, with dominance of one group over another often along these same structures (Sidianus et al. 2000, 2006; Levin 2004; Zakrisson 2008), 'gender' is the focus of this study. The social dominance orientation that arises from groupings is a key element of social dominance theory, reflecting a preference for hierarchical group relations in which one group has dominance over another (Pratto et al. 1994; Sidianus and Pratto 1999; Echabe 2010). Social dominance of males over females along gender lines appears to be relatively invariant across cultural, situational and contextual boundaries, including the Middle East (Levin 2004; Sidianus et al. 2000; Pratto et al. 2006; Zakrisson 2008), with exceptions perhaps in situations where women outnumber men (Zakrisson 2008). From Jackman (1994) perspective, however, male dominance is characterized by attempts to control women without rousing hostility because men desire relationships with women, unlike ethnic dominance, which usually involves hostility. Religion often entrenches gender stereotyping in accordance with biological roles, leading to hierarchical gender identities (Pratto et al. 2006). It is thus easy to imagine in Muslim societies, particularly if they are gender-segregated, with men viewed as the protectors of women, how gender inequality might (consciously or unconsciously) exist not only within the family but also in the workplace.

Taking into consideration the social and cultural context of this study, the following questions framed the interviews with the male and female clerks:

- To what extent do female and male medical students perceive a gender-dominated practice of medicine in the UAE?
- To what extent do they perceive this will affect how they will practice medicine following graduation?
- What advantages and disadvantages do they associate with their gender in the practice of medicine in the UAE?

The results of the current study are discussed against a backdrop of traditional Islamic and cultural values associated with being male or female medical students in a gender-segregated society that is undergoing rapid economic development.

2. Methods

2.1. Participants

After receiving ethical approval for the study, recruitment of final year medical students in the 2007/2008 academic year (n = 27) involved scheduling a number of sessions to provide female and male students on the various clinical rotations with a comprehensive explanation of the purpose of the research at a venue of their choice. This was invariably on campus or at a clinical site. Twenty-four of the 27 (89%—15 of the 18 women, 83%; 8 of the 9 men, 89%) students in the cohort consented to participate. Interviews were scheduled between October 2007 and March 2008. A unique code was assigned to each student to ensure anonymity. As UAE nationals, all participants were Muslim. While Arabic was their home language, they had been studying medicine in English for six years and so were relatively fluent.

2.2. The Researchers

At the time of the study, I (MM, Principle Investigator) had been employed at the College as a medical educator working across the six-year curriculum for about one year. Although I was not directly involved with the senior students, I became acquainted with their representatives on the various faculty committees. SBH-O spent a three-month sabbatical at the College during which time many of the interviews were conducted and the initial analysis undertaken.

Although we had worked in a multicultural South African academic setting with Muslim colleagues and students, we were new to undertaking qualitative research in the more conservative gender-segregated Middle Eastern context. It would therefore be prudent to consider the complexities involved in the cross-cultural and cross-gender interactions (Liamputtong 2010). First, as Anglo-Saxon women interviewing male students, we had to be culturally sensitive to the local customs, i.e., dressing appropriately, refraining from physical contact (e.g., no handshaking) and keeping a reasonable distance during the interviews. As cultural 'outsiders', we also needed to be flexible in terms of allowing students to identify the time and location of the interviews and allowing the students to dicatate the pace of the interview. We believe we developed a rapport with the participants by sharing personal stories about our South African students as well as our experiences of working and living in the UAE, a country of which they were very proud.

It was important that we were perceived as 'culturally competent', with a reasonable knowledge of the Emirati socio-cultural context and that we were genuinely interested in understanding what affected their careers as future doctors. We view the overwhelming positive response to recruitment as a reflection of the participants' genuine desire to share their stories and to contribute to research as a way of improving their education. It was my perception that Emirati students have a deep appreciation for education and are therefore highly respectful of academic faculty. Our willingness to learn more about Emirati culture was reciprocated, with participants openly sharing their aspirations, frustrations and even personal dilemmas.

From a personal perspective, this research was invaluable as it provided me with considerable insight into the UAE clinical setting, assisting in my role as a medical educator and academic counsellor. It later led to junior students researching the medical student and female Emirati patient experience in the gender-segregated UAE healthcare system (McLean et al. 2010, 2012).

2.3. Interviews and Analysis

This study was phenomenological in that it sought to explore male and female Emirati clerks' accounts of their experiences as they practiced medicine in a conservative, gender-segregated Muslim society. Semi-structured interviews were conducted in English by the researchers. They lasted about an hour and were digitally recorded. The research questions framed the interviews. Relevant issues raised by participants were explored further during the interviews. At the end of each interview, a summary was made to assist with the preliminary analysis while professional transcription was being undertaken.

As the research questions framed the interviews, data were analysed thematically within this framework (Braun and Clarke 2006). Initial themes and subthemes were identified independently by the two researchers who each read four transcripts (two male and two female participants). Once agreement had been reached in terms of the initial themes, the next level of analysis involved a more inductive approach of linking themes and subthemes. Verbatim quotes were identified at the same time. Regular checking took place as the remaining transcripts were analysed.

3. Findings

3.1. The Practice of Medicine in the UAE: Male- or Female-Dominated?

Only marginally did students perceive that medical practice in the UAE to be still male-dominated. While most clerks recognized that the majority of expatriate doctors were male, except in O&G (largely expatriate females), they identified several reasons for an increasing number of female Emirati residents and doctors. Reasons included there being more female medical students than males, the recent offering of a suite of local post-graduate training opportunities beyond family medicine and the fact that Emirati males are generally sponsored (and encouraged) to pursue both undergraduate and post-graduate medical studies abroad. Certain disciplines were, however, identified as being dominated (numerically but also in terms of the 'culture') by either men or women. To this end, female students identified surgery and orthopedic surgery as disciplines in which a female had to prove her worth before being accepted as a resident. When probed why this might be, both male and female clerks claimed that because surgery had on-call duties, which would be socially difficult for Emirati females, it remained a specialty for males.

> *"We are seeing many females, even local females everywhere in every hospital. We are seeing residents, specialists even consultants. Except maybe in Surgery, I can say there is a lack of female surgeons but other specialties they are there, I think"* [Female 3]

> *"According to the specialty. For example in Obs & Gynae, there are females more, but in Surgery, there is a limit of females, more males. And it's becoming, for residents in Internal Medicine, there is becoming more female residents"* [Female 13]

> *"I saw a lot of males [in Surgery] and some of them were like dominating. So, it was a problem and I didn't know how to deal with that. But, with time and what they saw with me, like a hard-working student and enthusiastic, they tried to give me support"* [Female 1]

Male students similarly identified O&G and pediatrics being serviced mainly by female physicians. Acknowledging their gender-segregated society, male students reported frequently being refused by female patients or doctors during their O&G rotation, resulting in them having little hands-on experience. The impact of the gender segregation characterizing UAE culture is evidenced by this description of a male clerk during his pediatrics rotation:

> *"The Pediatrics ward is ... again ... It's a funny ward where you rarely see a male resident. I came across only two male residents while all the rest were females. Usually, you see women gathering in the Pediatrics ward, sitting in the room, chit-chatting. So for a male in our culture, you can imagine a male invading a women's environment! It's like they are sitting with their children and it's like a cultural, I mean, like home"* [Male 8]

3.2. Implications of a Changing Physician Gender Profile

3.2.1. As Interns

Within a few months of the study, the clerks would enter their internship where they would besupervised by male and female residents and physicians. Generally, they did not foresee any difficulties, because, as one female pointed out, despite a gender-segregated education system, they were used to dealing with male doctors as this reflected the clinical profile in the hospital and at the medical school. Similarly, male students acknowledged that they had all had contact with female residents (Emirati Nationals) and were comfortable with this.

> *"I know for example a student doing training at the hospital, elective and so on, and my supervisor was a male and I had not difficulty. I can conduct with them easily and they can help me. So, I don't see any difference between the male and female supervisor"* [Female 15]

> *"I have many experiences with female residents. They were really helping me as a student. Enthusiastic and dedicated to teach me"* [Male 7]

Only two female students indicated a gender preference, one for a female supervisor and another for a male supervisor. The latter student who was married with children appeared to have had negative interactions with female clinicians and preferred to work within the professional boundaries of male and female colleagues.

> *"I feel more comfortable with female doctors. I learn from them a lot, more than from males"* [Female 4]

> *"For female practitioners, the problem is the attitude of the female doctors. Sometimes it is hostile. I think the male-female relationship is more professional, more, uh . . . clean"* [Female 14]

3.2.2. Beyond Internship

Based on their clinical experiences as clerks, students generally did not foresee any issues in terms of the increasing number of local female residents and doctors. One male student, however, anticipated that he might have to undertake additional after hours on-call duties as female residents and physicians would take maternity leave and would have family responsibilities. In his view, even in Canada, where he had undertaken his external elective, there appeared to be a lack of consideration for male physicians who had families (e.g., no paternity leave).

> *"The main obstacle I face is the she [the female] will not want to be on call on the week-ends. She will get pregnant if she is married. After pregnancy, delivery, she will take lots of holidays and the work will not move (laughs). This was also for Canada. The females refused to do on-calls so the males had to do. The males also have families and the children want their father to come home, but he has the weekends on call. Many weekends"* [Male 2]

3.3. Career Intentions and Medical Practice in the UAE: Gender and Mobility

When students were asked about their 'gender' and the practice of medicine in the UAE, the themes identified related to the repercussions of the local cultural context, most specifically in terms of 'gender'. Their responses are discussed in relation to the restrictions (e.g., travel) on females, gendered roles and responsibilities (e.g., wife and mother) and perceptions of being physically weaker.

3.3.1. Restrictions on Women

As a consequence of their social context, several female students identified obstacles, particularly in terms of travel, which had already impacted on their elective plans or would restrict how and where they might practice medicine. Also, for these women, choice was not always in their hands. Some had not been permitted by their families to undertake an external elective abroad and would certainly not be allowed abroad for post-graduate studies. While this situation largely reflects a religious 'requirement' of men to protect women, female students suggested that with considerable societal pressure for marriage and motherhood, finding a suitable husband for a daughter or a sister would probably take priority over a woman's career aspirations.

> *"As a female, the first obstacle ... I wanted to go abroad to finish my medical school but my family didn't agree"* [Female 14]

> *"My family will not accept it that much. My father is supportive and he wants me to go abroad but they still think if a girl wants abroad then she will not get a chance to get married"* [Female 8]

> *"I remember one thing. Maybe in the external elective. Because, uh, I am female and my relatives cannot go with me far away for a long period, for example, to Canada or the US, that's why this make me choose another country [Malaysia, also largely Muslim]. I went with my family but we, uh, we stayed there around two weeks only"* [Female 7]

For one female student, her desire to be independent (i.e., travel with no male chaperone) had culminated in her undertaking an elective in Saudi Arabia, which is a more conservative gender-segregated Muslim country than the UAE. Although Saudi Arabia was not her preference, this was where her family would allow her to travel and study without a male companion, although she was accompanied by other female students:

> *"For the elective, I get acceptance from Singapore and Malta. My family wouldn't allow me to go alone, so one of them was going to accompany me. I wanted to do it. I wanted to go alone to see, to experience the situation, more than just go to a specific place. Um, then we had another option to go to Saudi Arabia and my family accepted for me to go with some of my colleagues so I went there as I wanted to go alone [without a male chaperone]"* [Female 10].

On the flip side, one female student shied away from being 'alone' (meaning with no chaperone), separated from her family, claiming she did not have the *"personality"* to travel and study away from home. While this may be so, taking cognizance of the fact that in the conservative Emirati society, women are generally not allowed to travel alone, it is probable that she was not confident to be alone in a foreign country.

> *"But maybe this depends on person, personality and stuff, but for example for me, I think it will be difficult to go abroad alone and do my residency. I should have one of my family with me. But for a man, he can manage himself anywhere. Because of my personality I need that person. But because some female students could manage going abroad alone without anybody ... It is not a common thing, for a female to go abroad, but it does happen, not usually"* [Female 3].

For male students, a completely different picture emerged. Male clerks readily acknowledged (and verified by their female peers) that personal choice (rather than any social or cultural factor) would dictate where males would study and how they would eventually practice medicine. Males acknowledged that their gender allowed them to pursue any avenue of medicine, except perhaps O&G (because of refusal by female patients). Many openly acknowledged that their female peers would not be permitted to travel abroad to study and so would specialize in the UAE or the region where they would obtain a certification that was less recognized and valued than a North American qualification. As a result, not only would male physicians then be better remunerated than their female peers, but they were also destined for leadership roles on their return or shortly thereafter.

> *"Our families encourage us [to go abroad]. For females, the families somehow will not encourage. Males will usually sub-specialize. A female will never sub-specialize unless she stays long years outside. All local males or most of them, they sub-specialize in very important sub-specialties but females more general ... Males will be less but they will be given more responsibility. In the hospitals, the leadership will be males ... more highly qualified ... salaries depend on rank ... Males will be qualified by international boards. Females will have Arab Board. Not the same qualification"* [Male 2]

3.3.2. Gendered Roles and Responsibilities

As Emiratis generally marry at an early age, several students, females in particular, were already parents. Some lamented the fact that they were away from their families during the week on campus in the hostel. Male and female students acknowledged that for females particularly, it was going to be difficult to be a wife and a mother and have a professional career. At least one female clerk raised the issue of societal perceptions of women in medicine not being able to be a mother as well as a good doctor.

> *"Second thing. Children. I think medicine is hard work, it takes a lot of time and it's very difficult I think in imagination [i.e., in my mind] to balance between the home and the work. Very difficult"* [Female 4]

> *"For example, if she wants to be an ICU doctor, Cardiology, Surgery. Some specialties have many on-calls and might interfere with her social [family] life. So, as I can see, many of them will chose the uh, specialties so that they can have more social life [i.e., wife and/or mother]"* [Male 4]

> *"Because they think, for example, I am married, I have a baby, so I think they will think I will not be, uh, as dedicated for my job as a male, which is wrong"* [Female 14]

Males' comments were more likely to reflect gendered societal roles. From their paternalistic and Muslim perspective, protecting women is a man's responsibility and so women should be honored and not be made to work hard or long hours or be subjected to stress and physical effort.

> *"There are many advantages [to being a male]. Having on calls, it will be much easier for a male to do it. For females, it will depend on the location. But, mainly it's, uh being a male on the on-calls and the long working hours. If there are females who are having housework to do, it might be some problem. But for male, the timing is advantage. I can stay for long hours for on calls as well as maybe tough work, stress, stress-related and in, uh, musculo-skeletal [physical] effort"* [Male 1]

> *"We are also concerning about females to enlarge [increase in number]. In our societies, in our families, ladies first sometimes. If there is a work, or something troubling or something, we are focusing—do not make our females so tired. So, now for me, when I saw this girl working the whole night, it's like, it's tiring for us, so what about them? It's a bit difficult"* [Male 6]

One male student was of the opinion that Emirati men had a patriotic responsibility to specialize and sub-specialize in fields of medicine that better suited men, largely because of the roles women were expected to assume.

> *"For us, male doctors, we should have more roles taking the specialties that … there are sub-specialties that fit us more than females. I don't know, could be Surgery or Cardiology. The specialties that have more on-call duties because all females decided to stay in the country and do the specialties like Dermatology. That's OK, but for us, we have to take the action and get the specialties that our country needs"* [Male 4]

Both male and female students agreed that once married, a woman's life and her career (i.e., specialty choice, and even practicing medicine) depended on her spouse, i.e., where he lived and what he would allow.

> *"If I get married, for example, if he will agree to stay with me [where she does her residency] or will he keep me in Ras Al Khaimah [an emirate]? This is bad! The females here in our culture should follow her husband, not the opposite. In rare cases, you find the husband will follow"* [Female 4].

> *"If one is married, the husband may not be happy with you having many on-calls … So, some of the females who are married are getting into Family Medicine because Family Medicine has no [on call] duties. Maybe that will affect them more. Maybe she didn't want to do Family Medicine but because there is no duties, she will go to Family Medicine"* [Female 11]

> *"I think if they get married, they could have a few difficulties, unless the husband is open-minded and willing to help"* [Male 7]

3.3.3. Gender Differences in Physical Strength

Interestingly, while several males raised physical strength as a potential obstacle on behalf of their female colleagues, only two female students lamented the limitations of their physical strength:

> *"The difficulty that I encounter with myself. Sometimes when I encounter a male patient for examination. Sometimes it is difficult, not because he is male and I am a female. Maybe this problem also applies to females (laughs) when they are overweight. Sometimes I cannot examine them. I find it difficult (laughs)"* [Female 1]

> *"Maybe because it is difficult for females to practice Surgery. Because most of the time, the surgeons in the hospital are on call and the surgery may last more than five hours and she has to stand … "* [Female 3]

4. Discussion

The study coincided with a milestone for Emirati women in terms of the availability of local post-graduate opportunities beyond family medicine. Recognizing the travel constraints of most

Emirati women and the societal expectations of marriage and motherhood, these residencies would allow females to have professional careers whilst managing their expected social and domestic responsibilities. Residencies with few or no on-call duties, e.g., dermatology and ophthalmology were anticipated to be popular choices. Prior to these residency offerings, female Emirati medical graduates not permitted by their fathers, brothers or husbands to travel and study abroad (i.e., the majority) in reality had two professional choices—join the family medicine residency program or leave the profession.

Thus, in line with the global trend of a 'feminizing' medical profession, the male and female Emirati clerks interviewed in the present study agreed that as a result of female medical students and graduates undertaking local residencies (recently expanded beyond family medicine) due to restrictions on travelling alone and hence unable to study abroad, the face of the medical profession in the UAE would change from one serviced largely by expatriate males to one of female Emirati residents and physicians. There was agreement, however, that the situation was artificially skewed as male Emiratis were encouraged and sponsored (e.g., by the armed forces) to specialize abroad, leaving the women to specialize locally. It is important to note that although many of the males study abroad for several years to complete their residency and then a sub-specialization, often with their families, they almost all return to practice medicine in the UAE.

While recognizing the benefit of the recent local post-graduate offerings, both male and female clerks acknowledged that their career trajectories would, however, remain different. This they attributed to their socio-cultural context in which their gender (with associated expectations and restrictions) was an important consideration. Despite having aspirations of specializing abroad, most of the women were resigned to the fact that this would generally not be possible due to their inability to travel abroad without a chaperone unless permitted by their fathers, brothers or their husbands. If not already married, there was an expectation of they would need to marry soon. Whether married or unmarried, it was unlikely that they would find a chaperone for the duration of their post-graduate studies abroad. For the majority of the women, their professional careers thus rested largely with their immediate male family members or with their spouses. Like their male colleagues, these women were acutely aware of the implications on career trajectories of a local (Arab Board or other) certification compared with a more highly regarded American, Canadian or European board certification. Those returning with a North American Board certification (mostly males) would generally be offered consultant positions, whilst those with a local or Arab Board certification (mostly females) would be appointed at the lower rank of 'specialist'. According to the students, it would take a locally trained specialist 7–8 years to become a consultant. As several of the males in the present study indicated, if they returned to the UAE with an international sub-specialization, they would move relatively quickly up the professional ladder to be senior consultants or high-ranking administrators.

While Riska (2008) has described a vertical segregation in medicine (presumably with differential remuneration) along gender lines as a global phenomenon, it is likely to be exacerbated in societies where there is a more marked gender-based social dominance as is the case in many Middle Eastern countries. According to Echabe (2010), women in such societies are often relegated to jobs that display supportive behaviors, such as empathy, tenderness and understanding while men are appointed to high status positions involving decision-making, ambition, aggressiveness and assertiveness. Although Islam regards a woman's role in society as a wife and mother, she is, however, not forbidden to work provided there is a societal need and in positions which 'fit her nature'. While nursing, teaching and perhaps medicine appear to match these criteria (Badawi 1971), contexts requiring frequent contact with men, such as hotels and hospitals, are likely to be considered unacceptable workplaces for women by traditional fathers or husbands (Gallant 2006). Together with the travel restrictions and the expectation to marry and have children, Emirati women may thus not progress in their careers to the same extent as males. Although mentioned by a few students in the present study, Marmenout and Lirio (2014) female Emirati entrepreneurs reported having to show restraint in terms of their careers and income generation so as not to outshine their husbands. As *"culture is a macroconcept which subsumes religion"* and since *"Culture and, with it, religion are the sources of the gender construct … religion is derived from culture, and gender is, in turn, derived from both culture and religion"* (Raday 2003, p. 665), the context in which this study took place is indeed complex, particularly from an outsider's perspective.

With the relatively rapid economic development of most Middle Eastern countries, the position of women is changing as their societies modernize and as women become increasingly educated. Shaull (2005), in his foreword in the 30th anniversary edition of Paulo Freire's *Pedagogy of the Oppressed*, wrote this about education and freedom—*"Education either functions as an instrument that is used to facilitate the integration of the younger generation into the logic of the present system and bring about conformity to it, or it becomes "the practice of freedom," the means by which men and women deal critically and creatively with reality and discover how to participate in the transformation of their world."* (p. 34), which is particularly relevant in this context of a Bedouin culture with deep-rooted traditional religious values that is evolving as a result of progress. In a society described as paternalistic with a distinct gender hierarchy along biological roles, education is highly valued amongst females, who now account for almost three-quarters of college enrolments (Ridge 2009; World Economic Forum 2012). For some Emirati women, education may thus serve to liberate them from their socio-cultural shackles, mainly by delaying the age of marriage and motherhood. Heaton (1996) study of women in three Muslim countries (Egypt, Jordan, Indonesia) attests to the impact of an education in this regard: only 10% of women with a post-secondary education were married before the age of 20 (vs. 50% of women with no post-secondary education). A similar picture emerged for women with work experience in young adulthood (Heaton 1996). Schvaneveldt et al. (2005) study of cultural changes in Emirati family life over one generation found that while 93% of the mothers in that study were housewives with little formal education, almost 94% of their daughters (who were generally attending university) wanted professional careers. Compared with the mean age of marriage of their mothers (16.6 years), the ideal age identified by the daughters was 20.2 years, with a strong preference to select their own partner.

The dilemma facing Emirati women in terms of being a wife and mother and desiring a professional medical career has been voiced by women generally as it is they who are more likely to sacrifice their professional aspirations to raise children (Lempp and Searle 2006; Drinkwater et al. 2008; Mudaly and van Wyk 2015). As Allen (2005) pointed out, the career paths of women in medicine are different from their male colleagues: M-shaped, with an early peak, a dip in the middle (child-bearing years) and then the potential to peak later. The evidence also suggests that women do not usually drop out of medicine after childbirth, instead choosing to practice part-time (Allen 2005; McKinstry 2008). Several authors have suggested that with the changing physician profile, the profession should take a fresh look at the ingredients of professional status as well as lifestyle considerations in terms of flexibility of working hours, family leave and part-time training and support (e.g., on-site child care) for female physicians wishing to have a family (Allen 2005; Heru 2005). Today's medical students should therefore be able to choose specializations based on personal choice and not because of societal expectations of the professional strengths and weaknesses of males and females (Reichenbach and Brown 2004; Allen 2005). For Allen (2005), medicine should *"... consider some of the entrenched values and attitudes that reinforce the traditional pecking order in medicine and remain a source of implicit discrimination against women ... the most important thing for the medical profession to concentrate on now is how best to use the resources it has and will have in the foreseeable future ... It should be a matter of pride that so many brilliant young women are choosing to enhance the profession, and every effort should be made to throw out old fashioned practices and attitudes that inhibit the contribution they can make both in the early and later stages of their careers"* (p. 571). Bleakley (2013) continued this conversation, stating that female doctors entering the profession can *"resist and reformulate the current dominant patriarchy rather than reproducing it ... "* (p. 59).

Thus, gender, with all its social, religious and political complexities, particularly within the context of a gender-segregated patriarchal society where social dominance still exists, is likely to influence not only the day-to-day practices of male and female Emirati physicians but also their career trajectories. In a society where religion and culture are inextricably linked and one in which gender stereotypes and socialized roles culminate in men as protectors exerting (unconsciously or consciously) considerable influence over women, the career aspirations of many female medical students might for some remain just that—aspirations. The historical position of Emirati women has, however, changed and continues to change. For Muslim women in the Arab World who have clearly demonstrated a desire to be educated and have professional careers, their challenge lies in their often patriarchal society's traditional beliefs and values about the roles of women. In Jawad (1998) opinion, the persistent lower status of Muslim women (despite documented equality in the *Qu'ran*) and their apparent dominance by men can be attributed to several factors, including the reappearance of some pre-Islamic traditions (e.g., treating women as property) and the assimilation of some of the traditions and values of the conquering Turks and Mongols. Reformists have challenged Muslim women's lack of rights and control over their lives, claiming that this has arisen from different and perhaps incorrect interpretations of *Qur'anic* verses that bestow privilege on men over women, thereby reinforcing gender inequality and specific societal roles. In particular, the verse that states that men are 'guardians' (*qawamum*) has been used to entrench the women to roles of obedient wives and mothers and males as their guardians (Badawi 1971). Muslim women themselves are, however, challenging their status, with several forms of Islamic feminism having emerged (McDonald 2008) and with an increasing number of female entrepreneurs who have been able to navigate the constraints of their socio-cultural contexts (Goby and Erogul 2011; Itani et al. 2011; Marmenout and Lirio 2014; Tlaiss 2015).

5. Conclusions

Like the rest of the world, medicine in the UAE has become 'feminized', largely as a result of the increasing number of women studying at the tertiary level but also due to increasing opportunities for Emirati women to undertake post-graduate studies, which, at the time of the study, was mainly in the region or in the UAE due to travel restrictions. The young women in this study thus found themselves at the forefront of not only a changing profession but also in terms challenging the traditional values of their society. It is thus difficult to imagine, however, how a traditional gender-segregated society can withstand the pressures of modernization as well as the emergence of a generation of highly educated women who have clearly expressed a desire to enter the workforce. As more Emirati women enroll in higher education and become leaders in their respective areas, the 'gender' harness that tethers them to men will gradually loosen. Schvaneveldt et al. (2005) study of mothers and daughters concluded that the Emirati women of the present generation are *"core change agents for social revolution in this rich nation of desert history, oil wells, and traditional family life"* (p. 90) while the entrepreneurial women in Marmenout and Lirio (2014) and Tlaiss (2015) studies worked towards *"fulfilling their personal needs by negotiating the discriminatory cultural values of their societies, and positioning their entrepreneurship careers on the premise and promise that would allow them to meet their socially ascribed roles better"* (p. 576). Most of the female students in the present study were ambitious, with great career aspirations in medicine, but largely saw themselves constrained by societal expectations of marriage and motherhood and their status in society. Through education and persistence, a group of women will emerge who will go on to make their mark in the development of healthcare in the UAE. While some will have had to cope with the dual responsibility of parenthood and a career, they will nevertheless be role models for the next generation of female doctors.

Limitation: As this research involved cross-cultural and cross-gender interviews, limitations should be acknowledged. As female Anglo-Saxon researchers new to the Middle East, it is possible that in the gender-segregated Muslim context, participants may have 'positioned' themselves in terms of what they told us and how they told us. We do not think, however, that this was the case, with participants unreservedly expressing their individual perceptions of what it meant to be a male or a female in Emirati society. Male students were acutely aware of their potentially different career opportunities compared with those of their female colleagues, viewing this as 'normal', in line with their delineated biological roles in a young country that required local doctors. They, however, saw female doctors occupying roles that would allow them to have careers and families.

Acknowledgments: The researchers would like to thank the students for their willingness to share their experiences with us. This study as well as a similar one in South African was made possible from the research grant of Michelle McLean from funds accumulated while employed by the University of KwaZulu-Natal, South Africa.

Author Contributions: M.M. conceived the idea. M.M. and S.B.H.-O. designed the study and both interviewed the students. M.M. and S.B.H.-O. analyzed the data. M.M. wrote the first draft of the paper but S.B.H.-O. read and commented on. S.B.H-O has also agreed to the submission of the final version of the manuscript.

Conflicts of Interest: The authors declare no conflict of interest.

Ethical approval: Ethical approval for this study was obtained from the local district's Human Research Ethics Committee (Protocol No. 07/125, 23 August 2007).

Note: In 2010, a female participant provided an update on the status of her colleagues. Of the 15 female participants, six were married, four of whom had children. As Senior House Officers, the women had applied or intended to apply for local residencies as follows: Family Medicine (4), Dermatology (3), Internal Medicine (3), Emergency Medicine (2), Ophthalmology (1) and Radiology (1). After leaving the UAE, I lost contact with this student as she had transferred her residency to Saudi Arabia. Via LinkedIn, I was recently able to track one female and three male participants. The female participant is an Endocrinologist in Dubai, having completed her Internal Medicine specialty and Endocrinology Fellowship in Saudi Arabia. One male is currently a Sports Medicine Doctoral Fellow in France, following the completion of a Physical Medicine and Rehabilitation residency in France. Following completion of their Neurology residencies in Canada, the remaining two males are undertaking sub-specialties in Vascular Neurology and Epileptology in the USA and Canada, respectively.

References

Al-Jarallah, Khaled F., and Mohamed A. A. Moussa. 2003. Specialty choices of Kuwaiti medical graduates during the last three decades. *Journal of Continuing Education in the Health Professions* 23: 94–100. [CrossRef] [PubMed]

Allen, Isobel. 2005. Women doctors and their careers: What now? *British Medical Journal* 331: 569–72. [CrossRef] [PubMed]

Alromaithy, Abdulhamied, Layla Al Bloushi, and Dianne H. Saphiere. 2007. Cultural Detective: Arab Gulf. Available online: https://www.culturaldetective.com/ (accessed on 4 February 2012).

National Association of Universities and Higher Education Institutions (ANUIES). 2004. *Annual Estimates of Professions, 1990–2002*. Mexico City: ANUIES.

Arabian Business.com. 2016. Gulf countries still lagging behind on gender gap reforms. Available online: http://www.arabianbusiness.com/gulf-countries-still-lagging-behind-on-gender-gap-reforms-650493.html (accessed on 30 June 2017).

Babaria, Palav, Sakena Abedin, and Marcella Nunez-Smith. 2009. The effect of gender on the clinical clerkship experiences of female medical students: Results from a qualitative study. *Academic Medicine* 84: 859–56. [CrossRef] [PubMed]

Babaria, Palav, Susannah Bernheim, and Marcella Nunez-Smith. 2011. Gender and the pre-clinical experiences of female medical students: A taxonomy. *Medical Education* 45: 249–60. [CrossRef] [PubMed]

Badawi, Jamal A. 1971. The status of women in Islam. Available online: http://www.jannah.org/sisters/badawistatus.pdf (accessed on 4 February 2012).

Barakat, Halim. 1993. *The Arab World: Society, Culture, and State*. Berkeley: University of California Press. Available online: http://intersci.ss.uci.edu/wiki/eBooks/MidEast/BOOKS/The%20Arab%20World%20Barakat.pdf (accessed on 4 February 2012).

Barr, Donald A., and Elizabeth H. Boyle. 2001. Gender and professional purity: Explaining formal and informal work rewards for physicians in Estonia. *Gender and Society* 15: 29–54. [CrossRef]

Bleakley, Alan. 2013. Gender matters in medical education. *Medical Education* 47: 59–70. [CrossRef] [PubMed]

Braun, Virginia, and Victoria Clarke. 2006. Using thematic analysis in psychology. *Qualitative Research in Psychology* 3: 77–101. Available online: http://www.tandfonline.com/doi/abs/10.1191/1478088706qp063oa (accessed on 23 January 2017). [CrossRef]

Breier, Mignonne, and Angelique Wildschut. 2006. *Doctors in a Divided Society*. Pretoria: Human Sciences Research Council.

Breier, Mignonne, and Angelique Wildschut. 2008. Changing gender profile of medical schools in South Africa. *South African Medical Journal* 98: 557–60. [PubMed]

Ching, Susanne L., Elena A. Gates, and Patricia A. Robertson. 2000. Factors influencing obstetrics and gynecology patients' decisions towards medical student involvement in the outpatient setting. *American Journal of Obstetrics and Gynecology* 182: 1429–32. [CrossRef] [PubMed]

Dacre, Jane. 2008. Are there too many female medical graduates? *British Medical Journal* 336: 749. [CrossRef] [PubMed]

Dhami, Sangeeta, and Aziz Sheikh. 2000. The Muslim family: Predicament and promise. *Western Journal of Medicine* 173: 352–56. Available online: https://www.ncbi.nlm.nih.gov/pmc/articles/PMC1071164/ (accessed on 23 March 2017). [CrossRef] [PubMed]

Drinkwater, Jess, Mary Patricia Tully, and Tim Dornan. 2008. The effect on gender on medical students' aspirations: A qualitative study. *Medical Education* 42: 420–26. [CrossRef] [PubMed]

Echabe, Agustin E. 2010. Role identities versus social identities: Masculinity, femininity, instrumentality and communality. *Asian Journal of Social Psychology* 13: 30–43. [CrossRef]

Freire, Paulo. 2005. *Pedagogy of the Oppressed*, 30th anniversary ed. Translated by Myra Bergman Ramos. New York: Continuum International.

Gallant, Monica. 2006. Five Case Studies of Emirati Working Women in Dubai—Their Personal Experiences and Insights. Ph.D. dissertation, University of Southern Queensland, Toowoomba, QLD, Australia. Available online: https://eprints.usq.edu.au/1425/ (accessed on 23 March 2017).

Gallant, Monica, and James A. Pounder. 2008. The employment of female nationals in the United Arab Emirates (UAE): An analysis of opportunities and barriers. *Education, Business and Society: Contemporary Middle Eastern Issues* 1: 26–33. [CrossRef]

Goby, Valerie P, and Murat S. Erogul. 2011. Female entrepreneurship in the United Arab Emirates: Legislative encouragement and cultural constraints. *Women's Studies International Forum* 34: 329–34. [CrossRef]

Grasby, Devika, and Julia A. Quinlivan. 2001. Attitudes of patients towards the involvement of medical students in their intrapartum obstetric care. *Australian and New Zealand Journal of Obstetrics and Gynaecology* 41: 91–96. [CrossRef] [PubMed]

Hamilton, Alexander J. 2006. "GAMMS". Go away, male medical student. *Student British Medical Journal (Student)* 14: 112–13. Available online: http://student.bmj.com/student/view-article.html?id=sbmj0603112 (accessed on 4 February 2012).

Haug, Marie R. 1975. The deprofessionalization of everyone. *Sociological Focus* 8: 197–213. Available online: http://www.tandfonline.com/doi/abs/10.1080/00380237.1975.10570899?journalCode=usfo20 (accessed on 17 October 2009). [CrossRef]

Heaton, Tim B. 1996. Socioeconomic and familial status of women associated with age at first marriage in three Islamic societies. *Journal of Comparative Family Studies* 24: 41–58.

Heru, Alison M. 2005. Pink-collar medicine: Women and the future of medicine. *Gender Issues* 22: 20–34. [CrossRef]

Higham, Jenny, and Philip J. Steer. 2004. Gender gap in undergraduate experience and performance in obstetrics and gynaecology: Analysis of clinical experience logs. *British Medical Journal* 328: 141–43. [CrossRef] [PubMed]

Itani, Hanifa, Yusuf M. Sidani, and Imad Baalbaki. 2011. United Arab Emirates female entrepreneurs: Motivations and frustrations. *Diversity and Inclusions* 30: 409–24. Available online: http://www.emeraldinsight.com/doi/full/10.1108/02610151111150654 (accessed on 15 June 2017). [CrossRef]

Jackman, Mary R. 1994. *The Velvet Glove: Paternalism and Conflict in Gender, Class, and Race Relations*. Berkeley: University of California Press.

Jawad, Haifaa A. 1998. *The Rights of Women in Islam: An Authentic Approach*. New York: St. Martin's Press.

Kilminster, Sue, Julia Downes, Brendan Gough, Deborah Murdoch-Eaton, and Trudie Roberts. 2007. Women in medicine—Is there a problem? A literature review of the changing gender composition, structures and occupational cultures in medicine. *Medical Education* 41: 39–49. [CrossRef] [PubMed]

Lempp, Heidi, and Clive Searle. 2006. Medical students' perceptions in relation to ethnicity and gender: A qualitative study. *BMC Medical Education* 6: 17. Available online: http://www.biomedcentral.com/1472-6920/6/17 (accessed on 4 February 2012). [CrossRef] [PubMed]

Levin, Shana. 2004. Perceived group status differences and effects of gender, ethnicity, and religion on social dominance orientation. *Political Psychology* 25: 31–48. Available online: http://onlinelibrary.wiley.com/doi/10.1111/j.1467-9221.2004.00355.x/full (accessed on 15 June 2017). [CrossRef]

Levinson, Wendy, and Nicole Lurie. 2004. When most doctors are women: What lies ahead? *Annals of Internal Medicine* 141: 471–74. Available online: http://annals.org/aim/article/717826/when-most-doctors-women-what-lies-ahead (accessed on 4 February 2012). [CrossRef] [PubMed]

Liamputtong, Pranee. 2010. *Performing Qualitative Cross-Cultural Research*. Cambridge: Cambridge University Press.

Magrane, Diane, Jane Gannon, and C. T. Miller. 1994. Obstetric patients who select and those who refuse medical students' participation in their care. *Academic Medicine* 69: 1004–6. Available online: http://journals.lww.com/academicmedicine/Abstract/1994/12000/Obstetric_patients_who_select_and_those_who_refuse.23.aspx (accessed on 17 October 2009). [CrossRef] [PubMed]

Magrane, Diane, Jane Gannon, and C. T. Miller. 1996. Student doctors and women in labor: Attitudes and expectations. *Obstetrics & Gynecology* 88: 298–302. Available online: http://www.sciencedirect.com/science/article/pii/0029784496001913 (accessed on 17 October 2009).

Maiorova, Tanja, Fred Stevens, Jouke van der Zee, Beppie Boode, and Albert Scherpier. 2008. Shortage in general practice despite the feminisation of the medical workforce: A seeming paradox? A cohort study. *BMC Health Services Research* 8: 262. Available online: http://www.biomedcentral.com/1472-6963/8/262 (accessed on 17 October 2009). [CrossRef] [PubMed]

Marmenout, Katty, and Pamelo Lirio. 2014. Local female talent retention in the Gulf: Emirati women bending with the wind. *International Journal of Human Resource Management* 25: 144–66. [CrossRef]

McDonald, Laura Z. 2008. Islam and feminisms: An Iranian case-study. *Feminist Theory* 9: 347–54. Available online: http://journals.sagepub.com/doi/abs/10.1177/1464700108095857 (accessed on 15 June 2017). [CrossRef]

McKinstry, Brian. 2008. Are there too many female medical graduates? *British Medical Journal* 336: 748. Available online: http://www.bmj.com/content/336/7647/748 (accessed on 17 October 2009). [CrossRef] [PubMed]

McLean, Michelle, Salma Al Ahbabi, Mouza Al Ameri, Muneera Al Mansoori, Fatima Al Yahyaei, and Roos Bernsen. 2010. Muslim women and medical students in the clinical encounter: A United Arab Emirates study. *Medical Education* 44: 306–15. Available online: http://onlinelibrary.wiley.com/doi/10.1111/j.1365-2923.2009.03599.x/abstract (accessed on 4 February 2012). [CrossRef] [PubMed]

McLean, Michelle, Fatima Al Yahyaei, Muneera Al Mansoori, Mouza Al Ameri, Salma Al Ahbabi, and Roos Bernsen. 2012. Muslim women's physician preference: Beyond Obstetrics and Gynecology. *Health Care for Women International* 33: 849–76. Available online: http://www.tandfonline.com/doi/abs/10.1080/07399332.2011.645963 (accessed on 15 January 2013).

Metcalfe, Beverly D. 2006. Exploring cultural dimensions of gender and management in the Middle East. *Thunderbird International Business Review* 48: 93–107. Available online: http://onlinelibrary.wiley.com/doi/10.1002/tie.20087/abstract (accessed on 17 October 2008). [CrossRef]

Mudaly, Ronicka, and Jacqueline van Wyk. 2015. 'Pink collar' medicine: Medical students navigating the gendered landscape of a South African medical school. *South African Journal of Higher Education* 29: 229–43. Available online: https://journals.co.za/content/high/29/4/EJC182447 (accessed on 15 January 2017).

O'Flynn, Norma, and Janice Rymer. 2002. Women's attitudes to the sex of medical students in a gynaecology clinic: Cross sectional survey. *British Medical Journal* 325: 683–84. Available online: http://www.bmj.com/content/325/7366/683.long (accessed on 17 October 2008).

Paik, Jodi E. 2000. The feminization of medicine. *Journal of the American Medical Association* 283: 666. [CrossRef] [PubMed]

Phillips, Susan P., and Emily B. Austin. 2009. The feminization of medicine and population health. *Journal of the American Medical Association* 301: 863–64. Available online: http://jamanetwork.com/journals/jama/fullarticle/1152830 (accessed on 4 February 2012). [CrossRef] [PubMed]

Pratto, Felicia, Jim Sidianus, Lisa M. Stallworth, and Bertram F. Malle. 1994. Social-dominance orientation as an intergroup construct. *Journal of Personality and Social Psychology* 67: 741–63. Available online: http://psycnet.apa.org/?&fa=main.doiLanding&doi=10.1037/0022-3514.67.4.741 (accessed on 17 October 2008). [CrossRef]

Pratto, Felicia, Jim Sidianus, and Shana Levin. 2006. Social dominance theory and dynamics of intergroup relations: Taking stock and looking forward. *European Review of Social Psychology* 17: 271–320. Available online: http://www.tandfonline.com/doi/full/10.1080/10463280601055772 (accessed on 17 October 2008). [CrossRef]

Raday, Francis. 2003. Culture, religion, and gender. *International Journal of Constitutional Law* 1: 663–715. [CrossRef]

Reichenbach, Laura, and Hilary Brown. 2004. Gender and academic medicine: impacts on the health workforce. *British Medical Journal* 329: 792–95. [CrossRef] [PubMed]

Ridge, Natasha. 2009. *The Hidden Gender Gap in Education in the UAE*. Dubai: Dubai School of Government Policy Brief. Available online: http://www.mbrsg.ae/getattachment/2dee9885-631c-40a2-9e5f-d5c292a80e01/The-Hidden-Gender-Gap-in-Education-in-the-UAE (accessed on 7 September 2017).

Ridgeway, Cecilia L. 2009. Framed before we know it. How gender shapes social relations. *Gender and Society* 23: 145–60. Available online: http://journals.sagepub.com/doi/abs/10.1177/0891243208330313 (accessed on 4 February 2012). [CrossRef]

Riska, Elianna. 2008. The feminization thesis: Discourses on gender and medicine. *Nordic Journal of Feminist and Gender Research* 16: 3–18. [CrossRef]

Riska, Elianna, and Aureljia Novelskaite. 2008. Gendered careers in post-Soviet society: Views on professional qualifications in Surgery and Pediatrics. *Gender Issues* 25: 229–45. [CrossRef]

Roskovensky, Lindsay B., Douglas Grbic, and David Matthew. 2012. The changing gender composition of US medical school applicants and matriculants. *Analysis in Brief* 12: 1–2. Available online: https://www.aamc.org/download/277026/data/aibvol12_no1.pdf (accessed on 23 March 2014).

Salter, Alan. 2007. Gender and choosing a specialty. *Student British Medical Journal* 15: 313–15. [CrossRef]

Schiess, Nicoline, Halah Ibraham, Sami Shaban, Maria N. Perez, and Satish C. Nair. 2015. Career choices and primary care in the United Arab Emirates. *Journal of Graduate Medical Education* 7: 663–66. Available online: http://www.jgme.org/doi/10.4300/JGME-D-14-00780.1?code=gmed-site (accessed on 14 June 2017). [CrossRef] [PubMed]

Schvaneveldt, Paul L., Jennifer L. Kerpelman, and Jay D. Schvaneveldt. 2005. Generational and cultural changes in family life in the United Arab Emirates: A comparison of mothers and daughters. *Journal of Comparative Family Studies* 36: 77–91.

Searle, Judy. 2001. Women and medicine—A new paradigm. *Medical Education* 35: 718–19. Available online: http://onlinelibrary.wiley.com/doi/10.1046/j.1365-2923.2001.00975.x/full#references (accessed on 4 February 2012). [CrossRef] [PubMed]

Shaull, Richard. 2005. Foreword. In *Pedagogy of the Oppressed*, 30th anniversary ed. Translated by Myra Bergman Ramos. New York: Continuum International, pp. 29–34.

Sibbald, Barbara. 2002. Feminization of medicine—People say it is a bad thing. *Canadian Medical Journal Association* 167: 914. Available online: http://www.cmaj.ca/content/167/8/914.full (accessed on 4 February 2012).

Sidianus, Jim, and Felicia Pratto. 1999. *Social Dominance: An Intergroup Theory of Social Hierarchy and Oppression*. Cambridge: Cambridge University Press.

Sidianus, Jim, Shana Levin, James Liu, and Felicia Pratto. 2000. Social dominance orientation, anti-egalitarianism and the political psychology of gender: An extension and cross-cultural replication. *European Journal of Social Psychology* 30: 41–67. Available online: http://onlinelibrary.wiley.com/doi/10.1002/(SICI)1099-0992(200001/02)30:1%3C41::AID-EJSP976%3E3.0.CO;2-O/epdf (accessed on 17 October 2008). [CrossRef]

Sidianus, Jim, Stacey Sinclair, and Felicia Pratto. 2006. Social dominance orientation, gender, and increasing educational exposure. *Journal of Applied Social Psychology* 36: 1640–53. Available online: http://onlinelibrary.wiley.com/doi/10.1111/j.0021-9029.2006.00074.x/full (accessed on 17 October 2008). [CrossRef]

Tlaiss, Hayfaa A. 2015. Entrepreneurial motivations of women: Evidence from the United Arab Emirates. *International Small Business Journal* 33: 562–81. Available online: http://journals.sagepub.com/doi/pdf/10.1177/0266242613496662 (accessed on 30 June 2017). [CrossRef]

United Nations Development Program (UNDP). 2003. *Arab Human Development Report*. New York: United Nations Publication.

Van der Reis, Leo. 2004. Causes and effects of a changed gender ratio in medicine. *Medical Teacher* 26: 506–9. Available online: http://www.tandfonline.com/doi/ref/10.1080/01421590412331285405 (accessed on 4 February 2012). [CrossRef] [PubMed]

Van Wyk, Jacqueline M., Soornarain S. Naidoo, Kogie Moodley, and Susan B. Higgins-Opitz. 2016. Perceptions of final-year medical students towards the impact of gender on their training and future practice. *Advances in Medical Education and Practice* 6: 541–50. [CrossRef] [PubMed]

Weizblit, Natalie, Jason Noble, and Mark O. Baerlocher. 2009. The feminization of Canadian medicine and its impact upon doctor productivity. *Medical Education* 43: 442–48. [CrossRef] [PubMed]

Wildschut, Angelique. 2010. Exploring internal segregation in the South African medical profession. *Journal of Workplace Learning* 2: 53–66. Available online: http://www.emeraldinsight.com/doi/full/10.1108/13665621011012852 (accessed on 30 June 2017). [CrossRef]

World Bank. 2003a. *Gender and Development in the Middle East and North Africa: Women in the Public Sphere.* Washington: World Bank.

World Bank. 2003b. *Trade, Investment and Development in the Middle East and North Africa.* Washington: World Bank.

World Economic Forum. 2012. Global Gender Gap Report. Available online: http://www.weforum.org/reports/global-gender-gap-report-2012 (accessed on 30 June 2017).

World Economic Forum. 2016. Global Gender Gap Report. Available online: http://www3.weforum.org/docs/GGGR16/WEF_Global_Gender_Gap_Report_2016.pdf (accessed on 30 June 2017).

World Health Organization. 2017. Gender, equity and human rights. Gender. Available online: http://www.who.int/gender-equity-rights/understanding/gender-definition/en/ (accessed on 4 September 2017).

Wynn, Rhonda. 2000. Saints and sinners: Women and the practice of medicine throughout the ages. *Journal of the American Medical Association* 283: 668–69. [CrossRef] [PubMed]

Zakrisson, Ingrid. 2008. Gender difference in social dominance orientation: Gender invariance may be situation invariance. *Sex Roles* 59: 254–63. [CrossRef]

Article

Reimagining the Hajj

Robert R. Bianchi [1,2]

[1] University of Chicago Law School, Chicago, IL 60637, USA; beyazomar@aol.com
[2] Middle East Studies Institute, Shanghai International Studies University, Shanghai 200083, China

Academic Editor: Viola Thimm
Received: 25 February 2017; Accepted: 14 March 2017; Published: 24 March 2017

Abstract: Throughout the Middle East and the Islamic world, political and religious leaders are being pulled into sharpening debates over rival approaches to reforming the Hajj. For at least two decades, Hajj controversies have deepened with rising death tolls among the pilgrims and with soaring complaints about corruption and incompetence against pilgrimage managers in Saudi Arabia and dozens of other countries. Demands for Hajj reform are reaching new peaks after Saudi officials recently revealed stunning details of the scope and magnitude of pilgrim fatalities during the last 14 years. The Saudi data leave little doubt that the quality of care for Hajjis varies enormously depending on several key factors which policy makers and religious leaders must address with greater honesty and determination. Year in and year out, the most vulnerable pilgrim populations are poor people, women, and children from across Africa and Asia as well as foreign workers, refugees, and illegal migrants living in Saudi Arabia. Most of the current proposals for Hajj reform ignore these high-risk groups. Saudi planners focus on promoting year-round pilgrimage to boost tourism revenues and high-end infrastructure. In most other countries, government-run Hajj agencies are busy cutting market-sharing deals with private business cartels and their political patrons. The combined effect of these policies is to weaken what remains of already inadequate regulations that are vital to the protection of all Hajjis. Meanwhile, support is also growing for more sweeping proposals to reimagine and reinvent the Hajj instead of fine-tuning the status quo. Some of these reforms are particularly likely to test the ingenuity and influence of leaders from all backgrounds because they challenge longstanding custom. A few of the most unconventional suggestions include lengthening the Hajj season to several months as well as linking the Hajj to pilgrimages and festivals of other world religions throughout the year.

Keywords: Hajj; women's issues; migration; pilgrimage; refugees; international regimes

---

1. Reimagining the Hajj

Demands for wide-ranging reforms of Hajj management have been mounting for several decades. Year after year, rising death tolls and endless scandals highlight the failures of the current system created by Saudi Arabia and governments in a handful of the largest Muslim nations. (Bianchi 2016).

Reform proposals have become increasingly ambitious in scope and urgent in tone. Earlier calls to loosen the quota system and phase out the most dangerous rituals have given way to more daring suggestions for lengthening the pilgrimage season and diverting excess Hajj demand toward a year-round Umrah traffic sweetened with tourist visas allowing Muslims to travel—and to shop—anywhere in Saudi Arabia (oxfordbusinessgroup.com 2014; RT News 2016).

Religious authorities play only a modest—and reactive—role in these debates compared to the bureaucrats, travel agents, politicians, and interest groups that run the day-to-day negotiation and implementation of Hajj policy around the world. Nevertheless, religious leaders will be pressured to take greater responsibility for guiding Hajj reform as the system continues to falter and the rival remedies generate deeper divisions—internationally and domestically—between nations and citizens vying for the enormous power, wealth, and prestige that flow from pilgrimage enterprises.

For many years it seemed that the best path to reform was through internationalizing the Hajj—replacing Saudi claims of exclusive sovereignty over the holy cities with collective management by all Muslim countries under the auspices of the Organization of Islamic Cooperation (OIC). When Saudi rulers were fending off the challenges of the Islamic Revolution in Iran, they endorsed internationalization and even agreed to power-sharing arrangements with large Sunni countries that went far beyond Hajj-related issues. However, after Ayatollah Khomeini passed away, Iran gradually ended its pilgrimage boycott and the threat to Saudi primacy appeared to recede (Bianchi 2004).

Sensing a new lease on life, the Saudis backtracked on pledges to foster an international regime for Hajj management (Amiri 2011). Instead, they embarked on a rapid expansion of the pilgrimage sites and a thorough remake of Mecca's landscape—demolishing most of the city's ancient quarters and working class districts and replacing them with luxury hotels and shopping malls that were beyond the reach of ordinary pilgrims. In the meantime, the dangers and tragedies of the Hajj reached greater levels and sparked deeper outrage. The more lavishly the Saudis spent and the more grandly they built, the more disastrous the results—greater crowding, newer choke points, and higher body counts (Economist 2015).

Today, the neglected crises of Hajj management are back with a vengeance—aggravated by more strident Iranian challenges to Saudi authority throughout the Middle East and by deepening cracks in Saudi society that threaten the stability of the regime (Law 2015; Dorsey 2017). Moreover, by adopting a fiercely unilateral posture on pilgrimage policy, the Saudis have alienated all of the large Sunni countries that helped them negotiate international arrangements as a face-saving defense against the initial wave of Iranian criticism thirty years ago.

Hence, Saudi rulers are more isolated than ever precisely when they face the greatest opposition at home and abroad. The royal family's self-appointed prerogative as Custodian of the Two Holy Cities—supposedly a bulwark of their legitimacy—has become their Achilles' heel drawing fire from all quarters including former allies and dependents (Fisk 2016).

In this environment, internationalizing the Hajj may no longer be enough even if the Saudis once again come to view it as a necessary evil. The reformist momentum is shifting steadily from trying to fine-tune the Hajj to reimagining it altogether. Instead of seeing the Hajj merely as an annual religious festival, Muslims increasingly regard it as a permanent worldwide network of trade, migration, and political competition—a multifunctional and hierarchical system riddled with injustices and abuses that no state or coalition can address independently.

Perceptions of the Hajj as a global nexus of labor, goods, and power are widespread not only in the Middle East, but particularly in the Asian and African countries that have contributed the greatest number of workers to Saudi Arabia and its neighbors while suffering the highest casualties in repeated pilgrimage disasters. Demands for holistic reform of the Hajj are bound to soar as the Islamic world absorbs the stunning details of multi-year death rolls recently made public by whistle blowers in the Saudi Ministry of Health (Al-Akhbar 2016).

The Saudi records are breathtaking and heart breaking. They chronicle 14 years of pilgrim deaths in Mecca, listing the names, nationalities, genders, ages, and dates of death for 90,276 victims from more than 100 countries. The rolls take up 3100 pages, covering every day from 2002 through 2015 and including both Hajjis and Umrah pilgrims from overseas as well as within Saudi Arabia (Kingdom of Saudi Arabia, Ministry of Health 2016).

The strongest correlates of Hajj mortality are poverty and youth. High Hajj death rates also appear in countries where women comprise a high proportion of the pilgrim population and when the Umrah—the shorter and less regulated pilgrimage that can be performed year round—is growing in popularity. Female fatalities are closely tied to cultural and ethnic differences as well as economic inequalities. In addition to poor, young, and female Hajjis, heightened vulnerability appears among migrants, refugees, and Muslim minorities in many predominantly non-Muslim societies.

The Saudi whistle blowers have allowed us to glimpse the greater forces that drew these multitudes to Mecca and pushed them too soon into a world beyond. At a minimum, they force us to reconsider our most basic assumptions about the Hajj—as it should be ideally, as it is lived in today's reality, and as it might become in a better future.

2. Competing Views of the Hajj and Umrah

In Islamic teachings, there is little doubt that the Hajj is doctrinally and spiritually a supreme act of worship, which cannot be substituted by other pilgrimages to Mecca or any other sacred place. Hajjis are instructed to concentrate as fully as possible on devotion and purification, shunning all distractions that might cause God to question the sincerity of their intentions and to withhold the blessing and mercy that are the pilgrims' just rewards. In addition, the simplicity of the ubiquitous *ihram* dress constantly reminds Hajjis that, in God's eyes, all Muslims and all humans are equal regardless of worldly distinctions among ranks, classes, races, genders, and ages.

Naturally, the reality has always been more complex and far more mundane, frequently contradicting the core values of the Hajj and of Islam in general. Pilgrims commonly combine the Hajj and Umrah, at the same time or in sequence, and many people perform both devotions multiple times if they have the means and feel the need. Whenever possible, travellers to Mecca join worship to non-religious activities such as business, tourism, study, and job seeking (Bianchi 2007). Crime is commonplace: smuggling, pick pocketing, vagrancy, human trafficking, prostitution, illegal migration, resettlement in the floating underground of foreigners connecting the Persian Gulf countries with towns and villages across Asia and Africa (Bennafla 2005; Ghana Review International 2012).

Nowadays, the Hajj and Umrah are virtually fused into a year-round cluster of parallel economies—each with its multiple segments and price points—enlisting legal authorities when possible and defying them when necessary (Nehme 2016). Because the quota system has capped Hajj numbers, new growth in pilgrimage traffic has steadily shifted to the Umrah where arrangements are dominated by loosely regulated private sector travel companies. At the same time, most state-sponsored Hajj agencies across the Islamic world have gradually dissolved their monopolies, handing over the more lucrative markets to politically connected firms in tourism, transportation, and financial services.

This combination of unrestrained growth and haphazard privatization has created a regulatory nightmare for all countries with substantial Hajj and Umrah pilgrimages. It is an environment that breeds glaring hierarchy and endemic favoritism. Instead of being united in worship and equal in stature, pilgrims are divided by the strength of their patrons and the size of their money belts—with potentially fatal consequences for those at the bottom of the pecking order (Bianchi 2014).

Saudi Arabia's proposed remedy is to open its doors to Muslim tourists who want to travel beyond the traditional limits of the holy cities in the Hejaz. In this view, the Hajj crisis creates an opportunity to kill several birds with one stone. Saudi technocrats believe they can not only reduce the pressures of peak season bottlenecks, but also stimulate the rapid rise of a domestic tourism industry.

According to Saudi planners, higher Hajj revenues will spill over and prime the pump for much higher earnings during the longer Umrah periods. The presumed ripple effects will stimulate cross-investments in hospitality, construction, merchandizing, and services in multiple regions. Saudi Arabia's ever-elusive goal of economic diversification will come within reach just in time to cushion the country against the looming dangers of falling oil prices and slower growth in China (RT News 2016; Carey and Nereim 2017).

Even though most of Saudi Arabia still lacks the local infrastructure and experience to absorb foreign travelers demanding international standards, the government already has created a global feeder network of pre-approved travel agencies specially licensed to expedite cash-paying pilgrim-tourists. In nearly every country, intending pilgrims can access the website of the Saudi embassy to conduct their own market research and find referrals to recommended companies near their homes.

In a nutshell, the Saudi vision is a global franchise system of government licensed enterprises handling the high end of a consolidated Hajj-Umrah market generating year-round revenues from trade and tourism across every continent with new tributaries reaching into previously isolated corners of the Kingdom itself. It would leave a smaller and lower-end market of Hajjis to state-subsidized agencies in countries where government bureaucrats formerly monopolized the pilgrimage business. The remnants of the once mighty Hajj Directorates would provide bare bones services for economy-minded customers willing to stand in line for years or try their luck in quota lotteries.

By deepening the worldwide privatization of pilgrimage services, the Saudi Arabian government aims to put the entire industry under its protection and use the profits to bolster the Kingdom's struggling economy and political system. These policies threaten to undermine what is left of the regulatory resources the international community needs to rein in a pilgrimage system that is out of control. Perhaps some officials in the Saudi Ministry of Health arrived at similar conclusions before they leaked the extraordinary information we examine next.

3. The Correlates of Death in Mecca

Between 2002 and 2015, about 23 million overseas pilgrims came to Mecca for the Hajj. During the same period, about 30,000 overseas pilgrims died in all of the three month intervals that define the Hajj season—the Hijri months of Dhu al-Qi'dah, Dhu al-Hijjah, and Muharram. Another 29,000 foreign pilgrims perished during the remaining nine months that comprise the longer Umrah season. In addition, among the more than 11 million Hajjis who came from inside Saudi Arabia, over 31,000 died in Mecca—about 10,000 during the Hajj months and 21,000 over the Umrah months.

The most populous Muslim countries sent the largest delegations of Hajjis and accounted for the highest numbers of deaths, but at widely varying rates of mortality (deaths per 10,000 pilgrims). Eight countries stand out as the leading overseas sources of Hajjis (75 percent) and Hajj-related fatalities (73 percent). For the entire 14–year period, Iran and Turkey had the lowest death rates whereas Egypt and India had rates that were three to four times higher. In between, were Indonesia, Pakistan, Bangladesh, and Nigeria with death rates clustering slightly above the international average of 13 victims per 10,000 Hajjis (Table 1).

Table 1. Death Rates and Demographic Profiles for the 8 Largest Sources of Hajjis, 2002–2015.

Country	Hajj Death Rate	Total Hajjis	Hajj Deaths	Umrah Deaths	GDP Per Capita	Average Age	Female Percent	Umrah Deaths Percent
Iran	6.30	1,173,307	738	469	17,346	66.15	20.19	38.86
Turkey	7.20	1,291,338	935	483	20,420	66.90	27.91	34.06
Indonesia	15.83	2,770,000	4386	1451	11,149	63.67	37.65	24.86
Pakistan	16.80	2,127,112	3579	4413	4906	59.16	28.54	55.22
Bangladesh	17.28	1,032,088	1783	1836	3629	58.32	16.14	50.73
Nigeria	17.60	1,123,000	1988	3001	6121	54.24	46.28	60.15
India	18.91	1,480,186	2803	939	6187	64.40	28.11	25.09
Egypt	23.52	1,000,500	2353	3141	11,803	59.74	33.88	57.17

Source: Author's computations of raw data from Kingdom of Saudi Arabia, Ministry of Health (2016).

When trying to explain disparities in the performance of Hajj agencies, it is always helpful to begin by comparing their countries' relative living standards. Economic conditions directly influence the level of public resources available for government support of pilgrimage as well as the disposable income and health of the people they serve. More prosperous countries can afford to invest in agencies that screen, educate, and care for their clients, identifying at-risk populations and ensuring they receive timely medical attention. In a similar vein, travelers who are well-off can upgrade to safer and healthier accommodations in the public sector market or splurge on the frills and add-ons touted by competing private firms.

Indeed, per capita gross domestic product is a powerful predictor of the most basic goal of Hajj management—the ability to bring their charges back home safe and sound (Figure 1). Among the largest Hajj programs, Turkey and Iran are the best performers year in and year out and they also enjoy the highest income levels. Egypt's performance is much weaker than its living standard would suggest, particularly compared to Indonesia. On the other hand, Bangladesh and Pakistan are slightly more effective than India and Nigeria at similar income levels. Thus, even though adequate material resources are probably a necessary condition for effective management, there is still plenty of remaining variance to be accounted for—in some cases, by the experience and know-how of the Hajj organizations and, in other cases, by the characteristics and actions of the pilgrims themselves.

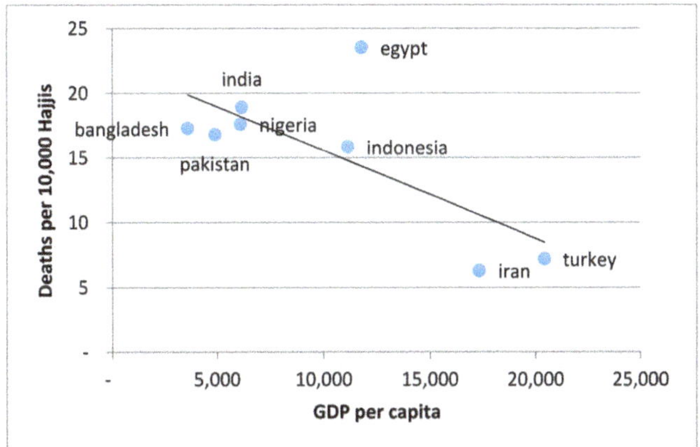

Figure 1. Hajj Death Rates and GDP per capita, 8 Largest Sources. Source: Author's computations of raw data from Kingdom of Saudi Arabia, Ministry of Health (2016).

Another strong correlate of Hajj mortality is the pilgrims' average age at their times of death (Figure 2). Older pilgrims fare much better than younger ones despite their obvious handicaps in terms of general health and physical stamina. A very high proportion of the Nigerian Hajj fatalities are working-age people less than 50 years old—33 percent of the men and 40 percent of the women. For Turkey and Iran, however, it is uncommon to find any fatalities in those age groups—4 percent of the deceased men and 6 percent of the women from Turkey and only 7 percent of the men and 8 percent of the women from Iran.

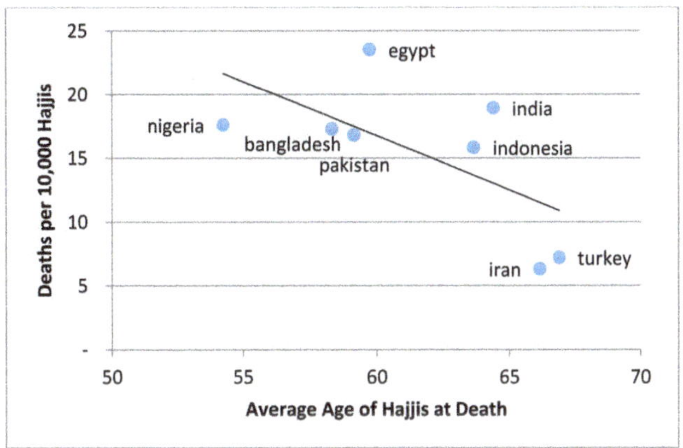

Figure 2. Hajj Death Rates and Pilgrims' Average Age, 8 Largest Sources. Source: Author's computations of raw data from Kingdom of Saudi Arabia, Ministry of Health (2016).

Why do fit Nigerian youths perish more frequently than wizened pensioners from Turkey and Iran? Probably because so many of the youngest pilgrims, hoping to flee poverty and unemployment at home, decide to plunge into a life of danger by absconding and seeking a niche in Saudi Arabia's vast pool of illegal foreigners. They are likely to engage in a host of risky behaviors, sleeping on the streets, scrounging for odd jobs, and trying to keep a step ahead of the law. The more time such fugitive pilgrims and visa overstayers spend in Mecca's underground, the more likely they are to end up on the death rolls—some to be identified by nationality, but not by name, and others to be coded simply as "African", "unknown", or "number 70,303".

In contrast, the Iranian shopkeeper and Turkish farmer enter the country fully vaccinated and primed with prescription medications (Razavi et al. 2013). Together with their spouses, they sleep in clean beds within walking distance of the Grand Mosque, watched over by teams of nurses and paramedics. Completing the Hajj, they shop and take in the sites before going back home where their breathless families can dote on the blessed couple and entertain their many well-wishers.

In addition to national living standards and pilgrim age, two other factors have a somewhat weaker correlation with Hajj deaths—the relative importance of the Umrah and the proportion of female Hajjis among the deceased (Figures 3 and 4).

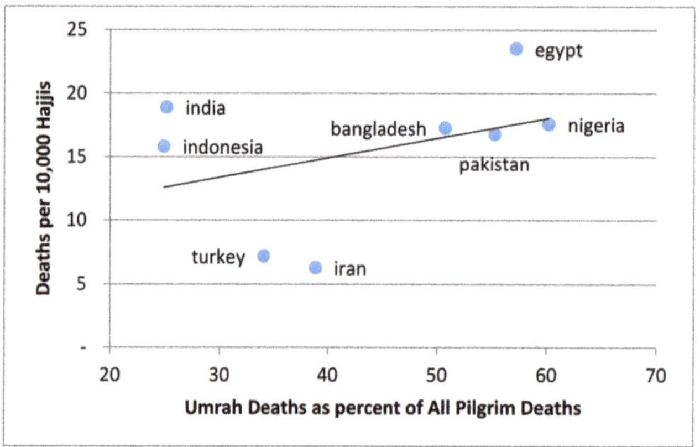

Figure 3. Hajj Death Rates and Umrah Predominance, 8 Largest Sources. Source: Author's computations of raw data from Kingdom of Saudi Arabia, Ministry of Health (2016).

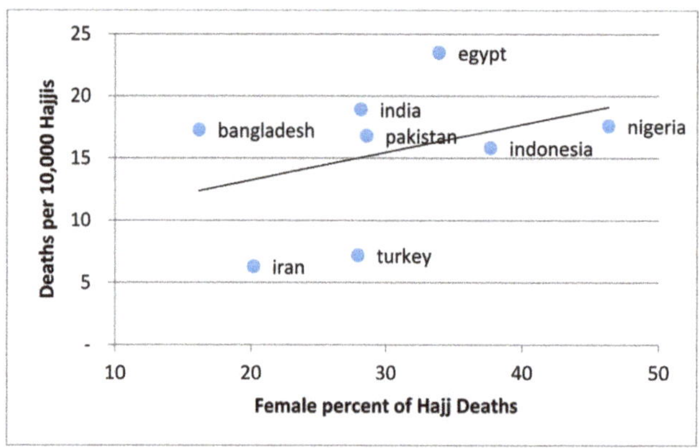

Figure 4. Hajj Death Rates and Female Hajj Participation, 8 Largest Sources. Source: Author's computations of raw data from Kingdom of Saudi Arabia, Ministry of Health (2016).

The Umrah, which is far less organized and regulated than the Hajj, is also more intimately tied to continuous transcontinental trade and migration linking Saudi Arabia and its neighbors with Africa, South Asia, and the Pacific Basin. While state agencies usually retain the upper hand in Hajj management, the Umrah has always been the preserve of private agents with extensive business connections and long experience in skirting legal formalities across borders. As Hajj growth has stagnated because of quota limits, the Umrah has skyrocketed around the world, generating a heavier and more constant flow of pilgrims that are less organized and supervised than during the Hajj.

In many countries, the total number of pilgrim deaths during the nine Umrah months now exceeds the body counts from the Hajj season. The countries with the largest Hajj delegations fall along a continuum of Hajj—Umrah prominence—Nigeria, Egypt, Pakistan, and Bangladesh lose most of their victims during the Umrah whereas Iran, Turkey, India, and Indonesia suffer most fatalities during the Hajj. Egypt stands out in this regard as a country where the Umrah is exceptionally popular—particularly during Ramadan—and where governments usually leave the Hajj in the hands of private businesses and religious groups (Whitman 2015). Little wonder that the death rates for Egypt's pilgrims are the highest in this group of countries.

Death rates also tend to rise when a larger share of fatalities are women. The most vulnerable women come from countries with longstanding grievances against Saudi abuse of their female pilgrims and migrant workers. Nigeria and Indonesia, which suffer the highest female tolls, are also the countries that have expressed the bitterest protests about mistreatment of their women in Saudi Arabia. For many years, Nigerians have complained that Saudi police falsely accuse their female pilgrims of prostitution, imprisoning or deporting them on mere suspicion. Jakarta waged a long battle with Saudi Arabia over widespread abuse of their female domestic workers during which the governments of both countries punished Indonesian women who sought employment in the Kingdom.

For Bangladesh, on the other hand, Hajj deaths are relatively high despite an extremely low proportion of women. In fact, Bangladesh's Hajj is so overwhelmingly dominated by males precisely because, for many years, it operated less as a pilgrimage than as a smuggling ring for young men who wanted to go overseas as illegal workers. Eventually, the Saudis pressured Bangladesh to clamp down on the travel agents that ran the business, leading to dozens of convictions for human trafficking (Financial Express 2013; Dhaka Tribune 2013).

Thus, we find reinforcing evidence from several directions that pilgrimage to Mecca—both Hajj and Umrah—is systematically related to high death rates for vulnerable travelers—both female and male—who swell the pool of migrant labor in Saudi Arabia and nearby countries. The common thread linking these deaths is that many of the weakest pilgrims could not control their own movements and finances. Regardless of whether they took the path of the Hajj or the Umrah, and whether they were male or female, it was the compounded handicaps of poverty and youthful inexperience that shaped their tragedies most of all.

4. The Rise of the Umrah Belt

The growth of the Umrah has been a pervasive and cumulative process, spreading across the Islamic world at varying speeds in different countries and cultural zones (Arab News 2016). There are many ways to track and map this evolution, including a closer analysis of the shifting seasonal patterns of pilgrim mortality that the Hajj and Umrah have generated in one country after another. The copious Saudi records allow us to view the data from multiple perspectives—finely grained pictures of month by month death counts for every country and every year or sweeping panoramas of entire decades and continents.

To grasp the powerful impetus propelling Umrah growth, there is no better starting point than the example of Turkey. Before the quota system was adopted, Turkey's Hajj was one of the largest and most volatile in the world, oscillating sharply in the wake of partisan clashes, military coups, and coalition governments. However, once the quotas kicked in, Turkey's pilgrim count settled into a stable range with only modest fluctuations in years when Saudi Arabia was willing to negotiate a temporary bonus with friendly politicians and bureaucrats in Ankara. During the 1990s, per capita Hajj rates actually declined in Turkey (T.C. Diyanet İşleri Başkanlığı 2016) (Figure 5).

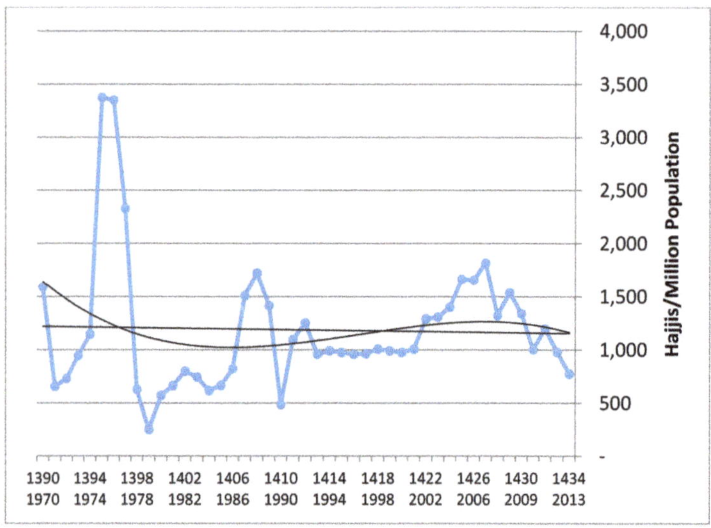

Figure 5. Turkey, Hajjis per Million Population, 1970–2013. Source: Author's computations of data from T.C. Diyanet İşleri Başkanlığı (2016).

Nonetheless, Hajj applications kept flooding in, creating waiting lists and backlogs that no government could hope to satisfy. In 2006, there were fewer than 3 applicants for each available place in the Turkish delegation. In 2010, the ratio was 11 to 1 and by 2013 it was nearing 30 to 1. This meant that new registrants would have to wait years or decades for their turn to come—longer than the remaining life expectancy of nearly everyone above the age of 60 (Yeni Şafak 2015) (Figure 6).

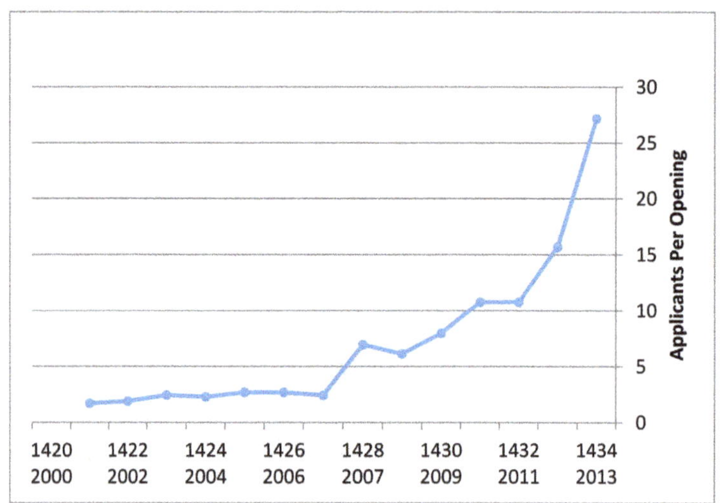

Figure 6. Turkey, Ratio of Applicants to Hajjis 2000–2013. Source: Author's computations of data from T.C. Diyanet İşleri Başkanlığı (2016).

When the Justice and Development Party consolidated power after 2002, its leaders devised a dual strategy to treat the problem. They adopted a vigorous campaign to promote the Umrah on an unprecedented scale while giving senior citizens the lion's share of the Hajj visas no matter how many younger applicants preceded them on the waiting lists. President Erdoğan personally urged intending Hajjis, including all the ministers in his cabinet, to make the Umrah instead and to take their spouses along as well (Daily Sabah 2015). For a couple of years, he also suspended new applications for the Hajj and reserved nearly the entire delegation for elderly first-time pilgrims who had been waiting several years already (Bianchi 2015a).

Thanks to Erdoğan, Turkey's Umrah traffic exploded. Before the Justice and Development Party era, Turkish Umrah goers were a small fraction of the number of Hajjis. By 2006 the total size of Turkey's Umrah was equal to its Hajj. In 2010, the Umrah was three times larger than the Hajj and in 2013 it was ten times bigger (Hurriyet Daily News 2011; Saudi Gazette 2016) (Figure 7).

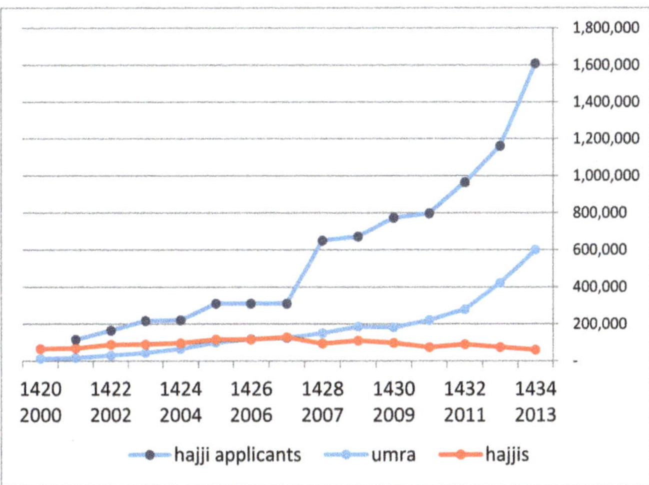

Figure 7. Turkey, Hajj Applicants, Umrah Goers, and Hajjis, 2000–2013. Source: Author's computations of data from T.C. Diyanet İşleri Başkanlığı (2016).

The combined opportunities for Umrah and Hajj still fell far short of the astronomical growth in Hajj demand, but the plan to grow and segment the overall pilgrimage market unfolded quite effectively. The rapid shift in the age profiles of Turkey's Hajjis and Umrah goers reveals the pattern with unusual clarity. A booming Umrah became the tour of choice for Turkey's pious middle classes with strong participation across all age groups and price points. In contrast, the greying Hajj became an old folks' refuge for those who saw their last chances slipping away while bureaucrats shuffled their paperwork and banked their down payments (T.C. Diyanet İşleri Başkanlığı (2014)) (Figures 8 and 9).

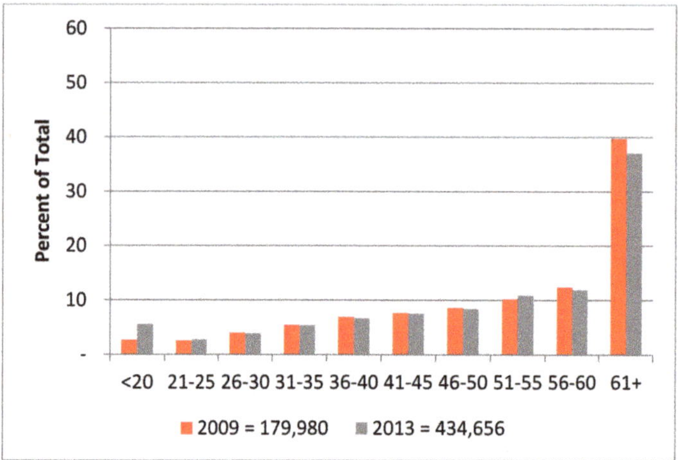

Figure 8. Turkey Umrah Age Groups, 2009 and 2013. Source: T.C. Diyanet İşleri Başkanlığı (2014).

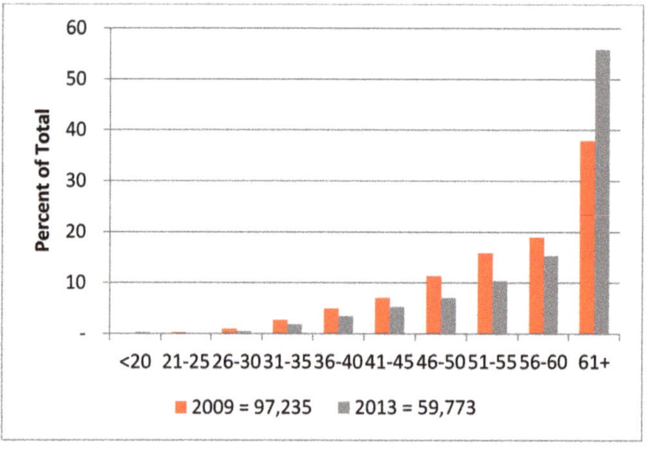

Figure 9. Turkey Hajj Age Groups, 2009 and 2013. Source: T.C. Diyanet İşleri Başkanlığı (2014).

Similar trends are playing out all across the Muslim world. A vigorous Umrah—entirely run by private travel companies with political connections at home and in Saudi Arabia—is eclipsing the once-mighty government Hajj monopolies—forced to farm out their markets to business cartels in tourism, transportation, and banking. The speed and circumstances of this transformation vary markedly from country to country. In some cases, such as nearby Egypt and Yemen, the Umrah has always generated year-round pilgrim flows which are simply increasing compared to past rates. On the other hand, several more distant countries, such as China and Senegal, remain solidly rooted in the Hajj-dominant pattern despite early signs that the Umrah is catching on there as well (Aw 2015; Ndiaye 2016).

Most countries fall in between these opposing trends and their pilgrim mortality figures reflect the quickening pace of the Umrah shift across time and space. For example, Pakistan took the lead in South Asia with Umrah deaths surpassing Hajj deaths around 2006. More distant Indonesia traveled the same path, but it began later and just recently crossed the threshold where Umrah deaths exceed Hajj fatalities (Onishi 2010) (Figure 10). One after another, dozens of countries have followed suit—Turkey, Bangladesh, the Philippines, Iran, Jordan, Oman, Malaysia, Thailand, Mali, Niger, Burkina Faso, Djibouti, Palestine, Kuwait, Ethiopia, Eritrea, Sudan, Libya, Afghanistan—and many more are close behind.

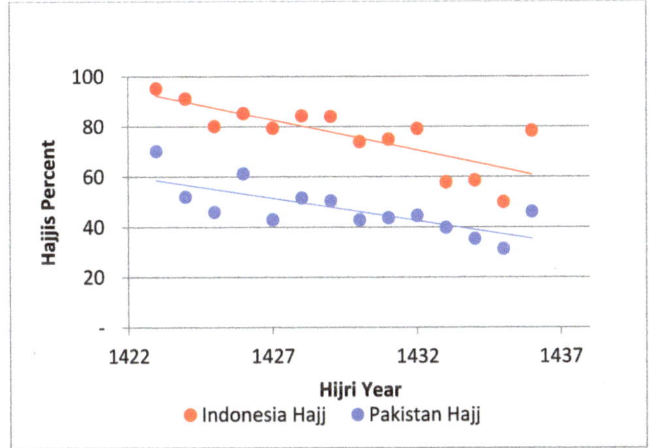

Figure 10. Indonesia and Pakistan, Hajjis as Percent of All Pilgrim Deaths. Source: Author's computations of raw data from Kingdom of Saudi Arabia, Ministry of Health (2016).

Together, these far-flung societies are forming a transcontinental Umrah Belt—overlapping megaregions linked by constant flows of migrants, cash, and merchandise between the Far East, Africa, and Europe using the Middle East as a central crossroad. The Umrah Belt rests on a long chain of neighboring regions that are becoming more integrated internally and with each other. From west to east, they span the African Sahel and Savanna, the Red Sea, Arabia and the GCC, South Asia, and Southeast Asia (Yamba 1995; Miran 2009; Tagliacozzo 2013; Boivin and Delage 2015) (Figure 11).

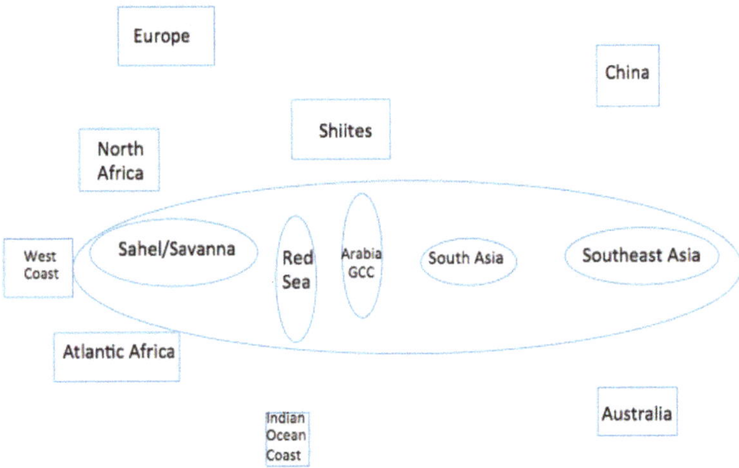

Figure 11. The Umrah Belt and Outlying Regions.

Just as important, the Umrah Belt is surrounded by several outlying zones and soft spots where many countries have preserved the older pattern of Hajj-centered pilgrimage despite the wider shift toward year-round Umrah travel. Some of the holdouts can be explained by the enduring barriers of long distances, but there also are clear examples of local clustering that suggest cultural and political reasons for their aloofness. The most notable holdouts include Western Europe, Australia, North Africa, and the Atlantic coasts of Africa both in the far west and the Gulf of Guinea. Francophone regions are particularly laggard in Umrah growth compared to their equally distant neighbors. Pockets of weaker Umrah participation also appear in countries with sizeable populations of Shiites and Ahmadis—Lebanon, Syria, Iraq, Bahrain, Kenya, and Tanzania (Ahmed 2009). China stands out as one of the few countries where the state still monopolizes the Hajj, discourages the Umrah, and tries to ban unsupervised international pilgrimage altogether (Hoshur 2016; Bianchi 2017).

The Umrah Belt is taking shape in the shadow of a far more ambitious project of mega-regional integration—China's New Silk Road linking the Atlantic and Pacific coasts of the Eastern Hemisphere with land and sea routes across all of Afro-Eurasia (Bianchi 2013). The Chinese ventures overlap and intersect the Umrah Belt at so many points that more and more people are calling it China's Islamic Road. The countries that Chinese planners have pinpointed as the prime areas of investment—Indonesia, Pakistan, Iran, Turkey, and Nigeria—exemplify the synergies and conflicts we can expect from interactions of the Umrah-Hajj Belt and the New Silk Road in the near future (Bianchi 2015b).

5. Women Pilgrims: The Importance of Cultural Empowerment and Uniform Protection

Women are a particularly vulnerable part of the pilgrim population. They are highly susceptible to contradictory cultural norms and to enduring gaps in regulatory protections needed to prevent their systematic abuse. Mauritania is the leading example of pernicious victimization of female Hajjis on both cultural and legal grounds. It has the dubious distinction of combining one of the world's highest Hajj death rates with the greatest proportion of female fatalities (Figure 12).

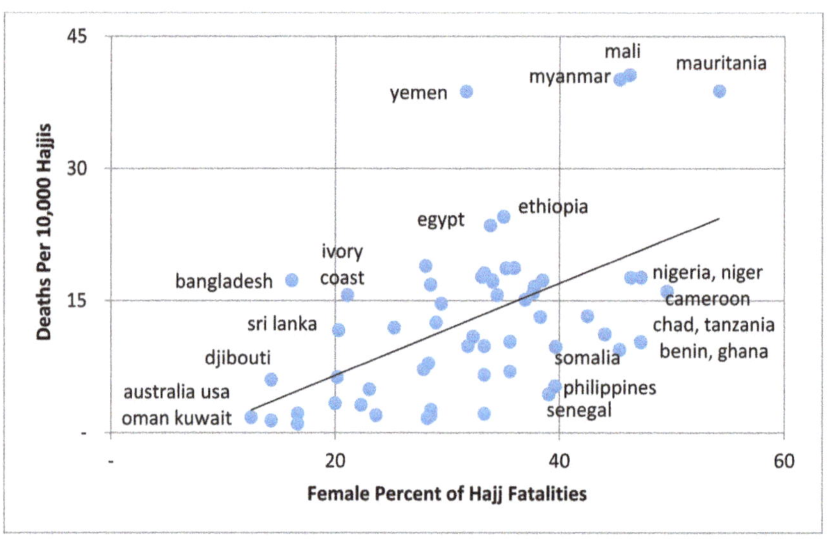

Figure 12. Hajj Death Rates and Female Percent of Fatalities, 2002–2015. Source: Author's computations of raw data from Kingdom of Saudi Arabia, Ministry of Health (2016).

When official protests from Indonesia and the Philippines interrupted the flow of female domestic workers from Southeast Asia to Saudi Arabia, recruitment shifted 8500 miles away to the farthest corner of North Africa (Dima-Macabando 2015). Mauritania's ongoing battle to stamp out slavery makes it a rich vein for people smuggling, especially when economic distress pushes recently emancipated groups to accept new forms of indenture. Labor recruiters have used the Hajj as both bait and cover in luring Mauritanian women to non-existent job opportunities and forcing them into virtual captivity as low-wage household servants to Saudi families (Donaghy and Alsaafin 2015).

In contrast to the youthful women usually imported from other countries, the Mauritanian domestics are conspicuously advanced in age—88 percent of the Mauritanian women who died during the Hajj season were more than 50 years old. By specifically targeting older women, the phony employment agencies manage to circumvent Saudi immigration and police officers who typically profile young women from Africa and Asia as potential sex workers.

The most striking feature of female Hajj mortality is its strong dependence on economic and cultural differences. The sharpest contrast is the deep split between the very rich and the very poor—Mali, Mauritania, Myanmar, and Yemen with extremely high female death rates versus Western and Persian Gulf countries with negligible mortality for both men and women. Hajjis from wealthier countries benefit from careful screening and ongoing medical attention. Pilgrims from destitute areas usually have to fend for themselves or rely on predatory gangs that have no intention of assisting their safe return home.

There are many instances of geographical clustering in which women's death rates are unusually high or low compared to the overall international pattern (Figure 13). The Malay-speaking Muslims of Southeast Asia stand out in combining high death rates and strong female presence. Indonesia, Malaysia, Singapore, Thailand, and Brunei cluster together in a tight cultural and regional grouping. All of these countries have flourishing economies and expanding middle classes that are fueling demands for higher Hajj quotas—demands that Saudi officials cannot satisfy short of a thorough overhaul of the quota system. In the meantime, Southeast Asia is teeming with illegal channels of pilgrimage that charge a premium for fake documents while providing no support for those who manage to slip through border controls at either end of the journey.

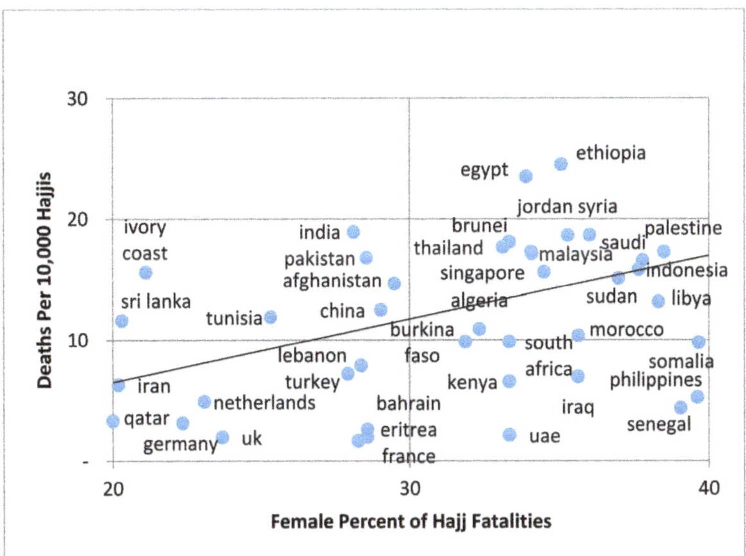

Figure 13. Hajj Death Rates and Female Percent of Fatalities, 2002–2015. Detailed View Source: Author's computations of raw data from Kingdom of Saudi Arabia, Ministry of Health (2016).

All of the South Asian countries have relatively high fatalities but with very weak female participation. Pakistan and India with professionally managed state agencies fare better than Sri Lanka and Bangladesh where private firms and labor brokers control the business. Nonetheless, the general trend in South Asia is for high-risk and male-dominated Hajj where female pilgrims are marginalized and poorly protected.

Countries in most parts of Africa—North, West, and East—have fairly low morality plus high proportions of women pilgrims. Nigeria and most of its neighbors as well as Senegal provide women both high opportunity and relative safety in performing the Hajj. West African women have long experience as business owners and recently they have extended their reach into pilgrimage markets, benefitting simultaneously from government set asides as well as privatization measures to open more doors for women traders to travel to Saudi Arabia. The widely noted achievements of Senegalese and Nigerian women in the Hajj business have been emulated in Cameroon, Ivory Coast, and elsewhere in West Africa (Hardy and Semin 2009; Adama 2009; Dioum 2014).

Arabic-speaking countries are notably less consistent than other regions in protecting the welfare of female pilgrims. Wealthy Arab nations provide relative safety, but only limited opportunities for women Hajjis. Most North African countries lean toward the Senegalese example, but Egypt and the Fertile Crescent nations of Syria, Jordan and Palestine trend toward the Malay pattern of high risk and moderate opportunity.

6. Political Insecurity and Muslim Minorities: India and Ivory Coast

In many societies where Muslims are a sizeable minority, the Hajj rests on shaky foundations, reflecting the politically charged role of religion in a delicate balance of power. India and Ivory Coast portray this dilemma poignantly, demonstrating that state-sponsored Hajj programs can both exacerbate and moderate communal strife. In India, publicly-funded Hajj agencies have stirred increasingly bitter clashes in national and state politics. On the other hand, the experience of Ivory Coast shows that ascending Muslim power can promote multi-faith pilgrimages in a concerted effort to recover from a decade of civil war and social partition.

India has one of the world's most politicized programs of publicly-subsidized Hajj. Knowing nothing more than the fluctuations in the annual number of state-supported pilgrims to Mecca, one can easily spot the turning points in the seesaw battle to control the central government in New Delhi (Haj Committee of India 2008–2016). When the Congress Party was in power, they spurred or maintained Hajj growth. When the Hindu nationalists of the Bharatiya Janata Party took over, they slowed or reversed the pilgrim flow (Figure 14 and Table 2).

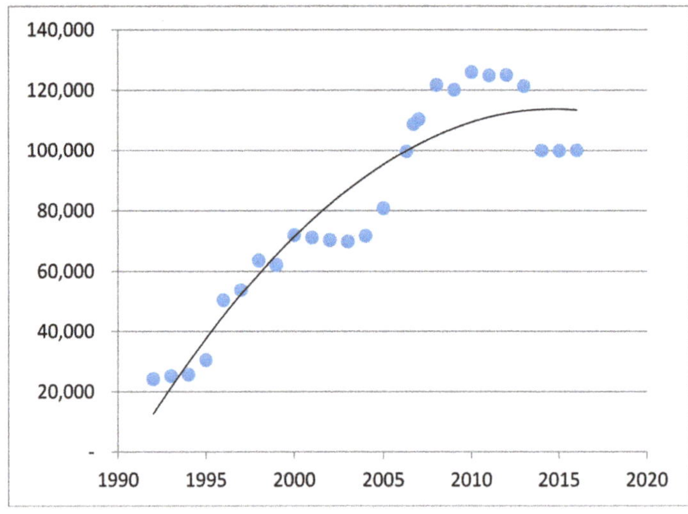

Figure 14. India Hajjis, 1992–2016. Source: Haj Committee of India (2008–2016).

Table 2. India National Election Winners and Hajj Growth.

Ruling Party	Years	Hajj Growth (1000)	Percent Change
Congress 1	1991–1996	23/50	116
BJP 1	1996–1999	50/72	43
BJP 2	1999–2004	72/71	−3
Congress 2	2004–2009	71/121	69
Congress 3	2009–2014	121/121	0
BJP 3	2014–2016	121/100	−17

Source: Author's computations of raw data from Haj Committee of India (2008–2016).

Comparing the performance of Hajj managers at the state level, we see a familiar trend in which pilgrim death rates closely track economic conditions (Haj Committee of India 2016). Well-endowed New Delhi is in a class by itself in dispensing Hajj services. At the other hand, the poorer states of the Ganges Basin and northeastern India provide shoestring aid that yields mediocre safety for its Hajjis (Figure 15). In between these economic extremes, two clusters of deviant cases stand out—a group of over-performing states where death rates are much lower than average and a set of under-performers where fatalities are far higher than local levels of prosperity would suggest (Figure 16) (Huda 2015).

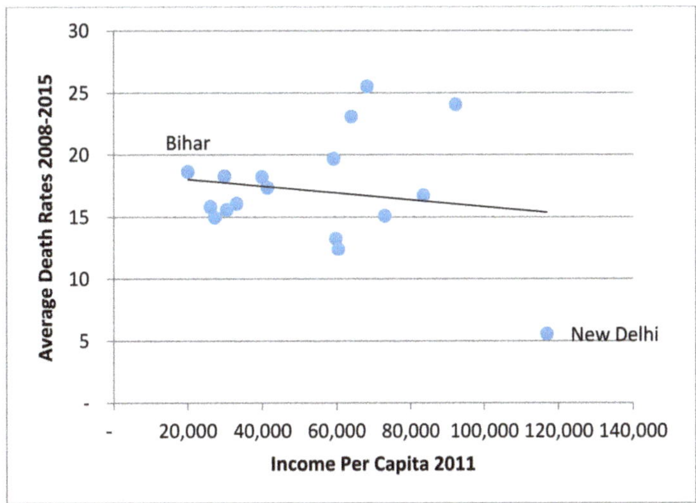

Figure 15. Hajj Death Rates and Income in Indian States. Source: Haj Committee of India (2016).

India's highest Hajj mortality appears in states where dominant parties consistently oppose using public funds to help Muslim minorities in religious activities. Three of the four high fatality states are northern bastions of the BJP—Gujarat, Haryana, and Uttrakhand (Figure 17). The Himalayan state of Uttrakhand hosts some of the most popular and profitable Hindu pilgrimage sites in the country. Politicians in this state are eager to subsidize pilgrimages, but only if they are both local and Hindu. The sole southern state in this group, Kerala, is a stronghold of leftists and secularists who discourage government aid for all religions.

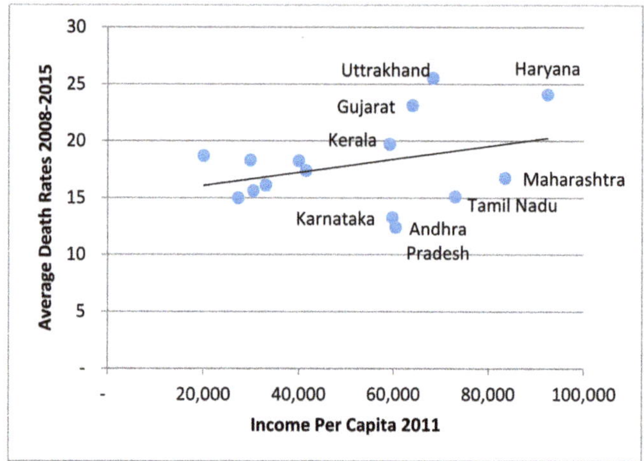

Figure 16. Hajj Death Rates and Income in Indian States. Detail without New Delhi. Source: Haj Committee of India (2016).

Figure 17. Map of Hajj Death Rates in Indian States Higher than Average in Red and Lower than Average in Blue.

All of the states with low Hajj fatalities are contiguous southern regions with large linguistic minorities—Maharashtra, Karnataka, Andhra Pradesh, and Tamil Nadu. These states are well-known for a combination of cultural diversity and political independence that blunts the spread of Hindu extremism beyond its northern heartlands. In this more pluralistic environment, politicians compete vigorously for Muslim voters and provide more generous support for their religious pursuits, including the Hajj.

India's Hajj-related headaches are growing more severe every year. The Supreme Court of India has ordered New Delhi to phase out central government Hajj subsidies, leaving each state to decide whether to fill the funding gap with local tax revenues (Vaidyanathan 2012; SahilOnline 2013). The Court's stance virtually guarantees an uptick in communal conflicts by stirring religious, regional, and cultural passions simultaneously in every state with a large Muslim population.

State-funded Hajj is enjoying greater success in Ivory Coast, but only after religiously motivated bloodletting nearly exhausted all sides. Much of the fighting revolved around protracted efforts to prevent one man from becoming the country's first Muslim president. Alassane Ouattara is an improbable demon. Often described as a secular Muslim, he is an aristocrat married to a French Jewish woman who became a Catholic. As an IMF-backed economist and protégé of founding father, Félix Houphouet-Boigny, Ouattara helped in navigating the Ivorian cocoa boom and tried to succeed H-B after his death in 1993 (Economist 2011).

Ouattara's rivals not only banned him from running for office, they also denied citizenship to a generation of Muslim immigrants from Burkina Faso and Mali who swelled the workforce of the southern fields and cities. Several army mutinies and market crashes paved the way for Laurent Gbagbo to seize power on a wave of xenophobia and religious extremism that tore the country apart both physically and politically (Human Rights Watch 2005). Eventually, Gbagbo accepted a South African-brokered truce and an electoral match up with Ouattara, but when he lost he unleashed a second civil war in which his militias targeted Muslim enclaves in Abidjan and across the south. French military intervention finally put an end to the slaughter, dispatching Gbagbo to the Hague where he currently faces trial before the International Criminal Court for war crimes and crimes against humanity (Kaplan 2012).

When Ouattara assumed the presidency, he sought to counter years of Islamophobia by rekindling Ivorian traditions of pluralism and religious tolerance. A key part of the campaign offered government aid for Christians and Muslims who wanted to travel abroad on pilgrimage. His administration has helped Muslims go on Hajj to Mecca, but it also sends Catholics to Lourdes and Protestants to Jerusalem (Conférence des Evêques Catholiques de Côte d'Ivoire 2016). Unlike the Indian politicians and judges who use rival pilgrimages as political weapons, Ouattara has tried to sweeten the transition to Christian-Muslim power sharing by reaching out to the very groups that slammed the door in his face over twenty years ago (Miran-Guyon 2014).

The coalition-building strategy is crystal clear when we compare Ouattara's regional shares of the vote in 2010 with the current pattern of Hajj participation in the Ivory Coast (Figure 18). Pilgrimage subsidies are going to the northern districts where Muslims predominate and where Ouattara handily carried the day in the first round of a three-man constant (Commission Electorale Independante 2010). However, the bulk of the aid reaches religiously mixed areas in the center of the country and Abidjan as well as Christian districts that Gbagbo's partisans once terrorized in the south and west (Direction Générale des Cultes Commissariat du Hadj 2016) (Figure 19).

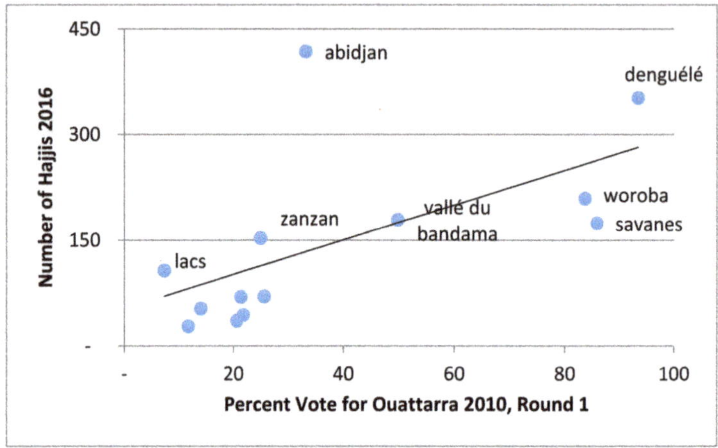

Figure 18. Hajj 2016 and Presidental Vote 2010, Districts Source: Author's computations of raw data from Direction Générale des Cultes Commissariat du Hadj (Direction Générale des Cultes Commissariat du Hadj 2016).

Figure 19. Lines of Control in the Ivorian Civil War 2007 (Cormier 2016) Rebels in the north, government forces in the south, and central buffer zone.

Today, most Ivorian Muslims live outside of their former northern heartlands among Christian and animist majorities that continue to dominate the coastal zones (Miran-Guyon 2015). Helping vulnerable Muslims—whether they are majorities or minorities—requires helping their struggling neighbors as well, not creating enclaves of privilege surrounded by hostile shutouts. Following that logic, Ouattara's supporters won over most of the non-Muslim districts in the second round of the 2010 election and even bigger majorities in his reelection of 2015.

India and Ivory Coast are not exotic cases. In contrast, they typify the pervasive intermingling of Muslim and non-Muslim peoples that has long characterized most of Asia and Africa and that is increasingly familiar in Europe and North America (McLoughlin 2013; British Muslim Experiences of the Hajj 2015). Their contrasting experiences with politically charged pilgrimages carry wider implications for the Hajj and its future evolution everywhere.

7. The Perpetual Pilgrimage of Myanmar Refugees

The most vulnerable group in Mecca may be the Muslim refugees from Myanmar. Many of them found shelter in Saudi Arabia during the 1970s, when their homeland was still known as Burma. King Faisal welcomed them as they were pouring into Bangladesh and most other countries were turning them away. Faisal's successors continued the practice on a smaller scale, but never granted legal residency status that gives foreigners access to employment, schooling, and health care (Ahmad 2009).

Today there are at least a quarter million Myanmaris living in Saudi Arabia, about half of them in Mecca's slums and working class neighborhoods—or what is left of them after years of demolition and gentrification. For this community, pilgrimage is far more than a seasonal festival. It is a livelihood and the pilgrims are their lifeline, dispensing a daily flow of sales, tips, and alms that sustains them and other members of Mecca's underclass twelve months a year (Jalabi 2016).

Those who ply the pilgrim throngs know the markets and side streets by heart. Many can sense danger before it erupts and flee in the knick of time. When tangled crowds brim with anger and panic, the street people—particularly children—are the first to react before stampedes trap the unwary in their own frantic footsteps. However, even the keenest survival instincts break down under constant stress and a steady stream of Myanmaris fills the morgues and death rolls where they are labeled as foreigners even if their birthplace is Saudi Arabia.

The Myanmari fatalities are extraordinary because of their enormous numbers—4193 over 14 years—but even more because of their nearly daily occurrence. During the 168 months covered by the Mecca death records, there were exactly six months when no Myanmari victims appeared—at least none whose remains and nationality could be identified. Yemen, Mali, and Mauritania suffer similarly bloated mortality rates—nearly three times the average for all overseas Hajjis—but none matches the ceaseless flow of Myanmari casualties (BBC News 2015) (Figure 20). Myanmari deaths include an unusually high proportion of women—almost 50 percent during both Hajj and Umrah seasons—and heavy tolls of children and teenagers—about 10 percent year-round (Figure 21) (World Bulletin 2016).

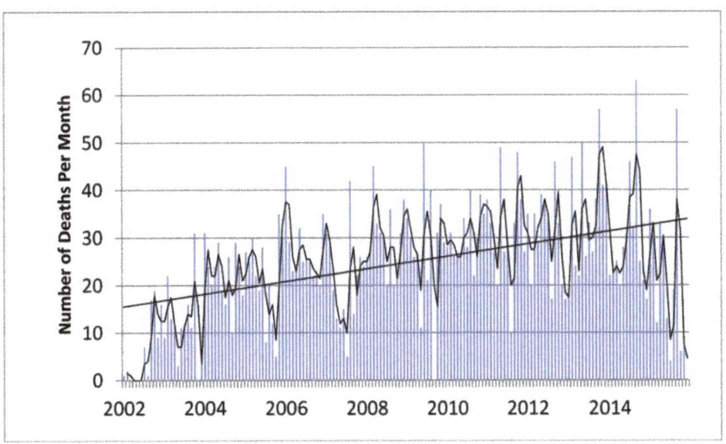

Figure 20. Myanmar Monthly Pilgrim Deaths, 2002–2015. Source: Author's computations of raw data from Kingdom of Saudi Arabia, Ministry of Health (2016).

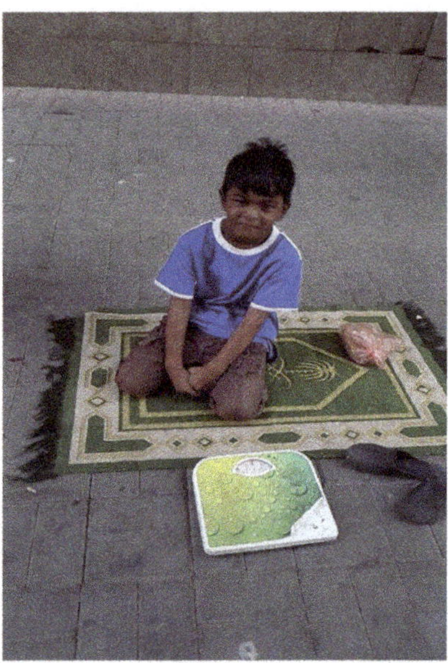

Figure 21. Naseem from Burma. Naseem: "People can weigh themselves for 1 riyal. My mother passed away in Burma and my father works at a car shop. I'm 8 years old and this gets me around 30–40 riyals a day (about $10). My father doesn't want me to work and discourages me but I want to work." Haji: "Why?" Naseem: "Because I want to study." Source: World Bulletin (2016).

8. Religious Imagination and Hajj Reform

The Hajj is long overdue for reform and reinvention. The yawning gap between its eternal ideals and its tragic realty is an open secret that every pilgrim shares as freely as the Zamzam water and dates she brings back home. The 'ulama are a necessary but flawed part of the reform equation. Divided and compromised by dependence on official patronage, they often lack both power and legitimacy. When they enjoy popularity, they have little influence on policy. When they gain formal authority, it erodes their credibility. A few of the more adaptive 'ulama acquire enough modern education to compete with lay professionals and intellectuals, but they usually find it hard to gain equal standing.

An invaluable contribution of the 'ulama is their constant contradiction of each other's views. For Muslims everywhere, this invites debate instead of stifling it. Rulers and ideologues who try to monopolize religious authority or to wrap themselves in self-spun legitimacy will always feel the stings of gadflies beyond their reach. Dissenters bucking the mainstream and innovators pushing the envelope can mine the countless principles, parables, and analogies that Islamic scholars put at everyone's disposal. Whenever Saudi Arabia and other states place new limits on pilgrim numbers and movement, preachers from every school will demand a solid justification for compromising the inherent right of free access to God's house and its sacred surroundings. Each time an egalitarian voice offers a critical reinterpretation of ritual practice, there will be a hadith, hoja's tale or poetic couplet that sounds tailor-made for the occasion.

With their distinctive blend of principle and pragmatism, Muslim scholars have eased the way for each generation to recreate the pilgrimage in light of changing times and needs. Focusing on sincere intention rather than ritual precision, clear-sighted 'ulama have given Hajjis permission to bury many outmoded and dangerous customs so that they can avoid burying one another. The examples are legion and multiplying year by year—saluting the Black Stone from a distance instead of rushing in to kiss it, pausing briefly on the chaotic Muzdalifa plain rather than spending the entire night, letting younger and stronger Hajjis stone the devils on behalf of the aged and infirmed, buying a ticket to share in the vicarious sacrifice of a common animal instead of slaughtering your own and leaving the remains to rot in the desert, and many other common-sense shortcuts that were once thought to make a Hajj invalid in God's eyes.

Today Muslims of all backgrounds—lay people as well as religious leaders—are debating further breaks with longstanding custom and doctrine as they envision a Hajj for the future. Most people are unwilling to limit their choices to the leading options—seasonal cycles of scandal and group funerals or the Saudi business plan for a year-round theme park. Many alternative proposals are coming into circulation, but three have stirred the greatest interest thus far—further internationalizing the current Hajj regime, refashioning the Hajj-Umrah calendar, and encouraging the cross-fertilization of global pilgrimages in all of the major faiths. Let us briefly consider each of these possible futures.

Internationalizing Hajj policy is a path that Muslim leaders supposedly embraced more than twenty years ago when Saudi Arabia was desperate for any help it could muster to fend off the Islamic revolution in Iran. When Saudi rulers had their backs to the wall, they did their best to appear open-minded. All Muslim states would run the Hajj together through the Organization of Islamic Cooperation (OIC). Saudi Arabia's sovereign territorial rights would be conditional rather than absolute. Sovereignty would be balanced by two God-given principles that no ruler could violate—the right of all Muslims to visit the holy cities as well as the duty to preserve their history and environment as part of the common heritage of mankind.

But as Iranian pressures abated, Saudi Arabia slid back into unilateralism—decreeing and demolishing first and consulting later, if at all. By allowing the Saudis to block substantial moves toward collective decision-making, Muslim governments have discredited the original agenda and themselves to an extent that may be irreversible. Even if Saudi leaders returned to the internationalization program—and there is no sign they ever will—it would probably be too late to matter. Popular support for the quota system is evaporating and historic Mecca has all but vanished.

In Hajj affairs, the OIC is just as toothless now as in the 1980s when it assumed the nebulous responsibility to supervise the Saudi supervisors. International regimes have fallen on hard times everywhere in the upsurge of geopolitics and Great Power rivalry. Under such conditions, Middle Eastern leaders will be less likely than ever to revive the waning enthusiasm for transnational institutions and norms. If the OIC ever gains the authority to fulfill its supposed Hajj mandate, it is likely to be under Turkish and Iranian auspices—perhaps in a post-Saudi era—and this time with more sympathy from Moscow and Beijing than from Washington and Brussels (Sola 2016).

Using Islam's lunar calendar to weave a tapestry of seasonal pilgrimages has deep roots in popular belief and practice. Nearly every Muslim society and subculture has evolved a comfortable rhythm of movement around sacred months and annual festivals with special meanings. These pilgrimage subsystems frequently overlap and constantly change in relative importance. All of them also have multiple non-religious functions, allowing pragmatic adaptation to economic, political, and international realities.

Reinventing pilgrimages has become an integral part of Islamic tradition. Shedding old customs in favor of new ones is not only customary, it is also authentic and progressive at the same time. When modern Muslims think about revaluing and reordering the Hajj and Umrah, they speak to urgent needs of the present and the future while also tapping into histories and collective memories that are older than Islam itself.

Today, the most radical proposals for adjusting the pilgrimage calendar are not the Saudi campaign to expand and commercialize the Umrah, but efforts to redefine the Hajj season altogether. If Muslims could perform the Hajj over a longer time period—two or three months instead of a couple of weeks—they could save countless lives throughout the year. According to this view, the next 14 pilgrimage seasons need not be marred by another 91,000 fatalities if Muslims honor the Hajj by making it in safety at flexible times (Karaca 2016; masjidtucson.org 2016).

These arguments are consistent with many trends that have already gained momentum in official policy and public opinion. Governments and religious leaders in many countries are urging Muslims to avoid multiple Hajjs in favor of going on Umrah or staying home and making more generous gifts to charities. They are telling younger and wealthier people to delay their Hajjs so that the elderly and disadvantaged can move to the head of the waiting lists. Individuals and families are putting a higher premium on comfort and value regardless of the months they choose for travel (BBC News 2004).

Sometimes policy-makers and religious authorities appear to be guiding mass behavior, but at other times they are simply bending to what they perceive as the wisdom of crowds and the shifting preferences of voter-consumers. A typical example is playing out in Egypt where government, business, and religious leaders have been arm wrestling over pilgrimage practices that most people regarded as long-settled and taken for granted. Saudi authorities decided to increase fees for Umrah visas and President Sisi objected, ordering Egyptian travel agents to boycott the Umrah until the previous rates were reinstated. Tourism firms saw a whole year's revenue flying out the window, but their state-dominated professional syndicate had to toe the official line (Mikhail 2016).

Egypt's religious scholars jumped into the fray, staking out positions on both sides. The Cairo-based leader of Dar al-'Ifta—a government mouthpiece—pronounced that the limits on Umrah travel were justified by the public interest in conserving scarce resources during a downturn in the nation's economy. In response, an al-Azhar scholar in Tanta denounced the ban as illegal because it violated Muslims' rights of unfettered access to the holy cities. Like good contract lawyers everywhere, these 'ulama marshaled unassailable principles to defend contradictory interests—a sure sign that horse trading was well underway and that all parties were counting the minutes to a deal.

In theory, the Hajj is also inviolable and immutable, but in practice it is eminently negotiable. The Saudis have used the quota system to reward and punish one country after another for political positions that have nothing to do with pilgrimage or religion. Hajj managers and politicians throughout the Muslim world have responded in kind—agreeing to implement Saudi directives if they could hand out a few thousand extra slots to their supporters in time for the next election (Adam 2016).

Eventually, we could witness similar bargaining over the length of the Hajj season and its connections to the wider pilgrimage calendar. Conventional religious authorities such as the classically-trained 'ulama might be reluctant to bring flextime to the Hajj. However, they long ago become followers and middle-men in such policy debates, deferring to the views of politicians, professionals, and citizens. If the 'ulama think the tides are moving toward an extended Hajj season—or even an uninterrupted year-round Hajj—they'll probably go with the flow instead of trying to push it backwards.

Yet another approach to Hajj reform looks beyond the Islamic world to consider the possible contributions of pilgrimage in improving relations among all global religions. This is certainly the most idealistic of the three agendas discussed here—audacious, utopian, and desperately needed by a world that seems determined to tear itself apart using religion as the most lethal weapon in its growing arsenals.

Islamic civilization has always overlapped and interacted with other transnational religions and those connections have become more intimate than ever as Muslim communities fill all corners of the globe. Millions of people across Asia and Africa are accustomed to participating in multi-faith pilgrimages—common sites where worshippers from different traditions share blessings from juxtaposed manifestations of the sacred. Muslims benefit from these pilgrimages whether they are labeled as predominately Islamic or partially Islamic or originally non-Islamic.

The Hajj was an Arabian pilgrimage long before it became an Islamic festival (Peters 1994a; Peters 1994b). It has never stopped evolving and could move in many future directions (Wolfe 2015). The Hajj could become an ecumenical gathering with room for non-Muslims. It could serve as a rotating opportunity to partner with the fixed pilgrimages of other faiths that hold their events on the same dates every year. In Malaysia and Singapore, Muslims and non-Muslims regularly celebrate together when Hari Raya Ramadan coincides with the Chinese lunar New Year. Lebanese Christians and Muslims open their doors to one another when the Prophet's birthday falls near Christmas time. In Nigeria, Yoruba families commonly include Muslim, Christian, and animist relatives who live under the same roof and intermarry with equally mixed neighbors. If Muslims in plural societies enjoy sharing their religious holidays with non-Muslims, then perhaps the Hajj can provide similar opportunities for all of humanity to become more cosmopolitan and more human.

Conflicts of Interest: The author declares no conflict of interest.

References

Adam, Shamim. 2016. Fears over Malaysia Mecca Fund Test Najib's Main Support Base. *Bloomberg*, March 9. Available online: https://www.bloomberg.com/news/articles/2016-03-09/fears-over-malaysia-mecca-fund-test-najib-s-biggest-supporters (accessed on 16 March 2017).

Adama, Hamadou. 2009. The Hajj: Between a Moral and a Material Economy. *Afrique Contemporaine* 3: 119–38. [CrossRef]

Ahmad, Syed Neaz. 2009. Burma's Exiled Muslims. *Guardian*, October 12.

Ahmed, Chanfi. 2009. Networks of Islamic NGOs in sub-Saharan Africa: Bilal Muslim Mission, African Muslim Agency (Direct Aid), and *al-Haramayn*. *Journal of Eastern African Studies* 3: 426–37. [CrossRef]

Al-Akhbar. 2016. Al-Mawt fi Diyafat al-Sa'ud: Wafa 90 Alf Hajj wa Mu'atamar fi 14 'Aman [Death in the Hospitality of al-Saud: 90 Thousand Hajj and Umrah Deaths in 14 Years]. September 23. Available online: http://www.al-akhbar.com/node/264560 (accessed on 16 March 2017).

Amiri, Reza Ekhtiari, Ku Hasnita Binti Ku Samsu, and Hassan Gholipour Fereidouni. 2011. The Hajj and Iran's Foreign Policy towards Saudi Arabia. *Journal of Asian and African Studies* 46: 678–90.

Arab News. 2016. Umrah Visas Closed: Egyptians Top List. June 26. Available online: http://www.arabnews.com/node/945176/saudi-arabia (accessed on 16 March 2017).

Aw, Samba. 2015. La Problématique au Sénégal du Pèlerinage à la Mecque ou aux Lieux Saints de l'Islam. *enqueteplus.com*, September 30. Available online: http://www.enqueteplus.com/content/la-problematique-au-senegal-du-pelerinage-la-mecque-ou-aux-lieux-saints-de-l%E2%80%99islam (accessed on 16 March 2017).

BBC News. 2004. Mecca Pilgrimage: Can It Be Made Safe? February 9. Available online: http://news.bbc.co.uk/2/hi/talking_point/3449239.stm (accessed on 16 March 2017).

BBC News. 2015. Hajj Crush: Mali Facebook Page Set Up to Find Missing Pilgrims. October 13. Available online: http://www.bbc.com/news/world-africa-34516133 (accessed on 16 March 2017).

Bennafla, Karine. 2005. L'instrumentalisation du pèlerinage à La Mecque à des fins commerciales: l'Exemple du Tchad. In *Les pèlerinages au Maghreb et au Moyen-Orient*. Edited by Sylvia Chiffoleau and Anna Madoeuf. Damas: Presses de l'Ifpo, pp. 193–202.

Bianchi, Robert R. 2004. *Guests of God: Pilgrimage and Politics in the Islamic World*. New York: Oxford University Press.

Bianchi, Robert R. 2007. Travel for Religious Purposes. Oxford Encyclopedia of the Islamic World. *Oxford Islamic Studies Online*. Available online: http://bridgingcultures.neh.gov/muslimjourneys/items/show/187 (accessed on 16 March 2017).

Bianchi, Robert R. 2013. *Islamic Globalization: Pilgrimage, Capitalism, Democracy, and Diplomacy*. Singapore and London: World Scientific Publishers.

Bianchi, Robert R. 2014. The Hajj in Everyday Life. In *Everyday Life in the Muslim Middle East*. Edited by Donna Lee Bowen, Evelyn A. Early and Becky Schulthies. Bloomington: Indiana University Press, pp. 319–28.

Bianchi, Robert R. 2015a. The Hajj and Politics in Contemporary Turkey and Indonesia. In *Hajj: Global Interactions through Pilgrimage*. Edited by Luitgard Mols and Marjo Buitelaar. Leiden: National Museum of Ethnology, pp. 65–82.

Bianchi, Robert R. 2015b. Islamic Globalization and Its Role in China's Future. *Journal of Middle Eastern and Islamic Studies (in Asia)* 9: 29–48.

Bianchi, Robert R. 2016. Hajj By Air. In *The Hajj: Pilgrimage in Islam*. Edited by Eric Tagliacozzo and Shawkat M. Toorawa. New York: Cambridge University Press, pp. 131–51.

Bianchi, Robert R. 2017. The Hajj and Politics in China. In *Muslim Pilgrimage in the Modern World*. Edited by Babak Rahimi and Peyman Eshaghi. Durham: University of North Carolina Press.

Michel Boivin Boivin, and Rémy Delage, eds. 2015. *Devotional Islam in Contemporary South Asia: Shrines, Journeys and Wanderers*. Abingdon and New York: Routledge.

British Muslim Experiences of the Hajj. 2015. Hajj Tour Operators and Pilgrim Markets. September 24. Available online: https://arts.leeds.ac.uk/hajj/exhibition/hajj-tour-operators-and-pilgrim-markets (accessed on 16 March 2017).

Carey, Glen, and Vivian Nereim. 2017. Saudi Arabia's Full Statement to Bloomberg on Its 2017 Agenda. *Bloomberg News*, March 6.

Commission Electorale Independante. 2010. Election du President de la Republique, Scrutin du 31 October 2010. November 3. Available online: http://www.ceici.org/elections/docs/EPR_31102010_RESUL_PROVI_CEI_03112010_A4.png (accessed on 16 March 2017).

Conférence des Evêques Catholiques de Côte d'Ivoire. 2016. Lieux de Pèlerinage. Available online: http://www.eglisecatholique-ci.org/index.php?page=lieu (accessed on 16 March 2017).

Cormier, Hégésippe. 2016. Location map of the «zone de confiance» created in Côte d'Ivoire after the Civil War. Available online: https://en.wikipedia.org/wiki/First_Ivorian_Civil_War#/media/File:C%C3%B4te_d%27Ivoire_ZDC.png (accessed on 16 March 2017).

Daily Sabah. 2015. Turkey's President Erdoğan Visits Mecca for Islamic Umrah Pilgrimage. March 1. Available online: http://www.dailysabah.com/religion/2015/03/01/turkeys-president-erdogan-visits-mecca-for-islamic-umrah-pilgrimage (accessed on 16 March 2017).

Dhaka Tribune. 2013. Riyadh Blacklists Thirty-One Hajj Agencies for Trafficking. April 30. Available online: http://archive.dhakatribune.com/bangladesh/2013/apr/30/riyadh-blacklists-31-hajj-agencies-trafficking (accessed on 16 March 2017).

Dima-Macabando, Labimombao A. 2015. Lanao Del Sur Pilgrims' Perceptions of Philippine Hajj Management 2010–2012: Basis for an Intervention Program. Paper presented at the 3rd Global Summit on Education, Kuala Lumpur, Malaysia, March 9–10.

Dioum, Cheikh Bamba. 2014. Organisation du Pèlerinage à la Mecque: Pourquoi la Privatisation est la Solution. *Rue Publique.com*, April 7. Available online: http://www.sunuker.com/2014/04/07/organisation-du-pelerinage-a-la-mecque-pourquoi-la-privatisation-est-la-solution (accessed on 16 March 2017).

Direction Générale des Cultes Commissariat du Hadj. 2016. Liste de Pelerins Pour Un Vol. August 16. Available online: http://radio-albayane.com/VOL08.png (accessed on 16 March 2017).

Donaghy, Rori, and Linah Alsaafin. 2015. Hundreds of Mauritanian Women Trafficked to Saudi Arabia Trapped in "Slavery". *Middle East Eye*, September 30.

Dorsey, James M. 2017. Think That 2016 Was a Tough Year for Saudi Arabia? Wait Till You See 2017. *International Policy Digest*, January 2.

Economist. 2011. Côte d'Ivoire's New President: The King of Kong. *Economist*, April 20. Available online: http://www.economist.com/node/18587205 (accessed on 16 March 2017).

Economist. 2015. The Economist Explains Why the Haj Is Safer Than Ever. September 21. Available online: http://www.economist.com/blogs/economist-explains/2015/09/economist-explains-14 (accessed on 16 March 2017).

Financial Express. 2013. Private Hajj Operators Suffer Blow over Human Trafficking Claim. June 22. Available online: http://print.thefinancialexpress-bd.com/old/more.php?page=detail_news&date=2013-06-22&news_id=173927 (accessed on 16 March 2017).

Fisk, Robert. 2016. For the First Time, Saudi Arabia is Being Attacked by Both Sunni and Shia Leaders. *Independent*, September 22.

Ghana Review International. 2012. Drug Baron Busted in Mecca: A Member of the Task Force of Ghana's Hajj Council Has Been Arrested in Saudi Arabia over Drugs. October 15. Available online: http://www.ghanareview.com/Restyle/index2.php?class=all&date=2012-10-15&id=55307 (accessed on 16 March 2017).

Haj Committee of India. 2008–2016. *Annual Reports, 2008–2016*. Mumbai: Ministry of Minority Affairs.

Haj Committee of India. 2016. Number of Deceased Pilgrims during Haj 1990–2016. Available online: http://www.hajcommittee.gov.in/previous_records.aspx (accessed on 16 March 2017).

Hardy, Ferdaous, and Jeanne Semin. 2009. Fissabililllah! Islam au Sénégal et Initiatives Féminines: Une Économie Morale du Pèlerinage à La Mecque. *Afrique Contemporaine* 3: 139–53. [CrossRef]

Hoshur, Shohret. 2016. Uyghur Muslims Detained in Turkey as They Attempt the Hajj. *Radio Free Asia*, May 18.

Huda, Kashif-ul. 2015. Hajj Pilgrim Numbers as Economic Indicator for Indian Muslims. *TwoCircles.net*, July 28. Available online: http://twocircles.net/2015jul28/1438057240.html (accessed on 16 March 2017).

Human Rights Watch. 2005. Country on a Precipice: The Precarious State of Human Rights and Civilian Protection in Côte d'Ivoire. Available online: https://www.hrw.org/sites/default/files/reports/cdi0505.png (accessed on 16 March 2017).

Hurriyet Daily News. 2011. Umrah Applications from Turkey on Rise. July 13. Available online: http://www.hurriyetdailynews.com/default.aspx?pageid=438&n=umrah-applications-from-turkey-on-rise-2011-07-13 (accessed on 16 March 2017).

Jalabi, Raya. 2016. After the Hajj: Mecca Residents Grow Hostile to Changes in the Holy City. *Guardian*, September 14.

Kaplan, Seth. 2012. Côte d'Ivoire's Ethnic, Religious, and Geographical Divisions. June 6. Available online: http://www.fragilestates.org/2012/06/06/cote-divoire-ethnic-division (accessed on 16 March 2017).

Karaca, Hüseyin. 2016. A Spiritual Season: The Three Sacred Months. April 5. Available online: http://www.lastprophet.info/a-spiritual-season-the-three-sacred-months (accessed on 16 March 2017).

Kingdom of Saudi Arabia, Ministry of Health. 2016. Statement of Deaths during Period from 1423 to 1437. Available online: http://www.al-akhbar.com/sites/default/files/pdfs/20160909/doc20160909.png (accessed on 16 March 2017).

Law, Bill. 2015. Hajj Stampede: Strain on al-Sauds amid Feuds, War and Incompetence. *Independent*, September 25.

masjidtucson.org. 2016. The Four Months of Hajj. Available online: http://www.masjidtucson.org/submission/practices/hajj/foursacredmonths.html (accessed on 16 March 2017).

McLoughlin, Seán. 2013. Organizing Hajj-Going from Contemporary Britain: A Changing Industry, Pilgrim Markets and the Politics of Recognition. In *The Hajj: Collected Essays*. Edited by Venetia Porter and Liana Saif. London: British Museum Press, pp. 241–52.

Mikhail, George. 2016. What's Behind Egyptian Campaign to Delay Saudi Pilgrimages? *Almonitor*, December 16.

Miran, Jonathan. 2009. *Red Sea Citizens: Cosmopolitan Society and Cultural Change in Massawa*. Bloomington: Indiana University Press.

Miran-Guyon, Marie. 2014. Côte d'Ivoire: Bouake, capitale de l'islam cosmopolite. *Agence Anadolu*, April 28.

Miran-Guyon, Marie. 2015. Côte d'Ivoire: Un civisme musulman à toutes épreuves. *La Revue du Projet*, May 23.

Ndiaye, Fatou. 2016. Sénégal: Pélerinage 2016 aux Lieux Saints de—Craintes d'une édition ratée. *All Africa*, February 2.

Nehme, Dahlia. 2016. For Illegal Pilgrims in Mecca, God's Blessings Transcend Secular Law. *Reuters*, September 14.

Onishi, Norimitsu. 2010. In Indonesia, Many Eyes Follow Money for Hajj. *New York Times*, August 5.

oxfordbusinessgroup.com. 2014. Stay for a While: New Visa Regulations Give Umrah Pilgrims the Chance to Extend Their Visit and Explore the Kingdom. Available online: https://www.oxfordbusinessgroup.com/analysis/stay-while-new-visa-regulations-give-umrah-pilgrims-chance-extend-their-visit-and-explore-kingdom (accessed on 16 March 2017).

Peters, Francis E. 1994a. *The Hajj: The Muslim Pilgrimage to Mecca and the Holy Places*. Princeton: Princeton University Press.

Peters, Francis E. 1994b. *Mecca: A Literary History of the Muslim Holy Land*. Princeton: Princeton University Press.

Razavi, Seyed Mansour, Ahmad Sabouri-Kashani, Hossein Ziaee-Ardakani, Aminreza Tabatabaei, Mojgan Karbakhsh, Hamidreza Sadeghipour, Seyed Abdolreza Mortazavi-Tabatabaei, and Payman Salamati. 2013. Trend of Diseases among Iranian Pilgrims during Five Consecutive Years Based on a Syndromic Surveillance System in Hajj. *Medical Journal of the Islamic Republic of Iran* 27: 179–85. [PubMed]

RT News. 2016. Saudi Arabia to Move from Oil, Earn More from Hajj. March 25. Available online: https://www.rt.com/business/337135-saudi-hajj-revenues-oil/ (accessed on 16 March 2017).

SahilOnline. 2013. Three More Government Hajj Houses in Karnataka. June 3. Available online: http://www.sahilonline.org/newsDetails.php?cid=1&nid=18383 (accessed on 16 March 2017).

Saudi Gazette. 2016. More Than 5m Arrive for Umrah. May 26. Available online: http://saudigazette.com.sa/saudi-arabia/5m-arrive-umrah (accessed on 16 March 2017).

Sola, Katie. 2016. Breaking with Iran Could Cost Saudi Arabia Billions in Revenue from Pilgrims. *Forbes*, January 5.

Tagliacozzo, Eric. 2013. *The Longest Journey: Southeast Asians and the Pilgrimage to Mecca*. New York: Oxford University Press.

T.C. Diyanet İşleri Başkanlığı. 2016. *Din İstatistikleri, 2005–2015*. Ankara: T.C. Diyanet İşleri Başkanlığı.

T.C. Diyanet İşleri Başkanlığı. 2014. Yaş gruplarına göre hacca umreye gidenlerin sayısı [Number of Hajj and Umrah Goers by Age Groups]. *dinihaberler.com*, December 31. Available online: http://www.dinihaberler.com.tr/html/diyanet-1.html (accessed on 16 March 2017).

Vaidyanathan, A. 2012. Phase out Haj Subsidy in Ten Years, Supreme Court Tells. May 8. Available online: http://www.ndtv.com/india-news/phase-out-haj-subsidy-in-ten-years-supreme-court-tells-govt-10-big-facts-481470 (accessed on 16 March 2017).

Whitman, Elizabeth. 2015. Ramadan 2015: Mecca Visits Top 14 Million, Breaking Record for First 16 Days of Muslim Holy Month. *International Business Times*, July 7.

Wolfe, Michael. 2015. *One Thousand Roads to Mecca: Ten Centuries of Travelers Writing about the Muslim Pilgrimage*. New York: Grove/Atlantic.

World Bulletin. 2016. Humans of Hajj is Bringing Stories of Pilgrims in Mecca. September 9. Available online: http://www.worldbulletin.net/news/177193/humans-of-hajj-is-bringing-stories-of-pilgrims-in-mecca (accessed on 16 March 2017).

Yamba, C. Bawa. 1995. *Permanent Pilgrims: The Role of Pilgrimage in the Lives of West African Muslims in Sudan*. Washington: Smithsonian Institution Press.

Yeni Şafak. 2015. Hajj Quota Reduction Puts Turkey in Tight Spot. September 15. Available online: http://www.yenisafak.com/en/life/hajj-quota-reduction-puts-turkey-in-tight-spot-2239701 (accessed on 16 March 2017).

Article

Gender, Madness, Religion, and Iranian-American Identity: Observations on a 2006 Murder Trial in Williamsport, Pennsylvania

Camron Michael Amin

Department of Social Sciences-History, University of Michigan-Dearborn, 1270 SSB (Social Sciences Building), 4901 Evergreen Rd, Dearborn, MI 48128, USA; camamin@umich.edu

Received: 12 June 2017; Accepted: 25 July 2017; Published: 1 August 2017

Abstract: Using participant observation, oral history interviews, and a study of court transcripts, Internet chats, and press coverage of a 2006 murder trial of an Iranian-American man in Williamsport, Pennsylvania, we can better appreciate the dynamic intersection of ethnicity, religion, and gender in constructing the social identity of Iranian-Americans. Brian Hosayn Yasipour, who immigrated to the United States in 1969, was convicted of murder in the third degree for killing his four-year-old daughter in 2001 during a custody dispute with his estranged, Iranian-born wife. He managed to avoid the death penalty. Debates about his guilt *in America* hinged on assessments of his mental state at the time of the crime and this, in turn, hinged on debates about how normative his actions would have been *in Iran*. Until his arrest, Brian had led a highly mobile life—moving back and forth between America, where he lived as a Christian, and Iran, where he visited as a Muslim. Was he a calculating Iranian-Islamic patriarch, outraged at the defiance of his wife and the attitudes of American courts toward his paternal rights? Or was he, per the court transcripts, a "white Christian" and survivor of childhood rape back in Iran, who lapsed into madness under the strain of his second divorce? Brian actively blurred these issues in court appearances before and after the murder—often expressing his agency in terms of preserving his imaginary and physical mobility.

Keywords: Iran; America; immigration; Muslim; filicide; gender; identity; mobility; Islamophobia; homophobia

---

1. Introduction

1.1. Overview

In this study I make use of a "regimes of im/mobility" approach (Schiller and Salazar 2013; Hackl et al. 2016) to analyze how ethnic identity, religious identity and gender ideology influenced the trial of an Iranian-American man in Williamsport, Pennsylvania for murder. Trial transcripts clearly illustrate how both the defense and prosecution exploited the ambiguity of Brian Yasipour's identity to bolster arguments for and against the proposition that Brian was legally insane at the time of the crime. But they also illustrate that Brian himself did not simply exist in a liminal state—not quite American, not quite Iranian—but deliberately moved between Iranian and American contexts both physically and conceptually from the time he arrived in the United States in 1969 until his arrest. He continued to assert his mobility conceptually while incarcerated, both before and after his conviction.

This study is also based on my observations as a pro bono consultant to pre-trial preparations of Brian's attorneys from 2004–2006, interviews with a number of participants conducted between 2010 and 2014, local media coverage, and the Internet postings of individuals who monitored the trial. These sources clearly illustrate the instability of the social categories applied to Brian Yasipour and his family by the Court and local community. The trial accomplished a sort of judicial assimilation of Brian. The verdict transformed him from an Iranian immigrant, who was free to move between Iranian/Muslim and (White) American/Christian contexts, into an American murderer who was confined to prison. The final judicial word on the case by the Superior Court of Pennsylvania in 2008 provided no indication that Brian's identity was ever an issue at trial. Brian's appeal was entirely focused on whether or not the Lycoming County Court had fairly accounted for evidence in his insanity defense (Superior Court of Pennsylvania 2008, para. 7–8). The words "Iran," "Iranian" or "immigrant" are nowhere to be found that final legal record. Taking a "regimes of im/mobility" approach to available sources restores to the narrative the fact that ethnicity, religion, and gender ideology were inextricably entwined in the trial process itself, despite being erased in the verdict and subsequent legal opinions.

1.2. Structure of Article

It is beyond the scope of this article to develop all of the lines of inquiry that might emerge from a detailed case study such as this one. Section 1.3 describes the evolving methodology of this study and considers it in relation to the genre of microhistory and studies of the "cultural defense" trial strategy used to insulate foreign-born defendants from criminal liability. It argues, however, that there are compelling analytic possibilities related to gender, ethnicity, and religion. Section 1.4 argues further that the interrelated nature of gender, ethnicity, and religion in this case is most usefully analyzed through a "regimes of im/mobility" approach. It also presents the important contexts provided by different prisms: Iranian-American Studies, Middle Eastern/Islamic Studies, Women and Gender Studies and studies of the phenomenon of filicide itself. Sections 2.1–2.3 apply the "regimes of im/mobilty" approach to illustrate how Brian's gender ideology, ethnicity and religion influenced assessments of his sanity, which, in turn were the key to assessing his guilt. Section 3 offers a concluding discussion of the implications of both the findings and limitations of this study for future research.

1.3. Brian Killed Susan: Trial as Applied Microhistory

Criminal trials, it should be noted, are unusual in the United States, and this was certainly the case in Pennsylvania. In a study of convictions of 12 different criminal offences from 1997 to 2000 in Pennsylvania, only 3.7% (2537) of convictions were obtained by bench trial, and 2% (1365) by jury trial. The remaining 63,899 convictions were the result of plea deals (King et al. 2005). So, for a historian, having a rich criminal trial transcript to examine is both a windfall and a challenge. Transcripts of trials have long served as an important source of social history. Beginning with the work of Ronald C. Jennings (Jennings 1999, for his collected works), studies of court records have had an enduring impact on Middle Eastern, Islamic and Women and Gender Studies (e.g., (Tucker 1998; Pierce 1999)). In Iranian Studies, fieldwork in contemporary Iranian family courts has catalogued not only patriarchal practices in the Islamic Republic of Iran but also women's resistance to such practices (Mir-Hosseini and Longinatto 2003; Osanloo 2006a, 2006b).

The genre of microhistory—the study of a discrete, short-term event as a microcosm of a wider social world—was arguably born with the close study of a trial record. Like Menocchio in Carlo Ginzburg's classic microhistory, *The Cheese and the Worms: The Cosmos of a Sixteenth-Century Miller* (Ginzburg 1980), much of what we know about Brian is through his interaction with a judicial process that put his idiosyncrasies into relief against other cultural norms. There are, of course, crucial and essential differences between the circumstances under study here and those taken on by Ginzburg. Menocchio's life was forfeit for articulating his beliefs—beliefs deemed heretical by a Catholic church in the midst of the brutalities and polemics of the Counter-Reformation. Brian's life was in jeopardy for a brutal act of murder. If Menocchio had recanted, his life would have been spared. Brian's crime, if proven, could not simply be excused.

Much ink has been spilled, including by its practitioners, to define microhistory to everyone's satisfaction (Brown 2003; Findlen 2003, 2005; Ginzburg et al. 1993; Ginzburg 2005; Lamoreaux 2006; Lapore 2001; Putnam 2006; Ze'evi 1998). How is it different from biography or closely descriptive field notes? Why lose the historically significant "forests" amidst close study of local or short-lived "trees?" How might a microhistorical approach be applied in this or that subfield of history? For me, microhistory is the closest description of the result of my evolving research methodology. Brian Yasipour's trial was "exceptional typical"—to follow Matti Peltonen (Peltonen 2001). The most essential sources—the trial transcript and interviews—were "local" and form an inherit limit on the focus of study. At the same time, they are connected to a wider socio-cultural order and raise issues that are part of broader academic conversations—too many to elaborate upon equally within the scope of this article (See Section 1.4).

One reason we have such a rich transcript in this case is because up until a month before the trial, it was set to be a death penalty case tried before a jury. Both sides had spent years preparing for that eventuality. Then, on 22 February 2006, the prosecution agreed to drop the death penalty in exchange for a bench trial. Yet, they proceeded initially with what they had prepared for a jury trial. Stephanie Farr, then of the *Williamsport Sun-Gazette*, covered the trial. She wrote, "Although it was not necessary ... the defense and prosecution opted to present opening statements to county Judge Dudley N. Anderson, the presiding judge in the bench-trial case (Farr 2006a)." For two days, calling on 22 witnesses, the prosecution laid out its case in exhaustive detail (YT, March 6th and 7th). "A class of junior and senior students from Montoursville High School who attended the trial on Monday were surprised by the monotony of the proceedings but more so by the photographs of young Susan ... 'The stuff on TV looks fake now,' Dawn Bennett, 18, of Montoursville said (Farr 2006a)."

The prosecution's theory of the case depended on a particular narrative of the day of the murder—an applied microhistory, if you will, built upon the testimony of police officers and forensic experts and eyewitnesses to a few key events in the days leading up to the murder. What follows is a summary of that applied microhistory, reflecting facts of the case that *were not contested* by the defense in the first two days of the trial. Brian killed Susan—of this, there is no doubt:

> He attacked her in an upstairs bedroom of a shabby green house on 1024 Memorial Drive in Williamsport, Pennsylvania. After sixty knife wounds, sometime between 4:00 and 4:30 p.m. on 24 August 2001, Susan succumbed. The coroner could not tell which wound killed her, but she could tell that Susan had tried to defend herself. She had no real chance of surviving the brutal attack. Brian was 52 and little Susan had not yet turned five. Her birthday was but three days away.
>
> After killing her, Brian checked the street. He went to a nearby Bi-Lo store and bought flowers. He came back and washed her clothes; he washed her body. He placed her back into bed and surrounded her with the flowers and with her favorite stuffed animals. He washed the two knives that he had used to kill her. They were his knives. This was his house. Susan was his daughter.
>
> At 7:15 p.m., a missionary stopped by the house. Brian sent him away saying it wasn't a good time. At 7:20 p.m., he went out to a dumpster and threw out some pornographic videotapes. At 7:25 p.m., Brian called 911 to report that he had found Susan dead. Police arrived at 7:27 p.m., and it was not long before Brian was taken into custody. He cooperated with police; he even helped them find Susan's mother, Amaneh, known in Williamsport as Mellie. She would be at the McDonald's on East 3rd, across from the Learning Works. Mellie and Brian were legally separated and just coming to the end of a long and bitter custody battle over Susan. That morning, Brian's visitation was reduced so that Susan could attend kindergarten. Brian was supposed to hand Susan back over to Mellie at the McDonald's at 8:00 p.m. that evening.
>
> At the police station, officers tried to build on Brian's cooperative behavior and coax a confession from him. He sobbed, looking at a picture of his daughter. For a while he maintained that he had found Susan after going to the Bi-Lo store to buy flowers. She looked scared, he said, so he had cleaned her up and placed her in his bed in new clothes,

> and with the stuffed animals and the flowers he had bought. He complained that he was hungry (and a diabetic), so an officer was sent to McDonald's. There, Mellie approached the officer. Brian had done this before—been late with Susan. Once before, in fact, he had kidnapped her. The week before Brian had followed Mellie and Susan from the McDonald's to the Learning Works and had threatened Mellie (but not Susan). Because of the way a custody hearing had gone earlier that day, she was worried that Brian had kidnapped Susan again. He had lost some of his visitation time so that Susan could start kindergarten in September, but she had agreed to let Brian have Susan for the afternoon following the hearing. Kidnapping was likely the worst thing Mellie could imagine Brian doing in response. Almost no one who testified—and certainly no one who knew the family well—had imagined Brian could do this.

The trial focused on the day of the murder, but it also examined many aspects of Brian's life before the trial (See Table A1 in Appendix A). For all that detail, it also left some information out of the discussion completely. Brian had not just sobbed at the sight of his daughter's photograph. Later that night he had confessed. Because Brian had not been properly Mirandized on the night of his arrest, Judge Anderson ruled his confession inadmissible on 22 November 2002 (Anderson 2002). All of the attorneys present at court in March 2006 and, of course, Judge Anderson himself, were aware of the confession but did not present it in open court or debate in any recorded sidebar in Judge Anderson's chambers. I, as a consultant to the defense, was not aware of the confession at the time. But since a record of it exists as part of the 22 November ruling, Brian's confession can be included in this analysis (Section 2.3).

Winning the motion to suppress Brian's confession was an important victory in the pre-trial period for his attorneys provided by the Public Defender's office, William Miele and Nicole Spring. Given the physical and circumstantial evidence, however, they also knew that the facts of the case would not exonerate Brian. "We ruled out self-defense pretty quick," Miele quipped. They were, of course, horrified by the crime but also obligated to provide a defense for Brian. Brian's history of mental illness would be crucial in defending his life, not his actions on 24 August. Miele had been worried about a jury trial, "for two reasons: one was the victim and the other was his nationality. Because this is a small, conservative, narrow-minded community." Nicole Spring added, "Any kind of Middle Eastern (*background*). The fear being that he killed a female child and is that going to be 'Okay, he thinks he has the right to' (Miele and Spring 2010, Time Index 7:38–8:28)?" Furthermore, Miele and Spring became aware of the prosecution's plan to use Brian's own words to help play to those biases and to undermine Brian's insanity defense. Prosecutor Michael Dinges was going to argue that Brian killed Susan in accordance with Iranian patriarchal norms. So, as part of preparations for what they assumed would be an inevitable "penalty phase" of the trial, they recruited me as a "cultural expert" on Iran to argue that Brian's actions would not, in fact, be considered "normal" in Iran. Rather, they intended to argue, Iran was the place where Brian's mental troubles began with the trauma of being raped by an older boy when he was twelve. I served in that role *pro bono* from late 2004 until the trial's conclusion in 2006 and, therefore, participated in the crafting of the hybrid cultural-insanity defense to counter the "cultural prosecution" Brian faced.

I raise these two issues here to highlight the essential methodological challenge of this study: I did not participate in the trial with the intent of observing it for academic study. But, as the trial date approached and I caught more glimpses of how the defense team was managing the issue of Brian's identity using my input about Iranian history and society, I resolved to reflect on what was happening as soon as the case reached its legal conclusion; this turned out to be the Superior Court of Pennsylvania's rejection of Brian's last appeal in 2008. With some funding from my campus, I ordered the full trial transcript (approximately 1200 pages, double-spaced) and traveled to Williamsport twice in 2010 to interview key participants. The transcripts were supplemented with several other court opinions on the case made available by the Lycoming Law Association (http://www.lycolaw.org).

I also revisited media coverage of the trial. My first impression of the local media coverage happened during the trial. This is because shortly before the trial, the defense team decided that the report I wrote for the Court would be sufficient and that it was unlikely that I would be called to testify about it. So, I did not attend the trial itself. As the trial progressed, they became less sure of that decision and wanted me to be available to testify by phone. So, each day during the trial, I scoured the Internet for glimpses of media coverage to supplement the brief updates I received from Miele and Spring. The most thorough coverage came from the *Williamsport Sun-Gazette*. But my search turned up something more: an active discussion on a web forum called *Forums for Justice*. Participants in this particular form of "non-institutional" media coverage of crime (Wheeler 2008) seem to obsess over abduction and murder cases—that of JonBenet Ramsey, in particular, with posts continuing to the time of writing. Two individuals dominated the five pages of posts on the "Yasipour thread" from 7 March to 19 April 2006: "Quinn" and "LurkerXIV." Quinn attended the trial and re-posted *Williamsport Sun-Gazette* coverage. In 2014, I had an opportunity to interview Stephanie Farr about her time covering the trial; she had not been aware of the FFJ discussions. At times, the substance of the virtual dialogue between Quinn and LurkerXIV epitomized the Islamophobic bias that Miele and Spring were afraid might exist in a local jury pool. But, as we shall see, their engagement with the Yasipours was more complicated than that.

In addition to the genre of microhistory, there was another academic prism through which I reflected upon this case: studies of "cultural defense." Volpp (2012) notes that the state employs metaphors about the legally imagined space of the homeland; these metaphors can change in accordance with attitudes about immigrants to support rulings against the interests of "non-White" immigrants and refugees. She also points out that both domestic and international legal orders divide the world into "failed states" with "pathological cultures," whose calling card is violence against women, versus (Western) states with functioning civil societies and "a monopoly on legitimate violence (Volpp 2006)." The prosecution's case might be thought of as an attempt to portray Brian as a typical product of a pathological foreign culture. In this reading his hyper-patriarchal gender ideology would have nothing to do with his damaged psyche. Instead, it was marker of his foreign-ness. A study of "cultural defense" in Belgium notes how it can be seen as a kind of performance in which a defense attorney actually emphasizes the foreignness of a client so that the jury will see the client's attorney as part of their society and be more receptive to the defense's argument (D'hondt 2010). A similar dynamic was evident in the transcript of the sidebar in Judge Anderson's chambers discussed in Section 2.2. Miele emphasized Brian's Iranian Muslim roots every bit as much as District Attorney Dinges, but to a different end: portraying Brian as the victim of a pathological culture. For the most part though, academic studies of "cultural defense" rest on close readings of legal opinions and related academic and journalistic commentary (For examples, see (Levine 2003; Demian 2008; Sharafi 2008)). The researchers in this field do not often engage with the participants in trials. They focus on case studies to examine the efficacy and policy consequences of cultural defenses. The only large-scale and long-term study of "cultural defenses" seems to have been undertaken in Israel. That study found that, in addition to the phenomenon of cultural defense, there were also many instances of cultural "offense" where convicts received harsher sentences because of their perceived difference from the dominant culture (Tomer-Fishman 2010). Furthermore, the most common reaction to cultural factors was to ignore or discount them. This is very much what happened, at the end of day, with Judge Anderson's verdict: the cultural offense and defense cancelled each other out to highlight "the science," in Judge Anderson's words (TY 2006, p. 136, 21 March), of expert psychological testimony.

Nevertheless, transcripts and press coverage of the trial illustrate that discussions of Brian's ethnicity, religion and gender ideology were entwined with debates over his sanity. And the question of his sanity was essential to his conviction. Brian's identities as an Iranian immigrant, as a convert from Islam to Christianity, and as a person afflicted by mental and physical illness were not overlooked or ignored by Judge Anderson. The microhistory of the process of judicial assimilation is lost in the final verdict, but preserved in all the sources being marshaled here. And there is another fact that emerges from those sources: Brian was not a passive recipient of this judicial assimilation. His agency was often expressed in terms of his mobility between Iranian and American culture. Just as it would be possible to consider the history of this trial entirely within the scholarly conversations about microhistory and "cultural defense," it would be possible to consider it within the subfields of Iranian Studies, Middle Eastern/Islamic Studies, Iranian-American Studies and Women and Gender Studies. However, the "regimes of im/mobility" approach allows us to benefit from the insights of those fields while permitting us to appreciate the dynamic way in which these insights would resonate with what participants did at the time and how they viewed the trial in retrospect.

1.4. Im/Mobilities as an Analytical Framework: Navigating the Intersection of Gender Ideology, Ethnicity, and Religion

Let's briefly consider some other academic conversations in which we might situate the history of this trial, beginning with the sub-field of Iranian-American/Diaspora Studies. The extraordinary circumstances here are precisely what make it challenging as "exceptional typical." Aside from the tragedy itself, there are other contrasts between Brian and the "typical" Iranian-American assimilation narrative. For example, the Yasipours do not seem to be well off financially in 2000, at a time when per capita income of Iranian-Americans was estimated to be more than 38% higher than for native-born Americans (Public Affairs Alliance of Iranian Americans 2014, *Iranian Americans: Immigration and Assimilation*, p. 12). Also, the Yasipours did not live in one of the states with a large concentration of Iranian-Americans: New York, Texas, Maryland, California, Virginia, Florida, Washington, D.C, and Georgia. Pennsylvania was estimated to have had a population of "foreign-born Iranians" of 2129 in 1990 and a population of "Iranian descent" of 4657 ca. 2000 (Fata and Rafii 2003, p. 11; Modarres 1998, p. 41). There was no Iranian enclave in Williamsport, and the Yasipours attended a church in nearby Montoursville.

It is difficult to score Brian's circumstances with the classic measures of assimilation, which are problematic in any case (Walters and Jimenez 2005; Alba and Roe 1997; Mostofi 2003). The rate of marriage outside of one's group is one such measure, with one Iranian-American advocacy group claiming it "to be estimated" at 50% (Public Affairs Alliance of Iranian Americans 2014, *Iranian Americans: Immigration and Assimilation*, p. 11). Aside from any skepticism about that estimate, was Brian's first marriage to American-born Betty Keller the one that should count toward this metric or his second marriage to the Iranian-born Amaneh/Mellie? Even the consideration of socioeconomic success—a metric to which Iranian American advocacy groups proudly point—is hard to resolve. Was Brian a more representative Iranian-American when he was a successful life insurance salesman in the 1980s, when he was disabled by mental illness in the 1990s, or when he was convicted of murder? The ephemeral position Brian occupied with respect to such analytical categories during his life does not invalidate those categories, of course. Nevertheless, it serves to remind us how much an individual's or a family's social standing can fluctuate relative to any group norm we may wish to deploy analytically.

When Judge Anderson and William Miele debate whether Brian should be fairly considered a "White Christian," this does touch on something that has been the subject of scholarly investigation in Arab-American Studies (Gualtieri 2009, especially pp. 52–80) and Iranian-American Studies, which examine the history of Middle Eastern immigrants attempting to assimilate "through the ultimate prize of White recognition ((Tehranian 2008, p. 1235); see also (Tehranian 2009))." A forthcoming study of "whiteness" by Neda Maghbouleh emphasizes the "instability" of that category in the identity of Iranian-Americans (Code Switch 2017, April 19, Time Index: 10:29–18:41), and that is certainly evident in the case of Brian Yasipour. Furthermore, it is not as though modern Iranian national identity itself has not also been subject to racialization (Zia-Ebrahimi 2016) or that Iranian society was immune from racist traditions of its own. Iranian visitors and immigrants could (and can) be alert to racism in America without reflecting on their own attitudes. For example, visiting the United States in 1945, the editor of Iran's main daily newspaper expressed shock at the Ku Klux Klan while also offering his own racist descriptions of minority neighborhoods in New York (Amin 2014, p. 171). In this case, however, the sources do not grant direct insight into whether the Yasipours thought of *themselves* as "white" or in racial terms at all.

And, as we shall see in Section 2.1, religion was a more visible component of Brian's presentation of his ethnicity in court. Brian did not just invoke Iranian ethnicity to remove himself imaginatively from American legal jurisdiction, but Islamic law and a highly patriarchal reading of Islamic/Iranian family norms. What the literature on Women and Gender Studies within Islamic Studies offers us is clarity on just how idiosyncratic and reductive Brian's expressed views on his "heritage culture" were. Iranian legal culture has been a hybrid system of European and Islamic jurisprudence for decades, no less dynamic than the American legal culture in which he was being tried. This point will be revisited in greater detail in Section 2.1.

Even if we were to ignore the Iranian/Muslim aspects of this story, it would be hard to describe this tragedy as typically "American" or representative of the filicide phenomenon in the USA or around the world. Based on a study of U.S. arrest records from 1976 to 2007, 15% of all homicides can be classified as filicide (involving victims of all ages). Mothers and fathers were equally likely to kill sons and daughters who are between the ages of one and 17 (3/4 of victims were under the age of 6). Only 5.5% of filicidal parents used "edged weapons" (including knives), compared with 49.2% using their bodies (e.g., fists) as weapons and 23.3% using firearms. Most alleged offenders arrested were white (the category to which Brian was classified). At age 52, Brian was among the 15.1% of alleged offenders in the USA aged between 41 and 60 years (Mariano et al. 2014). Researchers are still uncertain of the predictive value of known risk factors such as history of abuse, mental illness, family discord, and substance abuse to filicide. It is very difficult to predict and prevent filicidal ideation and action. Brian was in and out of family court for almost two decades before Susan's murder, but all who knew him were blindsided. For all his litigious and difficult behavior, Brian had no prior history of violence. Furthermore, per a Finnish study, the only certain way to prevent a filicidal parent from acting (on impulse or in some deliberate way) is to deny the parent access to the child (Lehti et al. 2012, p. 16). What is hard to predict is also hard to understand in retrospect. Simply constructing a new narrative with these prisms in mind will miss something important: the "real-time" fluidity and instability of Brian's social identity. Brian's assertions of different social identities and the variable ways in which he and his family were perceived during the trial rested on interrelated markers of their "otherness:" gender ideology, ethnicity and religion. A "regimes of im/mobility" approach can help us trace how different aspects of Brian's identity became visible and salient over the course of events and influenced the final verdict.

In formulating their "regimes of im/mobility" approach to the study of migration and transnationalism, Schiller and Salazar (Schiller and Salazar 2013) encourage a multi-faceted analysis. Analyses should try and account for individual agency in relation to "unequal globe-spanning relationships of power," as well as the "unequal relationalities" of local contexts, state actors, and class that can operate on an individual's mobility—facilitating it, restraining it (to the point of stasis) and interpreting it in a given contemporary moment, as well in historical context (Schiller and Salazar 2013, p. 200). With this 2006 trial in Williamsport we have a specific historical context with a lot of documentation relating to the actions of an individual. It involved a very high-stakes decision about that individual's mobility (imprisonment/execution versus death). And although there was never a doubt that the primary legal context would be local and "American," there was a lot of doubt about whether Brian was fully a member of that local American context and if some consideration should be given to a "foreign" cultural context in determining his guilt or innocence. Hackl argues in *Bounded Mobilities* (Hackl et al. 2016) for the need to move beyond the material manifestations of mobility to the conceptual. This is to bring into focus the interplay between identity and boundaries, the dynamics of imaginary, virtual and gendered im/mobilities and diverse combinations of mobility and immobility that can affect both the most confined and the most "hypermobile" individuals and groups (Hackl et al. 2016, pp. 19–34). As we shall see, on the conceptual level, Brian was "hypermobile"—moving back and forth between imaginary

Iranian/Muslim and American/Christian contexts. But, it was not just a flight of fancy on his part. Prior to his arrest he had moved back and forth between Iranian and American contexts. All this made assessments of his "true" cultural home by others more fluid also. The "interplay" between identity and boundaries in this case was almost entirely conceptual (as the crime and trial took place in Williamsport). That interplay comes into view most clearly through interrelated discussions of Brian's gender ideology (and whether his obsessive patriarchal outlook was "normal" in Iran), ethnicity (where the use of Persian serves as additional marker of his "otherness"), and religion (where Islam is "Iranian" and Christianity is "white" and American).

The most consistent feature of Brian's agency was his insistence on *mobility*—physical and cultural—between Iran and America. The trial process depended, in part, on deciding between competing implications of Brian's mobility. According to his defense attorneys, he could never fully abandon his Iranian origins or the trauma of childhood rape that he suffered there. According to the prosecution, he would never fully abandon his Iranian origins—particularly its uncompromising patriarchy—because it justified in his mind what he did to his daughter. In both legal arguments, a reductively Islamic and Iranian culture was not confined to another place. Iran was either where Brian made sense or it was the root of his madness even when his was in Williamsport. In both depictions, "Iran" formed a boundary around Brian's "American-ness." This was much less the case for his victims, his family.

State actors (the judicial and public health system in Williamsport) and societal actors (the Williamsport community, the press, and the public that followed the case online) acted to punish Brian, support Mellie, and memorialize Susan. Each of these actions had real and symbolic *immobilizing* aspects, finally assigning them into a local American context. For Brian, ultimately, this meant prison. For Mellie, it was acts of generosity such as a local church donating a plot for Susan's burial and Susan's inclusion in a local memorial for victims of child abuse. Mellie and Susan are never discussed as anything other than *natives* of Williamsport—they became conceptually fixed in that locality. There are two reasons this is important. First, Mellie's immigration to the United States depended on her relationship to Brian. As their relationship deteriorated, she needed the protection of the state and the support of the local Williamsport community to escape from him. Testimony regarding a bi-lingual confrontation between Mellie and Brian a week before Susan's murder highlights the unraveling of a "gendered immobility" in which women's mobility can depend on acts of "gender-related bargaining over their status, including the 'microphysics of domestic power' usually held by male householders (Bonfanti 2016, pp. 183–208, in (Hackl et al. 2016, pp. 30))." Second, it underscores the fact that the conceptual and imaginary aspects of im/mobility are at least as important as physical im/mobility in understanding the assimilative effects of the trial. No matter how it is discussed, "Iran" is only ever *an idea* that is invoked by state and individual actors to explain events that took place in America.

The most visible "state actor" in this analysis is the court system, as seen through court records and interviews with participants other than myself. And certainly my participation from 2004 to 2006 did limit my access to some of the other participants after the fact, notably the prosecutors, Michael Dinges and Kenneth Osokow. Accordingly, it was not possible to develop this analysis as a fully realized oral history, in which the recollections of all key individuals are analyzed in comparison with each other and other evidence. For the most part, though, my participation facilitated my access to information and people. The most visible individual actor in the study is Brian. My ability to interview Brian and reflect on accounts of his confession (in Section 2.3) provided evidence that is crucial to understanding how central mobility was in informing his actions, and, how concepts of mobility were entwined with Brian's transformation from an Iranian immigrant into an American murderer. The im/mobilities framework cannot and does not help explain every aspect of this narrative, but it does help us navigate the interrelated effects of gender ideology, ethnicity, and religion on the unfolding of this tragedy.

2. From Iranian Immigrant to American Murderer

The following three subsections discuss im/mobility with respect to gender, ethnicity and religion in turn. However, because gender, ethnicity and religion are interrelated in the sources they remain interrelated in the three discussions. Sections 2.1 and 2.2 analyze events that took place during the trial or were discussed during at trial (though not always in open court). Section 2.3 analyzes events and discussions that happened outside the courtroom but were closely connected to the trial process as it unfolded or in retrospect. These events and discussions informed the process of Brian's conviction even though they are absent from the verdict in 2006 and in subsequent legal opinions on the case.

2.1. Gendered Im/Mobility between Iranian and American Legal Systems

In 2002, Mellie had sued to finalize her divorce from Brian as he awaited trial for Susan's murder. In the course of court proceedings to bifurcate the marriage on 10 December, Brian said this:

> I am contesting the divorce because I do not believe in divorce, okay, and if she wants to get it, I have written her a letter. She has to go through proper channels [in Iran] to get it. Muslim marriage is not a sacrament but a simple legal agreement in which either party is free to [include] conditions. It's not a sacrament, so it's like a prenuptial agreement. I have another one [i.e., Iranian law in translation] from the Library of Congress. If you kill your child, you will not be charged. I can let you read it. It is in English. Okay, that's the law. If you like it or not. If a father, not a mother, if a father or grandfather or the father's side kill the child, you have to pay like $5000 to the mother, but you can't be charged. That's the law, you know, that—*we are really family oriented back there* (Yasipour vs. Yasipour, 10 December 2002 cited in (TY 2006, pp. 142–43, 7 March). Emphasis added.).

Brian's 2002 courtroom declaration became the centerpiece of the District Attorney Michael Dinges' case against Brian—a window on his motivation for killing Susan. Dinges could point to other facts and circumstances. The day of the murder Brian had lost some of his visitation privileges and had been effectively barred by Judge Nancy Butts from further legal action. Yet, he was able to use the possibility of granting Mellie a divorce to negotiate access to Susan on that afternoon even though it was not his turn to have her. Not only had he tried to cover up the crime by tampering with the scene, but he also had several thousand dollars in cash at the time of his arrest, consistent, they argued, with the intent to flee. To where? Iran—the place where Brian had opined—incorrectly—"If you kill your child you will not be charged." In 2002, Brian was asserting a kind of magical extraterritoriality that invoked two aspects of Islamic law—Iran's marital laws and criminal code at the time of the crime—in defense of his of marital rights under American law. In Brian's mind, the stigma of divorce in America would jeopardize his standing *in Iran*. This point was emphasized in the 2006 testimony of David Irwin, who represented Mellie in the 2002 divorce hearing:

> [Brian] didn't necessarily testify. He sort of made a speech. The speech repeatedly went into the fact that under Iranian law the parties are married pursuant to a contract between them, and talked about it being a multiple page contract with all of the contingencies and that the [American] Court didn't have jurisdiction over them under Iranian laws because they can't undo the contract. He said that repeatedly. He also said something to the effect, and I will paraphrase here, that if the Court in America were to grant the divorce and his wife were to remarry, that if he went to Iran he would be teased or harassed, or something along that line. He spoke for, it seemed, quite a long time about that. He was very coherent and clear in his position. The judge then made his ruling and made it clear that under American law that things are different and the elements to bifurcate the divorce are present. I think, if I recall, Mr. Yasipour thanked him when it was over. (TY 2006, pp. 136–37, 7 March)

Brian's representation of Iran's "family orientation" was hyper-patriarchal to the point of excusing paternal filicide and preserving male prerogatives in initiating divorce in Iranian law, which was governed by Twelver Shiᶜite Islamic jurisprudence. In rebuttal to this cultural prosecution Brian's attorneys argued that Brian was wrong about Iranian law. But it is important to understand that they were pushing back against an argument by the prosecution that also reductively portrayed Iranian and American cultures as irreconcilably different. The courtroom debates about Brian's true "cultural home" conceptually restricted Brian's efforts to move back and forth between Iran and America at will for his own benefit. Brian's transcultural mobility was not just conceptual. In fact, he had been utilizing it ever since he settled in the United States. He was well-established in Williamsport and well-known in the local courts. This was underscored early in the pre-trial process when Brian unsuccessfully petitioned Judge Anderson to recuse himself on 31 August 2001. Though it was just six days after Susan's death, Brian recalled with rancorous bravado that Anderson had represented his first wife, Betty, in 1989: "I remember that day very well that you were yelling 'Mr. Yasipour pay your child support, you have recent *inheritance* [emphasis added] ... (Anderson 2001, pp. 3–4).'" The only way Brian could have inherited from his Muslim family in Iran is if he was thought to be Muslim in Iran. Did Brian present himself differently when he lived in America after 1969 to how he presented himself when he visited Iran?

On 11 June 2010, I had an opportunity to ask Brian about this. "Are you a Muslim in Iran and a Christian in America?" I asked. "Yes," he said. Whether due to the stroke or the anti-depressants he was prescribed, Brian's face and voice were largely emotionless, but not cold, subdued, or robotic. There would be, at times, the faintest bit of urgency in his voice as he sought to clarify a point.

"If you were on Mars would you be a Christian or a Muslim?" I asked.

"Christian."

"What did you like about Christianity?"

"Love your neighbor."

A number of studies have shown that Iranian-Americans of Muslim origin tend to be either less committed to Islam ("spiritual," agnostic, or atheist or otherwise affiliated) or, to a lesser extent, to take the step of converting to some denomination of Christianity (Chaichian 1997; Mobasher 2012). What is unusual here, beyond the fact that Brian converted while still in Iran in 1968, was Brian's insistence on the advantages he perceived in Iranian law and society while simultaneously insisting on the advantages of living as a naturalized American and Christian convert in 2002. District Attorney Dinges was, in effect, calling his cultural bluff in 2006. Judge Anderson, however, did not take Brian's assertions about Iranian law at face value. He said, "I have trouble believing that any *even third world country* would have a law that says, 'Okay, you can buy your way into and out of murders of your children.' ... I kind of accept that is not the law of Iran (Emphasis added. (TY 2006, 21 March, pp. 7–8)." Anderson's intuition was correct. The Iranian legal system that Brian was attempting to conjure in defense of his marital rights and his legal culpability for Susan's death was not trapped in some patriarchal, "family-oriented" amber. It had been changing in the face of modern, globalizing cultural forces.

In 2001, Mohammad Eshaqi published a treatise on filicide in Iranian law that was a call for reform framed around equal punishment for fathers and mothers. The proposed reform was presented as both a defense of Islamic legal norms and of "dynamic jurisprudence" (*feqh-e puya*) in Twelver Shiʿism that is an Islamic Republican answer to pre-1979 legal reform in Iran. Eshaqi argued that all schools of Islamic law traditionally excluded filicide committed by fathers from *qeṣāṣ* (retaliation, i.e., the death penalty administered by the state on behalf of families who chose not to forgive the convict). Thus, filicide was outside the realm of *ḥadd* (required Koranic) punishments for crimes, and fell into the much larger realm of "discretionary" punishments, *taʿzir*, which have typically constituted the bulk of the criminal code in countries observing Islamic law.

In the Islamic Republic of Iran in 2001, filicide fell under Article 202 of the *ta'zir* criminal code. The question for Eshaqi was not whether the punishment was just but whether Article 202 could be revised to clarify that it would be applied equally to mothers and fathers who kill their children:

> [Current Article 202]: The father or grandfather that kills his own child should not be subject to *qesās*, yet shall pay a *diyeh* ("blood money") to the heirs of the victim and be subject to *ta'zir* (3–10 years for "intentional murder").

Proposed revision:

> The *father or grandfather or mother or grandmother* that kills their own child shall not be subject to *qesās*, yet shall pay the murder *diyeh* to the heirs of the victim and be subject to *ta'zir*. (Eshaqi 2001, p. 194)

Comparing Iranian law to British law, Eshaqi noted that "diminished capacity" (particularly its presumption in the case of mothers and the infanticide of children under 12 months) in British law is the functional equivalent of excusing parents from *qesās* in Islamic jurisprudence. In Eshaqi's view, the consensus opinion of Islamic jurisprudence is that no parent in their right mind would kill their own children; therefore, such acts of murder could never be fully intentional. While parents who kill their children cannot themselves be killed, they can very well be punished (Eshaqi 2001, pp. 197–202). True to form, Brian seems to have simply seized on the first clause of Article 202 that exempted him from *qesās* and omitted the punishment that was provided for in law. Brian did, however, get one thing right. Mothers who committed filicide were not given the same automatic exemption from *qesās* as fathers. They were liable for it, and, unless they had a sympathetic judge who could be convinced of a mitigating factor by an attorney, a mother who committed filicide (including infanticide) could be executed at the demand of the father's family. This is what indeed happened to one Sohayla Qadiri in 2009 after she was convicted of killing her five-day-old son (Parsā-ālipur 2009). Eshaqi's proposed reform was not just about sexual equality, but would also have had the effect of mitigating the disproportionate application of the death penalty to women compared to men who commit the same crimes. So, while Iranian-Islamic law assumed diminished capacity on the part of filicidal fathers and provided a (slim) chance to seek leniency for filicidal mothers, American law required diminished capacity to be decided case by case. The distance between the two legal worlds on the question of filicide was not as great as Brian represented it.

The clumsiness of Brian's impromptu attempt at legal hybridization notwithstanding, pre-modern Islamic jurisprudence in the Middle East (including in Iran) was a hybrid of regulations that flowed from religious precepts (though interpretations of the Koran and teachings of the Prophet Muhammad) and pragmatic concessions to matters of governance (notably in taxation) and custom. In the modern period, Western legal codes and procedures were adapted into Middle Eastern legal practice, either through indigenous reform or colonial imposition. Those Western layers and strands remained durable even in the face of recent Islamist rejection (Osanloo 2006a, 2006b; Bedir 2004; Spannus 2013; Kia 1994; Hoffman 2010). The process of legal reform in Muslim-majority states generally reached personal status and family law later than other areas of law.

In Iran, the process of legal reform relating to family law intensified during the authoritarian reforms of the Pahlavi Dynasty (1925–1979) and reached an important milestone while Brian was still living in Iran. Even "progressive" legislation like the Marriage Law of 1931 (Amin 2002, pp. 114–41) or the Family Protection Law of 1967—enacted two years before Brian left Iran—sought to regulate rather than abrogate the religious underpinnings of male privilege in family law. It has been observed that women's quest for equality in Iran, as in Europe and elsewhere, has been entwined with (and often undermined by) maternalism across the political and ideological spectrum (Kashani-Sabet 2011). When the Islamic Republic overturned the FPL in February 1979, it was soon compelled to use European models of procedure to implement the "restoration" of Twelver Shi'ite legal norms in matters of marriage and divorce, often with the same regulatory effect as the FPL. Ironically, Brian's dogged insistence on personally arguing for his rights in so many court appearances in the United States was similar—in style, not at all in substance—to the courtroom behavior of women in family court in Iran observed by Arzoo Osanloo and might also be considered a form of "rights talk (Osanloo 2006b, p. 200)," albeit a version informed by a striking degree of narcissism and an almost pathologically patriarchal mindset. The husbands of women seeking a *kholʿ* (as distinct from male-initiated *talāq*) divorce in Iran would have come into an Iranian family court with expectations of some sort of financial consideration (usually giving back the required *mehriye* or "bridal gift") before consenting to a divorce. It is this often tortuous process that takes up the time of family courts in Iran (Mir-Hosseini and Longinatto 2003). And that is for the dissolution of a regular marriage (*nekāh*), not the variety of marriage possible in Shiʿism, and legal in Iran, that allows for time-specific contract marriages (Haeri 2014). The rejection of Brian's imaginary effort to remove himself from an American legal jurisdiction to Iran was, of course, rejected in 2002 and 2006. But it did not entirely settle the question of Iran being Brian's true "cultural home" that validated (in Brian's mind) his hyper-patriarchal efforts to control Mellie and Susan.

A crucial episode in the prosecution's theory of the crime was the confrontation between Mellie and Brian in the Learning Works Store on 17 August 2001, a week before Susan's murder. It was the focus of Miele's cross-examination of Mellie on the second day of the trial. It revealed how use of language marked a mobile, permeable cultural boundary between Iran and America. Judge Anderson also participated in the exchange, to seek clarification:

> Judge Anderson: Why was [Brian] angry?
>
> Amaneh: Oh, I told him, "Why you here? Because we just said goodbye." We left the McDonald [*sic*] and came to the [shopping] center. And I asked him, "Why are you here? Why are you following us?" And he said, speaking Farsi, "Shut up and speak Farsi [*Persian*]," and I said, "I am asking why you here? [Sic] Is that a big question?" He said, "Speak Farsi. [Or] shut up ... "
>
> Miele: And then he got mad at you *because you were questioning him for being around his daughter* [emphasis added]?
>
> Amaneh: He was mad at me because he was speaking Farsi and I did not want to speak Farsi because he was saying something that was not okay to say, you know, I didn't want to hear.
>
> Miele: The only reason he's mad at you is because you won't speak Farsi with him?
>
> Amaneh: Because he was telling me bad words and he didn't want me to speak English so people wouldn't hear [the Persian threats] because the way he talks so friendly like [in English], but if you know the divorce, you know what's going on.
>
> Miele: I still don't understand why he's mad at you.
>
> Amaneh: Because I asked him, "Why are you followed [sic] me?" *Then I spoke English and he did not want me to speak English* [emphases added] ...
>
> Miele: As a result of this fight, argument, and the fact that Mr. Yasipour allegedly threatened to cut you up, were you afraid for Susan at that time?
>
> Amaneh: No.
>
> Miele: Why?

Amaneh: Because at the time I thought he—

Mr. Dinges: Objection to the relevance, Your Honor. We are offering it to show anger at [Amaneh].

Mr. Miele: Their theory is that the child's in danger because [Brian] is angry at [Amaneh]. She is there. She can give her opinion as to why she wasn't fearful for Susan at the time. How is that not relevant?

Anderson: [Ma'am] Mr. Miele's question was, did you have any fear for your daughter at that time? You answer was no. And he's asked you the question then, why not? Are you able to express that?

Amaneh: Well, he said he would kill me. He didn't say he would kill Susan.

Miele: You were aware, were you not, on that particular day that Mr. Yasipour had had a history of mental problems, weren't you?

Amaneh: Kind of ... I knew he was difficult. I knew we have gone to many counselors. He had gone to many counselors, but I am not a psychologist so ...

Judge Anderson: Okay. (TY 2006, 7 March, pp. 69–75)

Brian deployed Persian to try and isolate Amaneh and Susan in the Learning Works and transport them all to an Iranian cultural context in full view of the American one. Amaneh refused him, in Persian and in English, preserving a line of defense that Brian was clearly trying to breach: the limits of his visitation time with Susan. She was also trying to deprive Brian of his ability to "talk friendly like" in English and obscure from observers his naked hostility towards her. English gave Mellie a measure of mobility away from the "family-oriented" version of an "Iranian" family Brian was trying to maintain. After his divorce from Betty Keller, his sister and oldest sibling, Fakhri, encouraged him to remarry. She arranged the marriage between Brian and Amaneh in Iran in 1992. I asked what Amaneh's *mehriye* was. "500,000 *tumān*," he said, "It's like $500, cheap." It was his first victory over Amaneh, and there was only the slightest hint of a satisfied smile on his face. When I asked if the college-educated Amaneh had a job when they were together, he quickly asserted, "No, no she was just a housewife."

In court in 2006, Amaneh was also defending herself against Miele's tactical (but, still cruel) insinuations that, perhaps, she bore some responsibility for what happened to Susan. Didn't she know Brian was unbalanced? Implicitly: Couldn't she appreciate the looming danger to Susan? At the end of the exchange, Amaneh took a swipe at the insanity defense by refusing to agree that she observed signs of mental illness in Brian that would, in any way, mitigate or excuse his abusive behavior. Miele did not explore Amaneh's divorce and remarriage. Brian's suspicions about Amaneh's fidelity—for a time he doubted that Susan was his child—would later be introduced as evidence of Brian's pathological paranoia. Brian's defense team had to push back against the notion that his patriarchal paranoia was "normal" in Iran. However, Brian's behavior and the even the supportive testimony of other members of Brian's family made that difficult.

Brian's "Iranian" gender ideology came under scrutiny again on 13 March, the third day of the trial. The prosecution's witnesses had all completed their initial testimony and the defense began to call its witnesses to the stand. Miele began with Brian's sons, Brian Junior and Timothy S. (who went by Sam). The struggle for the narrative here centered on whether Brian's heated and protracted struggle for custody of his sons with Betty Keller informed his motive in killing Susan or not. Did the years of acrimonious and failed efforts to establish his control over Brian Jr. and Sam in the 1980s make him murderously desperate to retain control over Susan in 2001? Dinges prodded Brian Junior and Sam to admit that Brian was essentially frustrated because American courts denied his patriarchal authority, which he would have been able to take granted in Iran. The testimony of the sons drove the press coverage the next day (Farr 2006c). After testifying to his sense of his father's increasing mental instability in the weeks before Susan's murder, Brian Jr. provided some ammunition for the prosecution under cross-examination:

> Dinges: I mean, they [Brian and Betty] disagreed?
>
> Brian Jr.: Yeah. I mean, he would get upset. We was living in housing projects, trailer parks, and he always felt as if he had a good job, he was making good money, and he could never understand why the courts would not let him have custody of us, being that he was trying to get us out of an unsafe environment, and it really—in the long-run he was right because we was just out of control.
>
> Dinges: Exactly. He never—he was always upset because the courts weren't doing what he knew was right, correct?
>
> Brian Jr.: No. *What he didn't understand, that's the way it is in America. He's from a different country. I understood that and I'd try to help him, but he just didn't understand that.*
>
> Dinges: He's from Iran and pretty much what the father says goes?
>
> Brian Jr.: Yeah, much so, yeah. *It's a totally different culture* [emphasis added] ...
>
> Dinges: And that's probably the same thing he was going through with Susan, frustration?
>
> Brian Jr.: It's just something that—it was about to be the same thing all over again .... (TY 2006, 13 March, pp. 151–53)

In trying to represent the complexity of the situation—cultural differences, an acrimonious divorce, a sense that his mother's home may not have the best place to grow up after all, the fact of his father's obsessive nature—Brian Jr. handed Dinges something he had been looking for: that Brian's murderous rage was fueled by a "totally different" Iranian cultural norm. Even if what Brian did was unacceptable in Iran, how he *felt* would have "made sense" in Iran. If Brian was essentially Iranian, then his motive was informed more by an alien cultural logic than mental instability. Even under cross-examination, Brian Jr. pushed back, "I know what you are trying to insinuate. But, come on, I have to live with this from my own soul ... I really think my father meant to hurt himself that day ... I think he was on the verge of killing himself (TY 2006, 14 March, pp. 153)." The challenge for the defense was not to simply "assimilate" him as an American with mental problems, but to portray him sympathetically as an Iranian immigrant whose mental problems were ultimately rooted in Iranian origins.

2.2. *"If He Is Not a White Christian, What Is He?": Mobility, Ethnicity, and Religion*

The next day, 14 March, the defense sought to bolster its case that Brian's behavior had been erratic for some time prior to Susan's murder and that, nonetheless, Susan and Brian's relationship had been normal and loving before 24 August. It was also on this day that there was a debate regarding whether or not to admit into evidence my "cultural expertise" in the form of a report with the cringe-inducing title of "The Perso-Islamic Context for the Actions of Brian Yasipour." In that report I pointed out the religious and legal norms against female infanticide. I noted that Brian's claim that his rape was ignored in the 1960s was plausible not least because state initiatives to prevent child abuse do not seem to have gotten underway in Iran until the 1990s. I also noted that Brian's conversion to Christianity in Iran just before immigration would have been unusual as well as problematic given his origins in a conservative South Tehran merchant family. The details of my report were not discussed in the press or in open court. Judge Anderson, Dinges, Miele, and Spring debated the admissibility of my report in chambers. Miele argued that my report would "certainly counter any argument that the Commonwealth is alluding [to] and actually brought up specifically in cross examination yesterday about [Brian] being Iranian the way [Iranians] controlled their situations and families." Dinges argued my report was irrelevant because the accuracy of Brian's perspective on Iranian culture was not as important as his state of mind at the time of the crime. The debate developed from there:

> Judge Anderson: [You're] going to attempt to show me was the state of mind by Mr. Yasipour at the time of this killing, that he could not distinguish between right and wrong [i.e., the McNaughton standard for legal insanity]?
>
> Mr. Miele: We're going to show you a state of mind that complies with McNaughton on all the requirements of McNaughton and that being certainly one aspect, one component of it. What we're trying to do is buttress, if you will, [the defense's psychiatric expert] Dr. [Pogos] Voskanian's opinions based on some cultural considerations. He is not a white Christian, as the Court once referred to him. He is not. He is Iranian. That's where he was born, raised, [and] lived his formative years. He was raised in the Muslim religion. That is what his core is. Whether he's changed to Christianity, whatever, that doesn't change what happened to him as a child when he was 12 or so and where—how he had to deal with it as a child and the environment that he lived in.

Judge Anderson pressed, "If he is not a white Christian, what is he?" Miele reached further into the logic of his cultural defense. "This is about culture, not the color of his skin. We're talking cultural differences." Judge Anderson reminded him of the pre-history of the trial, when they all thought it would be a jury trial. At that time Miele's concern was Brian would not get fair trial because the jury would be "white Christians ... They would be seeing [an] Iranian, who I said was a citizen and appears to be white and who I believe is Christian ... Now, you are taking *me* to task saying *the Court* has this preconceived notion [emphasis added] ... " The discussion became at once personal and theoretical:

> Mr. Miele: You just—you do have a preconceived notion. You just acknowledged if only based upon his appearance and he's neither ... I didn't want him to be portrayed as a white Christian. I knew before then—before trial started, we'd discussed it on the defense that the Commonwealth at some point if we didn't they would certainly mention the fact that he is Iranian, and that's already happened, not through us, but through the Commonwealth's case.
>
> Judge Anderson: ... [Your] concern was that the jury would see him as something else, and that's why the whole issue came up.
>
> Miele: You're right, Judge.
>
> Judge Anderson: I don't care if he is Iranian frankly.
>
> Mr. Miele: I know you don't care. I understand that you don't care. I'm not accusing you of caring. I'm just saying you have to understand that because he is Iranian he comes from a different culture. They have different values. They have different ways of looking at things than you and I do, having been born and raised here in the US, and those things impact on him and how he deals with things, and Doctor—or Mr. [Anonymous'], I apologize, testimony will address that in part, particularly as it relates to how do you deal with being the victim of sexual abuse as a child in a Muslim country? How do you deal with that? What support is there available to you? I don't understand for the life of me how that isn't relevant. (TY 2006, 14 March, pp. 81–86)

By insisting on the relevance of Iranian culture, but to a different end than Dinges, Miele and Spring were deploying a cultural defense to persuade the court to a more sympathetic version of Brian as a "whole client (Goel 2004)." Dinges again protested that the cultural testimony was not relevant because what mattered was Brian's motive as established by the record of his conduct, not conjecture about cultural influences from Iran that may or may not have been on his mind when he acted. Judge Anderson had already begun to turn—not on the question of whether the McNaughton standard had been met, but on whether the cultural defense was relevant to the insanity defense. Anderson ruled that "I will try and understand the connection you are making, Mr. Miele," and that my report would be admitted into evidence as advisory to the court. It is possible that all the men knew something had changed in the discussion. Not only was the insanity defense not going to be undermined by the "logic" of Iranian culture, but, to the contrary, it might be strengthened. Brian's rape in Iran might be seen as more traumatic (because he received no help there), and, therefore, more plausibly the psychic epicenter of Brian's PTSD. Dr. Voskanian opined that Brian's PTSD was somehow activated the morning after Brian lost his bid to gain more visitation rights and induced the "dissociative state" in which he killed Susan later that afternoon. In this rendering, Brian's trauma in Iran was the real root of the tragedy in Williamsport. If accepted as true, this might admit some glimmer of Brian's humanity into the dark horror of his act.

The Yasipour family's humanity was portrayed in the earliest press reports on the trial—even Brian's humanity. "Brian A. Yasipour Sr. clenched his eyes but no tears would come as photographs and video of his slain daughter—her pale lips slightly open, her stuffed animals and dolls surrounding her and bouquets of 'sweetheart' roses on her lifeless chest—were shown on Monday, the second day of his trial in Lycoming County court (Farr 2006a)." Farr's coverage of this closed with a humanizing depiction of Brian and his family:

> For much of the day, Yasipour—a hirsute man who was dressed in a forest-green prison jumpsuit—stared blankly at the ground. His two sons, Brian Jr. and Timothy, sat behind him in support. The only time Yasipour expressed any emotion was when graphic pictures and videotape of his dead daughter's body were shown. (Farr 2006a)

Looking back on this episode in her life, Farr told me that she felt some compassion for Brian, despite the horror of what he did:

> The brutality of it never left me—those autopsy slides. Seeing just such a small body so cut up was really, it was ... It was a shock. It was a realization that the world may be, you know, wasn't as kind a place as I had previously hoped. I also felt, like, I felt a tinge of—I don't know—sadness for Brian in a way because he was painted ... as a very lonely man. And I didn't understand why if he was so lonely that he would take the one thing out of this world that seemed to matter most. (Farr 2014)

The room for mercy for filicidal parents—seen both in Iranian and American law—is rooted in an assumption that before there was a murderous mother or father, there was a "normal" mother or father and that some unusual circumstance or disease must have changed the equation. There is evidence of this in Pennsylvania's colonial history—underscoring the fact that legal and cultural norms are not static in any context: it was not until after 1785, when the penalty in Pennsylvania for maternal infanticide provided for imprisonment rather than execution, that the conviction rate increased from 26% to 42.8%, (Rowe 1991). For a similar sense of mercy to be activated for Brian in the 21st century, it was essential for Miele and Spring to make credible the idea Brian was in a dissociative state at the time of the crime. It had to be a state of mind resulting from PTSD rooted in the trauma of childhood rape back in Iran. That had to become a more plausible scenario than Brian acting vindictively, even impulsively, after a bad day in court. This aspect of the argument was discussed in open court during the dueling testimony of psychological experts.

Decisive for Anderson, in the end, was the psychological testimony, not of the expert witnesses for the prosecution or defense, but of one of the psychologists who had evaluated Brian in 1995, Dr. Jacqueline Sallade. She had written this:

> Mr. Yasipour is preoccupied with depressive obsessions such as the feelings of worthlessness, hopelessness, frustration, [of being] mistaken, blameworthy and pessimistic, as tearful, suicidal, and at times homicidal. *He has thoughts when he is rejected of hurting people, burning their houses down, killing them, etc., but he has never hurt anyone.*

Judge Anderson applied the implications of this assessment for the events of 24 August 2001:

> Picture Mr. Yasipour this day. Marriage gone. Job gone. Wife is against him. Attorney Mr. Felix fired the night before because he would not agree with him. Mr. Yasipour felt that he [Felix] turned on him for a decision that he'd [Yasipour] made. Mr. Yasipour went through a litany of witnesses that showed a pathetic effort to get people to come to his custody hearing. He went to neighbors. He went to people he thought were friends. He went to Molito's Sub Shop where he bought subs to try to get the people that worked at the sub shop to come down and testify for him. He was rejected. He went to his sons. They would not come up. He was running on a bad batch of road. The next day he gets there [i.e., the custody hearing]. What happens? Man, not only is he rejected, he's dressed down in severe style, and then he leaves. What's he got left? He's got Susan. He's got Susan. . . . First Susan says, "I don't want to go with you." [Brian asks Amaneh], "Will you help?" She goes with him. Now they get into the quiet of the home. What's she [i.e., Susan] want to do? Calls Mom. A form of rejection. It's the ultimate and the final rejection. And I believe that Dr. Sallade, who opined this six years before the fact, had it right on. (TY 2006, p. 15, 24 March; Sallade's testimony was on 15 March, per (TY 2006, pp. 143–44, 15 March))

Anderson rejected the "cultural defense" to the extent that it supported Voskanian's diagnosis of PTSD from a trauma experienced in Iran. He also rejected the "cultural prosecution" advanced by Dinges that Iranian norms informed and reinforced Brian's ability to form the intent to murder Susan. In convicting Brian of murder in the third degree, Anderson was accepting that Brian's ability to form intent consistent with murder in the first degree was compromised by his mental condition. In a sense, he wound up in the same place Brian would have started from under Iranian law: diminished capacity that reduced but did not eliminate criminal responsibility. Stephanie Farr covered the verdict with the headline, "Guilty but Mentally Ill: Judge Develops His Own Theory of Why Yasipour Slew His Daughter" (Farr 2006d)."

What was pointedly missing in Anderson's verdict, and much of the reaction to it, was any reference to Iran. The cultural defense had neutralized the cultural prosecution to the extent that the whole debate was absent in the verdict. From the standpoint of the Williamsport community at this point, Brian was assimilated into the American context physically and conceptually; it also immobilized him as a convicted murderer. A report of the verdict posted on WNEP's website at 4:57 p.m. made no mention of the family's immigrant background though it referred to Mellie by her Iranian name, Amaneh (WNEP 2006). Of course, it is not as though everyone suddenly forgot the Yasipours' background. What it is important here that the Yasipours' background could be framed differently at different times. It could be framed differently for Brian than for his victims. In 2014, news of Brian's death in the *Williamsport Sun-Gazette* referred to him as an "Iranian immigrant living in Williamsport when he stabbed his daughter in August 2001, saying he feared his wife planned to *take the girl back to their native country* (Williamsport Sun-Gazette 2014, *Man Jailed for Murder Dead at 64*)." Susan was born in the United States; she died in her native country. In the immediate wake of the verdict in 2006, the family was "native" to Williamsport. Brian, who never forgave Judge Anderson for not finding him innocent by reason of insanity and who had sought Anderson's recusal because of their history, may have benefitted from Anderson's ability to see his humanity, to see him as a person who had somehow changed and became incapable of restraining a murderous impulse. Even though he knew of Brian's difficult history, Judge Anderson had been as surprised as everyone else at Brian's violent turn. "No, to answer your question," he later told me, "I did not see this coming (Anderson 2010)."

Anderson also felt that Brian was not capable of true remorse, and this was reflected in his response to Brian's post-sentence motion (Anderson 2006, p. 2). It was a view I came to share after interviewing Brian and reflecting on something that was not presented at trial: Brian's confession. Anderson had ruled the confession inadmissible because Brian had not been properly Mirandized—a very American legal rationale. The content of the confession—the way Brian articulated his filicidal delusion—reminds us that immobilizing Brian physically and even in a specific discursive context does not exhaust the imaginary possibilities of im/mobility.

2.3. *"I Am a Good Father": Imaginary Im/Mobility in Brian's Confession and Internet Debates about Brian's Religion*

Outside the court and on the Internet was another forum in which the trial was being discussed. The *Forums For Justice* discussions of Brian's insanity defense and ethnicity, although they were happening in real time and involved some people who attended the trial and knew some of the participants, were not being monitored by the press. It was the other way around, actually, with FFJ posters updating the group with copies of press coverage (usually authored by Stephanie Farr for the *Williamsport Sun-Gazette*) and commenting on both the coverage and reports from the members who attended the trial.

As noted earlier, I became aware of FFJ when I was looking to follow events from afar at the time of trial. It was immediately apparent that the sympathies of the FFJ posters were with the prosecution and Mellie. These sympathies were refracted through an Islamophobic (and homophobic) ideological prism. Their compassion for Mellie (and even Brian's other family members) animated the FFJ postings almost as much as their wrath for Brian. The most frequent posters—often in direct dialog—were "LurkerXIV" and "Quinn." Quinn was a local woman who was able to attend the trial, often serving as the reporter for the group.

> LurkerXIV (15 March, 5:06 p.m.): The sooner this freak Yasipour is put behind bars for life, the better. I hope Mellie is holding up OK. This must be agonizing for her.
>
> Quinn (16 March, 10:49 p.m.): Mellie is an amazing women [sic]. She has a strength and understanding that I would never have. Brian has two older sons whom I have met and like, today we had lunch together. They are in an awful position as well; they love their father and don't deny that this happened but are strong in thier [sic] belief that he was not in his right mind at the time because of a (questionable IMO) history of mental problems and have forgiven Brian. Mellie and the boys have a wonderful relationship even tho they have different opinions about the case.

Quinn did not confine herself to observing the trial and engaging with the Yasipours. As the defense's theory of the crime played out it court, she desperately looked for ways to pushback and actually bolster the prosecution's case:

> LurkerXIV (17 March, 4:05 p.m.): Thank you [Quinn] for actually being there at the Court House for her during the trial.
>
> Reading the news reports makes me really detest some psychiatrists. The ones the defense has hired will say anything for the money. They are just hired hands. As for Yasipour being molested while he was a boy in Iran...that culture (Muslim) accepts and encourages male homosexuality, so I don't know why it would upset him so much.

> Quinn (17 March, 4:30 p.m.): The defence [sic] is saying that that is not accepted or acknowledged in Iran. They conceed [sic] that one man would never do that to another. There is no help for those that confess to a man on man rape. Miele is saying that is why he came to America, changed his name from Huessain (SP) to Brian, changed religion and the beliefs and way of living. They are supposed to have a culture expert coming in to testify . . .
>
> LurkerXIV (19 March, 11:20 p.m.): I wonder who their "culture expert" is and what he/she will say. Homosexuality in the Islamic world is a very convoluted business. Culturally, it is most certainly a common practice in Iraq and Iran; whether it is punished or not depends on who is in power.
>
> Here is a good article that explains why:
>
> http://www.frontpagemag.com/articles...le.asp?ID=5704
>
> Quinn (21 March, 12:03 a.m.): Thank you for the article. Any suggestions how I could get in the hands of the D.A. Dinges? I would like him to see this. I will be in court tomorrow. If it helps I do know the invesigater [sic] Steve Sorage.

The link to the article on *FrontPageMagazine*, whose motto currently is, "Inside Every Liberal is a Totalitarian Screaming to Get Out," results in a "not found, error 404." However, a quick search for "homosexuality" on the site yields dozens of articles lamenting both the prevalence of homosexual rape and intolerance towards the LGBTQ communities in majority Muslim Middle Eastern countries. It is an odd mix of Islamophobic orientalism and homophobia that animates many of the headlines on this site. The article that most seemed to resonate with LurkerXIV's description was an excerpt from Serge Trifkovic's *The Sword of the Prophet: A Politically-Incorrect Guide to Islam* adapted by Robert Locke on 23 January 2003 and entitled, "Islam's Love-Hate Relationship with Homosexuality (Locke 2003)."

Brian's sexuality was part of the courtroom debate about his state of mind at the moment of the crime. The prosecution's evidence of his sexual deviancy took two forms: testimony about him leering at a young (female) swimming instructor during one of Susan's lessons and a selection of pornographic video tapes that he tried to dispose of the day of the murder that featured transgender sex workers. For the defense, these same videos were presented as evidence of Brian's lingering trauma from being raped by an older boy back in Iran (the prosecution never stipulated the fact of Brian's rape, much less its effects). However, LurkerXIV and Quinn's "research" on Islam and homosexuality was part of a cultural framing of Brian that was at once Islamophobic (in that it embraced the idea that Brian's Muslim background defined him more than any other attribute and framed that Muslim background as inherently inimical to America/Christianity) and homophobic (in conflating rape with consensual sex). Quinn seems to have assumed that these biases were somehow a fact that their government should embrace and act upon. Quinn and Lurker XIVs' reaction to Anderson's verdict, then, was hardly surprising. The verdict prompted posts from a few others who had not commented on the trial while it was in progress, including, as we shall see, from Mellie Yasipour. Lurker XIV fumed, "I'm going to keep an eye on Anderson, and if he does a repeat performance of going easy on a child abuser or child-murderer, I'm going to get Bill O'Reilly on his case! (FFJ 2006, March 24, 7:04 p.m.)."

The importance of these Internet posts is that they reflect precisely the attitudes that Miele and Spring worried would influence a jury pool in their part of Pennsylvania. The combination of the transcript of sidebar in Judge Anderson's chambers and the *Forum for Justice* posts serve as proxies for the local mindset and how it might have impacted understanding of the Yasipour family, Brian in particular. As perhaps a further indication of the accuracy of Miele's characterization of Lycoming County Pennsylvania, Trump carried the county 70.46% to 25.75% in the 2016 Presidential election (http://www.electionreturns.pa.gov), the best margin of victory for a Republican presidential candidate recorded there this century.

The temptation here, perhaps, is to assume that this vitriolic and essentially Orientalist "othering" of Brian by the FFJ was simply a local manifestation of a prevailing hegemonic discourse. Mohsen Mobasher has analyzed the effect of a changing national discourse about Iran on Iranian-Americans in Texas. Many that he interviewed in his study reported a sense of alienation from the rest of American society—despite enjoying other measures of professional and economic success in America—because of the negative image of Iran in American culture stemming from the Iranian Revolution of 1977–1979 and Hostage Crisis of 1979–1981 and reawakened with Iran's inclusion in the "Axis of Evil" in the aftermath of 9/11 (Mobasher 2012, pp. 7–8, 53–60, 64–66). Brian killed Susan in a different America than the one he was tried in. On 24 August 2001, President George W. Bush was going to be in Williamsport for the Little League Baseball Championships. Most police resources that night were deployed to provide security for the Little Leaguers and the President. Because it was a bench trial, the defense team did not have not to contend with an anti-Iranian jury pool whose animosity would factor in the horrors that would unfold just 18 days after the murder.

It is worth noting that the Williamsport-based posters to the FFJ were not just supportive of Mellie in their posts. They distinguished between Brian Sr. and the rest of his family and expressed empathy for them throughout their posts even as they expressed outrage at Anderson's verdict. But the FFJ posters did not hear everything at the trial. For an obvious reason—the Fifth Amendment—they did not hear from Brian at trial. They also did not hear about Brian's confession during the trial. This revised narrative can include both.

Brian did not feel defined by his crime or by his national or religious identity, as far as I can tell. Certainly, as we have seen, he did not seem conflicted about his mobility between Iranian-Muslim and American-Christian contexts, nor was he particularly articulate about either religious doctrine. And, as I spoke to him in June 2010, his hyper-patriarchal gender ideology seemed more idiosyncratic—even as he discussed it in terms of mobility between "Iranian" and "American" contexts.

> "What should people know about you?" I asked.
>
> "That I am a good father."
>
> I paused [*I could scarcely believe what I was hearing*]. "Why do you think you are a good father?" I asked.
>
> "Because I care."
>
> "Anything else? Anything you did to be a good father?"
>
> No answer.
>
> "Why do you think others might *not* think you are a good father?"
>
> "Because of divorce."

I asked him what he remembered about Susan's death. He said he remembered stabbing her, but not why. This surprised me. All previous statements attributed to him indicated that he did not remember the act of killing Susan. I asked if he remembered why he had cleaned Susan up after he killed her. At trial, the debate was whether he was trying to cover up his crime or was engaging in some sort of confused mourning ritual (Farr 2006b). He said, "I did not want them to know which knife I had used, so I washed them."

> I said, "You were trying to convince the police that you did not kill Susan?"
>
> "Yes."
>
> "Did you plan to flee at some point, to escape?"
>
> "No."
>
> "So you thought you might convince everyone you had not harmed Susan and just continue living in Williamsport."
>
> "Yes."

I asked why, in his view, Amaneh wanted to leave the marriage. *Could he see her side at all?* I wondered to myself. "Because I was too obsessive."

I asked if anything happened that made it more likely that Susan would die. He mentioned that the custody hearing that morning had gone badly. He was only going to have Susan for three hours, three days a week, not eight. But, I reminded him, those five hours were going to be school. It is not as though Amaneh would actually have Susan with her more of the time.

"I wanted to get weekend visitation in exchange."

Even so, how did this inform his filicidal thoughts? I asked him, "Were you afraid that Amaneh would take Susan to Iran?"

"Yes."

I asked him what would be so bad about Amaneh living in Iran with Susan.

"It would not be nice to have a woman alone with her child."

"Well, couldn't you just go to Iran yourself and win your rights more easily?" I asked.

"I did not want to live in Iran," he offered. The reductive implication of what he was saying was that he killed his daughter so he would not have to live in Iran. This was at odds with the prosecution's theory that he planned to flee to Iran, but also with Brian's own attempts to be judged by Iranian legal standards in America. Could a man kill his daughter just to preserve the power of his own mobility? A member of Brian's former church in Montoursville, a witness for the prosecution, had said, "Brian Yasipour is the focus of Brian Yasipour's life (YT, 13 March, p. 20)." But, even with that, there were so many other options than murder. Filicidal ideation often includes a notion that killing the child is necessary to avoid a worse fate. I did not get the sense that he believed that when I spoke to him. What about the day of the crime?

It was not until I reviewed Brian's suppressed confession that I felt I understood the tortured logic of his filicidal delusion—the fate worse than death that would "inevitably" result from Susan growing up without him in Iran. Judge Anderson ruled on a pre-trial motion to suppress Brian's confession on the night of the murder on 22 November 2002 (Anderson 2002). The text of Anderson's order preserved the remarkable substance of Brian's confession itself. In his confession Brian drew a direct causal line between Judge Butt's decision to reduce his visitation and "the fact his child would be forced into prostitution (Anderson 2002, p. 4)." Why would this happen? Because, somehow, Amaneh might take Susan to Iran. Somehow the loss of his visitation rights, the loss of his control over Susan made this fear more concrete to him. But, he allegedly added, "she [Susan] did not have to worry about it anymore and she was better off now (Ibid.)." Anderson did not find police to be lying about Brian's statements, just that the confession was inadmissible because Brian had not been Mirandized. In these alleged statements, we see the scope of Brian's fears about losing control of Susan's mobility. In his mind at the time, the loss of control would lead to her sexual violation, if not through an assault (as had been his own experience) than through circumstances reducing her to sexual slavery. Even though Susan was much too young to be held to cruel account by a deranged father for sexual impropriety in a classic honor killing case, he could imagine an "inescapable" future when she would be old enough to "dishonor" him in Iran and destroy his wish to be a "good father." Nevertheless, despite his protestations in court about Iran being "family oriented," despite his attempts to import a more "Iranian" marriage into the United States, and despite his efforts to avoid imprisonment and responsibility for his crime, Brian wanted to stay in America. In the immediate wake of Susan's murder, it appears that Brian decided to risk being an American convict rather than being a repatriated Iranian fugitive from American law.

3. Concluding Discussion: "Regimes of Im/Mobility" and Historical Analysis

One of the limitations of this study, besides the obvious limitations of any case study, is that its methodology evolved from a non-research context and without a premeditated research design to explore the explanatory power of the many theoretical paradigms that might be reasonably applied. For example, it is unlikely that if I had begun with the intention of exploring regimes-of-im/mobility (or any other theoretical paradigm) in a given court system that I would have begun with a particular case. Rather, I would have established a long-term research project that relied on established relationships with a particular court that facilitated courtroom observations, routinized the review of court records and established protocols for interviewing participants in trials. I would have more deliberately integrated field research methodology with historical methodology to see what specific lines of inquiry emerged. Thinking about the most important sources for this study—the trial transcript and interviews—I can well imagine them, as part of a future study, being read comparatively with similar sources or even with literary/poetic sources for resonant themes and issues. That would have been far beyond the scope of this article, but there is extensive academic literature on the literary and memoir output of Iranian-Americans to take as a point of departure for such a future study (See, as examples, (Elahi 2006; Malek 2006; Karim and Rahimieh 2008); the last reference is an introduction to several studies in a themed issue of MELUS).

Nonetheless, the use of a "regimes of im/mobility" in a more retrospective way in this case has been helpful. And I would not claim to have exhausted its potential here. I applied it to a multi-focal analysis of gender and ethnicity and religion because those factors seemed linked at several points in the narrative of trial and were expressed in terms that resonated with the im/mobility framework. We are increasingly called upon to assess the intersection of multiple factors in social and historical analyses. The regimes of mobility approach can help us with this challenge. It can help us see and describe all "moving parts" in an unfolding event or process—even in the face of a considerable detail as in a microhistorical case study. It can do this because im/mobility—like gender—is such an elemental part of the human experience. Its expression is likely to be observable in a variety of sources, and, it will be part of any process we might choose to examine. To paraphrase Joan Wallach Scott, im/mobility is a "useful category of historical analysis (Scott 1999)." Furthermore, rather than compete with other lines of inquiry, it can add visibility to them.

It would, of course, be wrong to suggest that Brian was a typical Iranian, American, or Iranian-American, or, that the tragic experiences of the Yasipour family were a representative microcosm of the Iranian-American experience. But the very uniqueness of their circumstances generated an extensive record from a variety of vantage points. This allows us to appreciate the relationship between the specific (personal and local) to wider frames of analysis. In any microhistory, the challenge is to see the forest though a careful examination of a tree. In this case, however, we have two "forests"—Iranian and American. We found certain aspects of these "forests"—gender, religion, ethnicity—were important to examine together through a complicated set of circumstances using the prism of im/mobility. In Brian, though, we had a very strange "tree" in the foreground of the analysis. I will conclude by briefly reviewing how the "regimes of im/mobility" approach can draw the analytical eye not just toward the wider context but enrich our understanding of the particular. Brian was not the only tree in the forest.

Though I only met with lead investigating officer Stephen Sorage once, on 10 June 2010, I think of him as the man who came to know Brian best. He coined a most apt term to describe Brian's default state of mind: "Brianland". In Brianland, one did not have to answer for any harmful action to others or stick with any idea or commitment that conflicted with one's narrow interest. When I presented my preliminary research about this case at the Iranian Studies Conference in 2014, Ali Akbar Mahdi commented that Brian's agency was most visible in apparent moments of *cultural vacuum*, when it seemed to others (e.g., officers of the court, members of the community) that none of the imaginable identities—Iranian, American, Iranian-American, Muslim, Christian, White—applied to Brian. Rather than simply embracing or accepting a liminal status, Brian seemed to actively project a social identity that suited his immediate circumstances best. This suggests that Brian's erratic agency was not about embracing a "core identity," but about the freedom to move among different social identities in Iran and America. Brian's idiosyncratic picking and choosing of American and Iranian cultural values (or his readings of them)—his imaginary "hypermobility" in Brianland—bewildered observers in Williamsport because of the cultural plausibility of each of the identities he projected into the "vacuum." Furthermore, the cultures that he navigated between were not static and representations of them were not settled. Though the images of Iran constructed by the prosecution and defense were essentially negative, they were not identical. Judge Anderson came to accept that Brian's frightening version of "family-oriented" Iran was not accurate.

In reflecting on this study as a microhistory in the introduction, we noted the differences between Brian's situation and that of Ginzburg's Menocchio. There is also a similarity. In both cases, the legal culpability of the accused rested on the question of their sanity. Assessments of their sanity rested, in part, on how "alien" these individuals were: there was an imaginary banishment to another cultural place. Among the books used to establish Menocchio's deliberate indulgence of heretical doctrines was an Italian adaptation of the Koran (Ginzburg et al. 1993, p. 43). By contrast, the courtroom debates about Brian's ethnicity and sanity led to a nullification of those issues, letting the reality of his mental illness become a mitigating factor in his crime. Factoring in im/mobility into the microhistorical analysis of Brian's trial facilitates our ability to follow Brian's imaginary mobility between Iran and America. It also helps us notice the shifts in his social identity over time as perceived by others. As bewildering as Brian's imaginary hypermobility seemed to others during the time of his trial, it was built on a history of actual, physical mobility. At the same time, imaginary mobility seems to be at work in shifting community perceptions of the Yasipour family: sometimes they were Williamsport natives (Americans) and sometimes they were Iranian immigrants. Thinking of the relationship between imaginary and actual mobility helps the qualitative researcher reflect on these conceptual shifts as integral to an historical process rather than as disruptions. This is no less true in a microhistorical analysis with many details to consider. Consider a detail that illustrates the material consequences of imaginary im/mobility; they did not just apply to Brian, but to the court itself. In 2005, Miele and Spring sought a continuance to find and depose Brian's brother about Brian's medical history and in anticipation of the need for family testimony regarding mitigating factors in the (death) penalty phase of the trial. Anderson denied the continuance with this explanation:

> The difficulty lies in obtaining the brother's testimony. No one has spoken to [the] defendant's brother, no one has an address, and therefore the content of his testimony is at this time uncertain. If alive, [the] defendant's brother is in Iran, a country [with] which the United States has limited diplomatic relations. *Counsel concedes they cannot travel to Iran and it is highly unlikely that defendant's brother would be able to travel to the United States.* Counsel's plan, if the continuance is granted, is to find [the] defendant's brother through a law office in Chicago. This law office maintains contacts in Iran. If found, defense counsel feels that arrangements can be made through the Pakistani Embassy to obtain a Visa for [the] defendant's brother to travel to Dubai in the United Arab Emirates. Counsel would then either arrange for some type of video conferencing or, as a last resort, proceed to Dubai to take his deposition for trial. The Court is keenly aware, and is sensitive to the fact this is a death penalty case and, accordingly, wishes to proceed in a manner that is cautious and accommodating to the defense. But, while the Court applauds defense counsel for leaving no stone unturned, the logistics of this particular situation are far beyond speculative. There is no assurance that anything can be accomplished by *this intricate and costly procedure* [emphasis added]; no one can represent to the Court what the testimony of [the] defendant's brother will be, or even that he can be found. Accordingly, the motion for continuance must be denied. (Anderson 2005, p. 2; emphasis added.)

However much the defense might want to emphasize the role of Brian's Iranian origins, there were practical limits to that. This small example may not be what first comes to mind as a governmental "regime of im/mobility" rationally regulating the movement of "people, goods, capital and certain forms of knowledge (Baker 2016, p. 152)," but it was certainly an instance of that phenomenon with direct consequences for Brian. The writ and resources of the Lycoming County Court system could not contend with multiple "regimes" that added time and cost to the process of preparing Brian's defense to the fullest possible extent. Furthermore, there was no getting away from the fact that Brian was a part of the Williamsport community—especially its court system. The trial focused on his hyper-patriarchal paranoia as a function of his Iranian origins. At the same time, Miele, Spring, and Anderson recalled that he was briefly active in a *local* men's rights group (though, unfortunately, I do not have a clear sense of what that involvement entailed). Spring had worked with Brian while she defended his sons against criminal charges. Miele vaguely remembered Brian striking up a conversation with him about father's rights when their paths crossed in the Lycoming County Court Building. In Williamsport, Brian was chafing not against a major regime of im/mobility rooted in U.S. immigration policy, but against the regulation of his power in "his" household: when and where he could see his child. From that vantage point, a "family-oriented" Iran that would accommodate his (by his own admission) obsessive personality might be a compelling mirage to run towards. Yes, Iranian law has more lenient defaults for filicidal fathers, as Brian opined, but not at all to the extent that he claimed. Also, Brian did not know about efforts like that of Eshaqi to change that. Egalitarian reformism, though unsuccessful so far, is also part of Iran's actual, diverse, living, and changing culture. In a qualitative analysis informed by considerations of im/mobility, the unbridgeable contrast between reductive conceptions of America and Iran falters in the face of observable similarities between Iranian and American responses to the horrors of filicide.

Even reductive constructions such as "Iranian" or "American" may not be consistently applied. The same FFJ posters that expressed such vitriolic orientalism in their judgment of Brian's actions also embraced Mellie and Susan as their own—and as being American Christians. They could have read Mellie, in particular, as a Muslim Iranian immigrant who was the victim of the patriarchal norms of her culture of origin—a version of "colonial feminism" that scholars like Leila Ahmed (Ahmed 1992) and Lila Abu-Lughod (Abu-Lughod 2013) have critiqued with reference to European and American foreign policy in the Middle East. Williamsport's embrace of Susan and Mellie does not seem to have been expressed that way. And Mellie seems to have felt that embrace. Other than court records, we have two other public records of Mellie's perspective at the time. The first was one of the last FFJ posts about the trial, "I am finding people across *the country* who acknowledge this brutal murder. I wish Susan (whose love toward every individual was under no condition [*i.e., showed unconditional love to others*]) was here to experience the love and compassion once more (FFJ 2006, 28 March, 8:35 a.m.)." Quinn reported visiting Susan's grave in the cemetery the previous day, leaving an "Easters gift" and meeting with Mellie afterward.

It was a member of Stephen Sorage's church who donated the plot for Susan's burial. Sorage, who broke down at the sight of her autopsy, kept a picture of her on at his desk. It kept him focused on seeking justice for Susan. In our one and only meeting, he showed the picture to me. In the picture, Susan was smiling and safe, as if nothing could ever happen to her. It reminded me of the picture on a website memorializing her among other victims of domestic violence in her American home of Williamsport, Pennsylvania (An Empty Place at the Table 2005). The site mentions a "history of domestic violence" in Mellie and Brian's relationship prior to the murder—the only assertion of that we have in the historical record. Mellie and Susan, again, are just Williamsport natives—no mention of Iran. As a child, of course, Susan's mobility was always constrained. The microhistorical examination of her father's crime gives us a window on her agency and mobility between Iran and America also. She had visited Iran with her parents and knew Persian. We know she defended her mother when Brian threatened Mellie in Persian in their confrontation in the Learning Works. We also know that she tried to reassure her father that Mellie was not going to take her to Iran. When her father was selfish and cruel, Susan was kind and brave. In remembrance of lost loved ones, Iranians often quote a couplet by the 14th-century poet Hafez, "One whose heart is born into love never dies; what remains of us is written upon the record of the world." Susan's place in that record is no less valuable for being all too brief.

4. A Note on Methodology

In the end, I have to defer to readers to judge whether I have accounted for my own role sufficiently in the analysis because there is no way to write it out of the story. One unavoidable consequence of my role is that some participants would not talk to me after the fact, notably the prosecutors and Amaneh. My interviews with Judge Anderson (Anderson 2010), Stephanie Farr (Farr 2014), Nicole Spring, and William Miele (Miele and Spring 2010) were recorded, in keeping with my preferred approach to oral history. After an initial meeting on 10 June 2010, Agent Sorage would not respond to requests for a recorded interview. I was not permitted to bring recording equipment to interview Brian Yasipour in prison (Yasipour 2010). Therefore, my descriptions of those interviews rely on extensive notes that I wrote up within hours of those meetings. Transliterations of Persian words follow a modified version of the Library of Congress system, without diacritics except for the *ayn* and *hamza*. Vowels were rendered as follows: e/i, o/u, a/ā.

Acknowledgments: This research was supported by a University of Michigan-Dearborn Office of Research and Sponsored Projects Campus Grant (2009–2010). There are many colleagues I would like to thank for their input and advice as I worked on this project and presented aspects of it at conferences over the years (or went and on about it over coffee!): Carolyn Kraus, Elaine Clark, Arzu Osanloo, Kathryn Babayan, Firoozeh Kashani-Sabet, Persis Karim, Amy Malek, Ali Akbar Mahdi, Kristin Poling, Arang Keshavarzian, Ali Mirsepassian, Sally Howell, Marty Hershock (my microhistory guru), and Georgina Hickey. I also wish to thank Lycoming County Court staff—in particular, Dawn Sweeley—for their assistance in securing transcripts of the trial. I also should note the help provided to me by student assistant in 2008-9, Maryam Abbas, as I began to gather information to work on this project. I also wish to thank Viola Thimm for generously introducing me to im/mobility as an analytical framework. I benefitted very much from the comments of the anonymous peer reviewers. My wife, Amelia Amin, always provides loving support, but I simply could not have completed the revisions to this article successfully this summer without her patient and insightful feedback. All remaining mistakes of interpretation or detail are mine.

Conflicts of Interest: As noted, I did participate *pro bono* as a "cultural expert" for the attorneys representing Brian Yasipour at trial. My decision to study this event came after the trial was concluded and all interviews occurred after the legal process was over. Furthermore, as Brian Yasipour is now deceased, there is no way my analysis can have any impact on his sentence. The funding sponsors had no role in the design of the study, in the collection or interpretation of data, in the writing of the manuscript, or in the decision to publish the results.

Appendix A

Table A1. Chronology.

1950	Hosayn Yasipour born to a South Tehran merchant family.
ca. 1962	Many years later, Brian reported that he was raped by an older boy around this time.
1968–1969	Brian (Hosayn) leaves Iran in 1968 (converts secretly to Christianity before leaving), arrives in the United States in 1969, drops out of junior college, and begins a series of sales jobs while marrying and starting a family in Williamsport, Pennsylvania.
ca.1980–1990	A decade of custody battles with first ex-wife, Betty Keller.
1992	Brian and Amaneh (Mellie) Khatun marry in Iran as Muslims.
1994	Brian fired from his job at Monumental Life Insurance company; he begins a wrongful termination lawsuit.
1995	Psychologist Dr. Sallade assesses Brian for Social Security disability status.
1995–1996	Brian treated for Social Security disability status. Susan Marie Yasipour born 28 August 1996.
January 1999	Brian and Mellie separate; Mellie has primary custody.
June–October 2000	Brian restricted to supervised visitation after an attempt to kidnap Susan.
May 2001	Brian suffers stroke; his behavior becomes more erratic as custody litigation drags on.
24 August 2001	Brian kills Susan and is arrested the same evening.

Table A1. *Cont.*

2001–2002	Motion to suppress confession granted; Brian spends much of this time considered unfit to stand trial.
10 December 2002	Brian unsuccessfully challenges the divorce in a hearing; his courtroom declaration, the principal subject of this analysis, happens on this date.
22 February 2006	District Attorney waives the death penalty in exchange for a bench trial.
March 2006	Trial and verdict (third degree murder, and tampering with evidence).
June 2006	Brian sentenced to 22 and a half years, with time served.
August 2008	BBrian's 2008 appeal rejected by Pennsylvanian Superior Court.
2 August 2014	Brian dies of natural causes in Laurel-Highlands prison facility, Pennsylvania. He had suffered for years with untreated diabetes prior to his first stroke in 2001, and had several strokes while in prison.

References and Notes

Abu-Lughod, Lila. 2013. *Do Muslim Women Need Saving?* Cambridge: Harvard University Press.

Ahmed, Leila. 1992. *Women and Gender in Islam: Historical Roots of a Modern Debate.* New Haven: Yale University Press.

Alba, Richard, and Victor Roe. 1997. Rethinking Assimilation Theory for a New Era of Immigration. *International Migration Review* 31: 826–74. [CrossRef] [PubMed]

Amin, Camron Michael. 2002. *The Making of the Modern Iranian Woman: Gender, State Policy, and Popular Culture.* Gainesville: University of Florida Press.

Amin, Camron Michael. 2014. An Iranian in New York: Abbas Masudi's Description of the Non-Iran on the Eve of the Cold War. In *Rethinking Iranian Nationalism and Modernity.* Edited by Kamran Scot Aghaie and Afshin Marashi. Austin: University of Texas Press, pp. 161–78.

An Empty Place at the Table. 2005. Susan Yasipour. Available online: http://lycofs01.lycoming.edu/~estomin/violence/susan.htm (accessed on 18 March 2016).

Anderson, Judge Dudley N. 2001. *Commonwealth of Pennsylvania vs. Brian Yasipour, No. 01-11,465 Competency Determination: Opinion and Order.* Willimasport: Commonwealth of Pennsylvania, November 6.

Anderson, Judge Dudley N. 2002. *Commonwealth of Pennsylvania vs. Brian Yasipour, Sr. Defendant. No. 01-11.465. Pre-Trial Motion. Opinion and Order.* Willimasport: Commonwealth of Pennsylvania, November 22.

Anderson, Judge Dudley N. 2005. *Commonwealth of Pennsylvania vs. Brian Yasipour, Sr. Defendant. No. 01-11.465. Motion for Continuance. Opinion and Order.* Willimasport: Commonwealth of Pennsylvania, August 3.

Anderson, Judge Dudley N. 2006. *Commonwealth of Pennsylvania vs. Brian Yasipour, No. 01-11,465 Post Sentence Motion: Opinion and Order.* Willimasport: Commonwealth of Pennsylvania, August 21.

Anderson, Judge Dudley N. 2010. Interview with Judge Dudley Anderson. Williamsport, PA, USA, January 25.

Baker, Beth. 2016. Regime. In *Keywords of Mobility.* Edited by Noel B. Salazar and Kiran Jayaram. New York: Bergahn, pp. 152–70.

Bedir, Murteza. 2004. Fikih to Law: Secularization through Curriculum. *Islamic Law and Society* 11: 378–401. [CrossRef]

Bonfanti, Sara. 2016. Dislocating Pujabiyat: Gender Mobilities among Indian Diasporas in Italy. In *Bounded Mobilities: Ethnographic Perspectives on Social Hiarchies and Global Inequalities.* Bielefeld: Transcipt Verlag, pp. 183–208.

Brown, Richard D. 2003. Microhistory and the Post-Modern Challenge. *Journal of the Early Republic* 23: 1–20. [CrossRef]

Chaichian, Mohammad A. 1997. First Generation Iranian Immigrants and the Question of Cultural Identity: The Case of Iowa. *The International Migration Review* 31: 612–27. [CrossRef]

Code Switch. 2017. Interview with Neda Maghbouleh, Author of the Upcoming Book: The Limits of Whiteness: Iranian Americans and the Everyday Politics of Race. Redwood City: Stanford University Press, April 19. Available online: http://www.npr.org/podcasts/510312/codeswitch (accessed on 19 July 2017).

Demian, Melissa. 2008. Fictions of Intention in the "Cultural Defense". *American Anthropologist* 110: 432–42. [CrossRef]
D'hondt, Sigurd. 2010. The Cultural Defense as Courtroom Drama: The Enactment of Identity, Sameness, and Difference in Criminal Trial Discourse. *Law & Social Inquiry* 35: 67–98.
Elahi, Babak. 2006. Translating the Self: Language and Identity in Iranian-American Women's Memoirs. *Iranian Studies* 39: 461–80. [CrossRef]
Eshaqi, Mohammad. 2001. *The Punishment of Mothers and Fathers for the Crime of Killing a Child: Article 220 of the Islamic Penal Code Mojazāt-e Pedar va Mādar dar Jorm-e Koshtan-i Farzand: Māddeh-e 220 Qānun-i Mojāzāt-e Eslāmi*. Tehran: Safir-e Sobḥ.
Farr, Stephanie. 2006a. Prosecution: Yasipour 'Faking'. *Williamsport Sun-Gazette*, March 7, Cited by Quinn on *Forums for Justice*. (See FFJ).
Farr, Stephanie. 2006b. Yasipour Trial Set to Resume. *Williamsport Sun-Gazette*, March 13.
Farr, Stephanie. 2006c. Yasipour's Sons Testify at His Trial. *Williamsport Sun-Gazette*, March 14.
Farr, Stephanie. 2006d. Guilty but Mentally Ill: Judge Develops His Own Theory of Why Yasipour Slew His Daughter. *Williamsport Sun-Gazette*, March 27.
Farr, Stephanie. 2014. Author Telephone Interview with Stephanie Farr. Berkley, MI, USA, Recorded 20 May.
Fata, Soraya, and Raha Rafii. 2003. *Iran Census Report: Strength in Numbers: The Relative Concentration of Iranian Americans Across the United States*. Washington: National Iranian American Council, Available online: https://www.niacouncil.org/docs/irancensus.pdf (accessed on 27 July 2017).
FFJ. 2006. Forums for Justice. Susan Yasipour. March 7–April 19. Available online: http://www.forumsforjustice.org/forums/showthread.php?6760-Susan-Yasipour (accessed on 27 July 2017).
Findlen, Paula. 2003. The Singularization of Historytion of Historytory esMicrohistory within the Postmodern State of Knowledge. *Journal of Social History* 36: 701–35.
Findlen, Paula. 2005. Two Cultures of Scholarship? *Isis* 96: 230–37. [CrossRef] [PubMed]
Ginzburg, Carlo. 1980. *The Cheese and the Worms: The Cosmos of a Sixteenth Century Miller*. Translated by John, and Ann Tedeschi. Baltimore: John Hopkins Press and Routledge, Kegan & Paul.
Ginzburg, Carlo. 2005. Latitude, and the Bible: An Experiment in Microhistory. *Critical Inquiry* 31: 665–83.
Ginzburg, Carlo, John Tedeschi, and Anne C. Tedeschi. 1993. Microhistory: Two or Three Things That I Know About It. *Critical Inquiry* 20: 10–35. [CrossRef]
Goel, Rashmi. 2004. Can I Call Kimura Crazy? Ethical Tensions in the Cultural Defense. *Seattle Journal for Social Justice* 3: 443–64.
Gualtieri, Sarah. 2009. *Between Arab and White: Race and Ethnicity in the Early Syrian American Diaspora*. Berkeley: The University of California Press.
Hackl, Andreas, Julia Sophia Schwarz, Miriam Gutekunst, and Sabina Leoncini. 2016. Bounded Mobilities: An Introduction. In *Bounded Mobilities: Ethnographic Perspectives on Social Hiarchies and Global Inequalities*. Edited by Miriam Gutekunst, Andreas Hackl, Sabina Leoncini, Julia Sophia Schwarz and Irane Götz. Bielefeld: Transcipt Verlag, pp. 19–34.
Haeri, Shahla. 2014. *Law of Desire: Temporary Marriage in Shi'i Iran*, rev. ed. Syracuse: Syracuse University Press.
Hoffman, Katherine E. 2010. Berber Law by French Means: Customary Courts in the Moroccan Hinterlands, 1930–1956. *Comparative Studies in Society and History* 52: 851–80. [CrossRef]
Jennings, Ronald C. 1999. *Studies on Ottoman Social History in the Sixteenth and Seventeenth Centuries: Women, Zimmis, and Sharia Courts in Kayseri, Cyprus and Trabzon*. Istanbul: ISIS Press.
Karim, Persis M., and Nasrin Rahimieh. 2008. Introduction: Writing Iranian Americans into the American Literature Canon. *MELUS* 33: 7–16. [CrossRef]
Kashani-Sabet, Firoozeh. 2011. *Conceiving Citizens: Women and the Politics of Motherhood in Iran*. Oxford: Oxford University Press.
Kia, Mehrdad. 1994. Constitutionalism, Economic Modernization and Islam in the Writings of Mirza Yusef Khan Mostashar od-Dowle. *Middle Eastern Studies* 30: 751–77. [CrossRef]
King, Nancy J., David A. Soulé, Sara Steen, and Robert R. Weidner. 2005. When Process Affects Punishment: Differences in Sentences after Guilty Plea, Bench Trial, and Jury Trial in Five Guidelines States. *Columbia Law Review* 105: 959–1009.
Lamoreaux, Naomi R. 2006. Rethinking Microhistory: A Comment. *Journal of the Early Republic* 26: 555–61. [CrossRef]

Lapore, Jill. 2001. Historians Who Love Too Much: Reflections on Microhistory and Biography. *The Journal of American History* 88: 129–44. [CrossRef]

Lehti, Martti, Juha Kääriäinen, and Janne Kivivuori. 2012. The Declining Number of Child Homicides in Finland, 1960–2009. *Homicide Studies* 16: 2–22. [CrossRef]

Levine, Kay L. 2003. Negotiating the Boundaries of Crime and Culture: A Sociolegal Perspective on Cultural Defense Strategies. *Law and Social Inquiry* 28: 39–86. [CrossRef]

Locke, Robert. 2003. Islam's Love-Hate Relationship with Homosexuality. *The Front Page*. January 23. Available online: http://archive.frontpagemag.com/readArticle.aspx?ARTID=20145 (accessed on 15 June 2017).

Malek, Amy. 2006. Memoir as Iranian Exile Cultural Production: A Case Study of Marjane Satrapi's "Persepolis" Series. *Iranian Studies* 39: 353–80. [CrossRef]

Mariano, Timothy, Heng Choon (Oliver) Chan, and Wade C. Myers. 2014. Toward a More Holistic Understanding of Filicide: A Multidisciplinary Analysis of 32 Years of U.S. 2014 Arrest Data. *Forensic Science International* 236: 46–53. [CrossRef] [PubMed]

Miele, William, and Nicole Spring. 2010. Author Interview with William Miele and Nicole Spring. Williamsport, PA, USA, June 10.

Mir-Hosseini, Ziba, and Kim Longinatto. 2003. *Divorce Iranian Style*, Video recording. Film by Ziba Mir-Hosseini and Kim Longinatto, 1998; New York: Women Make Movies.

Mobasher, Mohsen M. 2012. *Iranians in Texas: Migration, Politics, and Ethnic Identity*. Austin: University of Texas Press.

Modarres, Ali. 1998. Settlement Patterns of Iranians in the United States. 1998. *Iranian Studies* 31: 31–49. [CrossRef]

Mostofi, Nilou. 2003. Who We Are: The Perplexity of Iranian-American Identity. *The Sociological Quarterly* 44: 681–703. [CrossRef]

Osanloo, Arzoo. 2006a. The Measure of Mercy: Islamic Justice, Sovereign Power, and Human Rights in Iran. *Cultural Anthropology* 21: 575–79. [CrossRef]

Osanloo, Arzoo. 2006b. Islamico-Civil 'Rights-Talk:' Women, Subjectivity, and Law in Iranian Family Court. *American Ethnologist* 33: 190–209. [CrossRef]

Parsā-āʿlipur, Keyārash. 2009. Qatl-e Farzand: Pedar Taʿzir, Mādar Eʿdām, The Murder of a Child: The Father *Taʿzir*, the Mother, Execution. *Radiyo Zamāmeh*. October 28. Available online: http://zamaaneh.com/humanrights/2009/10/print_post_446.html (accessed on 27 May 2014).

Peltonen, Matti. 2001. Clues, Margins, and Monads: The Micro-Macro Link in Historical Research. *History and Theory* 40: 347–59. [CrossRef]

Pierce, Leslie. 1999. Orality, Honor, and Representation in the Ottoman Court of ʿAintab. In *Women in the Medieval Islamic World*. Edited by Gavin R. G. Hambly. New York: St. Martin's Press, pp. 347–59.

Public Affairs Alliance of Iranian Americans. 2014. *Iranian-Americans: Immigration and Assimilation*. Washington: Public Affairs Alliance of Iranian Americans, Available online: http://paaia.org/wp-content/uploads/2017/04/iranian-americans-immigration-and-assimilation.pdf (accessed on 15 June 2017).

Putnam, Lara. 2006. To Study the Fragments/Whole: Microhistory and the Atlantic World. *Journal of Social History* 39: 615–30. [CrossRef]

Rowe, G.S. 1991. Infanticide, Its Judicial Resolution, and Criminal code Revision in Early Pennsylvania. *Proceedings of the American Philosophical Society* 135: 208–10.

Schiller, Nina Glick, and Noel B Salazar. 2013. Regimes of Mobility across the Globe. *Journal of Ethnic and Migration Studies* 39: 183–200. [CrossRef]

Scott, Joan Wallach. 1999. *Gender and the Politics of History*, rev. ed. New York: Columbia University Press.

Sharafi, Mitra. 2008. Justice in Many Rooms since Galanter: De-Romanticizing Legal Pluralism through the Cultural Defense. *Law and Contemporary Problems* 71: 139–46. [CrossRef]

Spannus, Nathan. 2013. The Decline of the *Ākhūnd* and the Transformation of Islamic Law under the Russian Empire. *Islamic Law and Society* 20: 202–41. [CrossRef]

Superior Court of Pennsylvania. 2008. *Commonwealth of Pennsylvania, Appellee v. Brian Yasipour, Sr. Appellant*. Decided: September 17. Available online: http://caselaw.findlaw.com/pa-superior-court/1438863.html (accessed on 19 July 2017).

Tehranian, John. 2008. Selective Racialization: Middle-Eastern American Identity and the Faustian Pact with Whiteness. *Connecticut Law Review* 40: 1201. Available online: http://heinonline.org/HOL/LandingPage?handle=hein.journals/conlr40&div=42&id=&page= (accessed on 11 June 2017).

Tehranian, John. 2009. *Whitewashed: America's Invisible Middle Eastern Minority*. New York: NYU University Press.

Tomer-Fishman, Tamar. 2010. "Cultural Defense," "Cultural Offense," or no Culture at All?: An Empirical Examination of Israeli Judicial Decisions in Cultural Conflict Criminal Cases and of the Factors Affecting Them. *The Journal of Criminal Law and Criminology* 100: 475–522.

Tucker, Judith. 1998. *In the House of the Law: Gender and Islamic Law in Ottoman Syria and Palestine*. Berkeley: University of California Press.

TY. 2006. Transcript of Commonwealth of Pennsylvania vs. Brian Yasipour. No. 01-11,465, Trial, Williamsport, PA, USA. March 6, 7, 13, 14, 21 and 22.

Volpp, Leti. 2006. Disappearing Acts: On Gendered Violence, Pathological Cultures, and Civil Society. *PMLA* 121: 1631–38.

Volpp, Leti. 2012. Imaginings of Space in Immigration Law. *Law, Culture and the Humanities* 9: 457–74. [CrossRef]

Walters, Mary C., and Tomas R. Jimenez. 2005. Assessing Immigrant Assimilation: New Empirical and Theoretical Challenges. *Annual Review of Sociology* 31: 105–25. Available online: http://nrs.harvard.edu/urn-3:HUL.InstRepost:3203280 (accessed on 29 May 2015). [CrossRef]

Wheeler, Marcy. 2008. How Noninstitutionalized Media Change the Relationship between the Public and Media Coverage of Trials. *Law and Contemporary Problems* 71: 135–53.

Williamsport Sun-Gazette. 2014. Man Jailed for Murder Dead at 64. *Williamsport Sun-Gazette*, August 5.

WNEP. 2006. Man Guilty of Killing Daughter. Available online: http://wnep.com (accessed on 1 June 2006).

Yasipour, Brian. 2010. Author interview with Brian Yasipour. Somerset County, PA, USA: Pennsylvania State Correctional Institution-Laurel Highlands, June 11.

Ze'evi, Dror. 1998. The Use of Ottoman Sharia Court Records as a Source for Middle Eastern Social History: A Reappraisal. *Islamic Law and Society* 5: 35–56. [CrossRef]

Zia-Ebrahimi, Reza. 2016. *The Emergence of Iranian Nationalism: Race and the Politics of Dislocation*. New York: Columbia University Press.

Section 4:
Intersecting Forms of Im/mobility

Article

Mobilizing Conflict Testimony: A Lens of Mobility for the Study of Documentary Practices in the Kashmir Conflict

Max Kramer

Department of Indology and Central Asia Studies, University of Leipzig, Leipzig 04081, Germany; max_arne.kramer@uni-leipzig.de

Received: 15 June 2017; Accepted: 31 July 2017; Published: 6 August 2017

Abstract: In this paper I introduce a lens of mobility for the study of documentary film practices and gender in zones of conflict. By drawing on my qualitative research regarding the practice of the independent filmmaker Iffat Fatima, I will argue that a lens of mobility helps to grasp highly mobile media practices both conceptually and methodologically. Through a lens of mobility, my focus lies on the potential of documentary film to open the imaginative boundaries of conflict zones and to politically and emotionally mobilize the testimony offered from everyday life in a highly militarized zone. This specifically requires the tracing of moments of political mobilization beyond cognitive questions of conflicting narratives and representations.

Keywords: conflict cinema; documentary film; mobility; Kashmir; gender

---

1. Introduction

My research focuses on the articulation of subjectivities through the form of an independent digital documentary film in relation to the Kashmir conflict[1]. I took approximately a year of fieldwork—mostly in northern India, Kashmir, and a number of places in Europe—following professional documentary filmmakers who were actively screening or producing their films on the Kashmir conflict from 2013 to 2014. In this paper, I will draw on my research into the practices of the filmmaker Iffat Fatima, broadening discussions on new methodological and conceptual approaches for transregional media studies. I will further embed my contribution within the emerging field of film practices in zones of geopolitical conflict.

Iffat Fatima was born and grew up in the valley of Kashmir. In the year 1989, she moved to Delhi for higher education and completed her Masters in Mass Communication at Jamia Millia Islamia in 1990. Since then, she has been working as an independent documentary filmmaker and installation artist. Her recent work in Kashmir is closely linked to a documentary film she made on the Sri Lankan conflict that is titled *Lanka: The Other Side of War and Peace* (Fatima 2005). In this film, she drives up the highway A9 that was closed during the high intensity conflict between the Tamil north and the Singhalese south of Sri Lanka. On the road, she encounters people whose lives have been afflicted by enforced disappearances[2]. Although Fatima regularly kept track of the events in Kashmir by visiting her relatives, it was through the previous film and the changed socio-political setting in the mid-2000s that she decided to undertake a project on disappearances in Kashmir. During those years the decline

---

[1] The independence of their practice must be understood in relation to other media formats (like the commercial Hindi-Film) and in consideration of the kind of restrictions that can be expected within the networks of documentary film.

[2] According to Amnesty International, one speaks of enforced disappearance when security forces capture and imprison people without officially acknowledging the imprisonment or giving any information about the whereabouts of the victim (Amnesty International 2015).

of highly militarized violence in Kashmir coincided with the emergence of digital film technologies. The fluidity of digital technology enabled a constant refinement and re-editing of the form in response to multiple test screenings during the eight-year long production that finally resulted in *Khoon Diy Baarav* (Fatima 2015).

At the end of the opening sequence of *Khoon Diy Baarav*, Fatima's voice-over states the intention that guided the making and screening of her film:

> Over eight years, I travelled with her [Parveena Ahangar; see Section 4] across the scarred landscapes of Kashmir, a witness to its brutalization, its trauma. The film is a testimony, a consequence of my baring witness.

My research questions follow this opening statement from the voice-over: How does Fatima organize the textures of the film so that it can work as testimony? In which way is this linked to questions of the representation of Muslim women's agency in conflict zones? How does she enable the film to become public in a way that makes this testimony palpable? What are the difficulties she encounters in such an attempt? And finally, what is the potential for opening up the hardened imaginations of the Kashmir conflict through such a testimonial practice?

In the background of my discussion of *Khoon Diy Baarav* is academic work that deals with gender and conflict in the Kashmir Valley (Kazi 2008; Shekhawat 2014), anthropological research on the category of "everyday life" within the Kashmir conflict (Bhan 2013; Duschinski 2010; Hoffman and Duschinski 2013) and studies pertaining to the visual regimes of the conflict zone, primarily in relation to the commercial Hindi film industry (Kabir 2009; Gaur 2010). These texts share a common concern for moving away from realist geopolitical approaches and research that focus on the conflict around the relations between India and Pakistan or the established conflict parties such as the Hurriyat, Indian and local parliamentary parties, the different Indian security forces, and the various militant outfits. The above mentioned authors have sensitized us to the multiple dimensions and stakeholders of the conflict and, in particular, to the lifeworlds of those who are forced to live under conditions of enduring militarization, refusal of citizenship rights, censorship, and torture (for a recent contextualization, see: (Hoffman and Duschinski 2013)). However, my own research is not primarily a contribution to this field which some have called Critical Kashmir Studies (https://criticalkashmirstudies.com/about/core-scholars/) and nor is it a contribution to media-anthropology, sociological theory, or film studies; however, I hope that it may be of interest to each of these disciplines. From the example of Fatima's practice, I aim to introduce an interdisciplinary approach meant to open up new theoretical and methodological avenues for the study of conflict cinemas. With this intention, my goal is to turn the sometimes-professed lack of method, theory and subject matter of "regional studies" into its strength by linking such work to the new interdisciplinary research paradigm of "new mobility studies" (Sheller and Urry 2006). Through this lens, I hope to further the study of cinematic practices that are concerned with conflict zones from a transregional media studies perspective.

In this paper I argue that, in Iffat Fatima's filmic practice, different mobilities intersect. In the social sciences, the research paradigm of "new mobilities studies" investigates a wide range of levels of mobility and concepts of mobility beyond the more traditional focus on social mobility. For example, physical and social mobility (Sheller and Urry 2006) are linked to imaginative, communicative, and emotional mobilities (Robins 2004; Schneider 2015, p. 226). A mobility approach will direct our attention towards intersections between these levels. For example, in *Khoon Diy Baarav* representations of the filmic subject's physical movements through the space of the valley of Kashmir create audio-visual testimony for—and at the same time *beyond*—a conflict narrative. I have said "beyond" because these representations are often creatively negotiated between film, audience and filmmaker. When Fatima travels with her film, the representations intersect with the affective mobilization and emotional and intellectual mobilities of audiences. In the following I will show, how the intersections of these levels are of specific significance for Iffat Fatima's film practice. Thus, "Mobility" is not used as a conceptual catch-all but as a metaphor (Urry 2000) that enables me to describe and analyse communicative moments of high importance and intensity to both, the filmmaker and her audiences. For this purpose, I will draw on Nadja-Christina Schneider's introduction of a "lens of mobility" (Schneider 2015; see my explanation in Section 3) for the analysis of transregional media practices. In the following paragraphs, some of these intersecting mobilities will be introduced, before I go into further detail in the Sections 4–6 of this paper.

Khoon Diy Baarav depicts everyday movements of women in a highly militarized zone. In Kashmir—as in other zones of geopolitical conflict—an infrastructure of checkpoints, curfews, and strikes restricts freedom of movement. In Fatima's *Khoon Diy Baarav*, depictions of the movements of women, together with the filmmaker's camera, create a testimony of everyday life in a militarized territory. These representations also portray the agency of her filmic subjects as women participating in a social movement of political self-determination by showing sequences of people marching through the streets and shouting slogans of "freedom" (*azadi*). These depictions intervene in dominant visual regimes. On the one hand, Fatima challenges the depiction of "immobilized Muslim women" in post-liberalization India (Schneider 2015). On the other hand, the film interrogates Kashmir's hypervisibility as a place of touristic pleasure and a terrorist threat for the national integrity of India: Kashmir as a "place of national affect" (Urry 2007, p. 254) and "symbolic centrality" (Gaur 2010) within Indian nationalist discourses. These national discourses are again linked to the trope of 'secularism endangered by the kashmiri muslim' (Kabir 2009): a threat to the Indian nationalist imagination of 'unity in diversity'.

Screenings of Fatima's film have often been accompanied by highly emotional engagements from members of the audience. Besides of travelling with her film beyond the physical boundaries of India, Fatima gave particular importance to screening her film within India and in front of audiences where individual members may feel patriotic and/or dismissive of narratives that represent a desire for Kashmiri political self-determination. In these instances she needs to negotiate "anger" by contextualizing the actualities of her film, but she also furthers "empathy" through the same process of framing her film in post-screening debates. Often, audiences are silent for a while after the film finishes; sometimes members of the audience cry. These highly affected individuals often say that they have had little contact with Kashmiri narratives and images of everyday life from Kashmir. Notably, there are sometimes aspects of their national and personal identities which are challenged by the visible evidence narrated through her film.

Connected to the question of affect, there is a particular danger pertaining to what Fatima considers to be the wrong kind of publicity: will angry groups from the Hindu right use the film as a scene for the creation of publicity, as they have done with other documentary films on multiple occasions (see Section 6)? Visibilities resulting from these performances may again harden around the binary of "national-antinational". This could prevent her film from retaining its intended effect when becoming public: it could break her attempt to open up the imagination of audiences and create empathy for the subjectivities she wants to articulate. The eight-year long work of refining the filmic form was intended to create a spectator's engagement that is compassionate and empathic. It should enable audience members to acknowledge her filmic subjects' desires for political self-determination. This spectator's engagement will be lost if she cannot to some extent protect her film from the particular kinds of affect-driven publicity that I will describe in Section 6.

Thus, the metaphor of mobility needs to be extended to the way filmmakers emotionally mobilize audiences for a particular testimony of a conflict. Representations and affect are interlinked: one is always mobilizing for something that is again part of a social distribution of affects and symbols. But how does Fatima protect the way her film becomes public from the above mentioned conundrum of emotional mobilization around an area of "national affect" (Urry 2007, p. 254) and "symbolic centrality" (Gaur 2010, p. 15). I will argue that her physical mobility helps her to protect the "skin of the film" (Marks 2000). This concept refers to the vulnerability and materiality of film practices, where small networks enable particular audience-film-filmmaker interactions. I use this concept to speak about ways in which becoming public may prevent the force of her film to work as she intends.

In short, through the intersecting mobilities of Fatima's practice both representations and affect need to be seen as deeply interwoven. Throughout this paper, I will show how Fatima interrogates dominant representations of the symbolic and affective importance of Kashmir within an Indian nationalist imagination (Section 4), as well as the way she examines the national public sphere as a space of media effect (Section 6). I shall first contextualize my contribution within the emerging field of research that Smets (2015) calls "Cinemas of Conflict" before I clarify the above mentioned intersecting mobilities first methodogically (Section 3) and later by drawing on examples from Fatima's filmic practice (Sections 4–6).

2. Cinemas of Conflict

Smets (2015) introduced the term "Cinemas of Conflict" as a field of research at the intersection of Cultural Studies and Peace and Conflict Studies. Cinemas of Conflict focus on filmmakers as participants in a given conflict: "[...] because they are encapsulated in a model that takes into account production context, the nature of the conflict, the impact of the conflict on everyday life, the situation of the filmmaker and crew, and the position that they occupy vis-à-vis the conflict" (Smets 2015, p. 2438). Through this focus "vis-à-vis the conflict," Smets develops typologies which are primarily drawing on Galtung (1969) and Bar-Tal (2003), organizing filmic practices in relation to cognitive conflict dynamics. In zones of geopolitical conflict, identities are often seen as being played out against each other in zero sum games (Bar-Tal 2003, p. 77): our history vs. their history, our memory vs. their memory, our trauma vs. their trauma. Zones of "intractable conflict" (Bar-Tal 2003, p. 84) are defined by Bar-Tal as places where cults of victimhood and socio-political interest have led to the impression of an unending reproduction of a respective conflict's logic. However, the opposing narratives are asymmetrically positioned, with evocations of security threats to national integrity in popular News-TV channels or in commercial war films having considerable more visibility than the (increasingly digitally "mass self-communicated" (Castells 2013, pp. 58–71)) narratives emerging from the region of the valley of Kashmir.

In a survey of studies concerning the field of war and cinema, Smets concludes that these—besides looking primarily at European and American films—are bound to the framework of national cinema. On the other hand, he also suggests that we think beyond the framework of exile and diaspora cinema where many studies on Palestinian and Kurdish cinema are located (see for example: (Shohat 2010; Horat 2010; Dabashi 2006; Naficy 2001)). Smets discusses in particular the influential work on exilic and diaspora cinema undertaken by Hamid Naficy:

> According to Naficy, the concept refers to films that signify [. . .] upon exile and diaspora by expressing, allegorizing, commenting upon, and critiquing the home and host societies and cultures and the deterritorialized conditions of the filmmakers. They signify and signify upon cinematic traditions by means of their artisanal and collective production modes, their aesthetics and politics of smallness and imperfection, and their narrative strategies that cross generic boundaries and undermine cinematic realism. (Smets 2015, p. 2438)

Smets also points to the predominance of textual analysis in relation to conflicts in non-Western areas (Smets 2015, p. 2438). He omits to refer to the work of Shohat and Stam (1994) which would have been helpful in showing a transtextual and transnational approach that does not focus primarily on questions of diaspora or exilic subject-positions, but densely contextualizes film practices in relation to particular conflicts.

In most of the above-mentioned studies, the cinema dealing with conflict zones has been addressed via the trope of memory, both collective and individual, that is sometimes thought to challenge official state narratives (see e.g., (Edwards 2015; Wang 2014; Macedo and Cabecinhas 2013; Chanan 2008; Pickowicz and Zhang 2006)). This relative 'dominance' of memory-cultural approaches is understandable because of the agents' attempts to render minor subjectivities visible by drawing on the enhanced possibilities of digital media. High quality films can be made with tiny crews and little budget, thus also supporting more individual film practices (Renov 2004) and new forms of observational realism—especially in the field of Chinese independent documentary (Berry et al. 2010). Recently, these memory and textual approaches within the field of media and conflict have been extended and partly circumvented by approaches of "political aesthetics" drawing on French philosopher Jacques Ranciére's "distribution of the sensible" (Rancière 2013, p. 7) by topographically tracing "practices in which time and space—that is the conditions for the possibility of subjectivity—are taken as the object of experimentation" (Tanke 2010, p. 15). This approach is meant to investigate artistic practices, where the limits of what can be seen and said are pushed and new ways of living are experimented with (Tanke 2010). This approach earned a certain popularity with the rise of the emancipatory, egalitarian potentials of digital media that make didactic media politics increasingly difficult to sustain in the light of a pro-sumer culture (Tanke 2010, p. 15). So, instead of looking at conflict–memory, political–aesthetic analyses are primarily interested in opening potentials (scholars drawing on Ranciére for the study of the visual culture of conflict regions include: (McLagan and McKee 2012; Hochberg 2015)). This again may be conceptually difficult to connect to both the politics of representation and a more sociological analysis, where one would be interested in the specific practices and limitations of individual agents within larger networks of documentary film (see the critique of (Kastner and Sonderegger 2014)). It also means that political-aesthetic approaches may not be helpful when we are trying to understand the moments when filmmakers inscribe themselves *within* pre-existing identity narratives or are negotiating a certain representation of testimony. The latter problem is of particular importance for the way I will further frame my question: how does Iffat Fatima mobilize testimony in the attempt to articulate a subjectivity *of and beyond* existing conflict narratives?

What is often left out of the way commercial cinema and news-television frame conflict zones is the everyday life, e.g., the mundane difficulties that result from living in usually densely militarized territories. A number of studies in an edited volume by Matar and Harb (2013) address this problem in relation to Palestine/Israel by showing the wide range of media practices in conflict zones that narrate conflicts "from below" (Matar and Harb 2013) by focusing on the everyday life of conflict zones. Amongst these media formats, documentary film has widened its potential since the emergence of digital technology in the field (in the late 1990s) to render visible the subjectivities of filmmakers who are deeply involved in the conflicts or themselves are numbered among the conflicts' victims. It has been argued that digital film practices often make it possible to circumvent state regulations pertaining to the visibilities of highly contested regions (Ezra and Rowden 2006). Thus via an independent digital documentary practice new forms of creating testimony and mobilizing audiences beyond the nation state's regulation are available. Indeed, Filmmakers not only participate in conflicts and are socially positioned in relation to the conflict's logic and the possibilities of the documentary field, but increasingly able to go beyond them without losing the grip on the local struggles they represent.

To extend the existing ways of looking at film practices in conflict zones, I draw on recent theorizations in "new mobility studies" (Sheller and Urry 2006; Urry 2000) and the data from my own qualitative research in order to introduce a "lens of mobility" (Schneider 2015) for the study of Cinemas of Conflict. Following Kevin Smets, my attempt is to point beyond studies of conflict zones that privilege exile and diasporic "in-betweenness" or reproduce the framework of national cinema. By researching the filmic practice of Iffat Fatima, I look into the ways through which she tries to challenge and open up the imagination of the Kashmir conflict. In this respect, typological categorizations through corpus-analytic approaches (as undertaken by Smets or Morag) are not helpful either when it comes to our understanding of the affective, opening and closing potentials of the documentary form. Thus, I have begun to investigate the form at the intersection of various mobilities—an approach which I shall outline in the following section.

3. A Lens of Mobility

Two recent works by Schneider (2015) and Mukherjee (2012) have suggested the framing of film practices through questions of mobility. The field of professional documentary practice is in many respects highly globalized and interconnected (e.g., in the funding and festival circuit). Thus, travelling with films, and pitching and negotiating them at various places which host festivals and workshops, is part of many filmmakers' practice. But how do these mobilities intersect and how could these intersections be conceptualized to capture which levels of mobility are at stake in (or even central to) independent documentary film practices of today?

Schneider (2015) looks at the "entanglement" between representations of mobility, politics of (im)mobility, and the mediation of mobility in the case of Indian Muslim womens' film practices. For Schneider, this includes questions of "emotional-","intellectual-", and "imaginative mobility" (Robins 2004, pp. 114–32), and the possibility of questioning stereotypes of Muslim womens "immobility". This lens would enable us to "sharpen our understanding of the interrelationship between new media configurations, emerging practices of mobility and processes of sociocultural change" (Schneider 2015, p. 225) enabling also an understanding of the various localities people appropriate within the media enviroments of today (Schneider 2015, p. 232). Mukherjee analysed the movements of "always-on-the-move filmmakers who attempt to connect place-based struggles, stitching together recorded footage from various places to bring out the commonalities and shared patterns among them" (Mukherjee 2012, p. 54). He points out the importance of both representations of movements—e.g., depictions of train journeys for labour migrants—and the affective registers of songs. In Biju Toppo's film *Kora Rajee—Land of the Diggers* (Toppo 2005), for Mukherjee, the use of songs "is an invitation to all of us to experience not only the spatial journeys with Toppo and his co-travelers, but also move across time joining the colonial and postcolonial coordinates of tribal suffering in India to question development's spatio-temporal logic" (Mukherjee 2012, p. 65). We get a sense of the intersection between the mobile lifeworlds of *adivasi* labour migrants and the film's mode of production and circulation. To flesh out these modes, the term "translocal" serves Mukherjee as an "analytical category to understand the circulation of documentary films in international festivals, the use of social actors in documentaries from various locales, or to explain the use of multi-sited documentary ethnographies to create critical 'geographical vocabularies' (Chanan 2010) for local-global audiences" (Mukherjee 2012, p. 65).

In what follows within this section, I shall argue that a lens of mobility is particularly helpful for the study of independent documentary film practices that engage with regions of geopolitical conflict. In this describtion, I shall link questions of representation to those of physical movements and emotional mobilization. In fact, what I have been mostly interested in are form-driven attempts by filmmakers to find ways out of the "intractable" and long-enduring Kashmir conflict, made to establish the conditions through which alternatives can be communicatively imagined and affectively mobilized. Iffat Fatima[3] often asks herself how to emotionally move and politically mobilize audience members who may have been exposed to nationalist rhetorics of mutually exclusive national/religious identities or invested in top-down geopolitical arguments about the strategic necessities of territory and national security. She considers her filmic form partly as an attempt to affect audiences through visible evidence that shakes the ground of discursive attempts by members of various audiences to explain away some concrete realities of "everyday life" in an occupied zone.

As taken up by Schneider (2015), an understanding of mobility refers beyond representations of mobility and the physical movements of filmmakers, including aspects of affect and creative negotiation through the audio-visual form of documentary film. To conceptualize these crucial attempts of

[3] When I speak about Iffat Fatima's intentions, I refer to a large number of recorded conversations I had conducted with the filmmaker since the end of 2013. Amonst them are conversations in New Delhi (28 February 2013; 27 October 2014; 16 December 2014) and via Skype (21 October 2015; 23 October 2015; 27 October 2015; 7 April 2016).

filmmakers, to think outside of the box of established narratives, she draws on Robins (2004) concepts of "intellectual-", "emotional-", and "imaginative mobility". Robins uses these terms to refer to media practices that not only inscribe themselves in one of the many already available identity narratives—or "imagined communities" (Anderson 2006)—but open up new subjectivities "beyond" (Robins 2004, pp. 114–32) them. In the case of my research on film practices that deal with zones of conflict, imaginative mobility refers to collective creative imaginations that challenge dominant frames of territoriality, sovereignty and public sphere(s). In his work on the media practices of Turkish labour migrants, Robins argued that individual agents challenge national imaginations by thinking outside of identitatarian logics (Robins 2004, pp. 114–32). He draws here—as do other mobility thinkers—on ontogenetics: the constant movement and change of *life as movement* that is epistemologically favored, instead of thought that epistemologically favors concepts which suggest a fixity of such social imaginaries as "national security" or "identity-politics" (see (Adey 2010; Urry 2000)). However, the danger may also arise here that one concentrates on opening potentials without contextualizing practices within the exisiting structural moments to which imaginations of the nation belong just as state regulations and the financial strictures of the field of independent documentary filmmaking. This is why I find Schneider's attention to the importance of representations of "im-mobilities", and (Sheller and Urry 2006; Göttsch-Elten 2011, p. 29) arguments to link processes of mobility as a reflexive category to immobility, fruitful. As Schneider (2015, p. 227) conceptualizes the term, processes of mobility would "also include the image distribution, circulation of perceptions, and information in local, national and global media. The politics of mobility as well as the representation of immobility should thus be central to any analysis [...] (Schneider 2015, p. 227).

In these above mentioned approaches, I regard immobility as a metaphor for structural moments such as sedimented narratives and visual regimes (e.g., memory and history writing, iconic depictions of conflict; media-discourses), social boundaries; social imaginations (the nation), and state and societal regulations (censorship, public shaming, etc.). I begin here with representations.

3.1. Representations

In zones of conflict, military presence leads to different kinds of physical immobility, such as roadblocks, checkpoints, id-controls, etc. Representing the everyday life in a conflict zone could be regarded as a particular strength of the independent documentary film, and often points towards the question of the (im)possibility of everyday movements (Morag 2013). Such everyday immobilities may not be very prominent in highly visible media formats where questions of national security frame images. The Hindi film industry is known for its allegorical treatment of the nation state and anxieties constructed around the "territorial integrity" of the mother nation being played out in relation to the "Muslim Other" (Gaur 2010). In the mediascapes of the Hindi film and 24/7 news television, and its convergent images as seen circulating through social media networks, we often witness how decontextualized images of violence coalesce at "places of national affect" (Urry 2007, p. 254). Representations of Kashmir in the Hindi film often resemble statements of India's first Prime Minister Jawaharlal Nehru, who saw the region as a place of pastoral feminine beauty and religious "otherness" while at the same time being central to the very idea of India (Anderson 2012, p. 80). In the Hindi film, the territory of the Kashmir Valley has been turned into an affect-loaded place, that is at the same time of "symbolic centrality" (Gaur 2010, p. 15)—especially to articulations of national secularism: the Kashmiri Muslim Other serves often to reaffirm a national secular self (Gaur 2010, pp. 36–38). From the 1960s onward until the beginning of the armed conflict in 1989, the region primarily figured as a touristic playground for Indian middle classes against the backdrop of mountains, lakes, and flower fields. After 1989, the same landscapes were re-framed through barbed wire, evoking the loss of paradise after an onset of armed conflict (Kabir 2009). The two main cinematic protagonists here, the terrorist and the tourist, are highly mobile agents, crossing boundaries for pleasure or/and for instilling terror and endangering national integrity. I have shown elsewhere (Kramer 2015) how the processes of touristic permeation (and linkages between the tourism industry, the Hindi film industry, and local government) and the framing of Kashmir as a security threat must be seen as symbiotic and take part in the continuation of the status quo. These well-known images of tourist pleasures and terrorist threats have been widely circulating through visual cultures in South Asia, overdetermining the political history of the conflict, which was one of central state misgovernance, militarization, and human rights violations by state agents (Bose 1997; Hoffman and Duschinski 2013).

3.2. Scales

An analysis of filmic mobilities makes it necessary to scale between the local and the global, looking at the dynamics through which the nation state gets challenged and sometimes transcended by transregional and translocal connectivities (see here the work in critical transnational film studies of Higbee and Lim 2010). To understand these connections, I draw on the word-pair territorialization/deterritorialization, defined by media culture scholar Andreas Hepp in the following way:

> Territorialization can be defined as the process in which an identifiable territory (a 'country', a 'region', a 'continent') is constructed as a physically anchored point of reference for a particular (media) culture, or as a form of communitization related to it. [...] Deterritorialization is, by contrast, the 'loosening' of this apparently 'natural' relationship between culture, communitization and territoriality. (Hepp 2012, p. 108)

I find it useful to extend this media cultural approach through the concept of (de)territorialization as it was established within the work of Deleuze and Guattari (1972). In short, this provides a framework for speaking about the potential of audience members being affected by film to open up beyond the already known narratives, categories and stereotypes. It involves attempts to capture new ways of thinking and feeling, thus offering imaginative and emotional mobility (Robins 2004). At the same time, a mobility focus on a filmmaker's agency must circumvent the anti-phenomenological positions of Deleuze and Guattaris' subjectless affect theory (no subject, no intentionality, no representation, etc.) to take the agent in an already more cohesive way as a human subject.

One of these new ways of reterritorialization attempted by the filmmaker Iffat Fatima (and other filmmakers who work on the Kashmir conflict such as Sanjay Kak and Uzma Falak) can be seen as the "translocal"—where local struggles are connected and broader scales of interaction established, that may or may not refer to the nation or region (Oakes and Schein 2006, p. 10). In the case of Fatima's practice, we are dealing with moments that are often "transnational" in scale because her film is sometimes negotiated by audience members through a national lens while her funding and film-networks are largly transcending the boundaries of the Indian nation-state. That some audience members negotiate her film via the category 'nation' has to do with Kashmirs above mentioned "symbolic centrality" (Gaur 2010) for the Indian nation-state. I shall follow the warning articulated by Higbee and Lim:

> [...] [W]hile the term 'transnational cinema' appears to be used and applied with increasing frequency as both a descriptive and conceptual marker, it also tends, for the most part, to be taken as a given—as shorthand for an international or supranational mode of film production whose impact and reach lies beyond the bounds of the national. The danger here is that the national simply becomes displaced or negated in such analysis, as if it ceases to exist, when in fact the national continues to exert the force of its presence even within transnational filmmaking practices. [...] [O]ne of the potential weaknesses of the conceptual term 'transnational cinema' [...] [is that] it risks celebrating the supranational flow or transnational exchange of peoples, images and cultures at the expense of the specific cultural, historical or ideological context in which these exchanges take place. (Higbee and Lim 2010, pp. 10–12)

Thus, if the transnational takes the normative and regulative presence of nation-state institutions and the imaginations of the nation state seriously, one needs to inquire into the moments when opening up our imagination of national sovereignty and security can be decribed as translocal. The concept of translocality is challenging to our understanding of a "public sphere", thus the referent of territory in which the films are seen to operate and cause effects. The next section deals with the methodological question: How can we investigate the opening and closing potentials of affect in the way films are "made public" (McLagan and McKee 2012, p. 10)?

3.3. Mobile Methods: Affects and Performances

While more text-based approaches from the humanties are helpful to understanding the politics of representation, the tropes of (im-)mobilities, and the discourses surrounding conflict, a lens of mobility as outlined above also requires a grasp of the way films mobilize and get negotiated. This could be achieved through mobile methods that imply: "to move with and to be moved by subjects" (Büscher et al. 2011, p. 7). Following the critical appraisal of mobile methods by Merriman (2014, p. 183), I do not see the focus of a mobilities approach resting solely on phenomenological, presentive aspects of social practices. Merriman warned that "non-representative" (Thrift 2008) methodologies should not be substituted for questions of text, discourse, and representation; otherwise, we would lose our grip on central aspects of social practices. They can serve, however, as an extension of the kind of phenomena and questions that matter to documentary film practices. From a media-culture perspective (Hepp 2012), one engages with the communicative form, of which representations are one important level amongst production, circulation, reception, and appropriation. In fact, without keeping an eye on the politics of representation (e.g., of evidence, memory, and history), the politics of documentary film cannot be understood. But by "following" film practices—by moving with the films and with the agents—I was able to capture the processes of negotations of filmic form in moments of high intensity contestations. These contestations, again, may not only say something about frames of representation through which the filmic form is negotiated between the filmmakers and audiences. These negotiations are also a central part of a mobile film practice, as in the case of Iffat Fatima, who often moves together with her films.

However, an approach that includes phenomenological questions demands that the researcher looks beyond dynamics of representative categories (e.g., the Kashmiri self-determination narrative vs. the Indian state narrative) towards not yet cognitive, affective potentials of filmic practices. Köhn (2016) recently pointed out the usefulness of film phenomenology for the mediation of mobility. For Köhn, this perspective offers "an understanding of audiovisual mediation that is attentive to the perceptive processes media involve the spectator in, and thus brings into view the meaningfulness of an embodied viewing experience" (Köhn 2016, p. 23). By drawing on film phenomenologist Marks (2000), I would like to refer to theories that conceptualize wider aspects of affect and sense perception for independent filmmakers. These aspects involve filmmakers, spectators, and researchers as embodied beings, who participate in the often ambivalent and contradictory sensory negotiation of a film—or, in the words of Merleau-Ponty (1968), "the thickness of flesh between the seer and the thing" (Merleau-Ponty 1968, p. 18; see also (Köhn 2016, p. 23)).

By following Iffat Fatima's practice, I became particularly interested in the affective politics linked to performances of films. How do they initiate and partake in forms of collective or individual "anger" and "empathy"? How do they create compassionate reactions and what do these imply for our understanding of who belongs to a group and who does not? By "performance", I understand the documentary film as something, which is negotiated between images of possible realities and possible interpretations of those realities (Bruzzi 2006, pp. 6–7). This understanding conceptually serves my study by moving away from older questions of 'what *the* reality of the documentary image is' while keeping its mimetic claim. Corner (2011) refers to this as "propositional realism" (Corner 2011, p. 72) that, by drawing on the words of documentary scholar Winston (2008), "claims the real". For Corner, this strongly links the form to the creation of "testimony", where audiovisual sequences and actualities testify for events expected to have happened in some reality.

In connection with social imaginations (such as "the nation" as an imagined community; Anderson (2006)), affects, when symbolized and negotiated via language, can become the basis for inclusions and exclusions within and beyond established narratives. Inclusions and exclusions can get sedimented in metaphors such as "our history", "our memory", "national integrity", or "the national public sphere". This also means that we have to look at the way the categories of "(the/a) public(s)" are performed and mediated through aspects of mobility, and as both moments where territory is marked by negotiations of otherness, and by increasing instances of deterritorialization. In the case of Fatima's practice, I argue that her movements and filmic form open up spaces beyond often normatively used categories of civil society or the "bourgeois public sphere" (Habermas 1990). This understanding builds on the critique of Jürgen Habermas concept of a "bürgerlichen Öffentlichkeit" put forward by a number of scholars (Negt and Kluge 1972; Fraser 1992; Warner 2002). In short, questions have been raised about who is excluded from Habermas conceptualization (Fraser 1992), what is the implicit territoriality of the public sphere (e.g., the nation-state; (Eley 1992)), where are liberal boundaries drawn between reason and affect (Warner 2002) and what does this imply in terms of the politics of mediation, form and address (Mazzarella 2013)? For the South Asian context, Bhandari (2006) and Mazzarella (2013) are important references regarding the plurality of publics and (affective) styles of public performances resulting partly from a post-colonial historical trajectory. I shall argue below in Section 6 that the plurality of publics—often different in style, in address, and in their potential for publicity—is taken as a serious concern by Fatima, who through her physical movements and emotional mobilization often renders the ideological boundaries (especially invested in normative ideas) of publics porous.

One rather obvious question may arise in relation to the above delineated approach: if so vastly different aspects are included—from emotional mobilization, to physical mobility, to representations of mobility and publics—where is the conceptual coherence that enables us to describe and explain these moments as significantly resulting from mobility? How does this instrument of analysis add anything to the way we understood film practices and subjectivities in conflict zones? Following Schneider and Mukkherjee, I argue that a lens of mobility adds to our understanding primarily when we draw on empirical data to show the intersections of those levels described above in specific descriptions and analysis of filmic practices. In the remaining sections of this paper, I shall outline aspects of my own research that led me to a conceptualization of a lens of mobility via the example of the filmmaker Iffat Fatima.

4. Representations of Gender, Islam and Mobility

The mothers and wives of the Association of the Parents of Disappeared People (APDP) holding pictures of their disappeared family members have in recent years become the subjects of some of the Kashmir conflict's more visible images. The APDP, headed by Parveena Ahangar, is an organisation which strives toward making the Indian army accountable for human rights violations, drawing attention to the enforced disappearances of the last 20 years as committed under the draconic Armed Forces Special Powers Act (AFSPA) which gives impunity to the operations of armed forces in "disturbed areas". In a number of documentaries and feature films, these individuals have been framed as depicting the 'human side' of the conflict, displaying the sorrows of the waiting women, while sometimes linking them up in a somewhat departmentalised way to the suffering of other groups—in particular, Kashmiri Pandit and Sikh women. Fatima's film *Khoon Diy Baarav* (2015) takes a rather different route in offering an explicit political positioning in an embedded production. The film was funded by the Norwegian women's rights' organisation Fokus as part of a long-term project supporting the APDP. Besides the support of Fokus, the production costs were limited because of the cheapness and malleability of digital film. While Fokus did not pressure the filmmaker to make any changes in the film, questions were raised regarding why she neither develops a character-driven narrative nor positions herself more reflexively in the film's textures. Fatima holds that this would be detrimental to both the political nature of the Kashmir conflict and the assertive political articulations of gendered resistance which have hitherto been rarely expressed outside of the discourse of human rights abuses with a focus on passive loss and suffering as inflicted by the ongoing conflict. In many reportages and documentary films on the Kashmir conflict Parveena Ahangar is depicted through a certain almost iconic sequence of mourning and a demand for justice directed at an unresponsive government. This sequence has now moved on in intermedial space and can be seen in a number of recent Hindi feature films as well (amongst them are: (*Lamhaa* (Dholakia 2010); *Harud* (Bashir 2012); (*Haider* Bhardwaj 2014)).

As mentioned above, women in conflict zones (Sharoni 2001)—and in particular Muslim women in India after the economic liberalization (Schneider 2015)—have often been represented only as (religiously) immobilized victims. Fatima's strategy was to challenge this visual regime by showing her female subjects in their everyday (im-)mobility and in their participation in the popular demands for political self-determination. Thus, she contextualizes this demand through the everyday and links it to the memory and passions that drive the subjects of her film to continue the demand for justice and freedom. In order to clarify this strategy of representation, let me discuss the beginning sequence of *Khoon Diy Baarav* that also serves as a signature for the formal approach of her film.

The film begins with a fade-in from black. We see Shamima Bano, whose husband Shabir 'disappeared', steering her boat through the backwaters of the quarters where she lives as a member of the Hanji community dwelling in the lakes of Srinagar (See Figure 1.). She speaks about the memory of her disappeared husband who came to her in a dream, saying, "I am Shabir"; she replied, "You cannot be Shabir, his face was the same, not his feet. I [Shamima Bano] tell him: I have put a mark on him [...] we have to do a DNA test." Next we see some images of the flora and fauna of the lake in winter. Shamima continues to recount her dream: Shabir tries to reassure her that it is actually him, but she tells him "No, no, no, we'll take blood from your father and test it to find out if you are his son, I woke up, my god what did I see". The boat passes by a group of men sitting in boats at the shore of the waterway. There is the close-up of one of them smoking his water pipe quietly while a little bird magically lands on his right shoulder. The next images show a few dogs—one puppy lost between barbed wire—and two children standing at the shore of the lake. We hear Fatima's voice asking Shamima, "Did you ever hear anything about him?" She replies: "Nothing, no trace of him."

Figure 1. *Khoon Diy Baarav* (2015), beginning sequence, by courtesy of Iffat Fatima.

Iffat Fatima stresses that her film attempts to reclaim the spaces taken away from the Kashmiris through the physical and imaginary occupation of the region. Commenting on what motivated her to include another boat scene with Parveena Ahangar positioned at the very end of the film, she pointed to a documentary by Zul Vellani called *Aatish-e-Chinar* (1998):

> which begins with this man sitting relaxed on the Dal Lake just rowing and [he] says something like: 'Oh what a wonderful thing this is, this great Kashmiri Culture!' Sitting on the boat as if he's in complete control, as if he's the maharaja there, that's why I put Parveena in that style. (Fatima in conversation, New Delhi, 4 April 2014)

Fatima attempts to show how these women exercise their agencies by moving through the militarised spaces of the valley, suffusing them with memories and dreams of loss and assertion. Shamima Bano's boat journey challenges the countless representations of the stereotypical male Hanji, who is always ready to serve Indian tourists as they enjoy their tours through the valley (Kabir 2009). The mention of the DNA test in a dreamlike sequence is a shocking testament of how the legal framework in which the APDP operate is pervading the women's lives, eating its way into their dreams. The sequence also shows Fatima's reflexivity concerning dominant depictions of the Valley of Kashmir. Extending an argument of Kabir (2009), I understand the image of the boat journey on the lakes and rivers of Kashmir as an inverted tourist gaze (Urry 2002) through which Fatima inscribes Kashmiri subjectivities into the overexposed landscapes of the valley. Through this representation, the enjoyments of the tourist figure exposed to a normalising gaze of consumption have been linked to the memory of those living in a region being held under the sway of an overwhelming military presence. I have shown elsewhere (Kramer 2015) that the trope of the boat journey pervades representations of the valley in both Hindi film and documentary films. In fact, the use of this touristic image enables Fatima to address an audience familiar with those tropes that widely circulate among South Asian publics (see (Kabir 2009)). But how do these images—invested in a natural movement—frame the larger presentational form of her film?

Fatima's film is distinctly organized around spatial moments. The women in *Khoon Diy Baarav* are depicted through the logic of "walking with", where in the process they show through carefully chosen actuality footage of everyday occurrences (e.g., encounters with the military, work in the field, walks in the forest, a wedding ceremony) the scars of conflict and their hopes for redress. During the production of the film, Fatima's own movements within the valley had also been at a certain risk, when she was—together with members of her crew—for one day imprisoned in an army camp for shooting footage of its surroundings. Her high social status as a filmmaker from New Delhi and her networks in Kashmir have enabled her to get out of this relatively dangerous situation. Approximately the first hour of *Khoon Diy Baarav* is largely dedicated to making the viewer acquainted with four women of the APDP. By accompanying them and hearing about their disappeared family members, we learn about their desires and dreams. The second half of the film is marked by highly emotive sequences of mass protest and mourning. Since these kinds of images are strongly contested, one could be tempted to read them—following Kevin Smets typology—as taking part in "victim cinema" where filmmakers share certain beliefs of patriotism via the victimization of their own group (Smets 2015, p. 2442). For Smets, following Bar-Tal (2003, p. 85), it is a cinema of "affected parties" (Smets 2015, p. 2442). Even though members of Fatima's audiences have sometimes commented on the one sidedness of her position (in favour of *azadi*) or tried to transcend the political intend of the images by referring to a shared humanity, I like to show that attempts to categorize her film as victim-centric, humanitarian or as being driven by *ressentiment* would fall short of the particular way the film is mediated in relation to highly affective images.

5. Refining the Form and Emotional Mobilization

The film has been more than eight years in the making. In the first two years of the project, Fatima did not shoot much footage because of a crisis the APDP was undergoing at that time. The money of Fokus was first used to stabilise the institutional set-up and later extended for three more years. A provisional version of the film called *On a Trail of Vanished Blood* (Fatima 2012) was screened three times, once in Norway and twice in India, where it garnered one rather heated discussion that provoked the filmmaker to rethink its modes of address. Such changes as were made include the beginning scenes of the film where, originally, groups of young men and women throw stones and perform a *ragḍa* around a blazing fire in the night. In Kashmir, a *ragḍa* has become a new technology of resistance, practiced since the year 2008: it entails a group standing in a circle and stamping their feet on the ground, often burning some object in the middle. This may be an Indian flag or a figure (straw man) of a popular Indian politician. See Figure 2.

Figure 2. *Khoon Diy Baarav* (2015), sequence of a *ragḍa*, by courtesy of Iffat Fatima.

Although in the scene the object between the stamping feet is not clear, the intensity of the rioting was later regarded by Fatima as a potential threat to Indian spectators' engagement with the politics of the film, and so it was shifted to a later positioning within *Khoon Diy Baarav*. At the same time, one could perceive a certain impasse between on the one hand the idea of a zero sum game between regressive discourses of victimization and on the other hand, anti-mimetic, experimental practices, that do not sufficiently engage with the politics of representation. She needed this image to show a certain anger, but at the same time this anger should not be conceived as simply regressive. To clarify this point, let me report a rather extensive excerpt from a conversation of mine with the filmmaker:

> I.F.: The first comment that comes out [of public debate on the film] is that it is a very powerful film. Now, the term 'powerful'—I do not know what is implied by that.
>
> M.K.: Perhaps that [sometimes] means "politically mobilizing in a problematic way" [...]; people want to be polite.
>
> I.F.: They also say they are very moved by it [...]; many of them have said that "the filmmaker is seducing us, but you don't know what actually is there. Look at the Kashmiri Pandits, look what they have done to them." So that these realities are wiped out and they seem to think that the film also can have the capacity to 'inflame'.
>
> M.K.: Yes, William Mazzarella describes this in his book (Mazzarella 2013): [A] postcolonial mindset is thinking about crowds that are easily emotionally mobilized: as soon as 'they' hear azadi-slogans, 'they' go out and demolish everything. But the way 'crowds' are functioning is at the same time very well organized as a kind of staged drama they play out. That is a form of delegitimizing political articulation. In Persistence/Resistance [filmfestival in New-Delhi, 18 February 2014] *Jashn-e-Azadi* (Kak 2007) [a film dealing with the articulation of Kashmiri political self-determination, directed by the filmmaker Sanjay Kak] was screened and it [was criticized to] work somehow similar in the way it

> creates affects of azadi. So you see movements, you see people marching, throwing stones, shouting "azadi" and so on. When you watch it you [may also] feel sympathetic...
>
> I.F.: [...] It takes you with it [...], but that is the objective of the filmmaker. The filmmaker does want you to empathize with those women, but that does not mean that people get out and start throwing stones. [...] But you also have to draw in your audience so that they can also engage with it. Those are very serious questions when one is making a film. [...] You have to create empathy; that is in some ways the objective of the film. That empathy factor can get disrupted—it can become a reactionary taste. It is a thin line. That is why I sometimes have a problem with that title, 'vanished blood'. I feel that maybe that also goes into that disruptive area. (conversation with Iffat Fatima, 27 October 2015)

The spectator should through the new position of the *ragḍa* -sequence open up to a Kashmiri experience of the conflict. In other words: The seemingly "resentful" image of a *ragḍa* must not be confused with the idea of ressentiment. Fassin (2013) differentiates between this nietzschean use of the French term "*ressentiment*" and "resentment" as two politically relevant ways of subjectivation, referring to the moral value of affects such as indignation, anger, ire, and bitterness (Fassin 2013, p. 250). For Nietzsche, it was a reactionary mode coming from dialectics where the position from below keeps the "evil one" as its Other and construes its own moral value as an afterthought to the same (Fassin 2013, p. 251). On the other hand, Fassin points to Adam Smith, who considered "resentment" as a normal yet disagreeable passion that "can be disciplined as long as a sense of justice prevails" (Fassin 2013, p. 251). Following Fassin's differentiation, the mode of political subjectivation of Fatima's film follows the memory trace of affective "resentment" that is articulated "from below" and conveyed forcefully through the re-positioning of the sequence at the end of the new film. At the same time, this portrays the deep engagement of Fatima with the temporalities of documentary film. The new positioning of the *ragḍa* sequence is the result of a careful elaboration upon the "everyday" in an occupied territory, which she mediates through the actualities documented and partly provoked by her walking together with the film's protagonists. For Fatima, the form resulted "organically" out of her long work together with the women of the APDP. In fact, this refinement of form may have led to a phenomena that Fatima has experienced after most of her screenings. A certain silence before people speak points perhaps towards a saturation of evidence throughout ninety minutes of documentary film, in which the consequences of military occupation become difficult to deny or bury under national or geopolitical rhetorics.

During this long period of production, Fatima did not apply for any pitching sessions of European funding institutions that are often accompanied by normative frameworks regarding the narrative form, such as the "journey of the hero" (Friedman 2015). On the other hand, she completely circumvented film certification, which would enable a TV-distribution in India. Since "questioning sovereignty and integrity of India" is amongst the guideline of certification, Fatima knew that there is little hope to maintain the presentational form of the film while letting it be certified. Even if screening documentary films without certification is common practice in a large number of grassroots film festivals in India, problems for uncertified films (and their makers) may arise in terms of opening space to political attacks from the Hindu right (see next section). Documentary filmmakers in India can certify more "balanced" versions of their films and travel with the uncensored cut. But for Fatima, the refinement of the filmic form needs also to be seen as part and parcel of her attempts at creating the specific conditions through which the film can be seen. This is going beyond the presentational form of the filmic artefact. Since she was especially interested in the way her film worked emotionally with audiences, she needed to follow it herself and—as we shall see in the next section—protect its vulnerable "skin".

In short: the form of the film is neither reducible to the digital or physical artefact of "film", nor to the negotiation of cognitive cues about its symbolic structure. The way in which I briefly framed a lens of mobility above requires us to search for possible openings between narratives, especially in relation to aspects of affect in documentary practices. I shall elaborate upon this question of affect more closely in the following section and link it to Fatima's practice of accompanying the screenings of her film.

6. Mobility and Publics: Protecting the Skin of the Film

I learned about the particular importance of affect while travelling with Fatima and having conversations with her about the interactions of audiences with her film. *Khoon Diy Baarav* touches a sensitive spot in the nationalist imagination of India—the very idea of national integrity. With audience members who identify themselves as national or patriotic in relation to Kashmir (or Pakistan), negative affective responses are imminent possibilities. These include not only reactions to screenings of the film, but the larger media environment, within which documentary films can become visible—even without being seen by those who are out to denounce them. When Iffat Fatima began showing her film in 2016, it was on the background of student protests at Jawaharlal Nehru University and at the University of Hyderabad, during which some Indian news anchors and journalists started a campaign against everything "anti-national" (Nair 2016, p. x). Well known to media practitioners in India, this term can—similar to questions of the defence of "Hindu sentiments" in the face of media liberalization (Ghosh 2010, p. 43)—become a rallying cry for the creation of mass-publicity. During her journey with the film, Fatima had one incident at the Indian Institute of Technology in Delhi where some students contested the film towards the end of the post screening debate (Joshi 2016). Most of the protesting students had not been present during the film screening and seemingly came just for the purpose of creating a particular visibility around the national-antinational binary and therefore reaffirm the normativity of the nation-state. During the documentary and short film festival ViBGYOR 2014 in Thrissur, Kerala, members of Hindu nationalist groups attacked the screening of Bilal Jan's film *Ocean of Tears* (Jan 2012), which inquired into a mass rape conducted by the Indian army in the Kashmiri village of Konan Poshpura. The filmmaker was protected by the audience of the festival, who stood between the entry point and the angry nationalists (Shyam 2014) One film screening of Sanjay Kak's film *Jashn-e-Azadi* (Kak 2007) that occurred during a festival that focused entirely on Kashmir, called "Kashmir before our Eyes" and which took place in Hyderabad in 2013, had to be shifted to another location after the opening screening was vandalized by a group of activists from a Hindu-nativist political organization that demands the creation of a separate homeland for exiled Kashmiri Pandits within the territory of the Valley of Kashmir (Saleh 2013). Performances to stop screenings from taking place—sometimes accompanied by the above mentioned forms of vandalism—do not require that participants even watch a film—the film can thus have publicity effects that are based on affects somewhat external to its presentational form (Mazzarella 2013).

In such an atmosphere, it becomes particularly important for Fatima to travel with her film. This is a way of protecting its vulnerable "skin" (Marks 2000) from the danger of crossing what I propose to call, following Mazzarella (2013), the "open edge of mass publicity" (Mazzarella 2013, p. 37). The "skin of the film" is a concept at the intersection of film-phenomenology and Deleuzian film studies introduced by Laura Marks. It refers to the haptic workings of small film practices, where:

> [...] the condition of being in-between cultures initiates a search for new forms of visual expression and leads to the hypothesis that many of these works 'call upon memories of the senses in order to represent the experiences of people living in Diaspora' (Marks 2000). But unlike Western ocular centrism (the prioritization of the eye as a sense for acquiring knowledge, truth, experience), intercultural cinema embraces the proximal senses (smell, taste, touch) as a means for embodying knowledge and cultivating memory. (Totaro 2002)

But there is another aspect of "skin" that is even more important to my argument than the question of "haptic vision" in relation to the category "memory". Marks (2000, p. 20) description of the conditions of film practices extends the "skin" to moments of circulation and reception: small screening sites at film-clubs and universities, screenings for friends and family, financial insecurity and strong support by personal networks, vulnerability of a video's material, and the importance given to the affective involvement of audiences. On the other hand, "viewers often take these contexts into account as part of their experience of the work. [...] Reproducible though they are, the media arts cannot be conceived of separately from the sets of viewers that give them meaning. Traces of other viewings, of differently seeing audiences, adhere to the skin of these works" (Marks 2000, p. 20). In other words: the skin is also a vulnerable boundary of a film's communicative surroundings and of its force. I have shown above how traces of former viewings have been weaved into the textures of the current form, to enable a refined emotional engagement. The skin opens to publics in highly context-specific ways. In films that deal with conflict zones and "places of national affect" (Urry 2007, p. 254), these small material screenings provide the possibility to stay below the radar of the "wrong kind of publicity". Still, the screenings of documentary films on Kashmir are often highly politically charged and open to all kinds of contestations. The ease of destroying the material skin of a video has now shifted to the difficult-to-estimate publicity potential of the more fluid digital media. It nevertheless constitutes a vulnerability, consisting now in the materiality and temporality of the digital: the dangers of decontextualization and fast-spreading anger. I see the mobility of Fatima's practice exactly as an attempt to protect this "skin" by being able to emotionally mobilize audiences into an understanding of what "moves" Kashmiri women to resist for many years in a struggle that often does not seem to offer any reasonable chance for success.

But how can we now establish a connection between the physical mobility of the filmmaker and the mobilizing force of Fatima's practice? How can we conceptualize the relationship between the protection of the vulnerable skin of the film and the potentiality of (anti-)national publicity that resides within media events which gather momentum by reiterating the dichotomy "national-antinational"? For this purpose, I turn to a discussion of the concept I have mentioned briefly above—"the open edge of mass publicity" (Mazzarella 2013, p. 37). Beyond empirical audiences, there are always imaginations of public(s) at play in any media practice. Michael Warner's distinction between *a* public and *the* public is a way of conceptually coming to terms with this "open edge". An empirical public or audience (*a* public) consisting of human beings that come together for some reason or another is always played out performatively at its intersection with an abstraction called "the public". The latter depends on a modern imagination of a community made up of strangers, but still connected (discursively and spatiotemporally, through media ensembles, etc.) as a unit of sorts. I understand this intersection with the symbolic boundaries of the nation-state in the sense of what William Mazzarella calls the "open edge of mass publicity" in the imagination of a modern public. Drawing on the work of Warner (2002), Mazzarella comprises the concept in the following way:

> [...] what I call the open edge of mass publicity: namely, the element of anonymity that characterizes any public communication in the age of mass publics; the sense that what makes a communication public is not just that 'it addresses me' by way of a public channel, but that 'it addresses me insofar as it also, and by the same token, addresses unknown others,' others who share my membership in an emergent general public. (Mazzarella 2013, p. 37)

This theorization helps to situate the potentials and dangers of working within a media environment in which, according to Fatima, the "wrong kind of publicity" can emerge easily and destroy the opening potentials of her practice.

By engaging with Fatima's practice, I was drawn to view the politics of affect—the way traces of affective memory are sedimented and can be reactivated in current events—as her attempts to make public the memory that perpetuates the desire for political self-determination. In this process of becoming public, it was not just the movement between spaces and the subject position "in-between" (e.g., Delhi and Kashmir, the Indian field of documentary, and the world of documentary film festivals and funding institutions), but the very situatededness in the transmission of a local memory that reinforced the importance of translocal movements and the co-presence of the filmmaker with the film. Fatima often told me how difficult it was to choose the right places of screening and also to establish—under the advice of a friend who is a human rights lawyer—a series of film screenings without the "wrong kind" of publicity effects. This, she was advised, would later result—if it was needed—in a legal defence against charges of her film "triggering communal unrest". All of these operations must therefore be seen as operating on that "open edge", defending the vulnerable "skin of the film". However, this leaves open the question of how Fatima may reach out, widening the scale of her film's communication in a paradoxical situation where scale effects—potentially enhanced by digital technology—are limited by the protection of the film's skin, as described above. The question of "letting the film go on its own" is thus crucial to a practice that refined for many years an artefact fit for communication while simultaneously addressing an issue that was constantly of high urgency to both the filmmaker and the film's protagonists. This happens within a situation where many Kashmiris strongly desire the widening of the conflict's scale to create transnational solidarity for their cause of political self-determination. Fatima told me that, by screening the film in the way described above, she may be able to reach influential people in academia and in other relevant positions in civil society. These agents may—after being moved by the testimony of her film—expand the scale of her film through their individual engagement and networks in more meaningful ways than uncontrolled publicity would enable. Measuring film effect is a complex and highly contested task, especially when one considers the categories of audiences and genre created in turn and the consequential levelling of different ways films move us and create testimony to expend a conflict's scale. However, this question is surely one that needs to be addressed more closely when one attempts to assess the transformative potential discussed here.

7. Conclusions

To make films on the Kashmir conflict means, for Iffat Fatima, not just interrogating dominant visual regimes by confronting them with images of "the everyday"—a category which is itself used to mediate these images, as they are captured as actuality footage—but engaging with questions of affect and its mobilization for political ends: will the audience show empathy, and will they feel what it means to live in an occupied zone, driven by a conflict memory to continue resistance against all odds? My use of a lens of mobility for the study of documentary films dealing with conflict zones is based on the observation that various levels of mobility are here entangled: representations, physical mobility and emotional and imaginative mobility. Regarding the politics of representation, I argue that Fatima challenges both touristic tropes of the Kashmir Valley and stereotypes of Kashmiri Muslim women as religiously immobilized victims. She achieves this by linking her filmic protagonist's everyday movements not only to an alternative vision of the Kashmir Valley, but—as in the sequence of Shamima Bano analysed above—by inscribing the agency of Kashmiri women into the tourist gaze itself. Seen through a lens of mobility, however, Fatimas practice of accompanying her protagonists for many years during the production of the film and later to represent them in the filmic textures, walking through an occupied zone, is just one half of the coin. Physically accompanying her film enables Fatima to create and control the conditions through which testimonies can be experienced and negotiated.

In the last section I have shown that this control of visibilities is particularly urgent in a media environment where the realization of nationalistically coded affects is an immanent possibility of the way films become public. By her travelling together with the film within the territorial boundaries of the Indian nation-state (the addressee of effective claims to legal redress) and addressing audience members with tropes known from the Hindi-film (a form known for its investment into an Indian nationalist imagination), the problem of (trans-)national address intensifies. I argue that Fatima achieves reflexivity through a long production in which the form was carefully refined through test screenings at various locations. This practice is meant to create the type of emotional and cognitive engagement that circumvents the pitfalls of documentary practices engaged with an affectively highly charged media environment. Visibilities are known to cut both ways: the moving-along-with-the film is partly meant to protect its vulnerable skin, and to control its visibility and its affective impact in the face of immanent possibilities for publicity creating performances from the Hindu-right that reaffirms the category of the nation. All these aspects of her practice achieve an intense calm of the performance and a saturation of visible evidence, enhanced by her presence after the screening as somebody who further contextualizes and authenticates the film's images. However, the problem of protecting her film from crossing the "open edge of mass publicity" remains ambiguous. A potential widening of the scale of the film via an open circulation of the presentational form remains bound to a significant break in the way she intends to mobilize audience members for an understanding beyond interlocked conflict narratives.

Thus, I argue that, for an understanding of these affective and narrative possibilities, the mobility of filmmakers is not just a secondary element of production (e.g., transnational funding, visiting pitching workshops in Europe etc.), but of central (and likely increasing) importance to the particular form through which documentary films will mediate testimony of conflict zones. This communicative form depends on entangled (im-)mobility between the politics of representations, physical and social (im-)mobility, and emotional mobilization. At the intersections of these mobilities, one can observe, describe, and analyze contemporary documentary film practices pertaining to conflict zones at their highest intensities, and in moments of political contestation and hope for possible openings beyond the deadends of the conflict. These are moments that matter to audience members, filmmakers, and researches alike, as they result from a multilayered investment in the documentary form as it is performatively negotiated. To capture these moments, mobile methods require the researcher to move with the filmmakers to sites of screenings and have conversations with both filmmakers and members of audiences.

To get hold of the social boundaries of the practice and the imaginative boundaries of representations, the opening potentials of imaginative and intellectual mobilities need to be seen as intrinsically linked to immobility, which captures the structural side of a practice. This includes institutional aspects regarding the lack of funding, governmental regulations, and sedimented discourses that seem to enclose conflict zones in always repeated narratives (often assymetrical in their relation to state power and hegemonic media discourses). Iffat Fatima not only attempts to open between narratives, but also to—reflexively—inscribe herself within certain, often less visible, narrative. The need to negotiate the political dimension of the conflict results in a critical appropriation of a narrative of Kashmiri political self-determination. By doing so, she re-territorializes through her movements new inscriptions in contentious conflict space. At the same time she creates possibilities of moving out of national frameworks, and into translocal and transregional subjectivities, because the everyday of a militarized zone may resonate with everyday experiences of other regions and localities.

Fatima's filmic practice stands widely apart from normative narrative schemes circulating through documentary pitching sessions in the global field of documentary (Friedman 2015; Wessely 2013) and the increasingly elaborated efforts by funding institutions of documentary film to measure and track "social impact" empirically with funding agencies dictating the terms of "impact" (Nichols 2016, p. 223). In this paper, I have pointed out some of Fatima's attempts at not being tracked through available categories (this or that pre-existing narrative, geopolitical argument or idea/space of effect) in highly affective and sometimes volatile media-environments. This avoidance of being tracked was partly enabled by her ability to open up new imaginations of the conflict that emerge from the specific location of her embedded, long term engagement with the APDP and its translation into a highly mobile film practice. In times where affects rush through social media, serving as means of capital-accumulation and 'information' on conflict zones, the search for practices of communication that draw on the emancipatory possibilities of digital technologies without falling into their often attached decontextualizing visibilities and temporalities becomes an urgent and pressing matter. A "lens of mobility" as suggested through my discussion of Iffat Fatima's practice may serve as an instrument to question new possibilities and problems of the independent digital documentary film.

Conflicts of Interest: The author declares no conflict of interest.

References

Adey, Peter. 2010. *Mobility*. New York: Routledge.
Amnesty International. 2015. The Day of the Disappeared: Enforced Disappearances Continue Unabated in Every Region of the World. Amnesty International USA. Available online: https://www.amnestyusa.org/press-releases/the-day-of-the-disappeared-enforced-disappearances-continue-unabated-in-every-region-of-the-world/. (accessed on 2 August 2017).
Anderson, Benedict R. 2006. *Imagined Communities*. London: Verso.
Anderson, Perry. 2012. *The Indian Ideology*. New Delhi: Three Essays Collective.
Bar-Tal, Daniel. 2003. Collective Memory of Physical Violence: Its Contribution to the Culture of Violence. In *The Role of Mentory in Ethnic Conflict*. New York: Palgrave Macmillan, pp. 77–93.
Bashir, Aamir. 2012. *Harud*. Directed by Aamir Bashir. Rotterdam: Hubert Bals Fund.
Berry, Chris, Xinyu Lu, and Lisa Rofel. 2010. *The New Chinese Documentary Film Movement: For the Public Record*. Hong Kong: Hong Kong University Press.
Bhan, Mona. 2013. Counterinsurgency, Democracy, and the Politics of Identity in India: From Warfare to Welfare? Abingdon: Routledge.
Bhandari, Vivek. 2006. Civil Society and the Predicament of Multiple Publics. *Comparative Studies of South Asia, Africa and the Middle East* 26: 36–50. [CrossRef]
Bhardwaj, Vishal. 2014. *Haider*. Directed by Vishal Bhardwaj. UTV Motion Pictures.
Bose, Sumantra. 1997. *The Challenge in Kashmir*. New Delhi: Sage.
Bruzzi, Stella. 2006. *New Documentary*. London: Routledge.
Monika Büscher, John Urry, and Katian Witchger, eds. 2011. *Mobile Methods*. London: Routledge.
Castells, Manuel. 2013. *Communication Power*, 2nd ed. Oxford: Oxford University Press.
Chanan, Michael. 2008. *The Politics of Documentary*. London: British Film Institute.
Chanan, Michael. 2010. Going South: On Documentary as a Form of Cognitive Geography. *Cinema Journal* 1: 147–54.
Corner, John. 2011. *Theorising Media*. Manchester: Manchester University Press.
Dabashi, Hamid. 2006. *Dreams of a Nation*, 1st ed. London: Verso.
Dholakia, Rahul. 2010. *Lamhaa: The Untold Story of Kashmir*. Directed by Rahul Dholakia. Mumbai: Viva Entertainment.
Duschinski, Haley. 2010. Reproducing Regimes of Impunity: Fake Encounters and the Informalization of Violence in Kashmir Valley. *Cultural Studies* 24: 110–32. [CrossRef]
Edwards, Dan. 2015. *Independent Chinese Documentary*. Edinburgh: Edinburgh University Press.
Eley, Goeff. 1992. Nations, Publics, and Political Cultures: Placing Habermas in the Nineteenth Century. In *Habermas and the Public Sphere*. Edited by Craig J. Calhoun. Cambridge: MIT Press, pp. 289–340.
Ezra, Elizabeth, and Terry Rowden, eds. 2006. *Transnational Cinema, the Film Reader*. London: Routledge.
Fassin, Didier. 2013. On Resentment and Ressentiment. *Current Anthropology* 54: 249–67. [CrossRef]
Fatima, Iffat. 2005. *Lanka: The Other Side of War and Peace*. Directed by Iffat Fatima. Sri Lanka: IAWRT.
Fatima, Iffat. 2012. *On a Trail of Vanished Blood*. Directed by Iffat Fatima. Norway: IAWRT.
Fatima, Iffat. 2015. *Khoon Diy Baraav*. Directed by Iffat Fatima. Norway: IAWRT.
Fraser, Nancy. 1992. Rethinking the Public Sphere. In *Habermas and the Public Sphere*. Cambridge: MIT Press, pp. 109–43.
Friedman, Yael. 2015. Guises of Transnationalism in Israel/Palestine: A Few Notes on 5 Broken Cameras. *Transnational Cinemas* 1: 17–32. [CrossRef]
Galtung, Johan. 1969. Conflict as a Way of Life. *Essays in Peace Research* 3: 484–507. [CrossRef]
Gaur, Meenu. 2010. *Kashmir on Screen: Region, Religion and Secularism in Hindi Cinema*. London: University of London.
Ghosh, Shohini. 2010. *Fire: A Queer Film Classic*. Vancouver: Arsenal Pulp Press.
Göttsch-Elten, Silke. 2011. Mobilitäten—Alltagspraktiken, Deutungshorizonte Und Forschungsperspektiven. In *Mobilitäten: Europa in Bewegung Als Herausforderung Kulturanalytischer Forschung*. Münster: Waxmann, pp. 15–30.
Habermas, Jürgen. 1990. *Strukturwandel der Öffentlichkeit: Untersuchungen zu einer Kategorie der bürgerlichen Gesellschaft*. Frankfurt am Main: Suhrkamp.

Hepp, Andreas. 2012. *Cultures of Mediatization*. Malden: Polity Press.

Higbee, Will, and Song Hwee Lim. 2010. Concepts of Transnational Cinema: Towards a Critical Transnationalism in Film Studies. *Transnational Cinemas* 1: 7–21. [CrossRef]

Hochberg, Gil Z. 2015. *Visual Occupations: Violence and Visibility in a Conflict Zone*. Paperback edition. Durham: Duke University Press.

Hoffman, Bruce, and Haley Duschinski. 2013. Contestations Over Law, Power and Representation in Kashmir Valley. *Interventions* 16: 501–30. [CrossRef]

Horat, Flavia. 2010. *Kurdisches Kino: Vom akzentuierten Exil—und Diasporakino zum internationalen Film*. Marburg: Schüren Verlag.

Jan, Bilal. 2012. Ocean of Tears. Directed by Bilal A. Jan. Jammu and Kashmir: PSBT India.

Joshi, Namrata. 2016. Are They Dead, Alive or Have They Turned into Ether? *The Hindu*. 13 February sec. Comment. Available online: http://www.thehindu.com/opinion/op-ed/iffat-fatima-talks-about-kashmir-documentary-khoon-diy-baarav/article8229909.ece (accessed on 3 August 2017).

Kabir, Ananya Jahanara. 2009. *Territory of Desire Representing the Valley of Kashmir: Representing the Valley of Kashmir*. Minneapolis: University of Minnesota Press.

Kak, Sanjay. 2007. *Jashn-E-Azadi*. Directed by Kak Sanjay. Delhi: Octave Communications.

Kastner, Jens, and Ruth Sonderegger. 2014. Emanzipation von Ihren Extremen Her Denken. In *Pierre Bourdieu Und Jacques Rancière*. Wien: Turia & Kant, pp. 7–30.

Kazi, Seema. 2008. *Between Democracy and Nation: Gender and Militarisation in Kashmir*. New Delhi: Women Unlimited.

Köhn, Steffen. 2016. *Mediating Mobility*. New York: Wallflower.

Kramer, Max. 2015. Filming Kashmir: Emerging Documentary Practices. In *New Media Configurations and Socio-Cultural Dynamics in Asia and the Arab World*. Edited by Nadja-Christina Schneider and Carola Richter. Baden-Baden: Nomos, London: Bloomsbury.

Macedo, Isabel, and Rosa Cabecinhas. 2013. (Post)-Conflict Memories and Identity Narratives in the Documentary Series I Am Africa. *Observatorio (OBS*) Journal* 7: 115–28.

Marks, Laura. 2000. *The Skin of the Film: Intercultural Cinema, Embodiment, and the Senses*. Durham: Duke University Press.

Matar, Dina, and Zahera Harb. 2013. *Narrating Conflict in the Middle East: Discourse, Image and Communications Practices in Lebanon*. New York: I.B.Tauris.

Mazzarella, William. 2013. *Censorium: Cinema and the Open Edge of Mass Publicity*. Durham: Duke University Press.

McLagan, Meg, and Yates McKee. 2012. *Sensible Politics: The Visual Culture of Nongovernmental Activism*, 1st ed. New York: Zone Books.

Merleau-Ponty, Maurice. 1968. *The Visible and the Invisible*. Evanston: Northwestern University Press.

Merriman, Peter. 2014. Rethinking Mobile Methods. *Mobilities* 2: 167–87. [CrossRef]

Morag, Raya. 2013. 'Roadblock' Films, 'Children's Resistance' Films and 'Blood Relations' Films: Israeli and Palestinian Documentary Post-Intifada II. In *The Documentary Film Book*. London: Palgrave Macmillan, pp. 237–47.

Mukherjee, Rahul. 2012. Travels, Songs and Displacements Movement in Translocal Documentaries Interrogating Development. *BioScope: South Asian Screen Studies* 3: 53–68. [CrossRef]

Naficy, Hamid. 2001. *An Accented Cinema: Exilic and Diasporic Filmmaking*. New Jersey: Princeton University Press.

Nair, Janaki. 2016. Introduction: A Teach-in for a JNU Spring. In *What the Nation Really Needs: The JNU Nationalism Lectures*. Noida: Harper Collins, pp. ix–xxv.

Negt, Oskar, and Alexander Kluge. 1972. *Öffentlichkeit und Erfahrung. Zur Organisationsanalyse von bürgerlicher und proletarischer Öffentlichkeit* 2. Auflage. Frankfurt: Suhrkamp.

Nichols, Bill. 2016. *Speaking Truths with Film: Evidence, Ethics, Politics in Documentary*. Oakland: University of California.

Oakes, Tim, and Louisa Schein. 2006. *Translocal China: Linkages, Identities and the Reimagining of Space*. New York: Routledge.

Pickowicz, Paul, and Yingjin Zhang. 2006. *From Underground to Independent: Alternative Film Culture in Contemporary China. From Underground to Independent: Alternative Film Culture in Contemporary China*. Lanham: Rowman & Littlefield Publishers.

Rancière, Jacques. 2013. *The Politics of Aesthetics*. London: Bloomsbury Academic.

Renov, Michael. 2004. *The Subject of Documentary*. Minneapolis: University of Minnesota Press.
Robins, Kevin. 2004. Beyond Imagined Community? Transnationale Medien Und Türkische MigrantInnen in Europa. In *Identitätsräume: Nation, Körper Und Geschlecht in Den Medien*. Eine Topografie. Bielefeld: Transcript, pp. 114–32.
Saleh, Abu. 2013. No 'Kashmir' in India: A Film Festival Vandalized in Hyderabad. *Cafe Dissensus Everyday*. October 8. Available online: https://cafedissensusblog.com/2013/10/08/no-kashmir-in-india-a-film-festival-vandalized-in-hyderabad/ (accessed on 2 August 2017).
Schneider, Nadja-Christina. 2015. Applying the Lens of Mobility to Media and Gender Studies: An Introduction. In *New Media Configurations and Socio-Cultural Dynamics in Asia and the Arab World*. Baden-Baden: Nomos, pp. 225–42.
Sharoni, Simona. 2001. Rethinking Women's Struggles in Israel-Palestine and in the North of Ireland. In *Victims, Perpetrators or Actors: Gender, Armed Conflict and Political Violence*. London: Zed.
Shekhawat, Seema. 2014. *Gender, Conflict and Peace in Kashmir: Invisible Stakeholders*. Cambridge: Cambridge University Press.
Sheller, Mimi, and John Urry. 2006. The New Mobilities Paradigm. *Environment and Planning A* 38: 207–26. [CrossRef]
Shohat, Ella. 2010. *Israeli Cinema: East/West and the Politics of Representation*. London: I.B. Tauris.
Shohat, Ella, and Robert Stam. 1994. *Unthinking Eurocentrism*. New York: Routledge.
Shyam, P.V. 2014. RSS Workers Stop Screening of 'Ocean of Tears' at Film Festival—Times of India. *The Times of India*, February 15. Available online: http://timesofindia.indiatimes.com/india/RSS-workers-stop-screening-of-Ocean-of-Tears-at-film-festival/articleshow/30453942.cms (accessed on 2 August 2017).
Smets, Kevin. 2015. Cinemas of Conflict: A Framework of Cinematic Engagement with Violent Conflict, Illustrated with Kurdish Cinema. *International Journal of Communication* 9: 2434–55.
Tanke, Joseph J. 2010. WhyRanciére Now? *Journal of Aesthetic Education* 44: 1–17. [CrossRef]
Thrift, Nigel. 2008. *Non-Representational Theory: Space, Politics, Affect*. London: Routledge.
Toppo, Biju. 2005. *Kora Rajee—Land of the Diggers*. Directed by Toppo Biju. Kathmandu: Film Southasia.
Totaro, Donato. 2002. Deleuzian Film Analysis: The Skin of the Film. Off Screen. Available online: http://offscreen.com/view/skin_of_film (accessed on 2 August 2017).
Urry, John. 2000. *Sociology beyond Societies*. London: Routledge.
Urry, John. 2002. *The Tourist Gaze*, 2nd ed. London: Sage.
Urry, John. 2007. *Mobilities*. Cambridge: Polity Press.
Wang, Qi. 2014. *Memory, Subjectivity and Independent Chinese Cinema*. Edinburgh: Edinburgh University Press.
Warner, Michael. 2002. Publics and Counterpublics. *Quarterly Journal of Speech* 88: 413–25. [CrossRef]
Wessely, Dominik. 2013. Notizen Zur Dokumentarfilmausbildung Im Zeitalter Der Digitalität. In *Dokumentarfilm*. Edited by Edmund Ballhaus. Berlin: Reimer, pp. 13–27.
Winston, Brian. 2008. *Claiming the Real: Documentary: Grierson and Beyond*. Basingstoke: British Film Institute.

Section 5:
Moving and Settling: Identity Negotiations in Muslim Migration Contexts

Article

Transnationalism among Second-Generation Muslim Americans: Being and Belonging in Their Transnational Social Field

Michelle Byng

Department of Sociology, Temple University, 1801 N. Broad Street, Philadelphia, PA 19122, USA; mbyng@temple.edu

Received: 15 June 2017; Accepted: 25 October 2017; Published: 30 October 2017

Abstract: An increase in transnationalism, the ability of individuals and families to travel and maintain relationships across national borders, has led to questions about its impact on identity especially for the children of migrants. When combined with concerns about global and national security such as those that are associated with Muslims and Islam, then questions about the strength national identity are particularly pertinent. This analysis uses the theories of transnational social fields and intersectionality to examine the transnational experiences of second-generation Muslim Americans. It relies on qualitative interview data. The data show the intersection of their national, religious, and gender identities. It demonstrates that they experience transnational being in their parents' country of origin and belonging in the United States. Nationality, religion, and gender influence what they experience in each location. The analysis demonstrates the stability and centrality of American national identity in what second-generation Muslims experience in both locations. Moreover, their belonging in the United States rests squarely on their perceptions of themselves as Americans and their construction of their Muslim identity as an American religious identity.

Keywords: transnationalism; second generation; Muslim Americans; being; belonging; social fields

---

1. Introduction

This analysis addresses identity among second-generation Muslim Americans. Through an examination of their transnationalism (i.e., experiences in the United States and their parents' country of origin), it questions their identity construction. Specifically, how does transnationalism inform expressions of religious, gender and national identity among second-generation Muslim Americans? Increases in transnationalism have led to social theory and research addressing identity as it relates to social membership (i.e., being and belonging) within a transnational social field (i.e., the nations of origin and residence) (Levitt and Schiller 2004). Scholarship on transnationalism takes in to account intersectionality or the multiple identity categories that inform experiences (Crenshaw 1991; Collins 2000). Research that addresses the second generation (i.e., the children of migrants) focuses on their participation in transnational practices and the influence of transnationalism on their identity (Levitt and Waters 2002). With regard to second-generation Muslims and transnationalism, there are analyses of identity especially as it relates to religion. Questions have been raised about the implications of transnationalism among Muslims in the West given Islamic terrorism. Research addresses the compatibility of Islam with western cultural values (Mandaville 2009; Mandaville 2011) and the possibility that Muslims in the West might use Islam rather than western laws and values to determine appropriate behaviors (Bowen 2004). While migration to western nations solidifies religious identity among Muslims, it does not necessarily lead to a corresponding increasing religious practice (Voas and Fleischmann 2012). Although parents are likely to invest in the religious upbringing of their children, second-generation

Muslims do not necessarily incorporate the cultural background of their parents in their practice of Islam (Voas and Fleischmann 2012).

One consequence of transnationalism is that identity is influenced by social relationships that are maintained across national borders and in more than one national context. In other words, by definition transnationalism means " ... identities and cultural production reflect their multiple locations" (Levitt and Schiller 2004, p. 1006). Transnationalism is carried out in places of attachment, signaling a " ... complex set of conditions that affect the construction, negotiation and reproduction of social identities" (Vertovec 2001, p. 573). Identity as a social construction rests on the view that societal circumstances, the reactions of groups and individuals to circumstances, and the relationships between groups and between individuals (often with regard to group membership) are the sites where the meanings of an identity are constituted and assigned (Lawler 2008; Berkhus 2008; Gergen and Gergen 2007). Identity can be understood as characteristics that individuals have in common, as the foundation of shared political interests, and/or as the basis for collective action (Brubaker and Cooper 2000). What identity references in this analysis is the relationship between self-understanding and social location or situational subjectivity. Situational subjectivity refers to " ... one's sense of who one is, of one's social location, and of how (given the first two) one is prepared to act (Brubaker and Cooper 2000, p. 17)." Understanding how second-generation Muslim Americans understand their identity given their transnationalism is especially pertinent. International political conflicts inform their religious identity. Yet as it the case with other Americans, political rights and obligations are associated with their citizenship and nationality (Faist 2000; Tilly 2003).

This analysis expands our understanding of transnationalism among second-generation Muslim Americans through a comparative analysis of what they say about their experiences when visiting their parents' country of origin and what they say about their American identity. It contrasts their experiences of being in their parents' country of origin with those of belonging in the United States. It notes the intersection of the respondents' religious, gender, and national identities to what they experience in their transnational social filed. The role that Muslim identity currently plays in international conflicts and the suspicions that surround Muslims in the United States since the 11 September 2001 terrorist attacks on the World Trade Center in New York, signal the need for continued research addressing how second-generation Muslim Americans understand their nationality. Qualitative interview data show the importance of national identity for second-generation Muslim Americans. The comparative social filed analysis expands our understanding of transnationalism among second-generation Muslim Americans by demonstrating that nationality is central to their identity in spite of the social and political conflicts that surround their religion. In contrast to past research, the analysis demonstrates that second-generation Muslim Americans do not simply rely on western values of religious freedom to validate their Muslim identity (Zevallos 2008; Henkel 2004; Salih 2004). Nor do they say that there is a parallel between western values and Islamic values that legitimates their religious identity (Schmidt 2004). What they say is that they live by American values and other Americans should too. Moreover, they do not become American as a result of vising their parents' country of origin (Purkayastha 2010). Instead, they arrive as Americans and they are American for their entire visit. They are appreciative and respectful of the bonds of family and the public visibility of Islam, but their interpretations and reflections are filtered through the fact that they are American. Finally, while the young women are consciously aware of restrictions on their activities in their parents' country of origin because they are female (Purkayastha 2010; Mirza 2013), the young men experience restrictions too. However, the explanations that the young men offer are not related to their gender.

The literature review that follows begins with the theories of transnational being and belonging, social fields, and intersectionality. These theoretical concepts are used to guide the analysis. Research literature on second-generation Muslims, transnationalism and the second generation, as well as transnationalism and intersectionality are reviewed. After describing the data collection and analysis methods the findings on transnationalism and second-generation Muslim Americans are presented. Second-generation Muslim Americans experience transnational being in their parents' country of origin and belonging in the United States. Their experiences are informed by the intersection of their national, religious, and gender identities. Their American national identity, as opposed to their religion, is central to their transnationalism and their belonging in the United States.

2. Theoretical Context and Background

2.1. Theorizing Transnationalism: Being, Belonging, and Intersectionality

Transnationalism captures the production of identities and cultures in multiple national locations (Levitt and Schiller 2004). It addresses the ability of migrants and subsequent generations in the families of migrants to participate in transnational social fields or networks of social relationships where resources, practices, and ideas are exchanged between migrants and non-migrants. Social fields do not discount the significance and durability of national borders. They take into account the ease with which geographical boundaries are crossed as well as the relationships and social practices that cross national borders with migrants. Participation in social fields varies in terms of being and belonging (Levitt and Schiller 2004). Being describes social relationships that do not impact identity. Social participation is characterized by simple engagement in relationships and practices. Individuals can be in a social filed or participate in social relationships where the cultural politics of those relationships are not an enduring part of how they define themselves. Even with regular participation, for ways of being to become belonging requires identification. Belonging, on the other hand, is about conscious participation that signifies connection and identification. Belonging is grounded in institutionally based actions that are the foundation for identification. In other words, belonging is expressed when cross border relationships and practices are used by an individual to express who they are (Levitt and Schiller 2004). These two concepts have allowed researchers to understand how formal and informal cultural, social, and religious practices in both nations of a social field influence experiences, the creation of meaning, and identity among migrants and their children (Levitt and Jaworsky 2007; Vertovec 2001).

The ability to maintain relationships across national borders has resulted in transnationalism becoming as influential to scholarship about migrants and immigration as are theories about assimilation, acculturation, and minority group inequality (Levitt and Jaworsky 2007; Waters 2014). Transnational migrants are socially embedded in multiple locations, sites, and modes of communication. They participate in organizations that assist in their settlement and that facilitate maintaining ties to their home country (Lacroix 2014). Familial, economic, political, cultural, and religious ties to country of origin influence identity and experiences in country of settlement for both migrants and their children (Gardner and Grillo 2002). Communication technologies, the ease of international travel as well as neoliberal political and economic relationships within and between countries have prompted some nations to redefine citizenship in light of transnationalism. However, other nations are wary of the influence of transnationalism on the assimilation and national identities of migrants and their children (Waldinger and Fitzgerald 2004; Heath 2014).

In nations such as the United States where the national loyalty of non-whites is questioned, transnational ties even among citizens can give rise to questions about loyalty (Waldinger and Fitzgerald 2004). In general, maintaining ties to the home left behind reorganizes family relationships in light of economic responsibilities (Osirim 2011; Binaisa 2013), gender roles (Das Gupta 1997; Fouron and Schiller 2001; Fouron and Schiller 2001; Viruell-Fuentes 2006) and religious identities (Abdelhady 2006; Al-Ali 2002) as they are carried out in both nations. Economic and business opportunities in the United States can provide resources for communities in migrants' home countries and for the revitalization of urban American neighborhoods (Osirim 2011). Migrant women in the United States become the carriers of ethnic culture (Das Gupta 1997) as well as the primary sustainers of family ties between both nations (Fouron and Schiller 2001). For first- and second-generation women in the United States, transnationalism has both liberatory and non-liberatory aspects. On one hand, it facilitates across generation integration into the United States and, on the other, transnationalism supports the maintenance of traditional gender roles (Viruell-Fuentes 2006). In addition because of the convergence of global, national, and local politics around Islam, Muslims and other Americans are conscious of the group boundary that marks Muslim identity (Abdelhady 2006; Al-Ali 2002). For the second generation, relationships with family members in their parents' country of origin, even without actual visits, allows them to develop a transnational identity (Viruell-Fuentes 2006; Louie 2006).

Intersectionality has expanded the analysis of transnationalism as it relates to identity. Intersectionality theory proposes that socially constructed identities categories, such as gender and race, organize social differences and inequalities (Crenshaw 1991). As a social theory, intersectionality captures how social devisions or categories work in concert to shape the lives of individuals and socially recognized groups (Collins and Bilge 2016). Identity categories and their resulting social consequeces expose and legitimate group-based resource and status inequalities (Crenshaw 1991). Global and national relationships of domination and subordination (i.e., matrix of domination) reveal the connection between transnationalism and intersectionality (Collins 2000). In other words, categories of inclusion and exclusion are just as informed by nationality as they are by other identities. The status that is assigned to a particular national identity is determined by the political and economic relationships between nations (Collins 2000). Transnationalism and intersecting identity categories inform the experiences of second-generation Muslim in the United States and when they visit their parents' country of origin.

2.2. Second-Generation Muslim Americans

In the United States research has focused on the ability of religious institutions to facilitate the reformulating ethnic identity to allow for assimilation (Wuthnow and Offutt 2008; Cadge and Ecklund 2007). Religion is argued to be one site where the second generation defines their identity with regard to the ethnic culture of their parents and their own nationality (Levitt and Jaworsky 2007; Cadge and Ecklund 2007). These general findings are complicated for second-generation Muslim Americans by national and global security policies that are enacted in the aftermath of the 9/11 terrorist attacks (Cainkar and Maira 2005). Islamic values, rather than those of western nations, are thought to guide the behaviors of some Muslims in the West (Bowen 2004; Grillo 2004). A shift toward Islamic values among the second generation is argued to be an outcome of national security policies that marginalize young Muslims (Mandaville 2009; Voas and Fleischmann 2012).

Racialized immigration policy and racial profiling results in Muslim Americans experiencing an infringement on their citizenship and belonging following 9/11 (Ahmad 2011). This finding is in contrast to the classic research that positioned Muslim immigrants and their religious institutions as similar to those of other ethnic immigrants to the United States (Haddad and Lummis 1987). However, the paradox of racializing Arab Americans with regard to their religion rather than by phenotype occurred prior to 9/11 (Naber 2000). As a direct result of post-9/11 security policies, young adult Muslim Americans are aware of not having the privileges of white race and of being socially positioned like other Americans who are not racially white (Alimahomed 2011). Anti-terrorism policies criminalize Muslims as persons who are not just culturally different but who hold beliefs that are opposed to core American values (Cainkar and Maira 2005). Given the global power of the United States and the association between Islam and terrorism, young Muslim Americans may construct forms of citizenship that are flexible, multicultural, polycultural, and dissenting (Cadge and Ecklund 2007). More importantly, their transnationalism maybe perceived as a national security risk to the United States that raises questions about their national loyalty (Maira 2004; 2008).

2.3. Transnationalism and the Second Generation

Transnationalism provides the second generation with a set of social relationships and/or a consciousness of global dynamics that inform their identity (Mandaville 2011; Salih 2004; Easthope 2009). Both citizenship and group boundaries shape their belonging in their parents' country of migration (Thomson and Crul 2007). However, visiting their parents' home country can increase their identification with that nation and decrease their identification with the nation where they are raised (Schimmer and van Tubergen 2014). Research on transnationalism among second-generation Muslims has focused primarily on Europe and Australia. These analyses highlight the influence of identity and values in the second generation's experiences of transnationalism. A comparative analysis of second-generation Muslims in the Demark, Sweden, and the United States specifically focuses on transnational identity formation. Research on second-generation transnationalism in the United States addresses its influence on female gender roles. The following begins with the transnational research on second-generation Muslims and then turns to that on second-generation women.

Second-generation Iranians think of their religious and national identities as synonymous (McAuliffe 2007). In contrast to the Baha'i, being Muslim makes them legitimately Iranian. As a result they deemphasize their Muslim identity. A comparative analysis of the Latin American and Turkish second generations in Australia finds that both groups have a sense of not fully belonging (Zevallos 2008). However Islam provides a pan-ethnic identity for those who are Turkish and Muslim. Yet when they visit Turkey their Australian identity is more important than their Turkish one. In other words, being Muslim is more important than being Australian but being Australian is more important than being Turkish (Zevallos 2008). Although they feel excluded in Australia, they also feel that they benefit from the nation's egalitarian ideals. A comparative analysis of second-generation Turkish Muslims in Turkey and Germany yields similar findings about social values. In both nations secularism in combination with the ideals of religious freedom allows them to practice Islam (Henkel 2004). An ethnographic account of a second-generation, young adult Muslim man in Italy yields similar findings. He legitimates his Muslim identity with universal values that go beyond a respect for difference (Salih 2004).

A comparative analysis of identity formation among second-generation Muslims in Demark, Sweden, and the United States about perceptions of western values in relation to Islam yields similar findings (Schmidt 2004). Western cultural values and democratic ideals allow for religious choice. In addition those values call for morally and ethically correct behaviors that are consistent with the values of Islam. As a consequence second-generation Muslims can practice Islam based on those values without the culturally informed religious practices of their parents. Alternately, they can adhere to western values that call for moral and ethical behaviors without Islamic religious practice and still lead a life that is consistent with their religion. Identity formation among second-generation Muslims in western nations is informed on one hand by their visibility and, on the other, in their relationships and conversations with one another (Schmidt 2004; Kibria 2008). The higher levels of religiosity among second-generation Muslim Americans in comparison to their parents correspond to their perception that Islamic values are consistent with American values of justice and equality (Cainkar 2004). The global and national contexts of Islam combine to create the transnational experience of religious identity for second-generation Muslims (Schmidt 2004).

The transnational experiences of migrant and second-generation women in the United States are defined by their roles as the carriers of ethnic culture (Das Gupta 1997) and the primary sustainers of family ties between both nations (Fouron and Schiller 2001) Transnationalism has liberating and non-liberating aspects for women. It can impose traditional female gender roles that subordinate women and it can provide second-generation women with an ethnic culture to combat western racism (Das Gupta 1997; Viruell-Fuentes 2006). For Haitian women transnationalism provides opportunities for political activism in Haiti while maintaining classic female gender subordination within their families. In other words, their family relationships reinforce gender inequality across their social field in spite of their transnational political activism (Fouron and Schiller 2001). Research on South-Asian Indian women demonstrates that their transnationalism frames the creation an authentic ethnic identity. First-generation women engage in the invention of ethnic authenticity that they impose on the second generation. Although the second generation rebels against the first generation's efforts, both generations of women are responsible for maintaining their community's ethnic identity (Das Gupta 1997). For second-generation Mexican women transnationalism allows them to adopt an ethnic, rather than a racial, identity in the United States (Viruell-Fuentes 2006). Even without visits to Mexico, their transnationalism means that second-generation Mexican women can position themselves outside of U.S. racism (Viruell-Fuentes 2006). In general, the transnational roles of first- and second-generation women facilitate across generation integration into the United States while supporting traditional female gender roles.

2.4. Transnationalism and Intersectionality

Intersectionality provides a more detailed analysis of transnationalism as it relates to identity. It expands the analytical lens of transnationalism to reveal the potential for an individual to live a life that is characterized by both majority and minority statuses (Purkayastha 2010; Purkayastha 2012). Moreover, transnational intersectionality allows for analyzes that take into account the racialization of religion and therein the ability of religion to inform the social relationships of domination and subordination (Purkayastha 2012). Recognizing this is particularly important for Muslims given their transnationalism in combination with national and global security policies that are directed toward them. Muslims' experiences of religion-based marginalization in the West in combination with gender-based marginalization of Muslim women speak directly to the transnational aspects of the "matrix of domination" (Collins 2000; Purkayastha 2012). Connecting intersecting identity categories to locations reveals contradictions in how identities are influenced by social structures as well as how they are experienced by individuals (Anthias 2012; Anthias 2008). Research demonstrating the inability of the South Asian and Muslim middle-class second generation to access American identity in spite of the parents' economic resources is evidence of transnational intersectionality. Their transnationalism provides them with other national foundations for their identity given the limits on their access to American identity in the United States (Purkayastha 2010). Muslim women living in western nations experience intersectionality given western cultural discourses about their religion and gender-based subordination of women. Although Muslim women's perceptions of themselves are different from how they are perceived by others in western nations, what they experience in their day-to-day lives are the implications of being thought of as dangerous, oppressed, or the embodiment of modesty. Others' perceptions of the intersection of their religious and gender identities shape their social experiences (Mirza 2013). Transnational intersectionality takes into account the possibility that participation in social norms, social relations, and elements of culture may be instrumental rather than an expression of identity (Anthias 2012). However, such participation can also indicate shared collective narratives of self and other that signal belonging and identity (Anthias 2008).

It is this context signals the need to further our understanding of transnationalism among second-generation Muslims Americans. Past research indicates that the second generation may experience some degree of bifurcated membership between the locations of their transnational social field. Research signals that anti-terrorism policies have negatively influenced the social membership of Muslims in the United States, including the second generation. These findings warrant a closer examination of how second-generation Muslim Americans understand their transnationalism. What do second-generation Muslim Americans say about their visits to their parents' country of origin? What do they say about their American identity? How does transnationalism inform expressions of religious, gender and national identity among second-generation Muslim Americans?

3. Data and Methods

Qualitative interview data is used to demonstrate what second-generation Muslim Americans experience in the locations of their transnational social field. Interviews were conducted between 2005 and 2009 with Muslim Americans living in Philadelphia, Pennsylvania USA and the surrounding suburbs. Philadelphia is home to a visible racially and ethnically diverse population of indigenous and immigrant Muslims. The Association of Religious Data Archives estimates the Muslim population in Philadelphia in 2010 at 39,540 or 26 out of every 1000 persons (Grammich et al. 2010). Respondents were recruited for this research based on their Muslim identity and their second-generation status. In other words, their parents had migrated to the United States.

This analysis is based on forty-seven interviews (thirty female and seventeen male respondents). Sixty percent of the interviewees were born in the United States and twenty-three percent are naturalized citizens. Only ten percent reported having a high school education, while fifty-five percent were currently enrolled in an undergraduate program. Eighty-one percent were between the ages of eighteen and twenty-three. Respondents were most likely to identify themselves as upper-middle class or wealthy (forty percent) and fifty-one percent reported household incomes above $65,000 a year. They are overwhelmingly of South Asian (68%) or Middle Eastern descent (21%). The parents of South Asian respondents are from Bangladesh, Pakistan and India. Middle Eastern ancestry is Palestinian, Syrian and Saudi Arabian. Six percent of respondents are of North African ancestry (Morocco and Egypt) and four percent have parents from West Africa (Liberia and Ghana). Forty-nine percent identified themselves as Asian, four percent as Black, four percent as White, thirteen percent said they were "in between" race categories and thirty percent chose a hyphenated identity such as Pakistani-American. I recruited study participants by attending and participating in organizational events held by the Muslim Students Associations at local college and university campuses, annual and monthly events held by the Council on American-Islamic Relations, Council for the Advancement of Muslim Professionals and other local groups, as well as attending events held at mosques in the city and surrounding suburbs.

Muslim identity is salient enough for the respondents to agree to participate in this project based on that identity. Their religiosity can be assessed through their responses to self-administered survey questions about religious practice. Their answers indicate that they are similar to Muslim Americans who participated in two Pew Research Center nationwide surveys (Pew Forum on Religion and Public Life 2007; Pew Forum on Religion and Public Life 2011). The participants in this project are more likely than those in either Pew study to say that they prayed five times a day and less likely to say that they never prayed (Table 1). They are more like the 2007 than the 2011 Pew respondents in terms of attending religious services. Eighty-seven percent of the respondents in this research indicated that they did fast during the month of Ramadan. Nineteen percent said that they read the Quran daily and 45% read it frequently. Overall, what the participants in this project say about their religious practices indicates that they similar to other Muslim Americans in terms of religiosity.

Table 1. Religiousity (Percent).

	Respondents	Pew 2007	Pew 2011
Prayer			
Five Daily	57.4	41	40
Fewer Daily	8.5	20	20
Less Often	29.7	26	29
Never	4.2	12	10
Service Attendance			
Weekly	38.3	34	47
Monthly	29.8	29	41
Seldom/Never	31.3	37	11

Sources: Pew Forum on Religion and Public Life Pew Forum on Religion and Public Life (2007): Prayer is for all US Muslims (p. 25). Note: Service Attendance is for native born not African American (p. 24). The Pew category "less often" is reported here as monthly attendance. Pew Forum on Religion and Public Life (2011): Prayer (p. 25) and Service Attendance (p. 26) are for those who are native born not African American.

Atlas-ti qualitative data analysis software was used to code and organize responses to interview questions by themes. Atlas-ti assigns numerical labels to coded sections of interview transcripts.

Those labels are included with the interview quotes that are presented in the analysis below. Interviews lasted for one to two hours and covered a range of topics: immigrant narratives, family and friendship relationships, 9/11 policies, media and Muslims, national origin discrimination, religion-based discrimination, American identity, Islam in the United States, and Muslims in the United States. All of the interviews were conducted and coded by the author. Interviews were recorded. They were transcribed by student research assistants. This analysis draws on what respondents say about visiting their parents' country of origin and their statements about their Muslim and American identities. It relies on data that were coded to highlight respondents' comments about the following topics: (1) the respondents' overseas family, (2) their family in the United States, (3) family ties: emotional ties and religious ties, (4) experiences in their parents' home county, (5) return travel to the United States, (6) Muslim identity in parents' home country, (7) Muslim identity in the United States.

The following analysis begins with what respondents say about visiting their overseas relatives. It notes what they say about their family relationships and how they experience their religion while traveling. Their comments are consistent with transnational being. They are engaged in social relationships and practices. However their engagement does not have a sustained impact on their identity. The analysis then turns to their belonging in the United States. It is expressed in the contrasts that they draw between themselves and their parents as well as the connections they make between their Muslim and American identities. It is important to note that interviewees were not asked to compare their transnational experiences to their lives in the United States. Nor were they asked to connect or compare their Muslim and American identities. The connections and comparisons appeared in how they structured their responses.

4. Results

The following analysis demonstrates that the intersection of the national, religious, and gender identities informs the transnationalism of second-generation Muslim Americans. Their descriptions of experiences in their parents' countries of origin and their understandings of their American identity demonstrate how they position themselves in their transnational social field. What they say about their visits to their parents' home country is consistent with transnational being. They are engaged in social relationships and practices, but those activities do not have a sustained impact on their identity. They are consciously aware of the difference between what they are experiencing and their lives in the United States. Their engagements are instrumental; they are simply participating in the social relationships of the moment. In contrast, their belonging in the United States is demonstrated in their use of core American values to construct Muslim as an American identity. Their comments go beyond the ideal of religious freedom to position themselves culturally within the pantheon of American citizens. This allows them to identify as both American and Muslim simultaneously and without contradictions. What they say indicates that they have the same social membership as other Americans.

4.1. Transnational Being: Family Makes It Home

How second-generation Muslim Americans experience, understand, and conform to family expectations in their parents' home country highlights their transnational being and intersectionality. They are consciously aware that they are visitors who are a part of their parents' family. They are living with their extended family, who can be strangers. They are engaged in family relationships and they have a sense of family membership, but their circumstances are temporary. Their American lives inform their understandings and interpretations. They are engaged in transnational being that is informed by the intersection of their nationality and gender identities.

In describing their visits overseas respondents say they are at home signaling the emotional connection and permanence of family relationships. Visiting family means that they are among different people but a bond exists between them because they are relatives. Alia describes the households of her four uncles who all live in the same apartment building. She notes everyday family conflicts as well as how she and her siblings are positioned as family members.

> "So like there's always some discussion about cutting trees in the front yard or some argument about who put the trash in the wrong place and a cat got in it and made a mess or something like that. So they were very sweet to us, me and my brother and sister, when we went and all of them made us feel like we were at home. But between the families themselves they have the same problems [as other families] . . . " (5:3; 18:18).

Alia describes the normalness of family conflicts while making it clear that she is comfortable in spite of them. Her comment hints at the hospitality that is extended to visitors and to the minor everyday tensions of family life. Foofer makes a similar comment. She is aware that she is in an unfamiliar set of relationships. She knows that she should be uncomfortable but she says that she is not.

> "So I didn't feel that awkward. Oh, I'm living with people I've never met before. ... I felt just very comfortable with it and I stayed with my mom's sister . . . I felt extremely at home even though I was traveling, just because I was with such close family members." (25:12; 23:24).

For Foofer what is significant is that she among relatives rather than the fact that her relatives are strangers. Her bond to the people she is visiting is based on their relationship to her mother. As a result, her sense that she is a member of the family is not disrupted by the fact that she does not actually know them. Ali's comment is like those of Alia and Foofer, although his focus is on how family membership is extended to him.

> "Like um, they saw me as still one of them. They didn't treat me like an outsider . . . [I]f I was at my aunt's house, I was like her son, you know. They were like, come closer." (4:6; 124:134).

Alia, Foofer, and Ali present what seems to be a paradox: they are visiting strangers but they experience the bonds of family. They describe relationships where they are identified as family members by others and they identify themselves as family members. The emotional bonds of family membership are a part of their transnationality although the practical side of knowing their relatives is absent. What they experience is transnational being. The experiences are important but they do not inform their identity. They aware that their relatives are strangers to them and they are strangers to those they are visiting. Their expressions of emotional connections demonstrate transnational being because the actual relationships of emotional bonding are absent. The emotionally grounded family relationships that exist with their parents are instrumentally extended to their transnational relatives.

There is a practical side of the second-generation's family membership also. They must conform to family rules and expected behaviors. What they say about expected behaviors highlights the differences between their American lives and their experiences abroad. Through comparisons they demonstrate the intersection of their American and gender identities. Although Ahmed and Alia provide similar statements what they say is informed by gender and explained through the lens of their American identity.

Ahmed says about his overseas family, "They want to know what you're doing at any moment of time, but it's perfectly fine." He goes on to provide details that are juxtaposed to his American life:

> "It's not like here where I could go out with friends at night . . . [T]heir family life is really oriented around be there at meal times, be there so you can communicate to each other. There's no, like as you can see our house is designed in a way where we have our bedroom sort of shut. Over there they hardly use their doors and everything is open. They know who's where and at what sort of times and things like that." (2:3; 32:34).

Ahmed is aware of and conforms to how he is expected to behave by his overseas family. He contextualizes the differences in social relationships through the architecture of houses. He tells us about differences in how family members interact with one another. He is conscious of differences with regard to privacy and that he is afforded more privacy in the United States.

Like Ahmed, Alia is also aware of more restrictions on her ability to be outside of the house and among friends when she visits her family. Note her description of going out and the role of gender in what she experiences:

> "And they want to make sure, especially me and Aisha my sister ... that we come home at a good time; we're not coming home late and if we come home late that at least our brother or cousin is with us ... Here my parents, they want to know where I'm going. They want to know what time I'm coming home. But they're not so when I come home, 'Where were you? What were you doing?' They don't really do that." (5:4; 24:24).

Both Alia and Ahmed conform to expected behaviors when they visit their relatives. They are conscious of the fact that they must provide an accounting of where they have been and what they were doing. They are both aware that there are restrictions on being out at night. For Ahmed the restrictions are about being available to participate in family interactions, while for Alia the restrictions are about her gender identity.

Although the practical side of what is expected of them is the same, the gender implications are different. The meaning and experiencing of Alia's gender identity is reoriented transnationally. She moves from being a person who simply needs to let her parents know where she is to being someone who is socially defined as unable to be public at night without a male relative. Additionally, Ahmed and Alia describe a similar freedom in their American life that they both say is absent in their parents' county of origin. They express a similar type of freedom to be out and among friends when they are in the U.S. This common characteristic of their American lives leads to a similar experience when they are in their parents' country of origins even though their explanations for the experience are different. For Ahmed it is about family relationships while for Alia it is about her female gender.

In their parents' home country second-generation Muslim Americans express an emotional connection to their relatives and a willingness to adhere to expected behaviors. Not actually knowing their relatives seems to be an anomaly in their visits to their parents' country of origin. However, it is not because their transnational being rests on the family bonds of their parents rather than their own. Their transnational being is expressed in their use of their American lives, or their national identity, as the comparative reference point for their experiences. In other words, what they say about their family relationships demonstrates transnational being or engagement that does not have an impact on their identity. The importance of their national identity and its intersection with their gender identities is expressed in how gender informs family relationships and the ability to go out. Second-generation Muslim American men and women face restrictions on going out in their parents' country of origin. However, their explanations the restrictions are different. In contrast, they provide similar descriptions of personal freedoms in the U.S. As second-generation Muslim Americans they have the freedoms of simply hanging out with friends or shutting their bedroom door that are common among American young adults without regard to gender.

4.2. *Transnational Being: Sights and Sounds of Public Places*

For second-generation Muslim Americans, transnational being in their parents' home country extends beyond family relationships to incorporate non-English language skills, the public visibility of religion, and their perceptions that they are identifiably American. What the respondents say indicates engagement in and an appreciation of what they are experiencing, but those experiences do not have a sustained impact on their identity. Their public place experiences and interactions are informed by the intersection of their national and religious identities. They are consciously aware that they are American and how it informs their interpretations and experiences. They are very appreciative of sharing the religious identity of those around them, but this does not displace the importance of their nationality.

The ability to speak the native language of their parents' home country informs the second generation's sense of shared ancestry and a connection to their surroundings. This is evidenced in a comment by Foofer: " ... [W]hen I got to India everyone was speaking in like Urdu and Hindi. So that was comforting because that's what I speak at home. (25:11; 21:22)". Note that her statement about "home" refers to the United States. Comments from Ali and Laila signal the importance that the second generation places on language to assess their membership in their parents' home country. Ali says:

> "I was very nervous because I'd lost my language, basically. I can still speak it, but broken up. So basically, it was me speaking my own language with an English accent. So I was very nervous, but they made me feel like I was really home. So it was great." (4:4; 84:94).

Ali identifies a language other than English as his own; that English is his primary language is a source of embarrassment for him. Laila's comment is similar, she says: " ... The language barrier is a big thing for me, because like I don't really know my native language very well" (36:15; 69:79).

For Ali, Laila, and Foofer language skills are part of their transnational being. They think of language as an indication of shared ancestry. Variations in their skills mean that they are positioned differently in social relationships when they are in their parents' country of origin. Foofer's is comfortable, Ali feels accepted because his American accent is overlooked, and Laila feels that the inability to speak her "native language" creates social barriers for her. Even though language is thought of as an indication of shared ancestry, their American nationality informs those skills. Foofer can speak Urdu and Hindi because it is spoken by her family in the U.S. In other words, the defining factor with regard to their language skills is not their ancestry but their lives in the United States.

Another societal site of transnational being in their parents' home countries is the public visibility of Islam. The second generation appreciates that their religion is a part of the nations they visit and they recognize it as a significant indication that they are in a different country. However, their American identity informs their understanding of what it means to have religion be an everyday part of public life. What they say indicates recognition and engagement (i.e., transnational being), but the intersection of their American and religious identities informs how they understand public place religion. Note Aminah's comment:

> "Okay, um over there they like play [the call to prayer] for every prayer and you can hear it.... I'd wake up at [dawn prayer] time hearing that. I loved it.... [I]t was very, that was very nice [and] meeting people talking Arabic as opposed to English. That was pretty interesting, because I understand Arabic a lot better than I speak it. I really liked it, a lot ... [B]ut also, I don't know if I'd go to like live there or something like that because I'm so used to it here." (7:1; 40:49).

Aminah's appreciation of the public visibility of Islam is clear; she loves being a part of the sights and sounds of her religion. This does not displace her American identity. Moreover, because she is American she doubts that she could actually live in a Muslim country. Leena's comment is similar but she is more direct in saying that her American identity means that in her parents' country of origin she is a visitor only. She says:

> "Well, I just, I like being there just for the fact that it's a Muslim country ... [Y]ou hear the [call to prayer] from the mosque. I like that and I like having the Arabic people everywhere and you are just one of them. But I still didn't feel like I was one of them, you know because I was from America ... I think differently." (37:1; 62:86).

Leena enjoys being a part of the crowd of people who share her religious identity and her ethnic ancestry. Yet she is keenly aware that her American identity shapes who she is all the way down to the level of her consciousness. Leena and Aminah feel emotionally connected to the Islamic culture that surrounds them, but they are temporary participants in those environments. Their ancestry and their religion allow them to be comfortable with their experiences. However their interpretations, their understandings, and how they position themselves socially are tempered by the fact that they are Americans.

A third indication that the second generation experiences being in their parents' home country is their perception that they are identified as American by other people. Laila describes being in a Pakistani marketplace with her mother when she was a little girl.

> "They definitely see that I'm foreign. I mean it just seems like the way that foreigners carry themselves ... people seem to pick that up really quickly. And I remember when I was young ... the beggars would come up to us ... [T]hey seem to know that we were foreign and that we had money. And I was like Mommy, how do they know this? She [said], 'I don't know, it's just the way we carry ourselves, it's just different.'" (36:15; 69:79).

That Laila is a "foreigner" is evidenced in her demeanor. Even as a small child she is aware that her American identity is readily observable, although she is not certain of how this is communicated. Nicole's experience is similar. Like Laila, being American makes her identifiable and, as a result, she experiences some discomfort when she is overseas. Nicole says:

> "In Jordan, you get off the plane and everyone just kind of looks at you, like they know you're not living in Jordan. They know you're like from America or somewhere else. So when [I] come here (return to the U.S.), I feel more comfortable, [because] I was raised here, this is my home." (47:1; 25:29).

Laila and Nicole's perceptions that they are visibly American indicate that the option to adopt the national origin identity of their parents is not available to them. They are not moving across a boundary that gives them access to Jordanian or Pakistani identity because of their ancestry matches that of the people in the country they are visiting. In those countries they are always American. The visibility of their American identity is an aspect of their transnational being. The second generations' experiences are embedded in family relationships and cultural practices (e.g., language and religion) that frame transnational being in the societies they visit. However, their American identity defines how they interpret what they experience in the parents' home country.

When the second generation is in public in their parents' home country they are conscious of the religion and ancestry that they share with the people of that nation. Their sense that language is an indicator of shared ancestry and that religion is a marker of common identity allows them to experience transnational being. Even when they do not actually know the people they are visiting, family relationships allow them to feel comfortable. Who their parents are creates the connection of family bonds. They do what is expected of them by their family and they are aware of implications of female gender with regard to those expectations. They are very conscious of being an American, also. Their American lives are a continuous reference point in shaping how they understand and interpret of their experiences. The intersection of their national, religious, and gender identities informs their experiences in their parent's country of origin. They are engaged in social relationships and practices that do not have a sustained impact on their identity. This is in sharp contrast to their belonging in the United States.

4.3. Transnational Belonging: Only in America

Belonging in a social field is evidenced in practices that enact identity. It is demonstrated through a conscious connection that utilizes a society's core values to legitimate one's identity and social membership. The second-generation Muslim Americans who participate in this research see their Muslim identity as an American identity. They do not argue that American ideals of religious freedom give them the right to be Muslim. They say instead that the two identities are consistent with one another. There is nothing about being Muslim that is inconsistent with being an American and there is nothing about being an American that is inconsistent with being Muslim. They express their belonging by separating their religion from their parents' ethnic culture, by framing their religious identity as an American identity, and by using core American values and ideals to support their social membership and participation as Muslims. What they say demonstrates the intersection of their national, religious, and gender identities.

The second generation sees their parents' religious identity as firmly embedded in the cultures of their countries of origin. They distance themselves from this understanding of what it means to be Muslim and, in doing so, from their parents. Ahmed, for example, tells a generational story highlighting the differences in culture between himself and his father. It is symbolized in his father's need to eat rice with every meal and his willingness to eat rice or pizza. He comes to these conclusions about his identity.

> "Whenever someone ask me what I am, I never say I'm Bangladeshi, I never say that I'm Arabian because I was born in Saudi Arabia. I do say I'm a Muslim ... So when you have these American values, it's not as extreme as double values, it's just a cultural lifestyle. But as long you don't violate your religious lifestyle, I believe it's perfectly acceptable." (2:6; 80:82).

In naming his identity Ahmed says that he is Muslim but that does not indicate that he is not an American. His identity and culture are based in the fact that he is both Muslim and American. He can eat rice with his meals or pizza. His American and Muslim cultural repertoires do not compete with one another. They do not pose conflicts for him. Living in the United States provides him with a particular style of living that allows him to be Muslim also.

Alia's comments are similar to Ahmed's. She sees cultural differences as dividing Muslims because migrants long for the home they left behind, but this is not a longing that she shares.

> " ... [A] lot of people come from other countries and they're all Muslim but they choose to stay with those who are like them. ... I mean we all see that we're Muslim, but people relate more to people who are like them. If they miss their country, they'll be reminded of [it] if they have friends who are like them. They want their kids to marry people from the same ethnicity, so they stay around those who are like them. It's a difference that I wish wasn't there but it's so apparent in the Muslim community, the separation." (5:7; 64:64).

Note that Alia is highlighting the boundaries between Muslims in the U.S. She frames those who are "like them" by pre-migration national cultures and not religion. From her point of view, pre-migration cultures divide Muslims among themselves and separate them from American society. Both Alia and Ahmed indicate that second-generation Muslim Americans can reject the influence of the country of origin cultures of their parents on their articulation of Islam. From their points of view, social boundaries exist among Muslims rather than between Muslims and American society. Alia and Ahmed frame their social belonging as culturally American and religiously Muslim.

Having been raised in the United States allows the second generation to be both Muslim and American. They see religion is one thing and culture is another. What amounts to religious practice can be specified, but religious practice need not be superimposed onto culture. This is reflected in the views of Ali and Eddie. According to Ali:

> "When I say Muslim I don't see it as a cultural thing, I see it as a religious thing. There's no such thing as Muslim culture which would be the way they look, the way they dress, the way they act. ... [I]f you migrate, what does that have to do to with your religion? Culture will always change no matter where you go, you'll adapt [to] a new culture. But something that shouldn't change is your religion ... unless you seriously think that it's wrong for you." (4:7; 140:146).

Ali is just as grounded in valuing his religious identity devoid of an articulation of Muslim culture as he is in the freedom to choose or reject religiosity. Religious practice is not culturally determined, nor is religion a culture in and of itself. Eddie's perspective is similar, religion can be influenced by culture but people who are raised in the United States are free to develop their knowledge of religion without relying on a reified Muslim culture.

> "But if you came here and you were raised here from [when you were] little and you grew up with a lot of Muslims who were basically the same, then your views are not as much influenced by your culture. You sort of get a chance to develop, to go to the mosque, and to the MSAs [Muslim Student Associations], and stuff. You sort of explore and you read more about your religion and you find out [about it]." (10:9; 79:79).

Eddie places the second generation's development of their religious identity firmly within their American experiences. His comment signals the ability of the second generation to engage in religious practice free from the influence of their parents and in a way that is shared with their peers. In other words, he understands religion as contextualized. Being Muslim in the United States is informed by learning and practicing Islam in the United States.

Living in the United States is the foundation of the second generation's Muslim identity. Not only are they Americans, they are not isolated from American culture. They use American values and culture as references points for their identity. In comparing herself to Muslims who are new migrants to the United States, Aminah makes this clear.

> " … [P]eople who come immediately from overseas, it's different for them; they still have grounding [in] how it was over there. But people like me [are] very Americanized. I don't have a lot of background culture in me. People who have grown up here [are] Americanized. … I think that once they realize that following the rules of the religion is what you're supposed to do then you can live your life around that. It's not a problem." (7:5; 81:81).

Aminah puts forward a very clear articulation of belonging as an American. She embraces American culture in the same way that she embraces her religiosity. She has the ability to practice her religion because she is an American. Moreover, her religious identity is not tethered to a set of cultural practices that would signify that she is not American.

Second-generation Muslim Americans situate their religious identity as an American identity. They separate their religion from their parents' ethnic culture thereby making it compatible with their social reality and nationality. They see themselves as simultaneously culturally American and religiously Muslim. Their identities are not in competition with or opposition to one another. They make the case that American society informs their identity. In doing so, they demonstrate their belonging in the United States.

The intersection of the second generation's national and religious identities is demonstrated in their deploying American values and ideals to defend being Muslim, to support their social membership, and their participation. Even when the second generation acknowledges the global and national political conflicts around Islam that heighten perceptions that Muslims are a threat to American society, they position themselves as Americans. Fatima Syed notes the media and the political visibility of Muslims in combination with an assertion of her American identity.

> "People think things about Muslims from what they see on television. We can show them that all Muslims aren't like that. We are Americans too and we're more like you than you think. … [Ethnic culture is] disappearing also over time. I mean we are the second generation. [Ethnic cultural is] probably more evident in the first generation that came but not so much now. I think that'll continue [to] happen over generations." (16:5; 88:91).

Fatimah Syed is speaking directly to the media images that construct Muslims as different from other Americans. She positions Muslims as Americans while acknowledging that migrants have cultural backgrounds that are different from Americans. Her point is that these differences are not a factor for second and subsequent generations of Muslims who are culturally like other Americans. Moreover, she projects the Americanization of Muslims into the future. Consciously or subconsciously, she invokes the classic narrative of immigrant incorporation to project the inclusion of the descendants of Muslim migrants into American society.

Fatimah makes a similar argument, just a little more vehemently. She feels that it is important for Muslims to be visible participants in American society. She frames social participation as a political right and a necessity. Her comment highlights the intersection of her national, religious, and gender identities.

> "I know for a fact that Muslims should be a part of their communities. If we're not there, than who [is going to] back up the stereotypes that we have? . . . If you're not, who's there to . . . stick up for us? If I wear hijab [a headscarf] and I'm hiding, than what's the use of my hijab? There's no definition to it if I'm not out there. . . . [W]e're in America. If you're in America, their rules are to be free. Practice your religion. So if that's what the Constitution is built upon, why not take it and move forward with it? . . . We're in America. ... I don't believe you can be here and not be a part of them. Once you're in America and you're born here, you are an American. You're just cosigned with Arabia and before that you're American, you're a Muslim American." (17:7; 34:34).

Fatimah clearly connects Muslim Americans active participation in American society to Constitutional rights, religious freedom, and citizenship. What she says is the very definition of transnational belonging in a social field. She signals the primacy of American identity over inherited or "cosigned" ethnic identities. She notes the absolute necessity for Muslims to be active social participants like other Americans, especially in light of negative stereotyping of Muslims. Additionally, she presents an articulation of Muslim female gender identity that is empowered. For her wearing hijab is an expression of her political rights as an American. From her point of view, political engagement and participation are social responsibilities. She speaks to the very heart of American ideals of rights, freedoms, and citizenship.

Belonging characterizes how second-generation Muslim Americans position themselves in the United States. On one hand, they eschew the ethnic identities of their parents that would create a boundary between their American and Muslim identities. On the other, they construct their Muslim identity as an American identity. They define what it means to be Muslim from within the context of their American experiences. Most importantly they use the values and ideals of American society to support the legitimacy of their Muslim identity as well as their membership and participation in Americans society. They step beyond the political right to religious freedom to construct Muslim identity as an American identity.

The positions of second-generation Muslim Americans in each location of their transnational social field differ. The differences signal shifts in social context that highlight the second generation's American identity. Fatimah's comments about wearing hijab indicate that female gender is experienced very differently in the United States in comparison the how it is experienced in the respondents' parents' country of origin. When in their parents' country of origin female gender is experienced as limitations on being in public at night without a male relative. In the United States Fatimah uses hijab as an expression of her American identity and as an assertion of political rights. She has a right to be visibility Muslim and female in American society. Similarly Ahmed and Alia's comments make it clear that, in contrast to their parents, they are American. While their parents use ethnic identity to cling to their migrant origins, Ahmed and Alia seek to eliminate migrant group boundaries that would separate Muslims among themselves and from American society. The American comparative reference point that the second generation uses to frame their overseas experiences is grounded in a full understanding and identification of themselves as Americans. Although the second generation enjoys experiencing the sights and sounds of Islam while overseas, Ali and Eddie's comments make it clear that for them Islam is an American religion. It is a religion that they learn in the context of their American lives and that they can chose to reject. Just as the use of American points of reference and interpretation are expressions of transnational being when the second generation is in their parents' country of origin, their insistence that their religion be framed, constructed, experienced, and understood from within the context of their American lives is an expression of belonging in the United States. For the second generation, Islam is not about the experiences and cultural references points of their parents; instead it is about who they are as Americans.

5. Concluding Remarks

The above analysis examines how second-generation Muslim Americans experience transnationalism. It uses qualitative interview data to assess what they say about their experiences in both locations of their transnational social field (i.e., their parents' country of origin and the United States). The intersection of their national, religious and gender identities inform their experiences in both places. In their parents' country of origin their transnational being highlights the importance of their nationality to their experiences. Not only are their American lives a continuous reference point for meaning making and interpretation, they are consciously aware that being an American makes them different from their relatives. They enjoy the public place visibility of their religion, but this is not enough to make them want to live in those countries. In addition, while they understand and accept the restrictions that are placed on young women because of their gender, young men simply offer a different explanation for similar restrictions that are placed on them.

In contrast, their belonging in the United States is institutionally grounded. They use the nation's core values to construct their Muslim identity as an American identity. Their nationality is American. They are not using the ideals of religious freedom to say that they have a right to be Muslim. They are saying instead that they are Americans. They are not attached to the ethnic cultures of their parents, nor are those cultures the foundation for their religious identity. Their religious identity is constructed inside of their American lives. Their national identity is American and their religious identity is Muslim. Their national identity empowers the expression of their religious identity.

A transnational social field analysis is important in revealing that being an American is central to the identity of second-generation Muslims in the United States. The national and global conflicts around Islam raise significant questions about the citizenship of Muslims in Western nations. Research has made the case for the negative impact of anti-terrorism policies on second-generation Muslim Americans. Assumptions that religious identity trumps national identity or that it at least poses problems for social participation are at the center of national and global security policies that target Muslims. In nations such as the United States that are founded on religious diversity that is represented in Christian denominations, recognizing that nationality is not hindered by non-Christian religious identity is extremely important. Clearly, the above analysis demonstrates that second-generation Muslims in the United States are Americans.

Conflicts of Interest: The author declares no conflicts of interest.

References

Abdelhady, Dalia. 2006. Beyond Home/Host Networks: Forms of Solidarity Among Lebanese Immigrants in a Global Era. *Indentities: Global Studies in Culture and Power* 13: 427–53. [CrossRef]

Ahmad, Muneer. 2011. Homeland Insecurities: Racial Violence the Day after September 11. *Race/Ethncity: Multidisciplinary Global Contexts* 4: 337–50. [CrossRef]

Al-Ali, Nadje. 2002. Gender relations, transnational ties and rituals among Bosian refugees. *Global Networks* 2: 249–62. [CrossRef]

Alimahomed, Sabrina. 2011. Generation Islam: Arab American Muslims and Racial Politics after September 11. *Race/Ethncity: Multidisciplinary Global Context* 4: 381–97. [CrossRef]

Anthias, Floya. 2008. Thinking Through the Lens of Translocational Positionality: An Intersectional Frame for Understanding Identity and Belonging. *Translocations: Migration and Social Change* 4: 5–20.

Anthias, Floya. 2012. Transnational Mobilities, Migration Research and Intersectionality: Towards a Translocational Frame. *Nordic Journal of Migration Research* 2: 102–10. [CrossRef]

Berkhus, Wayne H. 2008. Trends in the Qualitative Study of Identities. *Sociology Compass* 2: 1059–78. [CrossRef]

Binaisa, Naluwembe. 2013. Ugandans in Britain Making 'New' Homes: Transnationalism, Place and Identity within Narratives of Integration. *Journal of Ethnic and Migrations Studies* 39: 885–902. [CrossRef]

Bowen, John R. 2004. Beyond Migration: Islam in Transnational Public Space. *Journal of Ethnic and Migration Studies* 30: 879–98. [CrossRef]

Brubaker, Rogers, and Frederick Cooper. 2000. Beyond "Identity". *Theory and Society* 29: 1–47. [CrossRef]

Cadge, Wendy, and Elaine Howard Ecklund. 2007. Immigration and Religion. *Annual Review of Sociology* 33: 259–379. [CrossRef]

Cainkar, Louise. 2004. Islamic Revival among Second-Generation Arab American Muslims: The American Experience and Global Intersect. *Bulletin of the Royal Institute for Inter-Faith Studies* 6: 99–120.

Cainkar, Louise, and Sunaina Maira. 2005. Targeting Arab/ Muslim/South Asian Americans: Criminalization and Cultural Citizenship. *Ameriasia Journal* 31: 1–28. [CrossRef]

Collins, Patricia Hill. 2000. *Black Feminist Thought: Knowledge, Consciousness and the Politics of Empowerment. New York: Routledge*. New York: Routledge.

Collins, Patricia Hill, and Sirma Bilge. 2016. *Intersectionality*. Cambridge: Polity.

Crenshaw, Kimberle. 1991. Mapping the Margins: Intersectionality, Identity Politics, and Violence against Women of Color. *Stanford Law Review* 43: 1241–99. [CrossRef]

Das Gupta, Monisha. 1997. What is Indian about You? A Gendered, Transnational Approach to Ethnicity. *Gender and Society* 11: 572–96. [CrossRef]

Easthope, Hazel. 2009. Fixed Identities in a Mobile World? The Relationship Between Mobility, Place and Identity. *Identities: Global Studies in Culture and Power* 16: 61–82. [CrossRef]

Faist, Thomas. 2000. Transnationalization in International Migration: Implications for the Study of Citizenship and Culture. *Ethnic and Racial Studies* 23: 189–223. [CrossRef]

Fouron, Georges, and Nina Glick Schiller. 2001. All in the family: Gender, transnational migration and the nation-state. *Identities: Global Studies in Culture and Power* 7: 539–82. [CrossRef]

Gardner, Katy, and Ralph Grillo. 2002. Transnational households and ritual: An overview. *Global Networks* 2: 179–90. [CrossRef]

Gergen, Kenneth J., and Mary M. Gergen. 2007. Social Construction and Research Methodology. In *The Sage Handbook of Social Science Methodology*. Edited by Willam Outhwaite and Stephen P. Turner. New York: Sage Publicationa, pp. 461–78.

Grammich, Clifford, Kirk Hadaway, Richard Houseal, Dale E. Jones, Alexei Krindatch, Richie Stanley, and Richard H. Taylor. 2010. US Congregation Membership Reports: Philadelphia County. Available online: http://www.thearda.com/rcms2010/r/c/42/rcms2010_42101_county_cong_2010.asp. (accessed on 27 August 2013).

Grillo, Ralph. 2004. Isalm and Transnationalism. *Journal of Ethnic and Migrations Studies* 30: 861–78. [CrossRef]

Haddad, Yvonne Yazbeck, and Adair T. Lummis. 1987. *Islamic Values in the United States: A Comparative Study*. New York: Oxford University Press.

Heath, Anthony. 2014. Introduction: Patterns of generational change: Convergence, reactive or emergent. *Ethnic and Racial Studies* 37: 1–9. [CrossRef]

Henkel, Heiko. 2004. Rethinking the dar al-harb: Social Change and the Changing Preceptions of the West in Turkish Islam. *Journal of Ethnic and Migration Studies* 30: 961–77. [CrossRef]

Kibria, Nazli. 2008. The 'new Islam' and Bangladeshi Youth in Britain and the U.S. *Ethnic and Racial Studies* 31: 243–66. [CrossRef]

Lacroix, Thomas. 2014. Conceptualizing Transnational Engagements: A Structure and Agency Perspective on (Hometown) Transnationalism. *International Migration Reveiw* 48: 643–79. [CrossRef]

Lawler, Steph. 2008. *Identity: Sociological Prepsectives*. Cambridge: Polity.

Levitt, Peggy, and B. Nadya Jaworsky. 2007. Transnational Migration Studies: Past Develpments and Future Trends. *Annual Review of Sociology* 33: 129–56. [CrossRef]

Levitt, Peggy, and Nina Glick-Schiller. 2004. Conceptualizing Simultaneity: A Transnational Social Field Perspective on Society. *The International Migration Review* 38: 1002–39. [CrossRef]

Peggy Levitt, and Mary C. Waters, eds. 2002. Introduction. In *The Changing Face of Home: Transnationalism in the Lives of the Second Generation*. New York: Russell Sage Foundation, pp. 1–30.

Louie, Vivian. 2006. Growing Up Ethnic in Transnational Worlds: Identities among Second-Generation Chinese and Dominicans. *Identities: Global Studies in Culture and Power* 13: 363–94. [CrossRef]

Maira, Sunaina. 2004. Youth Culture, Citizenship and Globalization: South Asain Muslim Youth in the United States after September 11. *Comparative Studies of South Asia, Africa and the Middle East* 24: 219–31. Available online: http://muse.jhu.edu/journals/cst/summary/v024/24.1maira.html (accessed on 12 September 2007). [CrossRef]

Maira, Sunaina. 2008. Flexible Citizenship/ Flexible Empire: South Asian Muslim Youth in Post-9/11 America. *American Quarterly* 60: 697–720. [CrossRef]

Mandaville, Peter. 2009. Muslim Transnational Identity and State Responses in Europe and the UK after 9/11: Political Community, Ideology and Authority. *Journal of Ethnic and Migration Studies* 35: 491–506. [CrossRef]

Mandaville, Peter. 2011. Transnational Muslim Solidarities and Everyday Life. *Nations and Nationalism* 17: 7–21. [CrossRef]

McAuliffe, Cameron. 2007. A home far away? Religious identity and transnational relations in the Iranian diaspora. *Global Networks* 7: 307–27. [CrossRef]

Mirza, Heidi. 2013. 'A Second Skin': Embodoes Intersectionality, Transnationalism and Narratives of Identity and Belonging among Muslim Women in Britain. *Women's Studies International Forum* 36: 5–15. [CrossRef]

Naber, Nadine. 2000. Ambiguous Insiders: An Investigation of Arab American Invisibility. *Ethnic and Racial Studies* 23: 37–61. [CrossRef]

Osirim, Mary Johnson. 2011. Transnational Migration and Transformation Among African Women in the United States: Change-agents Locally and Globally. *Advances in Gender Research* 15: 185–210.

Pew Forum on Religion and Public Life. 2007. *Muslim Americans: Middle Class and Mostly Mainstream*. Washington: Pew Research Center.

Pew Forum on Religion and Public Life. 2011. *Muslim Americans: No Signs of Growth in Alienation or Sopport for Extremism*. Washington: Pew Research Center, Available online: http://www.people-press.org/2011/08/30/muslim-americans-no-signs-of-growth-in-alienation-or-support-for-extremism/ (accessed on 22 March 2015).

Purkayastha, Bandana. 2010. Interrogating Intersectionality: Contemporary Globalisation and Racialised Gendering in the Lives of Highly Educated South Asian Americans and their Children. *Journal of Intercultural Studies* 31: 29–47. [CrossRef]

Purkayastha, Bandana. 2012. Intersectionality in a Transnational World. *Gender and Society* 26: 55–66. [CrossRef]

Salih, Ruba. 2004. The Backward and the New: National, Transnational, and post-national Islam in Europe. *Journal of Ethnic and Migration Studies* 30: 995–1011. [CrossRef]

Schimmer, Paulien, and Frank van Tubergen. 2014. Transnationalism and Ethnic Identification among Adolescent Children of Immigrants in the Netherlans, Germany, England, and Sweden. *International Migration Reveiw* 48: 680–709. [CrossRef]

Schmidt, Garbi. 2004. Islamic Identity Formation among Young Muslims: The Case of Denmark, Sweden, and the United States. *Journal of Muslim Minority Affairs* 24: 31–45. [CrossRef]

Thomson, Mark, and Maurice Crul. 2007. The Second Generation in Europe and the United States: How is the Transnational Debate Relevant for Future Research on the European Second Generation. *Journal of Ethnic and Migration Studies* 33: 1025–41. [CrossRef]

Tilly, Charles. 2003. Political Identitys in Changing Politics. *Social Research* 70: 606–20.

Vertovec, Steven. 2001. Transnationalism and Identity. *Journal of Ethnic and Migration Studies* 27: 573–82. [CrossRef]

Viruell-Fuentes, Edna A. 2006. My Heart is Always There: The Transnational Practices of First-Generation Mexican Immigrant and Second-Generation Mexican American Women. *Identities: Global Studies in Culture and Power* 13: 335–62. [CrossRef]

Voas, David, and Fenella Fleischmann. 2012. Islam Moves West: Religious Change in the First and Second Generations. *Annual Review of Sociology* 38: 525–45. [CrossRef]

Waldinger, Roger, and David Fitzgerald. 2004. *Transnationalism in Question*. *American Journal of Sociology* 109: 1177–95.

Waters, Mary C. 2014. Defining difference: The role of immigrant generation and race in American and British immigrantion studies. *Ethnic and Racial Studies* 37: 10–26. [CrossRef]

Wuthnow, Robert, and Stephen Offutt. 2008. Transnational Religious Connections. *Sociology of Religion* 69: 209–32. [CrossRef]

Zevallos, Zuleyka. 2008. 'You Have to be Anglo and Not Look Like Me': Identity and belonging among young wome of Turkish and Latin American backgrounds in Melbourne Australia. *Australian Geographer* 39: 21–43. [CrossRef]

Article

Being a "Good" Son and a "Good" Daughter: Voices of Muslim Immigrant Adolescents

Cristina Giuliani *, Maria Giulia Olivari and Sara Alfieri

Psychology Department, Università Cattolica del Sacro Cuore, L.go Gemelli 1, 20123 Milan, Italy; mariagiulia.olivari@unicatt.it (M.G.O.); sara.alfieri@unicatt.it (S.A.)
* Correspondence: cristina.giuliani@unicatt.it; Tel.: +39-02-7234-2533

Received: 19 July 2017; Accepted: 14 November 2017; Published: 17 November 2017

Abstract: In the last decade, a growing empirical work has focused on adaptation processes of immigrants from Muslim-majority countries who live in the West, particularly Muslim youth born and/or educated in Western countries. The current study explored how Muslim boys and girls immigrated from Morocco, Egypt and Pakistan negotiate their identity on the base of interiorized social and cultural in-group norms associated to the representation of a "good" son and a "good" daughter within the resettlement society. Participants were 45 Muslim immigrant adolescents (30 females, 15 males) coming from Morocco, Egypt and Pakistan, who were interviewed through an in-depth semi-structured interview. Thematic analysis carried out on the interview transcripts permitted to identify four themes and thirteen subthemes, revealing interesting differences based on participants' gender and country of origin. The quality of being obedient and respectful of parents' desires was a significant common topic among all participants, although it was differently articulated by girls and boys. For girls, norms and expectations were strictly modeled around staying at home and preserving heritage culture. For boys, a heavy mandate—that is, gaining educational success in order to become the breadwinner—weights on them. Implications of these gender-based challenges are discussed in relation to specific vulnerabilities experienced by young Muslims living in Western society.

Keywords: Muslim; immigrant children; gender norm; identity

---

1. Introduction

Research carried out in the last decades on the experiences of immigrants in Western countries unanimously recognized the complexity and multidimensionality of the adaptation processes associated with living in a new socio-cultural context (Berry et al. 2006). Additionally, a large number of factors have been proposed as being associated with acculturation and adaptation of different immigrant generations. They include socio-demographic variables (e.g., gender, age, length of stay in the host country, socio-economic status), post-migration variables (e.g., acculturation factors), and social contextual variables (e.g., perceived discrimination, social support, ethnic network) (Berry et al. 2006; Bornstein 2017; Brubaker 2001; Marzana et al. 2016; Musterd and Ostendorf 2009; Sam and Berry 2016).

The migration transition is still more complex in the cases of family reunifications. Many patterns of serial migration exist and most of them are marked by a series of critical issues, well-illustrated in the psychological (Falicov 2002; Gonzales et al. 2006; Lashley 2000) and sociological (Bertolani et al. 2014) literature. From the point of view of the children, who are the object of interest in this study, this type of migration constitutes a challenge in multiple ways. In the first place, it imposes on children a double separation: the first between the parent who migrates and the children who remain in their country of origin; the second, at the moment of the family reunification, between the children and the social network where they had been settled until that moment. This aspect is particularly important as the children develop a referential relationship with other caregiver figures and then they have to separate from them in order to reunite with their parents (Lashley 2000). Secondly, the migration is often the parents' project and not the children's one, who must then take on the further challenge of having to adapt to someone else's plan. Finally, the separation from parents can be very long, and the reunification is not easy because over the course of time the family arrangements and bonds have changed (Falicov 2002; Gonzales et al. 2006). All these aspects inevitably affect the socialization process, which is more complex in reunification scenarios. Literature on the socialization in migration is flourishing (Vedder et al. 2009; Verkuyten et al. 2012) and has highlighted the complexity of parental task of transmitting to the young generations the values and norms of heritage culture within a new socio-cultural context. Much less is known about the children perspective. They interiorized social norms and values in their family and, as adolescents, they have to negotiate these aspects in light of the new experiences lived outside the family (peer, school, post-school activities, sport).

The present research was carried out in Italy, where the migratory phenomenon is quite recent and the policies implemented in the last two decades regarding familial reunifications have allowed a gradual process of immigrant families' stabilization in the host country. Therefore, alongside the growing number of children born in Italy (around 2/3 of the total population of foreign minors), a significant proportion of minors (especially the older ones) are immigrant children who experienced family reunification (Crespi 2014). Surprisingly, these latter represent a reality even less investigated in literature. We believe that the point of view of the children who experienced family reunification is very interesting from a psychological perspective, as they must negotiate multiple issues pertaining to their identity and to combine the feelings of belonging to their ethnic community with those of the host country. Since these aspects of negotiation become more salient and complex in adolescence, it is evident how being immigrant adolescents is an additional challenge. In adolescence, when the personal and social identity is already an object of negotiation, immigrant adolescents often live in between two different socio-cultural contexts, moreover, they have directly experienced mobility from their origin country to the host country and they have separated both from the extended family network and from their community.

In the present study, we limited our investigation to post-migration experience of reunified Muslim adolescents in order to explore how they negotiate specific cultural issues and social norms. This work employed a cross-sectional qualitative design and presents at least two points of innovation. The first one is the involvement of male participants, previous qualitative studies have indeed mainly involved female adolescents, young women, or adult women, neglecting males almost entirely. Findings from the current study revealed important aspects that have been verbalized by male participants, providing a complementary picture to that of their female peers. A second strength regards the involvement of Muslim adolescents coming from different countries: Egypt, Morocco, and Pakistan. This choice turned out to be fruitful because it sheds light on important differences among these three subgroups of immigrant Muslim adolescents. We believe it can help contrasting the outgroup homogeneity effect for whom "all Muslims are the same".

1.1. *Muslim Immigrants in Italy*

Despite the recent economic crisis, Italy is one of the major destinations for immigrants in Europe. The foreign resident population has increased over the years, reaching 5.9 million of individuals on 1 January 2016 (ISTAT 2016): this represents 9.58% of the total population.

Muslim immigrants and their descendants compose in Italy a large and increasing group, as in many European countries (e.g., Germany, France, and the United Kingdom; Pew Research Center 2010). In Italy, Muslim Arab, North African, and South Asian immigrants, account for approximately 20% of the legalized immigrant population (ISTAT 2016). Muslims are not a homogeneous group: in the Italian context, they comprise more than 20 different nationalities. In this study, we focused on three national groups (Morocco, Egypt, Pakistan).

The exploration of Moroccan, Egyptian and Pakistani immigrants' experiences is interesting for socio-demographic, political, religious, and cultural reasons (De Haas 2007; Giunchi 2012; Hermansen 1991; Zaman et al. 2006). Their immigrant experience is related to the political and social-economic conditions in their country of origin: Morocco and Egypt are considered to be more developed and dynamic countries with a Gross Domestic Product (GDP) per capita respectively of US $3169 and of US $2724 (World Health Organization 2016a), while Pakistan is a poorer country with a GDP per capita of US $1182 (World Health Organization 2016a). Furthermore, in Pakistan the overall status of women is among the lowest in the world and secondary education rates are still low for girls (World Health Organization 2016b). All the three are Muslim societies, but, whereas reformist and modernized ideas about women's rights have spread throughout Moroccan and Egyptian societies, in Pakistan the fundamentalist Islamic tradition is still strong (Giunchi 2012).

Their migration history in Italy is the result both of the policies of recruitment for manual labor since the 1980s and of the following immigration norms about family reunion (Legge Turco Napolitano, Act no. 286/1998). The 510,450 Moroccans (71% of them living in Northern Italy), 143,232 Egyptians (67% of them living in Northern Italy) and 122,885 Pakistanis (71.2% of them living in Northern Italy) officially residing in Italy on 1 January 2016 are among the largest Muslim minorities in the country. In particular, in Italy, Moroccan group is the largest national non-EU foreign group and Pakistanis are among the fastest growing immigrant groups (ISTAT 2016). In Italy, minors belonging to Moroccan, Egyptian and Pakistani groups number respectively 161,325, 49,141 and 33,598 (ISTAT 2016). These three groups have different migratory histories and characteristics. Migration from North-Africa (i.e., Morocco and Egypt) began in the mid-1980s, whereas migration from Pakistan started in the second half of the 1990s. In comparison with Egyptians and Pakistanis, Moroccans are much more deeply-rooted in the Italian context because of a longer migratory history.

For all groups, the first migration wave was male-dominated, though this trend was gradually counterbalanced by the arrival of women and children within the scope of family reunification (Ambrosini 2013; ISTAT 2016). Nowadays, only the Moroccan group gained a balance in the gender structure, on the contrary Egyptian and Pakistani immigrants are characterized by a very large imbalance in the gender structure (about 70% of the immigrants are males) (ISTAT 2016). Egyptians have higher educational level in comparison with Moroccan and Pakistani immigrants: the 64% of Egyptian immigrants has a medium level of education (i.e., they attended high school), whereas the 68% of Pakistanis and the 72% of Moroccans completed only elementary or junior high school. All these immigrants perform principally low-skilled work (building or handicraft sector, food and service sector, agriculture sector). These groups are also characterized by different levels of participation of women in the workforce: 23% of Moroccan women and 14.2% of Egyptian women are part of the Italian labor market, the same is true for only 4.5% of Pakistani women (Ambrosini 2013; ISTAT 2016). Most Moroccan, Egyptian, and Pakistani immigrants in Italy are living in the northern part of the country: the former settled predominantly in urban areas, while the latter settled in rural or suburban areas (Blangiardo 2013).

Overall, the presence of immigrants in Italy is characterized by high level of negative views and rejection, as highlighted by Ambrosini (2013), who suggested the concept of "subordinate integration" (p. 183). According to the author, immigrants in Italy seemed to be accepted in the labor market as long as they perform low skill jobs and remain at a low socio-economical level. Additionally, Muslim immigrants experience growing prejudice and hostilities originated by Islamism and terrorism and geopolitical tensions. The role played by young Muslims and those people whom Muslim faith is assigned (i.e., riots, recent terrorist attacks in Europe) has generated an atmosphere of fear and suspicion toward them (Allen and Nielsen 2002; Pew Research Center 2016). For these reasons, in many European countries and in Italy, the issue of integration and psychological adaptation of young Muslim immigrants has become urgent in public and academic discourses.

1.2. Identity Processes and Domain-Specific Norms among Muslim Immigrants

In the last decade, a growing empirical work has focused on adaptation processes of immigrants from Muslim-majority countries who live in the West, particularly Muslim youth, born and/or educated in Western countries.

The bulk of psychological studies on Muslims youth are based on the two-dimensional model of acculturation of Berry (1997). This theoretical model aims at evaluating how immigrants are able to both navigate between their own heritage culture and the host culture, combining customs, norms, values stemming from these two cultural frameworks (Arends-Tóth and Van de Vijver 2004). Many studies carried out in Europe using this framework show that Muslim youth living in Europe—in particular, Moroccans and Turks—remain strongly attached to own cultural heritage and struggle in combining loyalty to their cultural heritage and the host society norms and values (Berry and Sabatier 2010; Crul and Doomernik 2003; Stevens et al. 2004; Vedder et al. 2007; Verkuyten et al. 2012). Serious cultural conflicts between different contradictory norms and lifestyles are particularly stressful in adolescence when children have to face the normative tasks of identity redefinition. Although studies have rarely compared male and female Muslim immigrants adolescents, some authors (Stevens et al. 2004) suggested that Muslim girls are more vulnerable and seem to experience major cultural conflicts and ambivalences between loyalty to their family and community heritage and external pressures.

The above-mentioned acculturation studies offer an overall—but also oversimplified and static—picture of post-migration identity processes faced by Muslim youth. Despite its popularity in cross-cultural psychological research, several criticisms have been moved to Berry's acculturation model. In particular, authors criticized both the monolithic view on culture that ignore the diversity within cultural groups and the too simplified view of acculturation process that do not consider multiple dimensions and factors involved in acculturation (Bornstein 2017; Ngo 2008). Therefore, whether psychological studies have the merit of vastly underlining the centrality of heritage culture for Muslim young generations, they only partially allow a glimpse of the complexity of cross-cultural negotiations experienced by them in Western societies (Stevens et al. 2004). In fact, as suggested by authors (Arends-Tóth and Van de Vijver 2004), competing cultural pressures and norms regarding specific domains need to be deeply explored. These domains are generally classified as public or functional (i.e., language, contacts, news) or private (i.e., cultural habits, gender relationship, religion). Cross-cultural negotiations may differ across these different cultural domains: public domains of acculturation are more negotiable, whereas private domains, attaining norms and values that constitute core aspects of in-group identities, are more difficult to negotiate.

In this regard, studies carried out by Verkuyten et al. (2012) on young Muslims, based on the theory of social identity (Tajfel 1981; Turner et al. 1987), highlighted the importance of the in-group for the individuals, in terms of feelings, self-esteem, belonging, and behavioural norm acquisition. Research has shown that relationships with the in-group members increase the importance of ethnic identity and of the social norms linked to it (Ethier and Deaux 1994). As previously underlined, during the socialization process, parental normative pressures to maintain the own culture conflict with external pressures of larger society. Research demonstrated that among immigrants, attempts are frequent in order to maintain their core in-group norms and values so as to experience a feeling of continuity between their own origin country and their host country and to preserve the distinctiveness of their identity (Ethier and Deaux 1994).

Qualitative studies concerning domain-specific cultural issues among Muslims living in Western countries have been mainly carried out with Muslim female participants (mostly adult women), generally considered more vulnerable than their male counterparts because of their being "custodian of tradition" and "oppressed" by patriarchal norms and religious traditions. Researchers rarely take into account male immigrants' narratives about domain-specific cultural negotiations. In general, these studies highlighted three main cultural domains where cross-cultural negotiations are more challenging: gender expectations, the question of wearing the veil, and the importance of religious practices and duties.

Gender Expectations. Muslim adolescents negotiate their identity in light of cultural and religious prescriptions concerning appropriate gender roles and gender relationships (Abu-Ali and Reisen 1999; Ajrouch 2004). Studies (Dwyer 2000; Gilani 2005; Giuliani and Tagliabue 2015) have shown that Muslim girls and women face and sometimes creatively manage gender dilemmas experienced within the host societies. The immigration process and contextual factors (e.g., perceived discrimination) often tend to reinforce in the post-migration setting the cultural pressures regarding the woman's role as guardian of cultural and religious identity. Behavioural prescriptions regard appropriate dress, mating and dating rules, and marriage. Furthermore, girls are asked to maintain a strong connection to the country of origin of their family symbolically, but this is also reinforced through parents' choice to return to the country of origin in order to celebrate marriages (Reniers 2001). The geographical proximity and the recent and growing market of low-cost trips has contributed to the simplification of mobility (Bertolani et al. 2014; Leyendecker 2011).

Wearing the Veil. Frequently investigated in literature is the norm regarding the use of the veil. The veil is considered an "identity marker" that is clearly related to Muslim immigrant women (Crabtree and Husain 2012). Recently, researchers tried to investigate the deeper meanings of wearing the veil, highlighting the complexity of this phenomenon. They suggested that several different meanings coexist: the veil is a primary part of Muslim female identity (Hopkins and Greenwood 2013), it is frequently personal the choice to use it, and it not necessarily forced by in-group members (Lorasdaği 2009). Moreover, it is a ritual act that qualifies women as practicing the Muslim religion (Fadil 2011), or it is perceived as a religious duty (Killian 2003). It is moreover perceived an instrument useful to act in a pious way when there is a temptation to engage in non-religious acts (Patel 2012).

Islamic Religious Practices and Duties. Islam provides clearly core duties and practices that permit distinguishing between being or not being a "true" Muslim (Haddad and Lummis 1987; Hogg et al. 2010; Williams 1988). Studies about Muslim immigrants have revealed that religiosity (e.g., engagement in practices, beliefs, values) is a salient component of daily life and it is highly intertwined with ethnic aspects of identity (Maliepaard et al. 2010; Verkuyten and Yildiz 2007). Furthermore, studies comparing different generations of Muslim immigrants on religious identity show mixed results. On one hand, some studies confirmed the importance of religious commitment and practices among different generations of Muslim immigrants (Diehl et al. 2009; Güngör et al. 2011; Verkuyten 2007). On the other hand, other research indicates a progressive weakness of the religious engagement among the descendants of the first immigrants (Maliepaard et al. 2010). Among the less negotiable norms, there is the one concerning marriage. Traditional interpretations of the Quran state that men are allowed to marry a "chaste non-Muslim woman" (i.e., Christian or Jewish). A Muslim woman, however, is not allowed to marry a non-Muslim man (Leeman 2009). Besides what is dictated by religion, a main aspect of marriage management is linked to parental expectations. Research highlighted that some parents expressed strong disapproval of their daughters' marrying outside of their religion (Al-Yousuf 2006), and were more permissive with their sons' than with their daughters' marriages (Hanassab 1998). These gender differences are coherent with the woman's role and status within the household. Indeed, women are responsible for the upbringing of children and become therefore a primary means of cultural and religious continuity for future generations (Clycq 2012).

1.3. The Present Study

Although previous studies have highlighted cultural negotiations faced by Muslim immigrants in Western societies, to our knowledge, studies have rarely explored the post-migration experience of male and female Muslim reunified adolescents with respect to the negotiation of specific cultural and social norms.

Overall, the study adds to the literature in several ways. First, our focus is only on adolescent children of immigrants who experienced family reunification (foreign born children). Unlike studies where "second generation" is used by researchers as umbrella term including many different migration histories, in the current study we considered only the case of immigrant adolescent children who moved to Italy at different age through family reunification. These adolescent immigrants have been exposed during socialization process to different social and cultural contexts and need to combine contrasting social expectations (family, peer, school, host society).

Second, we explored both males'and females' perceptions, thus adding the male voices within a literature that has mainly focused on the female perspective.

Third, we included immigrants from Morocco, Egypt and Pakistan because of their representativeness within the Italian context, in particular within Northern Italy, where our study has been carried out. The choice of this regional area is due to the fact that it is the most industrialized and productive area in Italy, where Moroccans and Pakistanis mainly reside and work.

Considering these above-mentioned aspects, this study aims at exploring, through an in-depth semi-structured interview, in-group norms and meanings associated to the representation of a "good" son and a "good" daughter among male and female immigrant reunified adolescents coming from Morocco, Egypt and Pakistan. We considered these aspects in the light of gender and countries of origin.

2. Method

2.1. Participants

Forty-five immigrant adolescents participated in the current study and were recruited in the northern region of Italy using the "snowball technique". Among the participants, 30 female adolescents (11 from Morocco, 9 from Pakistan, 10 from Egypt) and 15 male adolescents (5 from Morocco, 5 from Pakistan, 5 from Egypt) met the following criteria and were thus selected: (a) the immigrant adolescent was aged 14–19; (b) the adolescent, born outside Italy, had immigrated to Italy from Morocco, Egypt or Pakistan through family reunification; (c) the adolescent had lived in Italy for at least two years. All participants identified themselves as Muslim. All participants were living in two-parent families with other sibling, the majority (n = 43) of mothers were housewives (except two Moroccan women employed in a full and part-time unskilled job respectively) and all fathers perform low-skilled work. All adolescents attended secondary high school. Participants demographic characteristics are presented in Table 1.

Table 1. Participants' demographic characteristics.

	Moroccans		Pakistanis		Egyptians	
	Female	**Male**	**Female**	**Male**	**Female**	**Male**
Age						
Range Mean (SD)	15–19 16.72 (1.61)	15–16 15.40 (0.54)	14–18 16.55 (1.81)	15–18 16.00 (1.22)	14–19 16.80 (1.61)	14–18 15.20 (1.78)
Age at time of immigration						
Range Mean (SD)	1–17 9.36 (5.08)	2–13 9.00 (4.79)	3–14 8.78 (3.97)	3–9 6.00 (2.45)	1–12 6.78 (4.24)	1–8 4.20 (2.86)
Years in Italy						
Range Mean (SD)	2–15 7.36 (5.25)	3–14 6.40 (4.97)	2–11 7.77 (3.41)	8–12 10.00 (1.58)	3–17 10.11 (5.80)	10–13 11.00 (1.41)
Family size						
Range Mean (SD)	5–6 5.45 (0.52)	5–7 6.2 (1.09)	3–7 5.33 (1.22)	5–7 6.00 (0.70)	4–7 5.80 (0.91)	4–6 5.00 (1.00)

2.2. Procedure

Data were collected from January 2008 to December 2011 within a broader research project entitled "Women experiences in Arab and Pakistani migration" (Regalia and Giuliani 2012). The research was granted approval by the University Ethical Committee (cod.01-14), which fulfilled ethical standards of the Italian Psychology Association (AIP, Associazione Italiana di Psicologia).

Adolescents' parents, when children were younger than 18 years old, were asked for written consent for their participation in the research under the condition of anonymity and for tape-recording the interviews. Adolescents older than 18 years old provide their written individual consent.

Participants were asked to complete firstly a brief demographic questionnaire, which gathered some personal information (country of origin, age, age at immigration, family size and condition, parental job). Then participants were administered an in-depth semi-structured individual interview conducted by two expert interviewers. All participants were fluent in Italian and all interviews were conducted in Italian.

The semi-structured interviews investigated different areas of immigrant adolescents' life: personal and family immigration history, life experience in the host country (family, school, work, leisure), parental expectations, comparisons between homeland and host country, social context and social relationship, future projects, and expectations about the future. In this study, findings from the qualitative analysis related to parental expectations and are based on participants' responses to four questions. We analyzed only the narratives stimulated by these questions. Questions 1 and 2 queried participants as follows: "What does it mean to be a good son?", "What does it mean to be a good daughter?". These two questions were designed in the attempt to explore adolescents' norms and values linked to the role of a good child. Questions 3 and 4 were posed as follows "How it should behave a good son?", "How it should behave a good daughter?". These two questions were developed to further explore the behavioral aspect linked to their representation of a good child.

The interviews took place in the respondents' homes or in public spaces (i.e., library, school), and respondents were offered a 10-euro gift certificate to a local market for their participation. The sessions were tape-recorded and later transcribed verbatim in Italian.

2.3. Data Analysis

The transcripts from the semi-structured interviews were analyzed separately for gender using thematic analysis, which is a method for identifying, analyzing, and reporting patterns (i.e., themes) within the data (Braun and Clarke 2006).

A 5-step process to conduct the thematic analysis was used (Olivari et al. 2015, 2017). Firstly, the researchers familiarized themselves with the text by transcribing the recordings, reading these transcripts thoroughly, highlighting keywords and phrases, and then noting initial ideas. Secondly, all the three authors independently began the coding process, which involved organizing the data into themes and subthemes. The three authors first reviewed all the transcripts separately and independently to determine the initial themes and subthemes. Subsequently, they met as a group several times to review and reach agreement regarding the themes and subthemes. Agreement was reached by discussion. Fourthly, the researchers reviewed and discussed the themes by reading them again and checking their coherency and consistency with each other and the entire dataset. Finally, the research team met again to define and label the themes and their underlying subthemes and to identify key participant quotations.

2.4. Limitations of the Study

The present work has some limitations that should be held in consideration. The first regards the small number of participants, which cannot be considered representative of the populations interviewed. Furthermore, these interviews were carried out six years ago, which cannot account for either recent socio-political vicissitudes that have marked some of these countries (e.g., the "Arab Spring"), nor for some recent debates on citizen rights that are now happening in Italy (e.g., such as "Jus soli"). Additionally, the size of our sample does not allow distinguishing the experiences of reunified children in relation to their age at time of immigration. Studies have demonstrated differences in speed and modes of the integration process among different young immigrant generations, in particular between those come in their early childhood (before 6 years old, generation 1.75) and those immigrated after a longer socializing process in the country of origin (1.25 an 1.50 generations). Further study could better investigate these aspects.

A second limitation regards the lack of detailed information with respect both to the contexts of origin of the adolescents (i.e., big city vs. rural village; specific ethnic group) and to the Italian contexts where they were living (i.e., discrimination, intergroup relationship, segregation). As widely suggested by literature (Musterd and Ostendorf 2009; Ngo 2008) these aspects play a significant role on acculturation and adaptation processes and should therefore considered in future investigations

The third limitation regards the exclusive use of interviews, which give us only the respondents' own views and may be, to various degrees, susceptible to social desirability. In order to avoid this problem, it would be important to include additional investigative tools, such as a questionnaire. Furthermore, we do not have information about the perception of integration of the adolescents interviewed, which would permit a better understanding of some facets of the aspects examined.

3. Results

Data analysis permitted to identity four main themes (Respect and obedience, Loyalty and attachment to the country of origin, Strict gender role differentiation, Strict rules about mating and dating) arising from adolescents' narrations and 13 subthemes. Each theme with its subthemes is presented in Table 2 and described below using direct quotations from the interviews. The reported quotations were translated from Italian into English, trying to respect the original verbal expressions related to the discursive context in which they were elicited.

Table 2. Summary of Themes and Subthemes that emerged from Thematic Analysis.

Theme	Subtheme
Respect and obedience	• To respect and to obey to parents • To respect adults in general
Loyalty and attachment to the country of origin	• To be proud of your origin • To be emotionally linked to the country of origin • To maintain the mother tongue • To observe religious practices • To wear the veil
Strict gender role differentiation	• To gain educational success (bread-winners) • To stay at home
Strict rules about mating and dating	• Prohibition to hang out with <<bad companies>> • Prohibition to hang out with a partner • Prohibition to hang out alone • Arranged marriage

Theme 1—Respect and Obedience. Among immigrant adolescents, respect and obedience to parents and adults appeared in general to be crucial and this aspect strongly emerged across all national groups. In particular, this aspect declined in two different ways: *"to respect and to obey parents"* and *"to respect adults in general"*.

The first subtheme *"to respect and to obey parents"* is common to boys and girls from Morocco, Pakistan and Egypt: obedience is a highly valued norm that governs family relations. In this regard, both boys and girls describe parents as older and wiser persons, who decide in the best interests of their sons and daughters. For our participants, parents are perceived as role models and final reference points for any choices and decisions made by the adolescents. According to our narratives, to be obedient also means not having any secrets from parents: all boys and girls believed that total self-disclosure is important in the parent–child relationship.

Males paid much importance to the rules that parents impose on them. In their representation very often these rules are aimed at preventing adolescents from getting into unpleasant and difficult situations, such as spending time in bad company or getting into trouble. Males recognized that these rules are difficult to follow, but they believed that their parents recurred to them because they are trying to keep them safe.

> You have to follow what they say to the letter, even if this goes totally in opposition to what you would like to do in life, unfortunately. (Moroccan boy, 15 years old)

> He has to respect his parents, he must obey, and then he must not go to trouble. (Pakistani boy, 15 years old)

As with boys, females gave importance to obedience to their parents and believed it was essential to try to take their perspective in order to better understand their rules and decisions. According to the female narrative, this perspective taking seemed to play an important role in guiding the females' way of behaving. Understanding their parents' point of view frequently led them to conform to their parental choices and desires. Besides this attempt to assume the perspective of their parents, girls considered it important to try to negotiate their choices with their fathers and mothers by expressing their opinions and their judgment. For them, obedience also meant to help and sustain their parents both practically and emotionally.

> I have to obey to my parents, because, according to me, children must have a model in their parents. (Moroccan girl, 18 years old)

> Listen to what parents tell her ... and if she does not agree with something, she does not have to do what she wants but she needs to understand why her parents want that thing and not what she wants. (Egyptian girl, 14 years old)

> You have to know how to listen to your parents and know how to support them when they are in a crisis. (Pakistani girl, 16 years old)

It is also interesting to note that males believed that females should listen to their parents more than males. Males recognized themselves as having a more "transgressive" role, but they do not grant it to females. In contrast, females do not report differences in gender.

> It is the same as for males, but they have to listen to their parents a little more than boys do. (Moroccan boy, 15 years old)

A second subtheme emerged strongly across Pakistani girls and that is "*to respect adults in general*". For Pakistani girls it appeared to be very important to show respect and to be polite with adults and in general with elder people (for example, an elder sibling), because their culture and religion suggest it. As the following quote suggested, Pakistani girls have formal ways of talking to their parents and elder family members as an expression of respect and good manners. They highlight the importance of respecting age and generational hierarchies, in familiar and extra-familiar contexts. They believe that it is essential to be nice and kind with older people, to address to them with respect by using formal ways to talk, as an expression of respect and good manners.

> First of all the respect for the other, be it Muslim, Italian or Pakistani. Many times I've seen my dad that ... there's a very nasty old man to whom I'd like to answer in a bad way, but then my father says: no, he's an old person, even if he doesn't respect you, I have to respect him. (Pakistani girl, 18 years old)

Theme 2—Loyalty and Emotional Attachment to the Country of Origin. From the adolescents' narratives, it emerged to be very important to keep alive and carry on the traditions of their countries of origin. According to the participants, loyalty and attachment to the origins are traits that are highly desired by the parents of Moroccan, Pakistani and Egyptian girls. Girls perceived that parents count on them for transmitting values, rules, habits and traditions to the next generation, in order to maintain a tight bond with their past and with their countries of origin. A strong connection with the country of origin and its culture takes a wider range of forms and meanings among girls in comparison with boys: a feeling of ethnic pride and emotional attachment to the country of origin, maintenance of the mother tongue, retention of traditional habits, engagement in religious practices, and wearing of the veil. The following quotes illustrate these aspects.

From the girls' narrations, it emerged that they felt it is important *"to be proud of your origins"*. This means that it is essential not to only remember their country of origin, and its traditions, but also not to be ashamed of it.

> The important things are those that, well, being foreigners living here, we don't have to be ashamed of being like this, in fact we have to be proud of it. So never forget your own origins. And also don't erase them, 'cause erasing them is a horrible thing. And so there are people who have lived in Morocco and come to live here and if you tell them like "Where are you from?" They answer "I'm Italian", not even telling you they're from Morocco ... that's awful according to me. (Moroccan girl, 15 years old)

> People should not be ashamed of their origins and culture, and should keep and maintain them across time. These aspects must be transmitted to heirs. If people are ashamed, a part of the transmission is interrupted, and then disappears at the end of centuries, these traditions disappears completely. (Egyptian girl, 15 years old)

> As a daughter, the parents tend to not let you forget the culture of your country... there is a pull and spring between parents and children ... sometimes you tend to have some behaviors like the peers who live around you, and parents on the other side tend to make you understand that we have another culture. (Egyptian girl, 17 years old)

> The girl is expected to follow the tradition; the male is expected to remain always close to them. (Pakistani girl, 18 years old)

Girls feel it is important *"to be emotionally linked to the country of origin"* and its traditions and customs, as following quotes suggested.

> I do not want to leave all the things that bind me to my country. (Pakistani girl, 18 years old)

> I want to go to Pakistan because I want to help people in trouble. This is my parents' passion... they want their children to do something for their country, for their own country. So if this identity does not save us, I do not think anyone else can do it. (Pakistani girl, 18 years old)

Another aspect connected to generational mandate is *"to maintain the mother tongue"*. Language is a salient marker of identity and many girls talk about the importance of preserving it as way of keeping connected to their cultural roots and heritage. Girls specified that frequently their parents asked them not to speak in Italian when they are at home, preferring the use of the Arabic, or that they are requested to watch television selecting and tuning on Arabic channels.

> [My father says:] you can take everything from me, but I want my kids to know Arab. (Moroccan girl, 14 years old)

Finally, a prominent aspect and this is common to both boys and girls, independent from their provenience, is "*to observe religious practices*" in order to stay connected with their country of origin. All the participants define themselves as Muslims but girls described religious duties and practices in a more detailed and intense way than males.

> My grandfather told me: Live the day as if you were the queen, but remember that Allah (that is, God) is with you. This phrase is valuable because it suggests how people should live. (Moroccan girl, 16 years)

> I go to the mosque once a week, on Friday, when I'm feeling like. If I finish school early on Fridays, there's usually the prayer, but I don't go every week, it depends on the school's schedule and if I manage to arrive on time, anyhow I sometimes pray at home.... (Egyptian boy, 18 years old)

An aspect that is linked both to the desire of keeping alive the traditional and religious habits is "*to wear the veil*". Modest dress code and veil are issues that emerged transversally in the girls' accounts, regardless of their ethnic origin. Egyptian, Moroccan and Pakistani girls described different experiences with the veil. Among the Egyptian girls, it seemed to be quite common to try to use the veil before deciding to use it forever. Moreover, it emerged that frequently parents sent their daughters in Egypt in order to get them used to it.

> At the beginning of high school I'll wear the veil [...] because I had tried to wear it for a few days this year and there were some that just did not talked to me anymore ... [...] My dad never talked to me about the veil, my mum yes because I had to wear it by 10 years. [...] My mom [...] told me in the sixth grade ... so ... in sixth grade, I wore it ... and this year I took it off, then I will wear it again in ninth grade and I think I will not remove it. (Egyptian girl, 14 years old)

> Before I didn't want to ... I didn't have it in Egypt ... here after one year ... my dad told me to put it on but I didn't want to ... I put it on in front of him at home ... and when I went out I took it off ... then I talked about it with my mum ... I came back to Egypt and I chose by myself 'cause everyone had it there ... and I was the only one ... (Egyptian girl, 16 years old)

From the Moroccan girls' narratives, it emerged that the use of the veil is not so common, even if it is perceived as a sign of their religion. It seemed that Moroccan parents left their daughters free to decide whether to use it or not, without pressuring them.

> Then there's the thing of the veil that anyway is part of our religion. But my parents let me choose, also because if my mother told me: you must put it on, I would answer her: but if you don't have it yourself! (Moroccan girl, 18 years old)

> I appreciate my parents for they do not oblige any of us to wear the veil ... So nobody wears it. (Moroccan girl, 17 years old)

On the contrary, for Pakistani girls the use of the veil seemed to be a sort of prescription coming from parents, from the family and from older people. There appears to be less space for negotiation in deciding to use it or not, and Pakistani girls conformed frequently to a habit that is strongly linked to their culture and religion.

> For example, when I was 16/17 I was in Pakistan, my parents didn't force me to put on, my uncle forced me. Because he said, because he, my two uncles are religious, they talk about politics, they pray, they stay in a group where they talk about politics, and like this, and so he didn't want he said that: 'no, you are a girl, you have to put on. (Pakistani girl, 18 years old)

> Yes, there's a lady who, since we had been very open-minded, bothered us a bit with putting the veil on, then we understood she's saying it also for our good and we listened to her too! (Pakistani girl, 18 years old)

Among males, only Egyptian adolescents described the importance of the use of the veil: some of them described it as a dictation, others as a personal choice.

> Do not wear the veil it would be a problem. Yes ... because if you do not wear it, it means that you do not respect your religion. (Egyptian boy, 14 years old)

Theme 3—Strict gender role differentiation. From the narratives of immigrant adolescents it strongly and transversally emerged that males and females have different family roles: boys have "*to gain educational success in order to become the breadwinners*", while girls have "*to stay at home*". Boys' and girls' narratives are similar in these two aspects and their narratives seemed to reflect each other.

Boys emphasize their future roles as the main family breadwinners. With the aim of financially sustaining and supporting the family, boys and their parents placed a high value on school and study.

> Going to school . . . I do it also for me, I do it also for him, for my family, because I'm the only one left that goes to school, apart from my younger sister, so everyone's counting on me to find a job and so on . . . (Moroccan boy, 15 years old)

> I have to study . . . I have to look forward, to my future . . . (Moroccan boy, 16 years old)

> In order to be a good son you have to make your family happy of you. You have to do something important to make you family feel good. You have to work, to earn . . . if your family wants you to be a lawyer, for example, you have to do it and give this happiness to your family. (Pakistani boy, 18 years old)

Also girls, in their narratives, recognize this role for their male peers.

> A good son must respect his parents, help them out, go to work, to earn, to lend a hand, to help them and the whole family. (Pakistani girl, 18 years old)

According to participant narrations, the female role, on the contrary, is bound to the domestic context. Within the domestic walls, girls are deputed to carry out daily domestic care, to care for younger siblings, and to help parents in their work, sometimes being "language" brokers in extra-family relationships.

> A good girl stays in the house. (Egyptian girl, 16 years old)

> Somebody says I am a prisoner in my home. I do not think in this way. I am not the only one. Too much freedom is not a good thing. (Pakistani girl, 18 years old)

Also boys, in their narratives, recognize this role for females.

> Women shouldn't work. (Egyptian boy, 14 years old)

From participant narratives, it emerged that females are also requested to study and to attend school. There is not a clear project involving a future job for girls and studying is only aimed at an increment of their knowledge and personal self-fulfillment that is unrelated to future professional engagement.

> It's my dad who wants us to study and I feel a bit like . . . being a girl, in my country the man is more valued, since he's stronger, but I don't like it, I want this to change and then for this reason my dad wants us to study, at least you don't face a situation in which you can't do anything. At least you have studied, that's the only thing you have, that is... knowledge, which no one takes you away. (Pakistani girl, 18 years old)

> A girl is different, if her parents don't want her to study and that she stays home, she cooks, respects her parents, it's alright, if they want her to study, then she has to study. (Moroccan boy, 18 years old)

Theme 4—Strict rules about mating and dating According to immigrant adolescents', in their family experiences, the management of peer relationships is based on several prohibitions around mating and dating. These norms could be differently divided according to gender and partially to the ethnic origin of participants.

A transversal subtheme, common to all boys is the *"prohibition of hanging out with <<bad company>>"*. Boys are requested by parents not spend time with peers who can put pressure on them to behave in a risky or deviant way. These parents strictly prohibit some occidental habits, such as smoking, drinking alcohol and taking drugs.

> To be a good soon you must avoid hanging out with smokers ... people that may affect you in a negative way [...] people who steal—they are always males and teens—so avoid people who steal cars and motorbikes and affect you negatively. (Egyptian boy, 16 years old)

> To be a good soon I do not have to do certain things, I shouldn't disappoint my parents ... I shouldn't drink, smoke, let them worry. (Moroccan boy, 16 years old)

> Boys shouldn't go around, they shouldn't do bad things. (Pakistani girl, 18 years old)

A transversal subtheme, common to all girls is the "prohibition of hanging out with a partner". Girls are requested by parents not to spend time with boys. Female adolescents should not have male friends or spend time with them. According to the girls' narrations, their parents do not want them to have any romantic relationship until their arranged marriage. Above all girls are prohibited to have sexual intercourse before marriage.

> [A good girl] shouldn't go out with boys, and if she goes out, she shouldn't have intercourse. (Moroccan girl, 18 years old)

> The engagement must be official. So, the two sides do not get around. Engagement is already a promise of marriage, in the sense that you cannot go back. (Moroccan girl, 19 years old)

For Pakistani immigrant females only, these strict rules extend to the *"prohibition to hang out alone"*. Pakistani girls in their narratives explained that, according to their culture, girls should not go out without being accompanied. Frequently Pakistani girls have the possibility of seeing their female friends only in the presence of their parents or other adults.

> I like to stay with friends, to stay with my friends, to go to the park, but when I go out, I do it with my parents. (Pakistani girl, 14 years old)

> I could not go out in the night, I could not go around when my friends, no! (Pakistani girl, 18 years old)

Dating norms are related among Pakistanis to the subtheme *"arranged marriage"* that is transversal and common to boys and girls, but mainly reinforced by girls. It is shared among them the opinion that arranged marriage last more than "romantic" ones, because in the latter love can end. Adolescents are requested not to have any romantic relationship until their parents chose a wife or a husband for them. Marriage is the responsibility of parents who act in the best interests of their daughters or sons.

> One thing about my country which is not bad is that a girl cannot choose their husband. I cannot say it is good or bad, because I do not want to be the one who chooses: my parents must choose for me, because they love me. (Pakistani girl, 18 years old)

> You should not believe in love. I read that it is such a drug. It last only for a while. (Pakistani girl, 18 years old)

The choice of the parents frequently is directed toward cousins (consanguineous marriages) or Pakistani friends from the country of origin. It is frequent that marriage is celebrated in Pakistan. Then, the spouses come back to Italy or stay and live in Pakistan. In the last case, marriage means that immigrant Pakistani girls have to leave Italy and return to live in their country of origin.

> I do not have a boyfriend. Not out of my family circle. I think I will marry one of my cousins. Or maybe my parents will let me marry a boy I have always known. (Pakistani girl, 18 years old)

> For my parents it is important the culture of origin. I do not think I could marry an Italian boy, nor an Egyptian one. In my country, parents look for a fiancé, we do arranged marriage. (Pakistani girl, 18 years old)

> I think my parents will choose for me a spouse. They will choose it in Pakistan. The family of the boy will decide to let him to come to Italy or not. If I have to move to Pakistan and live there it will be a little difficult for me. Because I lived here and to settle down again in Pakistan could be difficult. But I think is ok also to move to Pakistan. (Pakistani girl, 18 years old)

The appropriate age to get married is also strictly codified for Pakistani boys and girls.

> The other day I talked to my dad and he says: "Now, from the age of 18 to 25 you have to create your future, you have to study, you have to put yourself into the job world, so when you're 25 we find an agreement, we talk. Than we say to the girls who we are interested in, I do not say that I will choose and you will not say anything, but we will decide together who will be good for you. When you will be 27/28 we will make you marry". This is what he said to me. (Pakistani boy, 18 years old)

> The right age to get marry is 22. (Pakistani girl, 16 years old)

Girls describe a possible space for negotiation with their parents about marriage. Fox example, once the family has chosen a partner, boys and girls can express their opinions about it.

> They (parents) start to see and meet a boy they believe is compatible with me. Then, they come to ask to their daughter if she wants to marry him, and they let the boy and the daughter see each other. It depends on the girl to say yes or no, they cannot force the girl, if she doesn't want. (Pakistani girl, 15 years old)

> The parents choose the fiancé, and they ask you if you like it or not. I you don't they say that they will look for another one. (Pakistani girl, 15 years old)

> The parents cannot force you to decide, because it's your life. They simply do not want that you fall in love or love someone before getting married. (Pakistani girl, 18 years old)

4. Discussion

The aim of the current study was to explore through in-depth semi-structured interviews, in-group norms and meanings associated to the representation of a "good" son and a "good" daughter among male and female immigrant reunified adolescents coming from Morocco, Egypt and Pakistan.

Our study focused on the immigrant children who, during developmental age, had to leave behind their community of origin and to move to Italy through family reunification, directly experiencing mobility from one country to another. Secondly, we were interested in contrasting males and females' perceptions, adding the male voices within a literature that has mainly concentrated its attention on the female perspective. Thirdly, we were interested in exploring three of the main Muslim immigrant group residing in Italy (Morocco, Egypt and Pakistan).

Thematic analysis carried out on transcripts allowed us to identify four main themes and thirteen subthemes. Furthermore, a comparative analysis of the interviews allowed us to highlight both recurrent themes among reunified Muslim adolescents and specific ones based on participants' gender and country of origin.

Overall, these themes revealed that some in-group cultural and social norms play a significant role in identity processes of Muslims adolescents living in Italy. As suggested from previous studies (Ajrouch 2004; Maliepaard et al. 2010; Verkuyten and Yildiz 2007), the contents of these norms are highly interconnected, revealing an intersection between the dimension of gender identity and religious and ethnic dimensions. Moreover, the transcript analysis documented specific cross-cultural negotiations that participants face within Italian society when they meet with Western cultural models and values.

Irrespective of the participants' gender and country of origin, the qualities of being obedient and respectful of parents' desires were significant common topics among all interviewed adolescents. All participants depicted parents as role models and final reference points for any choices and decisions. This result is interesting in light of the migration history of these families, who lived a series of critical events (separation and reunification) affecting the quality of family relationships (Falicov 2002; Gonzales et al. 2006). For them being a "good" son and a "good" daughter mean first of all respecting and conforming to parents' desires and expectations. The emphasis on obedience and respect towards parents is a well-documented aspect in cross-cultural research distinguishing between collectivistic and individualistic cultures (Hui and Triandis 1986; Vedder et al. 2009). Within the collectivist culture, family needs precede individual needs. Interdependence and obedience are core values that are needed to maintain harmony, solidarity and loyalty between family members. In this regard, many studies have shown that first generation Muslim immigrant parents strive to defend their own cultural roots when they encounter individualistic values (e.g., independence, self-sufficiency, self-confidence) in Western societies and actively negotiate choices for their children (Gilani 2005; Giuliani and Gennari 2014; Killian and Johnson 2006). Women in particular are the ones who have the responsibility of keeping the family together, even at the cost of the happiness of their individual members. Our data clearly showed that in a post-migration context where these adolescents are being raised, obedience to parents is the main internalized value, which all participants talked about. Nevertheless, they also mentioned some possible spaces for negotiation within the family.

Several differences emerged in relation to participant gender. Firstly, it is worth noting that narratives of girls are articulated than male pairs. In fact, a wider richness of themes emerged from the females' interviews when compared with males' ones. Overall, girls also seem more engaged in norm negotiation processes within their family. It is likely that balancing tradition and "modernity" results a more challenging task for them than for males (Stevens et al. 2004).

Secondly, norms and expectations around being a "good" child are strictly modeled around gender-based specific contents, as widely documented in many studies that focused mainly on female perspective (Ajrouch 2004; Dwyer 2000; Gilani 2005). For girls this implies staying at home and preserving heritage culture (i.e., feeling of ethnic pride, maintenance of the mother tongue, wearing the veil), while for boys gaining educational success in order to become the bread-winner is key. In turn, these role mandates are linked to specific gender-based norms concerning extra-familial relationships. For girls, to different degrees dating and marriage norms regulate their heterosexual relations, while for boys there is a prohibition to engage in deviant activities (i.e., spending time in "bad company", smoking, drinking alcohol and taking drugs). Our findings about girls are consistent with previous studies that frequently documented that not only that first generation Muslim women take on a fundamental role in intergenerational transmission of culture (Abu-Ali and Reisen 1999; Giuliani and Tagliabue 2015), but also that a similar task is frequently assigned to younger female generations (Dwyer 2000; Gilani 2005; Killian and Johnson 2006). It is also apparent in our findings that educational concerns related to their future goals was the main normative issue for male participants. Success or failure of the family migration project seems to depend on males' school performances: they have to perform well at school in order to be able to assume financial responsibility towards family members in the post-migration context. Indeed, it seems to emerge the presence of a heavy mandate weighting on these male adolescents that confirms their future role as a breadwinner.

Migration, with the mentioned gender-based specific challenges it brings about, could result in an increased vulnerability for adolescent Muslims living in Western society. Girls are engaged in conflicts and negotiations between competing cultural models, as previously suggested by some studies (Sirin and Fine 2008; Stevens et al. 2004). They maintain a strong attachment to heritage culture but they also inevitably encounter Western models of female independence and self-fulfillment. Data showed that girls actively negotiate these issues with parents and family members, sometimes gaining small concessions, other times experiencing family conflict and ambivalence. For boys, the mandate on educational success is not negotiable and is particularly hard for them, as recent educational figures suggest (MIUR and Fondazione Ismu 2016). These children tend to leave school earlier than both native peers and second generation immigrants born in Europe. In Italy, like Spain and Greece (Aparicio 2007), immigrant students are more likely to leave school. Almost thirty-five percent of immigrant children living in Italy (versus 14.8% among native peers) fail to go beyond the level of compulsory education, they frequently do not obtain high school or vocational training degrees. Moreover, leaving school early is a more frequent phenomenon among males than females (European Commission/EACEA/Eurydice/Cedefop 2014). Research focusing on males is needed because of the risk of these male adolescents experiencing feelings of frustration and failure is high, taking into account the current precariousness of the Italian labor market, the economic and professional marginality of immigrants in Italy, and the negative prejudice towards Muslims (Ambrosini 2013).

Our data partially allowed pointing out some differences with respect to gender and cultural norms based on the participants' country of origin. One of the main ones concerns the dating and marriage norms that Pakistanis talked about. As other studies showed (Erricchiello 2011; Gilani 2005), the issue of arranged marriage—along with strict norms about extra-familial relationships—is common to Pakistani interviewed boys and girls who refer to parents the main decision-makers with respect to this choice. The value of arranged marriages (frequently with a cousin living in Pakistan) is particularly reinforced by girls who shared the opinion that they last longer than "romantic" ones. Girls imagined some possible space for negotiation with their parents about the choice of husband, but they also prefigured—not having a say in the matter—the possibility of leaving Italy and to go back to living in Pakistan if their future husband decided it. As for marriage, in our study Pakistani girls seem to experience stricter rules (i.e., about mating, dress and veil, religious duties, staying at home) in comparison with Moroccan and Egyptian ones. Certainly, the Pakistani post-migration experience reflects a more recent migration history in comparison with Moroccans and Egyptians who form ethnic communities with a longer history of stabilization in Italy (ISTAT 2016). Pakistanis' acculturation experience probably reflects also several cultural specificities linked to provenience areas of participants.

Finally, the current study clearly showed that the cultural mandates that immigrant adolescent experience in a post-migration context are mostly focused on a unique task, that is, maintaining and defending the integrity of own religious, ethnic, linguistic, and cultural roots. No quotations referred to family pressures to participate in and open towards the host society and mainstream culture. It is likely that migration transition and current post-resettlement contextual factors (e.g., conflictual intergroup relationship, perceived discrimination and prejudice) intensify in-group needs, in particular group cohesion, identification and conformism to in-group norms (Ethier and Deaux 1994). While this mandate is easily understandable as it safeguards in-group identity, on the other hand, the overall imbalance towards the heritage roots undermines a real process of integration of heritage and host cultures.

Author Contributions: Cristina Giuliani conceived and designed the research project, performed the interviews, analyzed the data and wrote the Introduction and Discussion sections. Maria Giulia Olivari analyzed the data and wrote the Method and Result sections. Sara Alfieri analyzed the data and wrote the Introduction and Method sections.

Conflicts of Interest: The authors declare no conflict of interest.

References

Abu-Ali, Azhar, and Carol A. Reisen. 1999. Gender role identity among adolescent Muslim girls living in the US. *Current Psychology* 18: 185–92. [CrossRef]

Ajrouch, Kristine. 2004. Gender, race, and symbolic boundaries: Contested spaces of identity among Arab American adolescents. *Sociological Perspectives* 47: 371–91. [CrossRef]

Allen, Christopher, and Jørgen S. Nielsen. 2002. *Summary Report on Islamophobia in the EU after 11 September 2001*. Vienna: EUMC.

Al-Yousuf, Heather. 2006. Negotiating faith and identity in Muslim–Christian marriages in Britain. *Islam and Christian–Muslim Relations* 17: 317–29. [CrossRef]

Ambrosini, Maurizio. 2013. Immigration in Italy: Between economic acceptance and political rejection. *Journal of International Migration and Integration* 14: 175–94. [CrossRef]

Aparicio, Rosa. 2007. The integration of the second and 1.5 generations of Moroccan, Dominican and Peruvian origin in Madrid and Barcelona. *Journal of Ethnic and Migration Studies* 33: 1169–93. [CrossRef]

Arends-Tóth, Judit, and Fons J. R. Van de Vijver. 2004. Domains and dimensions in acculturation: Implicit theories of Turkish-Dutch. *International Journal of Intercultural Relations* 28: 19–35. [CrossRef]

Berry, John W. 1997. Immigration, acculturation, and adaptation. *Applied Psychology* 46: 5–34. [CrossRef]

Berry, John W., and Colette Sabatier. 2010. Acculturation, discrimination, and adaptation among second generation immigrant youth in Montreal and Paris. *International Journal of Intercultural Relations* 34: 191–207. [CrossRef]

John W. Berry, Jean S. Phinney, David L. Sam, and Paul Vedder, eds. 2006. *Immigrant Youth in Cultural Transition: Acculturation, Identity, and Adaptation across National Contexts*. Mahwah: Lawrence Erlbaum Associates.

Bertolani, Barbara, Matteo Rinaldini, and Mara Tognetti Bordogna. 2014. Combining civic stratification and transnational approaches for reunited families: The case of Moroccans, Indians and Pakistanis in Reggio Emilia. *Journal of Ethnic and Migration Studies* 40: 1470–87. [CrossRef]

Blangiardo, Gian Carlo, ed. 2013. *L'immigrazione Straniera in Lombardia: La Dodicesima Indagine Regionale: Rapporto 2012 [Foreign Immigration in Lombardia: The Twelfth Regional Survey: Report 2012]*. Milan: Fondazione Ismu.

Bornstein, Marc H. 2017. The specificity principle in acculturation science. *Perspectives on Psychological Science* 12: 3–45. [CrossRef] [PubMed]

Braun, Virginia, and Victoria Clarke. 2006. Using thematic analysis in psychology. *Qualitative Research in Psychology* 3: 77–101. [CrossRef]

Brubaker, Rogers. 2001. The return of assimilation? Changing perspectives on immigration and its sequels in France, Germany, and the United States. *Ethnic and Racial Studies* 24: 531–48. [CrossRef]

Clycq, Noel. 2012. 'My daughter is a free woman, so she can't marry a Muslim': The gendering of ethno-religious boundaries. *European Journal of Women's Studies* 19: 157–71. [CrossRef]

Crabtree, Sara A., and Fatima Husain. 2012. Within, without: Dialogical perspectives on feminism and Islam. *Religion and Gender* 2: 128–49. [CrossRef]

Crespi, Isabella. 2014. Foreign Families in the Italian Context: Migration Processes and Strategies. *Journal of Comparative Family Studies* XLV: 249–60.

Crul, Maurice, and Jeroen Doomernik. 2003. The Turkish and Moroccan second generation in the Netherlands: Divergent trends between and polarization within the two groups. *International Migration Review* 37: 1039–64. [CrossRef]

De Haas, Hein. 2007. Morocco's Migration Experience: A Transitional Perspective. *International Migration* 45: 39–70. [CrossRef]

Diehl, Claudia, Matthias Koenig, and Kerstin Ruckdeschel. 2009. Religiosity and gender equality: Comparing natives and Muslim migrants in Germany. *Ethnic and Racial Studies* 32: 278–301. [CrossRef]

Dwyer, Claire. 2000. Negotiating diasporic identities: Young British South Ssian muslim women. *Women's Studies International Forum* 23: 475–86. [CrossRef]

Erricchiello, Giuseppe. 2011. Marriage strategies in migration: Analysis of a case-study within the Pakistani community in Italy. *Studi Emigrazione* 181: 123–36.

Ethier, Kathleen A., and Kay Deaux. 1994. Negotiating social identity when contexts change: Maintaining identification and responding to threat. *Journal of Personality and Social Psychology* 67: 243–51. [CrossRef]

European Commission/EACEA/Eurydice/Cedefop. 2014. *Tackling Early Leaving from Education and Training in Europe: Strategies, Policies and Measures. Eurydice and Cedefop Report.* Luxembourg: Publications Office of the European Union, Available online: https://webgate.ec.europa.eu/fpfis/mwikis/eurydice/index.php/Publications:Tackling_Early_Leaving_from_Education_and_Training_in_Europe:_Strategies,_Policies_and_Measures (accessed on 1 September 2017).

Fadil, Nadia. 2011. Not-unveiling as an ethical practice. *Feminist Review* 98: 83–109. [CrossRef]

Falicov, Celia J. 2002. Ambiguous loss: Risk and resilience in Latino immigrant families. In *Latinos: Remaking America*. Edited by Marcelo M. Suarez-Orozco and Mariela M. Paez. Berkley: University of California Press, pp. 274–88.

Gilani, Nighat. 2005. Identity development of teenage girls: A cross-ethnic perspective. *Pakistan Journal of Psychological Research* 20: 1–14.

Giuliani, Cristina, and Marialuisa Gennari. 2014. Intimate male partner violence: Voci dei migranti musulmani. *Maltrattamento e Abuso all'Infanzia* 16: 101–12. [CrossRef]

Giuliani, Cristina, and Semira Tagliabue. 2015. Exploring identity in Muslim Moroccan and Pakistani immigrant women. *Europe's Journal of Psychology* 11: 63–78. [CrossRef] [PubMed]

Giunchi, Elisa. 2012. Donne e diritto di famiglia in Pakistan, Morocco e Egitto: Un profilo storico-giuridico. In *Esperienze di Donne Nella Migrazione Araba e Pakistana [Women Experiences in Arab and Pakistani Migration]*. Edited by Camillo Regalia and Cristina Giuliani. Milan: Franco Angeli Editore, pp. 13–33.

Gonzales, Nancy A., Julianna Deardorff, Diana Formoso, Alicia Barr, and Manuel Barrera. 2006. Family mediators of the relation between acculturation and adolescent mental health. *Family Relations* 55: 318–30. [CrossRef]

Güngör, Derya, Fenella Fleischmann, and Karen Phalet. 2011. Religious identification, beliefs, and practices among Turkish Belgian and Moroccan Belgian Muslims: Intergenerational continuity and acculturative change. *Journal of Cross-Cultural Psychology* 42: 1356–74. [CrossRef]

Haddad, Yvonne Yazbeck, and Adair T. Lummis. 1987. *Islamic Values in the United States: A Comparative Study*. New York: Oxford University Press.

Hanassab, Shideh. 1998. Sexuality, dating, and double standards: Young Iranian immigrants in Los Angeles. *Iranian Studies* 31: 65–75. [CrossRef]

Hermansen, Marcia K. 1991. Two-way acculturation: Muslim women in America between individual choice (liminality) and community affiliation (communitas). In *The Muslims of America*. Edited by Yvonne Y. Haddad. New York: Oxford University Press, pp. 188–201.

Hogg, Michael A., Janice R. Adelman, and Robert D. Blagg. 2010. Religion in the face of uncertainty: An uncertainty-identity theory account of religiousness. *Personality and Social Psychology Review* 14: 72–83. [CrossRef] [PubMed]

Hopkins, Nick, and Ronni Michelle Greenwood. 2013. Hijab, visibility and the performance of identity. *European Journal of Social Psychology* 43: 438–47. [CrossRef]

Hui, C. Harry, and Harry C. Triandis. 1986. Individualism-collectivism: A study of cross-cultural researchers. *Journal of Cross-Cultural Psychology* 17: 225–48. [CrossRef]

ISTAT (Istituto Italiano di Statistica). 2016. Immigrati e Nuovi Cittadini [Report Monitoring Unit of Immigration]. Available online: https://www.istat.it/it/immigrati (accessed on 30 July 2017).

Killian, Caitlin. 2003. The other side of the veil: North African women in France respond to the headscarf affair. *Gender and Society* 17: 567–90. [CrossRef]

Killian, Caitlin, and Cathryn Johnson. 2006. "I'm Not An Immigrant!": Resistance, Redefinition, and The Role of Resources in Identity Work. *Social Psychology Quarterly* 69: 60–80. [CrossRef]

Lashley, Myrna. 2000. The unrecognized social stressors of migration and reunification in Caribbean families. *Transcultural Psychiatry* 37: 201–15. [CrossRef]

Leeman, Alex B. 2009. Interfaith marriage in Islam: An examination of the legal theory behind the traditional and reformist positions. *Indiana Law Journal* 84: 743–71.

Leyendecker, Birgit. 2011. Children from Immigrant Families—Adaptation, Development, and Resilience. Current Trends in the Study of Migration in Europe. *International Journal of Developmental Science* 5: 3–9. [CrossRef]

Lorasdaği, Berrin K. 2009. The headscarf and "Resistance identity-building": A case study on headscarf wearing in Amsterdam. *Women's Studies International Forum* 32: 453–62. [CrossRef]

Maliepaard, Mieke, Marcel Lubbers, and Mérove Gijsberts. 2010. Generational differences in ethnic and religious attachment and their interrelation. A study among Muslim minorities in the Netherlands. *Ethnic and Racial Studies* 33: 451–72. [CrossRef]

Marzana, Daniela, Sara Alfieri, and Elena Marta. 2016. The multidimensional nature of young immigrants' well-being. *Rivista Internazionale di Scienze Sociali* 123: 21–40.

MIUR and Fondazione Ismu. 2016. *Alunni Con Cittadinanza Non Italiana. Rapporto Nazionale 2014-15.* Milan: Graphidea.

Musterd, Sako, and Wim Ostendorf. 2009. Residential segregation and integration in the Netherlands. *Journal of Ethnic and Migration Studies* 35: 1515–32. [CrossRef]

Ngo, Van Hieu. 2008. A critical examination of acculturation theories. *Critical Social Work* 9: 1–6.

Olivari, Maria Giulia, Elena Santoro, Elisa Stagni Brenca, Emanuela Confalonieri, and Paola Di Blasio. 2015. Health workers' perceptions of Italian female adolescents: A qualitative study about sexuality, contraception, and caring practices in family health centers. *Health Care for Women International* 36: 1239–54. [CrossRef]

Olivari, Maria Giulia, Gaia Cuccì, and Emanuela Confalonieri. 2017. Italian Adolescents and Emergency Contraception: A Focus Group Study. *Journal of Pediatric and Adolescent Gynecology* 30: 41–46. [CrossRef] [PubMed]

Patel, David S. 2012. Concealing to reveal: The informational role of Islamic dress in Muslim societies. *Rationality and Society* 24: 295–323. [CrossRef]

Pew Research Center. 2010. The Future of World Religions: Population Growth Projections, 2010–2050. Available online: http://www.pewforum.org/2015/04/02/religious-projections-2010-2050/ (accessed on 15 July 2017).

Pew Research Center. 2016. Europeans Fear Wave of Refugees Will Mean More Terrorism, Fewer Jobs. Available online: http://www.pewglobal.org/2016/07/11/europeans-fear-wave-of-refugees-will-mean-more-terrorism-fewer-jobs/ (accessed on 15 July 2017).

Camillo Regalia, and Cristina Giuliani, eds. 2012. *Esperienze di Donne nella Migrazione Araba e Pakistana [Women Experiences in Arab and Pakistani Migration].* Milan: Franco Angeli Editore.

Reniers, Georges. 2001. The post-migration survival of traditional marriage patterns: Consanguineous marriages among Turks and Moroccans in Belgium. *Journal of Comparative Family Studies* 32: 21–45.

Sam, David, and John Berry, eds. 2016. *The Cambridge Handbook of Acculturation Psychology.* Cambridge: Cambridge University Press.

Sirin, Selcuk R., and Michelle Fine. 2008. Muslim American Youth. *Childhood* 24: 463–73.

Stevens, Gonneke, Trees V. M. Pels, Wilma A. M. Vollebergh, and Alfons A. M. Crijnen. 2004. Patterns of psychological acculturation in adult and adolescent Moroccan immigrants living in the Netherlands. *Journal of Cross-Cultural Psychology* 35: 689–704. [CrossRef]

Tajfel, Henri. 1981. *Human Groups and Social Categories.* Cambridge: Cambridge University Press.

Turner, John C, Michel A. Hogg, Penelope J. Oakes, Stephen D. Reicher, and Margaret S. Wetherell. 1987. *Rediscovering the Social Group: A Self-Categorization Theory.* Cambridge: Basil Blackwell.

Vedder, Paul, David L. Sam, and Karmela Liebkind. 2007. The acculturation and adaptation of Turkish adolescents in North-Western Europe. *Applied Development Science* 11: 126–36. [CrossRef]

Vedder, Paul, John Berry, Colette Sabatier, and David Sam. 2009. The intergenerational transmission of values in national and immigrant families: The role of Zeitgeist. *Journal of Youth and Adolescence* 38: 642–53. [CrossRef] [PubMed]

Verkuyten, Maykel. 2007. Religious group identification and inter-religious relations: A study among Turkish-Dutch Muslims. *Group Processes & Intergroup Relations* 10: 341–57. [CrossRef]

Verkuyten, Maykel, and Ali Aslan Yildiz. 2007. National (dis) identification and ethnic and religious identity: A study among Turkish-Dutch Muslims. *Personality and Social Psychology Bulletin* 33: 1448–62. [CrossRef] [PubMed]

Verkuyten, Maykel, Jochem Thijs, and Gonneke Stevens. 2012. Multiple Identities and Religious Transmission: A Study among Moroccan-Dutch Muslim Adolescents and Their Parents. *Child Development* 83: 1577–90. [CrossRef] [PubMed]

World Health Organization (WHO). 2016a. Regional Health Systems Observatory-EMRO. Available online: http://rho.emro.who.int/rhodata/?theme=country (accessed on 1 September 2017).

World Health Organization (WHO). 2016b. Eastern Mediterranean Region, EMROPUB. Available online: http://applications.emro.who.int/dsaf/EMROPUB_2016_EN_19169.pdf?ua=1&ua=1 (accessed on 1 September 2017).

Williams, Raymond B. 1988. *Religions of Immigrants from India and Pakistan: American Tapestry*. New York: Cambridge.

Zaman, Riffat. M., Sunita M. Stewart, and Taymiya R. Zaman. 2006. Pakistan: Culture, community, and familial obligations in a Muslim society. In *Families Across Cultures*. Edited by James Georgas, John. W. Berry, Fons J. R. van de Vijer, Çiğdem Kağitcibaşi and Ype H. Poortinga. Cambridge: Cambridge University Press, pp. 427–34.

MDPI AG
St. Alban-Anlage 66
4052 Basel, Switzerland
Tel. +41 61 683 77 34
Fax +41 61 302 89 18
http://www.mdpi.com

Social Sciences Editorial Office
E-mail: socsci@mdpi.com
http://www.mdpi.com/journal/socsci

www.ingramcontent.com/pod-product-compliance
Lightning Source LLC
Chambersburg PA
CBHW051313020426
42333CB00028B/3322

* 9 7 8 3 0 3 8 4 2 7 5 2 0 *